JAN & DEAN ARCHIVES
VOLUME 3

FOREWORD

IN THE 1980S, FANZINES offered fans the ability to get more information on their favorite bands and communicate with other fans. Without the internet as a resource, it was sometimes hard to get information on tours or even see articles in print if your band wasn't one of the majors.

While Jan & Dean had a very attentive fan base, it's safe to say that the band didn't rate a whole lot of media attention in general. Their hits were decades old, and even given Jan's motivating story, most publications could cover them once or twice at a 30,000 foot level and be done.

But fanzines were written by and for a very specific audience: rabid fans. Their audience was interested in nearly anything related to the band: musicians playing on the tracks, stories of the band members, what they ate for breakfast...you get the idea.

In particular, Jan & Dean offered a lot of interesting story points. In addition to the typical rock music-related topics, Dean was a talented and active graphic designer. The tangental connections to other bands made for interesting reading, as did Dean's connections to the lead singer of that "other" surfing music band.

Sunshine Music was one of these magic fanzines that filled the fan's demand for information. Run and edited by music writer Mike "Doc Rock" Kelly, the newsletter was welcomed by the fan community and contained the typical fanzine fare: letters from members, a bit of news, reprints of news articles and other tidbits to fill out the issues. His fanzine was the successor to Ripped Baggies Club, a fanclub that had been supposedly sponsored by Dean but faded after just a few years.

This book reprinting the first 20 issues of Sunshine Music is your chance to enjoy the excitement of those fanzine years without having to endure the wait between issues. Grab your board and go memory surfin' with Sunshine Music.

Original copyrights as stated in individual publications.
Collection copyright 2014 White Lightning Publications
None of the sale offers or addresses shown are presently valid.

SUNSHINE MUSIC

—SPECIAL REPRINT—

DJs See Page 5!

SUNSHINE MUSIC
c/o Doc Rock
Box 1166
Lawrence, KS 66044

To:

FIRST CLASS MAIL

SUNSHINE MUSIC

Jan • Dean • Papa

Editor
Michael "Doc Rock" Kelly

Graphics/Layout
Buzzie

Associate Editor
Frank M. Kisko

Issue 1' **Fall, 1979**

CONTENTS

Lyrics	2
You Have Received	3
Let Me Explain--Ripped What?	4
THE TURNTABLE -- DJ NOTES	5
After *Deadman's Curve* (The Movie)	5
What'$ It Worth to You?	6
Marney Koch's Tape List	7
Orville & Wilbur Pilots	8
Short Cuts	9

Contents not already copyrighted are © 1979 by Michael Bryan Kelly.

The Newsletter of the Official Jan and Dean
Authorized International Fan Club

YOU HAVE RECEIVED THIS PREMIER ISSUE OF SUNSHINE MUSIC
FOR THE FOLLOWING REASON(S):

( ) You are Jan   ( ) You are a DJ
( ) You are Dean   ( ) You are related to J&D
( ) You sent 50¢ for a sample issue ( ) You sent your 'zine
( ) You placed an ad in SM   ( ) You deserve it

SUNSHINE MUSIC
S. Dromenski/D. Girard
HIGH TIDE Music--ENDLESS SUMMER Music ASCAP

You should'a seen me and the rest'a the guys,
Crusin' in our T-shirts and our white Levis!
Jump in my car and we'd be ready to go,
Listenin' to the music on the ray-dee-oh!

Listen to the music of the SUNSHINE!
Funtime, funtime MUSIC
I love that music
SUNSHINE love that funtime MUSIC!

(Doo-do-doo)
Down at the drive-in we'd be playin' it cool,
Checkin' out the chicks to meet the New Girl In School!
All year around you know we'd always be seen,
Ridin' in our custom machines!

Little Duece Coupe, little Cobra, and a Bucket-T,
Bucket-T Bucket-T Bucket-T!
(Ahhh)
They were hot off the line, but the one that looked
so boss to me (so boss to me) was Little GTO!

(Get 'em, Get 'em, gotta get 'em)
Split to the beach an' try an' ride the big waves!
Everyone I know was wrapped up in the craze!
Spent all our night times draggin' on main!
All the single girls 'd drive the guys insane!

Everybody sing now SUNSHINE!
It's a funtime funtime MUSIC!
I love that music SUNSHINE!!!

SUNSHINE MUSIC 1

DJ FEATURE

THE TURNTABLE- - - DJ NOTES - - -AN OLDIE FOR YOUR RADIO SHOW

Twenty years ago this Fall, BABY TALK was #10 in the U.S.

Trivia: This was the first Jan and Dean song, originally recorded by the Laurels on the Spring record label. Herb Alpert worked on the session, and the record label it was on by Jan and Dean, DORE, was named after Alpert's daughter!

AFTER DEADMAN'S CURVE (THE MOVIE)

I haven't been able to confirm all the facts, but, it seems that all of the SRO concerts Jan and Dean have been doing up and down the coasts have not gone unnoticed in Hollywood. Word is that the guy who produced the Jan and Dean TV series (what, you never heard of *The Jan and Dean Show*, of which up to four episodes were filmed before Jan smashed his fiber-glass rod back in '66?) has a renewed interest in J&D.

First, this producer, Dale Davis, filmed a Jan and Dean concert, on stage with J&D were former Jan and Dean back-up musician Glen Campbell, actors Hatch and Davison, who played our heroes in the TV movie, as well as a Beach Boy or two. Second, he took Jan and Dean to Hawaii to film some new footage of the boys.

Anyway, evidently the old TV pilot, the concert, and the Hawaii footage will be put together to make a big Jan and Dean TV special this Fall! It may even be a pilot for a series! Well, we'll see. If true, it would be the greatest thing since they invented 45s.

If all this interests you at all, then mayhaps you best run your tired squinties over the article in this issue of *Sunshine Music*, titled:

JAN AND DEAN PILOTS
or
ORVILLE AND WILBUR FLY AGAIN

It has been suggested that the readers of *Sunshine Music* might also be interested in reading *Add Some Music*, the *Beach Boys Magazine*. If you wish to subscribe to this fanzine, send $1.00 to:
Add Some Music
Box 10405
Elmwood, Conn. 06110

"*ADD SOME MUSIC*" "*CALIFORNIA MUSIC*". That is what you get in *California Music*, primarily Beach Boys, but with other surf 'n drag artists as well. Surf with an Australian slant. Here's the address: 2 Kentwell Avenue; Concord 2137; Australia.

LET ME EXPLAIN

What happened to the *Ripped Baggies Club*? What happened to the *Ripped Baggies Newsletter*? What happened to the $5 sent to Mark Plummer for a one-year membership/subscription?

Well, fans, let me explain as well as I can. The story begins back in the '60s, when I had a dream of having a Jan and Dean Fan Club. Then, it zips up (the charts) to 1975, when I began to discover that I was not the onliest J&D freak in the land. At this time, I began looking into the possibilities of starting a fan club. And what did I find out? That a guy on the coast, recently stationed in LA, was starting a club! Since this guy was much closer in miles to J&D than I was, I gave him my support of his club.

So far, so good. He got Jan's and Dean's blessings. Dean did a logo for the club. Jan gave him acetates to sell to finance the club, which was great because it spread the rare sounds around, at the same time that it made the club newsletter free for two years.

If you got the old newsletter, then you know that I wrote articles for *Ripped Baggies*. Through correspondence, trades of tapes and records, and telephone conversations, I became great friends with MARK PLUMMER, originator of the *Ripped Baggies*.

Now comes the explaining. Within the last eight months or so, Mark has been separated from his wife, and is involved in a divorce. His. And she is apparently giving him a rough time.

Due I guess to personal pressures, Mark decided to step down as Club Honcho. Knowing my interest and fanaticism, he accepted my offer to take over the club. I intended to keep the same name for the club and simply pick up where Mark left off. Mark agreed, and said that, after he put out one last issue, he would send me the money people had paid for subscriptions/memberships, as well as the names and addresses of the 100 paid subscribers and the 200 unpaid persons who had received the free newsletter.

Then, I did not hear from Mark for literally months. And the one last issue never came out. Finally, July 24, I got a letter from Mark. To answer your questions, I will now quote from Mark's letter:

What about the $5 membership fees people paid?
"*If anyone wants a refund on their dues they can write me & ask for it.*"

What about the farewell issue?
"*There was supposed to be an April newsletter but I haven't heard from Marilyn since December.*"

What about the club?
"*It was fun for a while but it turned into a nightmare.*"

What about the badges, club LP's, etc.?

So, to cut it short, I have assumed leadership of *The Official Jan and Dean Authorized International Fan Club*. Authorization coming from Dean and Jan. And in that sense, and since Mark originally turned the old club over to me, the new club is in fact an extension of the old club. On the other hand, since I do not have Mark's membership list,
(*continued on page 9*)

SUNSHINE MUSIC 1

Official SUNSHINE MUSIC Tape List
Taping Editor: Marny Koch
285 White Oak Lane Winnetka, Il. 60093

Dean Torrence and Bill Lee (1973)--telephone interview, pretty good but fuzzy in places. 00:24:00

Jan Berry, Tom Sumner, Mark Plummer (April, 1976)--portable cassette recording in Tom's apartment, buzzing at beginning but improves-contains some songs not recorded as of 4/76-fair/good quality. 01:00:00

Dean talks about Jan & Dean and Papa Doo Run Run (1976)--Dean's side of phone interview, good quality. 00:22:30

Jan Berry "Live at the Falomino," (November 14, 1976)--almost studio quality stereo concert, contains a minor flaws from original. 00:45:00

Kathy Torrence and Mark Plummer (1977)--portable cassette interview in Kathy's (Dean's sister) apartment, good quality. 01:00:00

Papa Doo Run Run in concert (summer, 1977)--studio quality stereo concert-tape supplied by Papa. 00:43:00

Papa interviews, Vancouver (October 25, 1977)--portable cassette recording, interview in restaurant, background noise. 00:45:00

Papa interviews, Seattle (November 11, 1977)--portable cassette recording, quality good, VERY spontaneous. 01:00:00

Dean Torrence, Marny Koch, Alexandra Lee (November 23, 1977)--portable cassette recording in Dean's office, quality good, some noise toward end. 00:45:00

Jan Berry concert, Topeka KS (March 14, 1978)--portable cassette recording, fair/good quality-some words difficult to understand. 01:11:45

Myke Kelly reviews Jan's Topeka concert (3/78)-personal collection of seeing Jan, songs in background, good quality. 00:18:15

Jan Berry live at Macon County Light Company (March 16, 1978)--portable cassette recording, fair/poor quality. 00:35:00

Mr and Mrs Torrence, Marny Koch, Mark Plummer (August 24, 1978)--portable cassette recording, interview in the Torrences' home, slight noise in places. 00:26:00

Papa Doo Run Run, Marny Koch, Mark Plummer (August 24, 1978)--portable cassette recording between shows at Disneyland, some background noise (fireworks, people), good quality. 00:35:00

Backstage with Jan & Dean and Papa (September 23, 1978)--portable cassette recording, lots of noise, fair quality. 00:45:00

Jan Berry, Diane Osborne, Mark Plummer (December 9, 1978)--portable cassette recording made in Jan's apartment-part of a song being written-quality fair/good. 01:00:00

WHAT$ IT WORTH TO YOU?

This is a possibly regular feature of SM, relating how much Jan and Dean records are going for these days. It may help you to judge how much to offer for a record, and how much to offer a record for if you have extras to offer. One thing to keep in mind. A record is worth only what it is worth to you. Also, in 1973 records went for very average prices. Since then a few collectors have bid against one another, causing a great inflation in Jan and Dean record prices. So, go easy, and let's all work together to keep prices within reason!

June 1979 Feinberg, NJ

$12	Summer Means Fun, LMS	VG+
$6	Surf City	M-
$5	Little Old Lady	VG+
$7	Sidewalk Surfin'	M-
$7	Dead Man's Curve	M-

Summer 1979 Tannfelt, Sweden

$15	Dore LP cover split	G++
$7	Design LP (Challenge cuts)	M-
$25	Dead Man's Curve stereo	SS
$8	Batman stereo cut out	VG+
$6	Gotta Getta Date Arwin	VG
$B10	Baby Talk	M-
$B10	Clementine	M-
$3	There's A Girl	M-

July 1979 Goldmine Swapper

$2.50	Time Machine	M-
$2	Miss America (Imperial)	VG+
$3	Hits of the Hops	M-
$3	Sunday Kind of Love	M-
$3	Freeway Flyer	M-
$3	Anaheim Azusa	M-
$3.50	Popsicle	VG+
$1.50	Honolulu Lulu	VG
$2.50	Little Old Lady stereo	M-
$18.00	Folk & Roll	M-
$12.00	Command Performance mo	VG+
$6	Design split woc	VG+

Foreign LP Startrax 974 Has the 9 cuts by Dean & Papa

August 1979 Levin Ill.
$10	Yellow Balloon 45 NJ	M-

$3.00 per hr recording (5¢/min)
MRX₃ or TDK AD Cassettes: C-60 $3.25 C-90 $4.90
Or, send your own blank tapes.
Postage: 1st Class 1 tape-55¢
each add'l tape-40¢
Spcl. 4th Class, 2-10 tapes, 59¢

These are asking prices I have seen lately. I am not offering these records! Write and tell me what you have actually paid lately for Jan and Dean records!

SOLD OUT

SUNSHINE MUSIC 1

SHORT CUTS

***They say Dean got a platinum LP for his cover of Steve Martin's LP. Must look nice next to his gold record for Surf City, and the Grammy for the artwork on *Pollution*.

***Celebration does a medley in their concerts --Catch a Wave and Surf City. I hear that it sounds just great!

***There is a live J&D LP being put out by a Southern California news vendor. It is a concert from 1978. There are supposed to be only 500 copies coming out. If I can get some, I will make them available.

***Back in 1975, on Dick Clark's *Action*, Jan did Tinsel Town, and with Dean he did Surf City, out on a beach surrounded by teenagers. Many of those kids must have been in diapers when Surf City was #1. At any rate, Dick asked Jan how many hits they had had. Jan answered that they had had about six gold records and began to list them, but Dick interrupted. Was Jan making a mistake? The *Anthology* LP lists only one million seller. Perhaps such classics as Little Old Lady and Dead Man's Curve eventually sold a million on reissues such as the Liberty Golden Hit Series or the United Artists Silver Spotlight Series. Or, maybe Liberty padded their sales figures. This was a common practice among labels wanting their artists to look like real superstars.

***There still seems to be plans for a *Deadman's Curve* soundtrack LP. Some two dozen tracks have been laid down in two sets of sessions. The first set had Dean and Papa. The second set added Jan and Mike Love. There are some weird sounds there. If a label is ever found, the "soundtrack" lp may come out someday. There are enough surplus cuts for a Volume III

****Deadman's Curve* is probably to be released to theaters in the US, in a longer version. Enough scenes were filmed to have made a two-part TV movie, so a longer version is easily possible.

***If you have any news, send it in, all right?

EXPLAIN (continued from page 4)

and since I have not one penny of money from dues already paid, I feel it is best that I disassociate myself and the new club from the old one.

Hence, this all-new 'zine *Sunshine Music!*

By the way, the statement in the TBE ad and "formerly the Ripped Baggies Newsletter" was an error, not intended to be in the ad, not true, and something apparently dreamed up by the editors of TBE. Similarly, the phrase "bi-monthly" was stuck in by TBE. As yet, I do not know the frequency with which *Sunshine Music* will come out. Like, I'm new at this, you know. Also, I cannot set a price as I write this. I hope to arrive at a cost before I mail this to you.

A final word: Send all questions about anything to do with the old, now defunct *Ripped Baggies Club* to Mark Plummer/Box 2341/Alameda, CA/94501.

Your Editor,

Myke

JAN AND DEAN PILOTS
OR
ORVILLE AND WILBUR FLY AGAIN

April, 1970

SM: I was sitting there in the theater, paying no attention at all to the previews of coming attractions, and then all of a sudden, THEY'RE COMIN' FROM ALL OVER THE WORLD! And I jumped up, "WHAT! 'Cause I didn't know about that movie, and I had never heard the song yet. So I looked up on the screen and there you guys were on skateboards, Jan taking gas in a bush!

Dean: The TAMI Show. (Ed.: Teenage Awards Music International)

SM: Yes, the TAMI Show. Which I haven't seen since the movie run.

Dean: It was on TV, one week ago.

SM: They never show it on TV in Kansas. If they did, I would tape it, video tape it, audio tape it, film it...

Dean: Well, I just ran into the producer. As a matter of fact, that's who I was having this meeting with at five that I cancelled, he's the guy that produced it. He opened up his closet last time I was over there about three days ago, and said, "There it is, and I'll let you take it and make a copy of it."

That was too easy. I looked at it. I had been doing the same thing as you, if it were on. "Boy, jeeze, I would tape it and everything." So I said, "How much?" And actually I wouldn't care how much it is, I'd still want it.

SM: Why don't they put it on one night on TV, maybe ABC in Concert?

Dean: Well, I don't know if I'd go that far.

SM: This coming weekend they are gonna do a oldies show with Jerry Lee Lewis, and a whole '50s Midnight Special.

Dean: Everything hits TV about five years behind, or maybe not quite that long...

(Ed.: Maybe I had the right idea, because some two years after this conversation, Dick Clark hosted excerpts from the TAMI Show on ABC late night with Jan and Dean live!)

SM: I always look for the pilot of your series to be shown on TV.

Dean: Naw, they'll never show that.

SM: In the summer, they show old unsold pilots...

(continued on page 10)

Dean: Yeah, that's right.

SM: And I always get the TV Guide and look for it.

Dean: I've got it. Luckily, I got the pilot. It's terrible. Ha!

SM: All I ever knew about that show was a one liner in the Sunday Kansas City Star TV section.

"The Jan and Dean Show," half-hour color program featuring the young singers as themselves in various locations around the country.

That was the only thing I ever heard about that show, and it has always frustrated me.

Dean: Awww.

SM: And then the Monkees had their show right afterwards.

Dean: We were doing our pilots at the same time. And we both had spies on the others sets. Nesmith was in here just an hour ago. We've become pretty close, so I know what they were thinking, and they knew what we were thinking. We had spies on their set, and they had spies on our set to see what we were doing, so we'd all know what was going on.

And we would have opposed each other for at least the first year. Which would have been fun, because we were all kinda friends, and we would have interrelated our shows.

Matter of fact, we even had an idea of switching them. Because, you see, it would have been (seen as a rivalry by the fans) just like with the Beach Boys. Everybody would think they had to take sides, which they didn't because we were all close friends, and we were all on each others records. Yet everyone thought they either had to be for Jan and Dean or for the Beach Boys.

When it came down to the Monkees or Jan and Dean on TV, you would have had to decide (like with the Beach Boys) one was always better than the other, and the other was no good.

So we planned to switch. On our night, they would be on OUR show. And on their night, we would be on THEIR show. Doing their show. On their channel. We'd worked out some really fantastic things to keep it really, you know, to not pin ourselves down to one thing to the point that people got tired of us after a year.

Because we realized in the very beginning that even the pilot was boring! By the time we finished the pilot, we were bored. We were hoping it wouldn't sell. I just told somebody about that yesterday. And I said, "God, if this thing sells, we're screwed!"... Everybody else was counting on it. It meant money, success...

SM: But the TV show skyrocketed the Monkees. And I have always felt that if the *Jan and Dean Show* could have gone ahead, that if Jan hadn't had the accident, then Jan and Dean would have been back at the top again.

Dean: Ahh, you'd skyrocket for a second or two...

See, we had really been pacing ourselves for eight years. Making it able to last eight years. When the Monkees got on, well, actually they were lucky, they stayed on for two or three years, three seasons. They were pretty successful. But soon they burned themselves out, and they were gone.

(Dean, as devil's advocate) But all the bucks you make during that time is well worth...

(Dean's self-reply) Do you want to be a flash in the pan for two or three years, and make that kind of money, and pay that kind of taxes on it. Or, do you want to spread it out, because we were ending up with a lot more than if we were just flashes.

So, it was a questionable thing.

Monkees' Story: Seven top-ten records, all but two with flip sides on the chart as well, from September '66 to August '68. The TV show was on NBC from Sept. 12, '66 to Aug. 19, '68; CBS Sept. 13, '69 to Sept. 2, '72; and on ABC Sept. 9, '72, to Sept. 1, '73. Now it is in syndication.

SUBSCRIBE TO SUNSHINE MUSIC

I can't pin it down exactly, yet. However, it looks like my cost per copy of *Sunshine Music* is going to be well over 50¢. So I am going to have to charge more, $1, for a single issue. Subscriptions will be $5 for 7 issues. Until we reach 100 paid subscribers, I will still be losing money on each copy. On the other hand, costs may come down. A larger number of members could lower the cost per copy through volume; the number of pages may go down; postage could go down (HA!); Jan, Dean, or a record label may underwrite the effort.

If my costs do go down, I will pass the savings on to you, the subscriber. I will give you a refund, or credit, or a special issue, or more pages, or an extra issue, special photos, something. In any event, you will get your moneys worth. You have my word, sworn on a stack of Jan and Dean albums. Stereo!

Finally, I will put out a minimum of 4 issues per year, up to a maximum of 12 issues per year, if I can get my thing together that often. Sound OK? Hope so. Make checks payable to Michael Kelly.

"TIME BARRIER EXPRESS"

This is a slick pro-zine which covers all aspects of rock and rock and roll. You can learn a lot here. The table of contents of the current issue of *Time Barrier Express* includes the following, plus more:

Reparata and the Delrons
Elvis-- the Sun years
Carl Perkins
Major Lance
Otis Blackwell (Elvis Composer)
Disco, Soul, etc.
Fanzine Reviews
Book Reviews

SUNSHINE MUSIC 2

SUNSHINE MUSIC 2

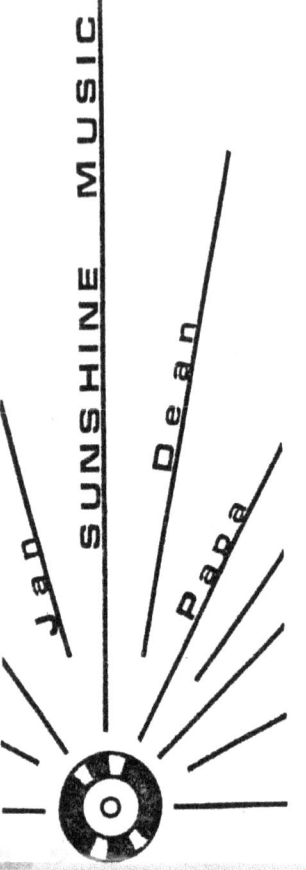

Jan Dean Papa SUNSHINE MUSIC

Editor
Michael "Doc Rock" Kelly

Graphics/Layout
eye design

Associate Editor
Frank M. Kisko

The Magazine of the Official Jan and Dean
Authorized International Collectors Club

Issue 2   Winter, 1980

CONTENTS

Lyrics: Frosty (the Snowman)	2
Let Me Explain	4
Mill Run Concert Review by Marny Koch	6
DJ Note	7
White But Alright, or Two Silhouettes on the Stage	8
Deadman's Curve Records	10
Survey of Favorite Songs	11
New Jan and Dean Records	22
The Centerfold	12
Letters	15
Cruising	23
Jan and Dean's LP Record	19

Contents not already copyrighted are © 1979 by Michael Bryan Kelly.

FROSTY
(The Snowman)

As sung by Jan and Dean on Liberty 55522
Arranged by Jan Berry/Produced by Lou Adler
for Nevins-Kirshner, 1962
Written by Steve Nelson and Jack Rollins
Published by Hill and Range Songs, BMI
Copyrighted

Bomp Bomp Bomp, Bomp Ba Ba, Ba Ba Dip Dip
Ding-a-dy, Ding Di-Ding, DONG!

Frosty the Snow Man, was a jolly, happy soul!
With a corncob pipe and a button nose, and two eyes made out of coal.
Frosty the Snow Man, is a fairy tale they say,
He was made of snow, but the children know
How he came to life one day.

There must have been some magic in that old silk hat they found!
For when they placed it on his head, he began to twist around
AND AROUND AND AROUND. WOO!

Frosty the Snow Man, was alive as he could be, and the children say
He could do the mash
Just the same as you and me.

Bomp Bomp Bomp, Bomp Ba Ba, Ba Ba Dip Dip
Ding-a-dy, Ding Di-Ding, Dong!

Frosty the Snow Man, knew the sun was hot that day
So he said, "Let's run and we'll have some fun, before I melt away."
Down to the village, with a broomstick in his hand,
Running here and there all around the square saying, "Catch me if you can."

He led them down the streets of town right to the traffic cop,
And he only paused a moment when he heard them holler, "Stop!"
Oh, Frosty the Snow Man, had to hurry on his way, but he waved goodbye,
saying,
"Don't you cry! I'll be back again some..."

Bomp Bomp Bomp, Bomp Ba Ba, Ba Ba Dip Dip
Ding-a-dy, Ding Di-Ding, DONG!

(voices over fade)
Jan: What ever happened to my abominable snow man 1st.
Dean: (falsetto) More snowballs, Igor?
Jan: He, heh, flying snowballs for Christmas.
Dean: That's what I pour snow for, Igor, hee hee hee.
Jan: Ha Ha, Yeah!
Dean: (unintelligible) bar B Q...

SUNSHINE MUSIC 2

LET ME EXPLAIN

There were three versions of SUNSHINE MUSIC Issue One. The first two versions had either a light pink or a light blue cover. They also were not proofread, due to a strategic error on my part.

The third version had a hot pink cover (looks like Pepto Bismol to me). Also, it was proofread. I think I like version three best! Pink and black are the SUNSHINE MUSIC colors, because those were the colors of Jan and Dean's car club in the old days, not to mention the Arwin record label colors. And proofreading speaks for itself.

SM#1 is now a back issue, available only in version three. I have sent out so many of those turkeys (a term of affection I picked up from Dino) that my mailman thinks it is a pinko-Communist conspiracy. I get from one to three or four letters each day, and the same day I slap on a 15¢ stamp (32¢ overseas) and send off the issue. The response has been gratifying, and I love writing to you all.

One thing. If you want a quick, personal reply to a letter, send an SASE (self-addressed stamped envelope). This will improve your chances of a speedy reply by many hundreds of percents. Otherwise, you are liable to have to wait until I send your next issue to you, with the letter stapled inside.

For the many of you who wrote asking about your Ripped Baggy money, I hope my opening article in issue #1 cleared things up for you. Let me reiterate, I do not have any money, or the names and addresses of the Ripped Baggies Club (now defunct) members. Write for recompense to Mark Plummer, Box 2341, Alameda, CA 94501.

More explaining. When I wrote for the ill-fated Ripped Newsletter, I ran a poll of readers to ascertain who liked what about J&D. Mark never published more than a tiny bit of the results, so I am beginning a series of reports on the survey results with this issue. Check the contents for the page number, and read a recap of what Mark published, plus hitherto unrevealed results.

And, finally, explaining who I am. That is, who is Myke, who is Michael, and who is Doc Rock.

Myke: When I was in high school, a friend and I used to sing J&D in the halls, in the boys' John (for the echo—we drew quite a crowd during the lunch show), and with local bands. My friend's name: Mike. Well, when people heard us coming down the hall (or out of the restroom), it was awkward to say, "Here come Mike and Mike," or, "Hi, Mike and Mike," so we said, "Just forget that and call us by the plural for Mike, which is Myke." So they did.

Later, when I began writing Dean, I wrote Myke on the SASE. And, when I drafted my J&D discography, on impulse I put Myke next to the page numbers. Then, when I sent the discog to other J&D fans, they took the unintentional hint and wrote to me under the name Myke. So that's the name of that tune.

Michael: My parents had that great idea. They wanted to give me an unusual name (true) and since they knew not a single Mike, they gave me that name. Since then, they have learned that Michael was the most popular boys' name of 1948! (Now you know my age.) Anyway, I like Michael, tho most people insist on calling me Mike against my suggestion that they try the longer form.

Doc Rock: That is the stage name I adopted for my weekly oldies show on KJHK FM-91. The Rock 'n' Roll PhD. I figure 9 years in college earns one certain privileges. Plus, it provides a good gimmick on which to center my show, i.e., the rock and roll lesson of the week, pop quizzes (trivia contests), etc. Works well, since Lawrence is a college town, and the university owns the station. My theme is Freddy Cannon's *Rock and Roll ABC's* ("It takes a whole lot of soulful music to get your rock 'n' roll Ph.D."). I also do private parties, and my post office box is under the name Doc Rock. Hence, the use of the name Doc Rock on SM. However, the P.O. staff folks have been willing to put anything in Box 1166, no matter if it is addressed to Doc Rock, Myke, Michael, Mike, Sunshine Music, or even Herbert Hawkins (I don't know who he is, but I get his mail in my box about twice a week. I wonder if his wife knows about the two.... Well, let's not speculate...).

P.S. I start and end each 3-hour Doc Rock Old Wave Show with a J&D cut. Sounds great, and I get a lot of J&D requests. Didn't know Dean's mom ever listened to Kansas radio stations....

SHORT CUTS

***Pickwick Records has bought the Doré label and masters. It would seem that there are some six heretofore unknown Jan and Dean tracks which may soon be released on Pickwick from the Doré vaults. Keep your fingers crossed.

***There is already a Pickwick LP release, with *Linda* on it, HISTORY OF ROCK 'N' ROLL VOLUME 3, Various Artists, Pickwick SPC-3677 (Stereo).

***In coming months, Jan and Dean will be appearing on many TV shows, including *DINAH* and *MIKE DOUGLAS*. They turned down a *HOLLYWOOD SQUARES*, because it was a nostalgia special, and Jan and Dean do not get involved in any situations that have anything to do with oldies for nostalgia sake, or anything that has legendary overtones! The reason for this is that the bulk of Jan and Dean's audience is under 20 and they are hearing Jan and Dean's music ("oldies") for the very first time.

***The Neil Young LP *TONIGHT'S THE NIGHT* on Warner Brothers (S2221) features the title song, which is about Jan's late brother Bruce, who was Neil's road manager. Also featured is the song *Don't You Just Know It*.

11

The Turntable — DJ Notes
An Oldie for Your Radio Show

Right this minute, *SURF CITY* is a giant hit in Holland and Belgium!

Trivia: In 1963, only 13-year-old girls and weirdos like yours truly bought records. Today, any top-ten hit goes gold. That is because, since the Beatles and Sonny & Cher made rock acceptable to adults, people from age 8 to 80 buy rock 'n' roll records. Not so in the days of early-'60s rock. That is why, over a ten-year career with over two dozen hit records, Jan and Dean had only one million seller, *SURF CITY*. Well, as of October 20, 1979, *SURF CITY* is #6 in Belgium and #3 in Holland the second week running! Put *that* on your turntable and play it!

★★

Subscribe to SUNSHINE MUSIC

SUNSHINE MUSIC will be published four times a year, with an issue coming out each Summer, Fall, Winter, and Spring. As I find it possible, special issues will be published in between the four seasonal issues.

The subscription rate is $5 for seven issues. This includes the regular seasonal issues and the special in-between issues. Thus, a subscription could run for one and 3/4 years if I put out only the regular seasonal issues. More realistically, the seven-issue subscription will last about one year.

As I promised last issue, if my cost of putting out this magazine goes down, you will reap the benefits. That is, if I have 1,000 subscribers, I can put out the magazine for much less per person than I can if I have 100 subscribers. Which means I can serve you better in one or more of several possible ways. I will make the magazine longer. I will add professionally half-toned photos, which really cost. And/or I will publish BONUS FREE ISSUES to all current subscribers, issues which will not count against subscriptions.

In other words, you will get your money's worth, or my name is not Myke..., er, I mean Michael... Doc Rock...?

Send $5 payable to Michael Kelly (that's the name my bank likes), and mail your subscription and correspondence to *SUNSHINE MUSIC*
Box 1166
Lawrence, KS 66044

Jan and Dean with Papa Doo Run Run
Mill Run Theater, Illinois — October 15, 1979

The Old Mill Run Theatre has 3,000 seats and all of them were filled. There was a second show added that night and that was quickly sold out as well.

The show started with Papa Doo Run Run. They came out and did some oldies and some original songs. As usual, they were full of energy and good sounds.

When Jan and Dean joined Papa on stage, things really took off. The show was absolutely fantastic! Jan sounded better than he had in performances before he got back with Dean. His voice and singing have continued to improve. I'm glad that Jan is now singing with a band that can sing and play the music.

There was a point in the performance when Dean got crazy. He asked if anyone had a skateboard and three of them were brought on stage from the audience. Dean did a quasimodo right off the stage.

When they left the stage, the audience demanded more. They came back on stage, did an encore, and left (they had a second show to do). The audience wanted still more when the house lights came on.

Everybody wanted more. But what we got was lots of fun and really a great experience.

I got backstage between shows. I talked with Dean for a while. And I met Jan (something I'd wanted to do for several years).

★PICTURES AND TAPES★

For Sale: Color pictures of Jan and Dean with Papa Doo Run Run in concert at the Mill Run Theater in Illinois on October 15, 1979. 20 pictures for $12.00.

There is also a variety of Jan and Dean related cassette tapes available. For a list of titles and rates, see Issue One of *SUNSHINE MUSIC*, or write directly to: Marny Koch
285 White Oak Lane
Winnetka, IL 60093

White But Alright
or
Two Silhouettes on the Stage

Such irony. Throughout the middle '60s, J&D were considered light-weight, frivolous, and not to be taken seriously (which produced the best music in two decades and suited Dean to a "T"). And here, in the early '60s Jan and Dean thrilled black audiences throughout the South as they toured with Little Richard's band as their backup group!

Myke: In 1968 I found a record store in Topeka, Kansas, called *Moser and Chubbs*, run by a very, very old man and woman. They opened the store in 1956 and never, never had sent back surplus 45's to the record companies after songs were no longer selling. As a result, in the late '60s she had boxes and boxes of old, dusty records. But she wouldn't let you browse through them. You had to ask for a specific want.

At the store, I got all my Doré singles, all my picture sleeves, and my first Jan and Arnie 45's. Since then, I have gotten several other *Gas Money*'s, *Bonnie Lou*....

Dean: From her, the old lady?

Myke: No, I ran across three brand new *Gas Money*'s in a 10¢ bin in the late '60s at a TG&Y sidewalk sale. All three are marked with a sticker which reads "Certified Top Ten," but I don't know who certified it. Certainly not *BILLBOARD*!

Dean: Did you buy all three?

Myke: Certainly, Dean! Why? Do you need copies of some of the early records?

Dean: No, no, I was just curious. That's what I would do. If I'm looking for something, you buy, you're so hungry for it, you buy them all. Then later you wonder why you have so many!

Myke: The last record I got from her was Billy Ward and His Dominoes *Jennie Lee*. A black group covering a white artist!

Dean: Well, they figured it was the other way around. They thought we were stealing the black sound. So, therefore, it was okay for the black artist to cover the white artist's song.

You know, one of the first tours we ever did, we showed up where we were supposed to meet everybody, and they were very surprised to find we were white guys and they just sounded (on records) black. We'd heard some of them, and we knew they were black, but we didn't know all of the acts were black. We were the only white guys in the tour!

Myke: This was when?

Dean: About '60, '61. I don't really remember what songs we had at the time. I know we had *Baby Talk* and a few of those. And in those days, those sounded black, I guess. So they booked us, just on the basis of those records, figuring that we must be a black group.

The first night of the tour we had no idea that nobody in the audience knew that we weren't black. So they introduced us, and we were standing backstage with Bobby Day [*Rockin' Robin*, *Over and Over*], Little Willie John [*Fever*], and the backup band for everyone, the Little Richard Band. All very heavy groups, but all very black!

So they introduced us, and the crowd went crazy! Just crazy! Until we walked out! Then it went suddenly silent! They were shocked.

Myke: And so were you?

Dean: And so were we! Cause we thought they would keep screaming 'cause then they knew we were white and they were still screaming for you in spite of it. But, it became obvious when we came out that they were screaming at the record they'd heard and thought was a black group singing it. And it was REALLY surprising to them when the two whitest people they'd ever seen walked out.

Myke: Blond, blue eyes!

Dean: Oh, blond hair, yeah!

Myke: Did you lip sync to a record, or did you do it live?

Dean: No, we did it live with the band, Little Richard's Band, which was a *damn* good band. And they really helped us out. They got the people enthused again, because the initial response to our color was... *quite noticeable*.

Then about half way through the first song they were starting to get over the shock. By the time we finished the second or third song, they were into it with us again. But that initial gasp, it was—well, really kind of funny.

[Editor's note: Here comes the old Dean:]

The first time, it was a shock. Then we decided it was something we could play for, each show! "Oh, just wait til they see! [cackles with glee]". So at each show we would have all the lights way down when we were introduced. Then we would go out there and start singing, and they would all be going crazy....

Myke: And then the lights would go on *as you were singing*!?

Dean: Yeah, and it used to really surprise them!

That was a very weird tour. We couldn't stay in the same hotels as they could. If they went to a black motel we couldn't stay there, and if we went to a white motel they couldn't stay there. And we played mostly the South, which made it very strange. They'd usually have to sneak us into their rooms, most of the time we did that 'cause it was much harder to sneak all of them into our rooms.

Very weird, like eating. We'd all eat together, but we got absolutely terrible service. Nobody would wait on our tables!

Hyke: Well, that's sho' biz!

SUNSHINE MUSIC 2

Survey of Favorite Songs

I ran a survey of favorite Jan and Dean songs in an issue of Mark Plummer's RIPPED BAGGIES Newsletter. But Mark never got around to publishing the results. The turnout was very good, with an awful lot of Jan and Dean fans sending me their opinions as to what were and were not the best Jan and Dean records. So, I will publish the results of the survey in SUNSHINE MUSIC, beginning right now. Five survey items will be reported this issue: Favorite 3 Doré songs.
Favorite 5 Liberty chart songs.
Favorite 5 LPs.
Favorite 5 Jan Berry songs.
Favorite 5 Dean Torrence songs.

I'd better explain the scoring method I used. It is a point system, based on how highly you ranked your favorite songs. Take the question of favorite Liberty chart songs. I asked for your top *five*. So, if you listed *Fiddle Around* as your number one favorite, it got *five* points. If you listed *Surf City* as your second favorite, it got four points. The song listed third would get three points, the song listed fourth, two points, and the fifth would get only one point.

This system was used so that a song you liked best would get more credit than one liked less well. On questions asking for three or seven favorites, the point scale went from three to one, and from seven to one. The points each song got is given next to its position ranking of first, second, etc. Also, in parentheses the number of people who answered that it was their first choice for that question is given. This number was used to break ties where two songs got the same number of points.

Everyone confused? Good, let's move on to the results.

1. Favorite three Doré songs.

Baby Talk was the clear favorite on Doré, getting more first-place votes than all the rest combined. The second choice, *Baggy Pants*, was a distant second, with about 1/3 the points of *Baby Talk*. One reason for this is that for many Ripped Baggies members, *Baby Talk* was the only Doré song they were familiar with.

```
 1.    57 (15)     Baby Talk
 2.    15          Baggy Pants
 3.    11   (1)    Clementine
 4.    10   (3)    Gee
 5.     8   (1)    We Go Together
        tied       White Tennis Sneakers
 6.     7          There's A Girl
 7.     6          Jeanette, Get Your Hair Done
 8.     4   (1)    Such a Good Night for Dreaming
 9.     3          Judy's An Angel
10.     2          Rosie Lane
11.     1          My Heart Sings
        tied       Jennie Lee (?)
        tied       You're On My Mind
```

BACK ISSUES & SAMPLE COPIES

Single back issues of SUNSHINE MUSIC #1 are available for $1. A sample copy of the current issue of SUNSHINE MUSIC may always be had, for $1. Send checks payable to SUNSHINE MUSIC
Michael Kelly to
Box 1166
Lawrence, KS 66044

★ ★ ★ ★ ★ ★ ★

DEADMAN'S CURVE RECORDS

Last issue I printed a note concerning an LP which was due to be available soon. Well, it is available NOW, and it is a real collector's item. The album is *JAN AND DEAN LIVE AT THE KEYSTONE BERKELEY*, September 22, 1978, with Papa Doo Run Run. This was the fourth gig J&D and Papa ever did together.

The black and white LP cover was designed by Dean. Pictures taken outside the Golden Bear are featured, and the record label design features a butterfly.

What kind of music is on the album? Well, there are 18 cuts:

Side One		Side Two	
Surf City	Little Deuce Coupe	Good Vibrations	China Girls
Help Me Rhonda	Shut Down	California Girls	Brown Sugar
Dead Man's Curve	Sidewalk Surfin'	I Get Around	409
Little Old Lady	Do You Wanna Dance	Fun Fun Fun	Be True to Your School
Dance Dance Dance		Barbara Ann	

There is some J&D joking featured on the LP, which was recorded in Mono on a portable cassette recorder, yet is supposed to be pretty good quality for a cassette recording.

Only 500 copies have been pressed as yet, but if response is good, a later pressing of 5,000 is hoped for. Either way, a copy from the first 500 would be a collector's item for sure.

Who has this LP for sale? Well, it is Larry Melton, a long-time J&D fan in Southern California. He has put his own money into this project and is counting on enough fan response to pull him out of debt. The LP is semi-authorized by the Titanic Twosome, who will get royalties on the sales of the LP. Larry has the 500 copies in his living room and will fill orders immediately. If you have questions, call him at 415-826-4982. To order send to:

Deadman's Curve Records $12.00 C.O.D.
Dept. SM $14.50 1st Class
858 Shotwell $12.81 Special 4th Class
San Francisco, CA 94110 $15.28 California Residents

SUNSHINE MUSIC 2

HUMO'S TOP-20 — VAN DE PLATENVERKOPERS (BELGIUM)

STAND OP 27-9-79

Stand op 13 Sept.	#	Titel	Aantal weken in Top-20
1	1	Quiero me mucho — Julio Iglesias (CBS)	7
6	2	We don't talk anymore — Cliff Richard (EMI)	7
3	3	Gotta go home — Boney M. (Ariola)	7
7	4	I don't like mondays — Boomtown Rats (Phonogr.)	5
10	5	Don't bring me down — E.L.O. (CBS)	3
2	6	I was made for loving you — Kiss (Vogue)	11
8	7	Gloria — Umberto Tozzi (CBS)	7
4	8	Angel eyes — Roxy Music (Polydor)	9
5	9	Voulez-vous? — Abba (Vogue)	9
9	10	Surf City — Jan & Dean (Fonior)	1
12	11	This is my life — Shirley Bassey (EMI)	9
13	12	A brand new day — Wic Stars (EMI)	1
15	13	Can't stand losing you — The Police (CBS)	1
17	14	Beat the clock — Sparks (Ariola)	3
15	Begin the beguine — Johnny Mathis (CBS)	1
11	16	You can't change that — Raydio (EMI)	7
16	17	In mijn caravan — Will Tura (Topkapi)	5
18	Eeny meeny miny mou — Luv' (Philips)	1
14	19	After the love has gone — Earth, Wind & Fire (CBS)	5
20	Bad girls — Donna Summer (Philips)	9

NEDERLAND singles Hilv. 3 (Buma/Stemra)

1	BRAND NEW DAY	Wic Stars	3
2	QUIERE ME MUCHO	Julio Iglesias	4
3	DEAD MAN'S CURVE	Jan & Dean	2
4	WE DON'T TALK ANYMORE	Cliff Richard	2
5	I DON'T LIKE MONDAYS	Boomtown Rats	2
6	DON'T STOP	Massada	20
7	ARUMBAI	Raydio	6
8	MARCHING ON	Boney M	8
9	GOTTA GO HOME	Jan & Zwaan	2
10	IK ZOEK EEN MEISJE	Willem Duyn	
11	WILLEM	Cindy	
12	NOELA HOEP	Kiss	11
13	I WAS MADE FOR LOVIN' YOU	Commodores	
14	SAIL ON	E.L.O.	9
15	DON'T BRING ME DOWN	The Specials	17
16	GANGSTERS	Bellamy Bros	19
18	IF I SAID YOU HAVE...	Michael Jackson	13
19	GIVE UP YOUR GUNS	The Buoys	10
20	EENY MEENY MINY MOU	Luv	

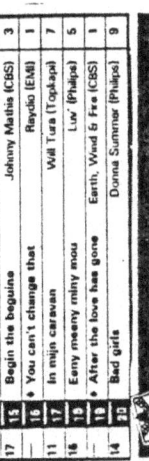

HOLLAND
(Courtesy TROS Radio)
As of 10/2/79
SINGLES

This Week	Last Week		
1	1	A BRAND NEW DAY, Wic Stars, EMI	
2	2	QUEREME MUCHO, Julio Iglesias, CBS	
3	3	SURF CITY, Jan & Dean, Bureco	
4	4	WE DON'T TALK ANYMORE, Cliff Richard, EMI	
5	18	DON'T STOP, Michael Jackson, Epic	
6	6	WILLEM, Willem Duyn, Philips	
7	7	ARUMBAI, Massada, Kendel	
8	8	I DON'T LIKE MONDAYS, Boomtown Rats, Mercury	
9	9	SAIL ON, Commodores, Motown	
10	10	GANGSTERS, Specials, Chrysalis	
11	11	MARCHING ON, B.Z.N., Mercury	
12	16	IF I SAID YOU HAD A BEAUTIFUL BODY, Bellamy Brothers, Warner Bros.	
13	13	ANGEL EYES, Roxy Music, Polydor	
14	NEW	SURE KNOW SOMETHING, Kiss, Casablanca	
15	9	GOTTA GO HOME/EL LUTE, Boney M, Ariola/Fleet	
16	13	CAN'T STAND LOSING YOU, Police, A&M	
17	NEW	WE BELONG TO THE NIGHT, Ellen Foley, CBS/Cleveland Int.	
18		LOST IN MUSIC, Sister Sledge, Atlantic	
19	NEW	TUSK, Fleetwood Mac, Warner Bros	
20	NEW	THE WORKER, Fischer Z, United Artists	

SUNSHINE MUSIC 2

CELEBRATE THE NEWSLETTER is a new Beach Boys fanzine that understands all too well the highly restricted leisure time schedule of the modern day fan. Consequently, editor Marty Tuber has thoughtfully scrapped his earlier FRIENDS OF THE BEACH BOYS policy of printing massive 60-page issues, chock-full of fun and fascinating facts and fiction, in favor of a new CELEBRATE THE NEWSLETTER policy of printing minimal 4- or 5-page issues which are still lots of fun. Send 50¢ ($1.00 for overseas airmail) and rest assured that you'll be able to read the next issue and still get in 18 holes of golf. Write to: Marty Tuber
33 Caroline Street
Albion, NY 14411

CALIFORNIA MUSIC!!!

It may seem strange to go to Australia to get "California Music," but at 2 Kentwell Avenue, Concord 2137 Australia, Stephen J. McParland puts it out! With an emphasis on Jan and Dean, this fine 'zine covers everything from the well-knowns (Beach Boys) to the unknowns (Tony Rivers). For the true collector, not the casual fan.

LETTERS

Dear Michael,

I heard on America Top 40 October 27, that Jan and Dean tied with the Everly Brothers as most popular duo. It seems that J&D had six American top 40 hits in 1964, while the Everly's had eight in 1958. Casey Kasem played *Surf City* as an extra the week before. I hope you can print this information, because it can encourage J&D fans to really buzz the radio stations.

Thank you,

Dave Rocke
Massachusetts

Dear Michael,

Yes, it is true that *Surf City* was on the hit charts in Holland. Belgium, the friendly neighbor of Holland, which always follows the trends of Holland, now has it on the Belgium Top-40, which is very serious in that field. In Holland they already have a new Jan and Dean number on the charts. *Dead Man's Curve*, which is in third place. Enclosed you will find Belgium charts.

Keep Rockin',

Vic Van Dessel
Editor, *THE ROCKIN' FIFTIES*
Leurshoek 74/1
B- 2750 Beveren Waas
Belgium

Clementine did well, in third place with 11 points, barely beating fourth-place *Gee* with 10 points. By noting that *Clementine* got only one first-place vote, compared to three for *Gee*, you can see that many more people included *Clementine* on their lists than included *Gee*. That is, *Gee* got nine of its 10 points from first-place votes, while *Clementine* got only three of her 11 from first-placers.

The humor-satire of Jan and Dean did well in the Doré voting, with humorous tunes placing seventh, fifth, second, and, if you count *Baby Talk*, first.

One more thing. Since I got to see all of your favorites, fair play dictates that I tell you my favorites:

1. Baby Talk (original, ain't I!)
2. Such A Good Night For Dreaming (good slow-dance song)
3. You're On My Mind

2. Favorite five Liberty chart songs.

It was close, folks. For a while I thought that *Dead Man's Curve* would win, but *Surf City* emerged victorious. So what else is new?

1.	90	(9)	Surf City
2.	77	(6)	Dead Man's Curve
3.	39	(2)	The Little Old Lady From Pasadena
4.	33	(0)	Sidewalk Surfin'
5.	30		Drag City
6.	29	(2)	The New Girl In School
7.	27	(5)	Linda
8.	25	(1)	Ride The Wild Surf
9.	12		Popsicle
10.	11	(1)	From All Over The World
11.	11		I Found A Girl
	tied		Anaheim Azusa
12.	6		Fiddle Around
13.	5		You Really Know How To Hurt A Guy
14.	2		Tennessee

Look at that *Sidewalk Surfin'*! With no first-place votes, it won slot four! Which means that is was nobody's favorite, but on almost everyone's list of top five. Compare this against *Linda*, coming in at only seventh in spite of *five first-place* votes! Virtually no one included it on their list unless as number one!

Sum surprises: Three of Dean's least faves did well: *I Found A Girl*, *Fiddle Around*, and *You Really Know How To Hurt A Guy*

(to p.18)

* * * * * * *

SUNSHINE MUSIC 2

Batman and *Honolulu Lulu* got nothin'! I like those two quite a lot, although my top five looks like this:

1. Linda (my first Jan and Dean record!)
2. Dead Man's Curve (my second J&D LP)
3. Sidewalk Surfin' (mono version only!)
4. Drag City (stereo version only)
5. AACSCBRATA (a masterpiece of studio work)

5. Favorite five LPs.

There is not much consensus on this question. With a choice of three Doré records, 11 different songs got votes. With a choice of five, 15 Liberty hits got votes. But with a choice of five, 23 LPs made the list.

Surprise! The number one choice was *RIDE THE WILD SURF*, the LP that Alan Betrock in the *ROCK MARKETPLACE*, July 1973, said was "rushed out" to coincide with the movie, and contained some "filler cuts." Still, it is a great surf LP.

1. 51 (3) Ride The Wild Surf
2. 45 (1) Drag City
3. 40 (3) Command Performance
4. 37 (2) Little Old Lady From Pasadena
5. 35 (6) The Sound of Jan and Dean (Dore)
6. 35 (4) Legendary Masters Anthology
7. 29 (2) Dead Man's Curve
8. 18 (1) Folk 'n' Roll
9. 17   Gotta Take That One Last Ride
10. 12 (1) Golden Hits Volume 2
11. 9   Filet of Shit
12. 8 (1) Jan and Dean (Sunset)
13. 8   Surf City
14. 7   Linda
15. 5 (1) Old Wax and New Waves
16. 5   Save For A Rainy Day (Columbia)
17. 4   Batman
    tied The Very Best Volume 2
18. 3   Popsicle
    tied Golden Hits
19. 1   Coke Jingles LP
    tied Save For A Rainy Day (J&D)
20. 0   LJ, Design, Challenge cuts
    tied Pop Symphony
    tied Golden Hits Volume 3
    tied The Very Best Volume 1

Second place went to *DRAG CITY*, my first J&D LP. To me, this is prime Jan and Dean.... fresh, young, well-financed, fully engineered, custom-written. The *LIVE--IN CONCERT!* album came in third, again something of a surprise since the "live" cuts do not resemble the hits at all (except *From All Over The World*). But my guess is that we all love the vicarious pleasure of J&D in concert, live; we love to hear them talking and joking (even if Liberty did cut out 99% of the fun); and we like to hear their voices in new arrangements.

The *ANTHOLOGY* came in at sixth, and *GOTTA TAKE THAT ONE LAST RIDE* at ninth! Pretty good, for reissues! *FOLK 'N' ROLL*, a "Jan" album that Dean wasn't much into, did quite well. *FILET OF SHIT* (as Dean calls it) also made a fine showing, considering it was a mish-mash and had no hit on it. Again, the "live" aspect probably attracts a lot of us.

POP SYMPHONY did nothing. Here are my choices:

1. DRAG CITY
2. FILET OF SHIT
3. LINDA
4. SAVE FOR A RAINY DAY (Columbia version)
5. COMMAND PERFORMANCE

Honorable Mention: POP SYMPHONY

6. Top five Jan songs.

Now, I LOVE Jan's post-wreck sides. I have them on a car tape that I play constantly. I think they are masterpieces of arranging, engineering, subtle mixing, and lively performances.

1. 42 (3) Little Queenie
2. 35 (1) Sing Sang A Song
3. 34 (5) Skateboard Surfin' USA
4. 33 (3) That's The Way It Is
5. 30 (3) Tinsel Town
6. 16   How, How I Love Her
7. 14 (1) Don't You Just Know It
8. 14   Fun City
9. 12   Mother Earth
10. 10 (2) Totally Wild
11. 6   Your Sweet Sweet Love
12. 5 (1) Tomorrow's Teardrops
13. 4   Blow Up Music
14. 4   Sing Sang A Song Singalong Version
15. 3   Fan Tan
    tied Laurel and Hardy
16. 2   Girl, You're Blowing My Mind
17. 1   Love and Hate

But I never cared much for *Queenie* or *Skateboard*, so I was really taken off guard when they placed one and three! And I like *Mother Earth* a lot, but better than the spirited anthem of adoration and love, *Totally Wild*?!

This was my hardest to select, because I love them all. But, when you gotta, ya' just gotta:

1. Totally Wild
2. Your Sweet, Sweet Love (slow version)
3. Sing Sang A Song (I don't understand it, but I love it)
4. Fun City
5. Love and Hate

SUNSHINE MUSIC 2

Jan & Dean's LP Record

We all know how popular each of Jan and Dean's 45's of the fifties and sixties was. As a matter of fact, they had 29 consecutive singles on the national charts. *Surf City* was the biggie, #1, while *The Universal Coward* missed the top 100 altogether, bubbling only as far as #105. But what about the Jan and Dean albums? how well did each of the famous Liberty LP's sell? Here is the Jan and Dean Liberty Top 101

#10.

The least successful Jan and Dean LP to hit the Billboard chart was FOLK 'N' ROLL. It stayed on Billboard's chart for only 3 weeks. Interestingly, this LP was probably Dean's least favorite, since it is so short on humor and satire and long on serious, "meaningful" songs. I don't even hear Dean on at least four of the cuts. Of three singles from the LP, only one made the top 40. The LP is uneven, with some very tight, fine cuts (*Turn, Turn, Turn, A Beginning From An End*, etc.) and some satire (*Folk City*) and even some "schlock rod" (*Hang On Sloopy*).

#9.

Next was a 5-week wonder, FILET OF SOUL. This was released after Jan's accident, against the team's wishes. A later issue will give a detailed account of this weird and wonderful LP.

#8.

GOLDEN HITS VOLUME 2 has all their big Liberty songs, from *Linda* to *You Really Know How to Hurt A Guy*. The only fault of this LP is that *Dead Man's Curve* is the wrong take, *From All Over The World* is not the hit version (I like it better anyway), and, in stereo, *Little Old Lady From Pasadena* is too slow and *Sidewalk Surfin'* is slow and missing sound effects. Those engineers at Liberty are sure sloppy. I guess that the Sinatra kidnapping had the artists too tied up to supervise the package. A real treat is the jacket, showing a lot of old pictures from the 45 and LP sleeves, sensational liner notes by Spleen himself, and the only publicity still I have ever seen from the Jan and Dean feature film.

#7.

Now we are getting somewhere. For a long 21 weeks, THE NEW GIRL IN SCHOOL hung on the chart. This was originally called DEADMAN'S CURVE by Liberty and given a black and pink cover photo. Later pressings, with DEADMAN'S CURVE the big hit, had a color photo. This LP gave the only good stereo version of *DMC*. It had *School Days*, which was the last single Liberty released after Jan and Dean left the label. It provided hits for the Rip (Bruce & Terry and Jan & Dean) Chords (*Three Window Coupe*) and Ronny and the Daytonas (*Bucket T*). The latter was *Jennie Lee*, again! I love it in stereo.

Two instrumentals fill out the album. Dean is on paper triangle, and Jan wails out on the pencil and pillow. Each side ends with a strong cut, real hit material, *Hey Little Freshman* and *My Mighty GTO*. GTO later appeared in another form on the flip of *Little Old Lady From Pasadena*.

---

7. Top five Dean songs.

From '67 to '70, I *lived* on Dean's cuts. Lived and breathed them, that is. There was not a clear winner here, with *Yellow Balloon* doing well in first and second places. As with the Dore and Jan items, many people were familiar with only a very few, usually hit songs.

1.	34 (4)	Yellow Balloon
2.	32 (1)	Summertime, Summertime
3.	22 (1)	Vegetables
4.	19 (2)	Gonna Hustle You
5.	19 (1)	Like A Summer Rain
6.	13 (1)	Summer Means Fun
7.	11 (2)	Sunshine Music
8.	10 (2)	I Only Have Eyes For You
9.	10 (1)	Sidewalk Surfin'
10.	9 (1)	Louisiana Man
11.	tied 7 (1)	Pocketful of Rainbows
12.	tied 5	California Lullabye
	tied	Taste of Rain
13.	tied 4	Laurel and Hardy (?)
	tied	Raindrops
14.	tied 3	Be True To Your School (?)
	tied	Rain On The Roof
	tied	I Get Around
15.	tied 1	Get A Job
	tied	Fan Tan (?)
	tied	Hawaii/Tiajuana (?)

It is interesting that while most of Jan's top ten sound much alike as far as vocals and backings go, all of Dean's top 12 are distinct sounds. Jan's are like cuts on an LP, while Dean's are almost like they were by different artists.

In many ways I prefer the post-wreck work to the Liberty material, and my favorite Dean songs are:

1. I Only Have Eyes For You (on the car radio in the movie)
2. Like A Summer Rain (of three versions or more, the 2:17 45 version)
3. Taste Of Rain (especially in stereo!!!)
4. Gonna Hustle You (stereo flip of UA Sidewalk Surfin')
5. Yellow Balloon
tied Cal Lullabye, Louisiana Man, Sidewalk Surfin' on UA!

That's all for this issue. Look for more results in coming issues of SUNSHINE MUSIC. Meanwhile, let me say how much I enjoyed hearing from you all. The letters that many of you sent were a pleasure. Just as important, it was gratifying to have concrete evidence that I was, in fact, *not* the only person who spent hours and hours listening to Jan and Dean between 1966 and 1975, the years of obscurity for J&D.

* * *

SUNSHINE MUSIC 2

Cruising

Let me take this opportunity to cruise issue number two of SUNSHINE MUSIC just before it "goes to press." Besides the TV shows mentioned in SHORT CUTS, it is rumored that Jan and Dean will be on Donahue. Unfortunately, I have not been able to confirm this, but I wanted to alert you to the possibility. Also unfortunately, I am not early enough to advise you that Jan and Dean were on the Midnight Special December 21.

With reference to the ads you see in SUNSHINE MUSIC, so far they have all been run for free or for trades. I know the advertisers or have personal knowledge of them, and believe they will be reliable in their dealings with you. Let me know if you have any trouble with any of them, and I will try to help and will quit running their ads, as well as let everyone else know of your problems.

The letters I printed this issue were just samples of the many I have been privileged to receive in recent weeks. If you write a letter which you would like to have me consider for printing in SUNSHINE MUSIC, then be sure to indicate that such is the case in your letter. Otherwise, I will assume you are just communicating with me and will not give your letter special consideration for printing.

I encourage you to write if you have any questions which I can in turn get an answer from Jan and Dean on. That is the whole idea of SUNSHINE MUSIC--to bring us, the fans, closer to them, the entertainers.

In case you wonder, the top-ten LP ranking of Jan and Dean's albums is based on the Billboard LP Charts. That is, the album ranked #1 reached the highest position on the charts, the album ranked #2 reached the second highest position, etc. The number of weeks each LP stayed on the charts is just noted for interests' sake.

The title track is a great tapestry of voices. *Drag Strip Girl* is a delightful parody of *Surfer Girl*. *Surfin' Hearse* (not to be confused with the later song by the Quads) sounds a lot like a California version of Dion and the Belmonts. *Schlock Rod* is freewheeling satire.

Popsicle Truck, released in '66 by Dean on a 45 as *Popsicle*, is basic bomp-surf. Jimmy Gilmer and the Fireballs' *Sugar Shack* was the source for *Surf Route 101*, where an unidentified girl makes surfing sound like real fun! *Sting Ray* was later done by the Routers by Bones Howe, engineer and co-composer. And *Little Deuce Coupe*, the weakest cut, features Glen and a Beach Boy or two.

The Jan and Dean Top Ten. Quite interesting, isn't it? I hope your favorite album did well. In case it didn't look at it this way. Ranked by duration on the chart, the line up is like this: 10, *FOLK 'N' ROLL* (3 weeks); 9, *FILET OF SOUL* (5 weeks); 8, *VOLUME TWO* (6 weeks); 7, *LINDA* (10 weeks); 6, *DRAG CITY* (14 weeks); 5, *COMMAND PERFORMANCE* (16 weeks); 4, *RIDE THE WILD SURF* (19 weeks); 3, *LITTLE OLD LADY FROM PASADENA* (20 weeks); and 2 & 1 tied with *SURF CITY* and *DEAD MAN'S CURVE* (21 weeks).

New Jan and Dean Records

It came as quite a surprise, but there were a lot of newly released records during the first part of this winter.

45	Netherlands	GIP 4067		Surf City/Dead man's curve (sic)
45	Netherlands	GIP 4071		I Get Around/Little Old Lady/Ride the Wild Surf
45	Belgium	Ariola 101047		Surf City/Deadman's Curve
45	Australia	UA 006 82726		Surf City/Little Old Lady
LP	Netherlands	GIP 33021		Surf City
LP	Australia	K-Tel NA 536		The Jan and Dean Story
LP	California	Deadman's Curve Records		Live Concert LP
LP	U.S.	United Artists LT 999		Deadman's Curve
LP	Netherlands	Sunset 128 60020/21		Jan and Dean

The Netherlands LP features Dean and Papa Doo Run Run recreating the Jan and Dean (and Beach Boy) hits. The Australian LP features the recreations plus old Dore and Challenge tracks. The California LP is an "Authorized Bootleg." The U.S. LP is a great reissue of original Jan and Dean tracks. The cover of the LP and the great picture of Jan are worth the price alone. Although uncredited, Dean controlled the graphics, as evidenced by the gulls, the yellow motif, and the fact that he picked the photos. The Netherlands Sunset LP has the Anthology LP cuts.

OCTOBER 20, 1979, BILLBOARD

HOLLAND
(Courtesy Billboard Benelux)
As of 10/5/79
SINGLES

This Week	Last Week		
1	2	BRAND NEW DAY, Van Shelton, EMI
2	1	DON'T STOP, Michael Jackson, Epic
3	4	SURF CITY, Jan & Dean, Dureco
4	3	QUEREME MUCHO, Julio Iglesias, CBS
5	17	WE DON'T TALK ANYMORE, Cliff Richard, EMI
6	6	WE BELONG TO THE NIGHT, Ellen Bos
7	12	IF I SAID YOU HAD A BEAUTIFUL BODY, Bellamy Brothers, Warner Bros.
8	8	SAIL ON, Commodores, Motown
9	14	SURE KNOW SOMETHING, Kiss
10	10	WILLEM, Willem Duyn, Philips
11	5	GANGSTERS, The Specials, Chrysalis
12	19	TUSK, Fleetwood Mac, Warner Bros.
13	13	I DON'T LIKE MONDAYS, Boomtown Rats
14	11	LOST IN MUSIC, Sister Sledge, Atlantic
15	18	MARCHING ON, D.J.M. Mercury
16	16	WHATEVER YOU WANT, Status Quo, Vertigo
17	NEW	YOU CAN DO IT, Al Hudson & Soul Partners, MCA
18	NEW	MESSAGE IN A BOTTLE, The Police, A&M
19	NEW	STREET LIFE, Crusaders, MCA

BELGIUM
(Courtesy Billboard Benelux)
As of 10/5/79
SINGLES

This Week	Last Week		
1	2	WE DON'T TALK ANYMORE, Cliff Richard, EMI
2	1	QUEREME MUCHO, Julio Iglesias, CBS
3	4	GOTTA GO HOME/AT LUFT, Boney M, Hansa
4	NEW	I DIDN'T LIKE MONDAYS, Boomtown Rats, Phonogram
5	3	I WAS MADE FOR LOVIN' YOU, Kiss, Vogue
6	5	ANGELO, Brotherhood of Man, Pye/Vogue
7	NEW	GLORIA, Umberto Tozzi, CBS
8	NEW	ALINE, Christophe, Vogue
9	NEW	SURF CITY, Jan & Dean, Dureco
10	8	VOULEZ-VOUS, Abba, Vogue

SUNSHINE MUSIC

Jan Dean Papa

Editor
Michael "Doc Rock" Kelly

Copy Editor
Dean O. Torrence

Associate Editor
Frank M. Kisko

Graphics/Layout
eye design

The Magazine of the Official Jan and Dean
Authorized International Collectors Club

Issue 3 **Spring 1980**

Contents not already copyrighted are © 1979 by Michael Bryan Kelly.

OK Jan and Dean fans world-wide, here is a simplified guide to getting SUNSHINE MUSIC into your mail box safe and sound:

SUBSCRIPTIONS

```
Subscription, 7 issues - - - - - - - - - - - - - $5.00
Sample Issue - - - - - - - - - - - - - - - - - - $1.00
Back Issue - - - - - - - - - - - - - - - - - - - $1.00
Overseas Postage
   Surface 7 issues, add - - - - - - - $1.00
   Surface 1 issue, add - - - - - - - - $0.15
   Airmail 7 issues, add - - - - - - - $3.50
   Airmail 1 issue, add - - - - - - - - $0.50
Brown Mailing Envelope (6x9)
   7 issues, add - - - - - - - - - - - - - - - - $1.50
   1 issue, add - - - - - - - - - - - - - - - - - $0.25
      Issue 1 sold out (temporarily?).
```

Make checks payable to Michael Kelly.

● **FIDDLE AROUND**

(As recorded by Jan & Dean/Liberty)
CLINT BALLARD, JR.
LARRY KUSIK

Woh, woh, who fiddle around
(Fiddle fill-in) they would fiddle around and
(Fill-in) they would fiddle around and
around
All over the town.

Do you remember Sally?
Her eyes were big and blue
Her kisses were so tender and warm
But her heart was so untrue
She used to (repeat chorus)

Sue said she'd be faithful
Irene gave me her heart
But they would start a-cheatin' on me
Each time we were apart...oh they would
(repeat chorus)

'Though I've had lots of girlfriends
When all is said and done
Baby, you're the only girl for me
'Cause you're the only one...who
doesn't (repeat chorus)

Copyright 1962 by Bourne Co.

21

SUNSHINE MUSIC 3

FROM JAN AND DEAN'S MANAGER

TELEX
237990 SHEF UR

SUITE 2004
375 PARK AVENUE
NEW YORK, N.Y. 10022

(212) 935-9330

Nov 26th, 1979

Mr. Michael Kelly
Sunshine Music
c/o Doc Rock
Box 1166
Lawrence, Kan. 66044

Dear Michael:

First of all, the main message that you should convey to your network of fans is that United Artists just released a new JAN & DEAN album entitled "Deadman's Curve" (United Artists LT-999) it is a single album of all the JAN & DEAN classics, but they are all re-mixed so that the entire recording sound is much brighter than the original. Also, the cover has some great pictures of JAN & DEAN today! I urge you to tell as many people as possible about this album. Also tell them to call up radio stations and request that they play JAN & DEAN's songs.

In addition, as for upcoming concert dates, JAN & DEAN and PAPA DOO RUN RUN will be embarking on a major tour around the middle of January, so if you want these dates, write and I'll forward them to you.

Thanks for everything, Michael, and I look forward to hearing from you soon, until then, I remain,

Sincerely yours,

C. Winston Simone

CWS/ns

DEAR JAN AND DEAN

This column is written by YOU, the fan and reader of J&D & SM.

Dear Jan and Dean,

After listening to you for 20 years (of dear) we finally saw your show in May at the Bush Gardens.

I wonder if you realize what was going on in the audience? Besides all the good vibrations going back and forth? There were those who were toddlers when you began recording, and there were second-generation fans, my daughter included. Since this was an open-air theater, people were walking by and suddenly becoming instant fans. "Hey! Who are these guys? Where can I get their records?"

We met an elderly couple who were waiting. They told us how their son had been killed in Vietnam. They had come to your show to remember him, because he had been a huge fan of Jan and Dean. We saw them later during the show, laughing and clapping their hands.

So, I guess what we're trying to say is that there are a lot of us out here who enjoy you two. We enjoyed your music in earlier years, when we listened with the tops down out on dates. You put the fun in the music then, and we will be here to support you again with future records. We will enjoy hearing your music grow, and still enjoy the past.

Sincerely,
Gorden and Carol '80

JAN AND DEAN

Back in the '60s there was a duo who was really fab.
Their names were Jan and Dean
And for their music we were really glad
for they gave us the California dream.

They sang of cars and surfin' and gave us all they had.
The songs we thought were really boss.
With "Sidewalk Surfin'" they set a brand new fad,
But soon through fate it all would seem lost.

In '66 there was a terrible accident
After which all seemed shattered.
Why was it so very coincident
That to me it so much mattered?

Now Jan and Dean are back again,
With the group Papa Doo Run Run.
With the records we make an awful din
And we're having lots of fun.

Their music should go on forever
For so many it will never die.
For me it is just like a lever
That I use to get myself high!

Charlene Copes, 1-12-80

SUNSHINE MUSIC 3

Jan & Dean and Papa in concert, Palo Alto, CA (Feb 23, 1979)
--good quality, 2 shows, 01:50:00 ($5.50)
J&D medley--every song released 1958-1978. 00:19:30 ($0.98)

$3.25 for blank 60-minute cassette*
$4.90 for blank 90-minute cassette*
$0.45 per cassette 1st class postage and handling
$2.00 per cassette international airmail

Also available: Jan & Dean albums on tape for $2.00** each
Jan & Dean singles on tape for $0.20** each
please write for lists

*you may supply your own cassettes--if you send me the money I will get either TDK-AD or MRX

**price of blank cassettes NOT included in this price

write to: Marny Koch
285 White Oak Lane
Winnetka, IL 60093 USA

When requesting lists, SASEs are preferred but not necessary.

SUZY HARVEY RECORD SALE

This group of records is for sale at set prices, first-come, first-served. Postage will be extra. Write directly to Ms. Harvey, and do not send money until she tells you what you were first in line for.

LP's

Golden Hits Vol. 2 (Lib. 3417) Mono VG+ $10.00
Dead Man's Curve/New Girl In School (Lib. 7361) Stereo VG $10.00
Very Best Of Jan and Dean (UA 515) Stereo Vol. 2 Sealed $6.50

45's

Little Old Lady/My Mighty GTO (Lib. 55704) New $3.50
Yellow Balloon/Noollab Wolley by the Yellow Balloon group
Canterbury 508 $2.00
Honolulu Lulu/Someday (Lib. 55613) VG+ $3.00
You Really Know How To Hurt A Guy (Lib.) VG PICTURE SLEEVE $4.50

Write to: SUZY HARVEY   Box 586   Whiting, IN   46394

TAPE LIST

Dean Torrence and Bill Lee (1973)--telephone interview, pretty good, but fuzzy in places. 00:24:00 ($1.20)
Jan Berry, Tom Sumner, Mark Plummer (Apr 1976)--portable cassette recording in Tom's apartment, buzzing at beginning but improves--contains some songs not recorded as of 4/76-- fair/good quality. 01:00:00 ($3.00)
Dean talks about Jan & Dean & Papa Doo Rin Run (1976)--Dean's side of phone interview, good quality. 00:22:30 ($1.13)
Jan Berry "Live at the Palomino" (Nov 14, 1976)--almost studio quality stereo concert, contains a few minor flaws from original. 00:45:00 ($2.25)
Jan at Home (Apr 1977)--pretty good quality. 00:39:00 ($1.95)
Kathy Torrence and Mark Plummer (Apr 1977)--portable cassette recording with Dean's sister, good quality. 01:00:00 ($3.00)
Papa Doo Run Run in concert (summer 1977)--studio quality stereo concert supplied by Papa. 00:43:00 ($2.15)
Papa interviews, Vancouver (Oct 28, 1977)--portable cassette interview, background noise. 01:00:00 ($3.00)
Papa interviews, Seattle (Nov 11&12, 1977)--good quality, VERY spontaneous. 00:45:00 ($2.25)
Dean, Marny Koch, Alexandra Lee (Nov 23, 1977)--portable cassette interview in Dean's office, quality good/fair, some noise toward end. 00:45:00 ($2.25)
Dean Torrence and Steve McParland (Feb 25, 1978)--phone interview from Australia to LA, very good quality, fades slightly in places. 00:30:00 ($1.50)
Myke Kelly reviews Jan's Topeka concert (Mar 1978)--personal recollection of seeing Jan, songs in background, good quality. 00:18:15 ($0.91)
Jan Berry concert, Topeka KS (Mar 14, 1978)--portable cassette recording, fair/good quality, some words difficult to understand. 01:11:45 ($3.59)
Jan Berry Live at Macon County Light Company (Mar 16, 1978)-- portable cassette recording, fair/poor quality. 00:35:00 ($1.75)
Dean interviewed in WVVW-FM, Chicago area (Aug 8, 1978)-- good quality recording from radio. 00:40:00 ($2.00)
Jan & Dean in concert, New York (Jul 15, 1978)--Pretty good quality, a little fuzzy. 00:19:00 ($0.95)
Mr&Mrs Torrence, Mark Plummer, Marny Koch (Aug 24, 1978)-- portable cassette interview in Torrences' home, slight noise in places. 00:28:00 ($1.40)
Papa Doo Run Run, Mark Plummer, Marny Koch (Aug 24, 1978)-- portable cassette recording between shows at Disneyland, some background noise, good quality. 00:25:00 ($1.25)
Jan & Dean and Papa in concert, Palo Alto CA (Sep 23, 1978)-- portable cassette recording, fair/good, 2 shows. 01:37:00 ($4.85)
Backstage with Jan & Dean and Papa (Sep 23, 1978)--lots of noise, fair quality. 00:45:00 ($2.25)
Jan Berry, Diane Osborne, Mark Plummer (Dec 9, 1978)-- Interview in Jan's apartment--part of a song being written --quality fair/good. 01:00:00 ($3.00)
(continued)

LETTERS

Dear Michael,
Did Jan ever marry the girl Annie (from the movie) and was the song Lovely Lady ever a record?
Robin Woodruff

Robin,
Neither Dean nor Jan has ever shared a skateboard on a permanent basis. And, the Lovely Lady song was written on the set of DEADMAN'S CURVE on five-minutes notice by Papa Doo Run Run specifically for the film. For reasons of copyright, Jan's real comeback-45, Mother Earth, a classic ecology ballad, could not be used. Mother Earth was released on Ode records in 1973, in three slightly different mixes.

Hello Doc,
--from Merry Olde England, where we are stationed for the time being. Our daughter goes to a public school here, which is to say a private school. Blazers, straw hats, headmaster, etc. The kids have to shake hands, say good-bye to their teacher, and curtsey to the headmaster!
The other day when I picked her up, I got a nod from the headmaster to go into his office. I thank my lucky stars that I was wearing a skirt and tweed jacket instead of my usual uniform-- blue jeans, Addidas, and stolen RAF sweater!
Well, there in the office sits the Music Mistress. Miss Jump! (I kid you not.) "Mrs. Newbill, your daughter has been teaching all the class a song, and I was wondering if you could tell me what 'bust your buns' refers to?"
"After all, I wouldn't want the other children to be exposed to an indelicate song."
Now, I have already had some wondrous experiences in the Headmaster's office explaining American eccentricities. Not the least of which was why my daughter was absent so we could cut up and consume a domesticated fowl in the middle of the last week in November!
To this day I have visions of future generations of British youth singing Sidewalk Surfin' right along with Yankee Doodle. You see, I told our Miss Jump that the melody in question was an olde American Folk-Surfing Song. And that it was perfectly delicate.
And I kept a straight face yet! (Thank you Jan and Dean!)
Carol N

Carol,
For propriety's sake, let's not expose Miss Jumps' pupils!

Mike, Just a note to thank you for the SUNSHINE MUSIC. I really enjoyed reading about J&D music (almost as much as listening to it)! I'm doing a radio show on Friday nights now (with give-aways and trivia) and the kids sure are turning on to Jan and Dean There are a lot of us out here (in New Mexico) who love that music, even though originally from New York City, like myself!
Frank Cavaliero

Dear Michael Kelly,
In Short Cuts you mentioned that Jan had said that they had "about six gold records" as of 1975. Well, a May, '79 Washington Post article reported the list having swelled to ten gold records (Little Old Lady and Dead Man's Curve were specified). So, either they are counting the sales of reissues, or else the legend hath grown with time!
Kathy Davis

Jan and Dean surf-rocking in D.C.

Sunday finds Jan and Dean, surf-rockers extraordinaire, harmonizing at G.W.U.'s Lisner Auditorium. I would imagine most of you already know about the band's struggle back to life (if not, wait for a rerun of "Dead Man's Curve," so I'll spare you the details and simply mention that at their last appearance in D.C. the faithful were standing on their chairs by the end. Whether that portends miracles or merely testifies to excessive enthusiasm I'll leave to you.

LET ME EXPLAIN

Thanks to all of you for your kind support of my efforts with SUNSHINE MUSIC. It is fun work! Keep writing to me, and keep including the SASE!

Concerning back issues, I have a good supply of Issue #2 on hand. Unfortunately, I am completely out of Issue #1. So, if you need #1, write me and let me know. If there is enough interest, I will get another batch made up.

Last time I told you about Larry Melton's live LP. Well, I have gotten strong feedback from those of you who have ordered the LP. Some of you have written praising the LP. Others have written complaining that Larry Melton has taken your money but never sent you an LP. I have checked on this, and Melton says he is innocent. Since I have no control over him, all I can say is, beware! Deal with him at your own risk. Order COD, perhaps. Whatever.

Many people have written asking about Jan and Dean's recording history. So, I am making available my 11-page Jan and Dean Discography available for $2.

Filet of Jan and Dean

A big part of the Jan and Dean Magic has always been the satire and comedy that they inject into rock and roll. In 1966, there was to be an LP which would bring this facet of J&D to the fore once and for all, and in a permanent form. But in those days, record companies did not give artists much "artistic freedom." But let's let Dean tell the story in his way...

"I guess FILET OF SOUL was the last thing we ever did. And yet, that was what the main breakup of of the Liberty label was about. Our contract was coming up, and we were holding the album over their head. Now, the original FILET OF SOUL album was what you got on LEGENDARY MASTERS, edited down to one side, side four. That's the original, basically, even with a lot of redundant crud cut out.

I WISH YOU HADN'T GONE FAST FORWARD OVER THE MAIN PART OF "DEADMAN'S CURVE."

"That's the way it was on the original album, the way we wanted to do it."

BUT, IT WAS GOOD!

"No, well . . , kind of. It was like all the rest. But, just as you said, how many albums was "Deadman's Curve" on up to that point. We said, 'Here it is, again--let's make it different.'"

BUT ON THIS LIVE VERSION, THE VOICES STAND OUT MORE, MUCH MORE.

"Yes, we let them stand out on this one. On the earlier LP, COMMAND PERFORMANCE, we wanted it to sound pretty exciting, and in a concert you wouldn't be able to hear the voices that well anyway, so that was the feel we were looking for. FILET OF SOUL was approximately the same thing, but, you see, FILET OF SOUL was relating to the other area we were into, which was comedy."

BUT WEREN'T SONGS LIKE "SIDEWALK SURFIN'" AND "DEADMAN'S CURVE" WITH ITS SKATEBOARD TERMS AND SOUND EFFECTS PRIMARILY COMEDY, A PARODY OF THE DRAG SONGS WITH THEIR JARGON AND ENGINE SOUND EFFECTS?

"Yes, that's basically what it was all about, but this was taking it even a step further. Now, on COMMAND PERFORMANCE you didn't hear the comedy. Here we wanted to get into some of the stuff we really did do, which was a lot more involved than one-liners, quick one-liners. Here we wanted to get into some of the stuff that were normally cut out (like on COMMAND)."

AT YOUR KANSAS CITY CONCERT SHORTLY BEFORE JAN'S WRECK, YOU TWO WERE REALLY FUNNY, THE COMEDY WAS THE REAL SHOW.

"Of course! We knew that! We were aware of that! Everyone heard your records, hopefully they were being played. Obviously, the only reason you are out there is because people have heard your records, paid money for them, and have come out to see you. So you figured, do you go and give them straight music, and we chose not to. After four or five years, you just don't want to do that anymore. You go out and you entertain, you go out and give them more, entertaining them and yourself, too. That way you don't get so bored doing the same old songs, and it's spontaneous. None of the stuff on LEGENDARY MASTERS was written. All of it just happened, up there on stage. And, it never happened the same exact way again."

YOU SAY LEGENDARY MASTERS SIDE FOUR IS THE SAME CONCERT AS USED ON SOME SONGS ON FILET OF SOUL? "LET'S HANG ON," WHICH STARTS OVER AND OVER ON LEGENDARY, IS THAT THE SAME EXACT CONCERT AS THE FULL VERSION ON FILET?

"Yeah, same concert, same concert!"

WHY TWO LPS OF THE SAME CONCERT, AND SO DIFFERENT FROM EACH OTHER?

"Well, you see, I guess the whole point of this conversation is that, in the fight over that album, they did it--that was their (Liberty records') album. They waited until we were off the label,"

THAT'S WHAT I THOUGHT!

"and then they did what they wanted to do. As you can hear, that was their solution, that album was totally, totally wrong. They missed the point of that album, which was the comedy. The point was, everybody else had a 'soul album' album, so we created a satire of everybody else's soul album. The Beatles had RUBBER SOUL, whatever esoterically that meant, who knew? You know, everybody was making up stuff. *'Well, RUBBER SOUL means. . .'.*"

WELL, THE BEATLES SAID THAT IT COULD MEAN WHATEVER THE INDIVIDUAL WANTED IT TO, DIDN'T THEY? THAT IT DIDN'T HAVE ANY REAL OR SPECIFIC MEANING?

"Exactly! So, it was with FILET OF SOUL, it didn't have any meaning though everybody could read into it whatever they wanted to. And that was what was fun.

"OK, RUBBER SOUL, which was, abstract, kinda pretty. Then, the Righteous Brothers had come out with BLUE-EYED SOUL, which was kind of nice because you really did have blue-eyed soul. That was a little more relevant. Then James Brown came out with SOULFUL SOUL, soon everybody had some kind of soul. Everybody picked up on it and got so serious. So we said.

SUNSHINE MUSIC 3

26

"Well, that was wrong. That was the wrong theory, they told us. "This is the time that you should do something serious. Not screwing around. Boy, I mean, you haven't had a big hit since last summer, and now you are really taking a chance putting out this silly thing. It sounds like you're not serious at all!'"

BUT THE SERIOUS STUFF, THE PROTEST SONGS, DIDN'T LAST VERY LONG.

"Exactly! This LP was getting back into what we were doing before FOLK 'N' ROLL, but they didn't look at it that way. They wanted us to do the serious songs. They felt that sooner or later we were going to make it on those. As a matter of fact, we almost had Jan convinced of that.

"Yet at this period, we were still loose, still having a lot of fun with it, and not frustrated. Until they started confronting us with 'You can't put out an album with three or four songs on it. We said, 'Yes, we can,' so there was a big battle, throwing people up against walls and swearing at one another. Finally, we said to each other, 'OK, we'll please them 'cause we do want the album to come out, and as it is now they just won't release it. Let's go back into the studio and put a few more songs on it.'

"We went back in, and did a second version of it. We put on three more songs, feeling we just couldn't compromise the project any more by putting any more songs on the album. We felt even that was too many. We had maybe six songs on it now, and said, 'OK, here it is!'

"'That's still against all music biz rules! You guys are nuts. We're not going to put out this album!'

"Around this time we left on the tour, and I can remember calling them from some place in Alabama, I think Birmingham, to see what the status of the album was. They said, 'We are not going to release it. Nobody here likes it. Instead, we are going to have someone else change it, re-edit it, pull out all the talking all together, and re-do it.' And they could, because they had the master tapes."

SO THEY STUCK ON OLD VERSIONS OF "DEADMAN'S CURVE"...

"They wanted this guy, Dave Pell, to re-do the album. Jan told them from Birmingham, "If Dave Pell touches that thing..."

DAVE PELL DID A COVER VERSION OF "MANAH-MANAH" MUCH LATER.

"Pell's now working at Bob Smith Porsche up the street; if you want to go visit him! So Jan said, 'If Dave Pell touches that album I'll break his neck, and I'm not kiddin'!'

"Well..., if the Beatles have RUBBER SOUL..., and the Rightous Brothers have BLUE-EYED SOUL, and James Brown and the black artists have soulful soul/whatever, then we must have... (chuckle) FILET OF SOUL! I mean, (ironically) it's obvious!"

"So that's how the title came about. Then everybody asked, 'What's FILET OF SOUL?' To us, our soul wasn't really in just the music, rather it was in the presentation of the music, it was in the overall satire and the dryness, and we promoted that, over time. With each record, I think, we got a little more obvious with the humor. Finally, we wanted to give them an album where they can really see how obvious it had become, and see how they would pick up on it.

"So the original FILET OF SOUL has four songs on it; the rest is all talk. Introducing people in the audience that we knew. Mistakes. People falling off the stage. Introducing individually the entire band."

BUT THERE ARE NO COPIES OF THAT ORIGINAL ALBUM, JUST THE ORIGINAL TAPE?

"I have one copy, and I have it on tape, too. Eh, some day I'll see if I can get you a copy of it, or a tape copy."

YEAH!

"I'd like to make a copy of it. At least 1 finally got to get a part of it out on the Anthology Album (side four), which I'm glad about. But even that is not as radical as the original.

"We took that original in to Liberty. We had spent a lot of time on it, and a lot of money. They said, "THREE SONGS!!! Before they even heard it, they looked on the cover and vetoed it. *"You guys are crazy!"*"

WHAT ABOUT "IN-A-GADDA-DA-VIDA" JUST A FEW YEARS LATER, A WHOLE SIDE OF AN ALBUM WAS JUST ONE SONG.

"OK, we were avant garde. Being too early is as bad as being too late.

"We told Liberty, 'But that's it! C'mon, listen to it! Listen to it and you will understand!' So, picture it, here are all these guys in their seersucker suits, thin ties, management guys. What did they know? All they were interested in, as I told you before, were sales, sales, SALES! *"Gotta get the album out there!"*"

WITH LOTS OF SONGS.

"There wasn't a new Jan and Dean album in the stores at that time, so we said why not do something a little bit different? Something off the wall?

27

of "Popsicle" on the flip--more vocal emphasis, fading on the uh-huh-huh-huh, leading to Glen Campbell's guitar solo (sounds like a banjo, but it's not).

Liberty mailed the 45 to a few stations, with "Norwegian Wood" marked. Dean sent it to an extensive list of stations with "Popsicle" marked, and a note pleading that they play "Popsicle," and not the "A" side as previously marked, which he felt was not as good commercially as "Popsicle." He mailed "Popsicle" with this note to every station over and over for five or six days in a row. Then, on the last day, he mailed the note without enclosing the copy of the 45, using his humor to emphasize his point, saying thanks to them and the record was selling so well we don't have any left to mail! And sure enough, "Popsicle" was a hit, and no one ever heard "Norwegian Wood."

Even if it were not for the FILET OF SOUL fiasco, Jan and Dean would not have stayed with Liberty. The label was offering them a renewal of their expiring five-year contract at the same rate they had signed for in the early sixties, ignoring how much bigger they had become, not to mention how much bigger rock and roll had become, how much other artists were getting, and how much other labels were offering Jan and Dean!

But there is one thing I wonder about. What are the songs that Dean mentioned, the ones they had "boxes" of. What unreleased treasures? Besides that, I heard Dean on KOMA, Oklahoma City a few days after the wreck. The DJ was conducting an interview over long distance, because he had interviewed them on his show the night of one of their last concerts before the wreck. On the phone interview, Dean revealed that he and Jan were all set to cut the vocals on a new album the day of the wreck. Dean said that they had a whole new LP of instrumental tracks, ready for vocals to be added! What was this? Satire? Harmonies? More Folk 'N' Roll? Sloan and Barri? Stuff that Lou Adler gave to the Mamas and Papas? "Louisiana Man" and "Like a Summer Rain"?

Perhaps we will never know. But at least now we know why "One Two Three," "I Found a Girl" with Dean's mike "unhooked," and two versions of "Norwegian Wood" all turned up on this FILET OF SOUL hodge podge. And consider the irony. Pell, as Liberty's agent, picked, out of all the "boxes" of songs available from the vaults, the other record that Liberty had suppressed in 1963, against Jan and Dean's wishes: "Gonna Hustle You"!

★★★★★★
★★★★★★
★★★★★★
★★★★★★
★★

He who laughs last, he who, he, who, ha, ha, CHOO!

And they knew he wasn't kiddin', so they said that was tough and they just wouldn't release it at all. Jan says, 'OK!' and hung up on them.

"That was about the last communication we had with Liberty. We came off the road, and the next day Jan had his accident. After that they say, 'Hey, there's no road blocks!' 'Hey, there's an accident, his name's on the news, whew, let's get that album out there!' So they jammed that album fast."

BUT IT WASN'T QUALITY!

"It was terrible! Which is a shame. You spend eight years trying to build something and then in one month they can destroy you. If they want to. Six years later I had a chance to put it out the way, or almost the way it was meant to be. I only had room for one side so I did some real radical editing to get it to fit on one side. Maybe someday Part Two will get a chance to be heard.

"Even on the back of FILET OF SOUL, where it says 'Ha-Ha-Ha-Choo!'? On the Anthology Album you hear all the sneezin'. Right?"

RIGHT.

"Well that back cover was supposed to relate to all that sneezing, and the laughing, and the coughing. . ."

AHHHH! THEN YOU DID DESIGN THE BACK COVER OF THE ALBUM AND WRITE THE LINER NOTES AFTER ALL.

"Yes, I did do the liner notes, which don't correspond with what is on the album!"

I NEVER COULD RELATE THOSE TWO THINGS.

"Yeah, the record and the cover didn't relate at all. The HA-HA-HA-HA-CHOO doesn't relate to anything, even the title FILET OF SOUL doesn't relate to anything. They blew it all the way around. It's too bad to see a concept go right into the gutter.

"The album didn't do too well. Then they said, "Let's put out a single! Let's put out a single quick, while everybody's still talking about him! He's in a coma! That's great! He could be in a coma for a year! We could keep milking it!"

"Nice guys."

To cut the story short, Dean wanted to release "Popsicle" instead of Liberty's choice: "Norwegian Wood." Dean didn't care for their choice, so he got Liberty to put his re-mix

SUNSHINE MUSIC 3

JAN AND DEAN RECORD AUCTION

This is an auction of Jan and Dean records. For each record listed below, a minimum bid and a condition is given.

The minimum bid amount is where the bids should start. If you want a record, offer any amount over the listed minimum. Offer only what a record is worth to you. The minimums are based upon how good of condition the record is in, how much it cost me, and to some extent the age and rarity of the record.

Each record has a condition assigned to it, as follows:

```
Sealed - - - - - an LP that has never been opened
New - - - - - - a record that is new or like new
VG - - - - - - - very good, some visible &/or audible wear
G - - - - - - - good, looks & sounds used, but plays well
P - - - - - - - poor, a garage-sale item, plays but is
                nothing to be proud of.
```

Remember, the more you bid, the more likely you are to win a record, but be sure to bid only what a record is really worth to you. Postage will be added later, and for Special 4th class is 59¢ up to one pound. First class, postage over one pound, and insurance will be extra and up to you, too.

S.A.S.E. with bids, please!

45 RPM

M I Found A Girl/   Lib. 55833   MB $4
   It's A Shame To Say Goodbye   *unique sound!*
   The first side is as close to Folk music as J&D ever got, thank goodness. The second side features Jill Gibson singing "Dean's part," the high part.

G+ Freeway Flyer/   Lib. F55766   MB $3.75
   From All Over the World   *exciting!*
   "Flyer" is about getting caught speeding by CHiPs! "Big John Law don't take no lip, unless you're a chick and you're really hip!" This song was never on an LP. The second side was a bigger hit (both got airplay) and was also never on an LP in this version. These seem to have been recorded in the same sessions as the Coke commercials. Flyer features sound effects!

M Little Queenie (mono)/   A&M 1957   MB $5
   Little Queenie (stereo)   DJ Copy   *Jan!*
   This is one of the last singles Jan put out before he and Dean began working together regularly again. Originally done by Chuck Berry, it is a great rocker!

G- The Little Old Lady/   Lib. 55704   MB $2
   My Mighty GTO   *Hit City!*
   Old Lady 45 is a different mix than on any stereo LP. GTO is not the same version as on any LP, including out-takes LP. This record has writing and sticker on label, put there by a radio station.

N+ Gonna Hustle You/   includes picture sleeve
   Summer Means Fun   MB $7
                                        Dean uncensored!
   Dean put this out in 1973 as THE LEGENDARY MASKED SURFERS. The sleeve has 2 pictures on Dean and a chick getting it on on a phony beach with phony palm trees, etc. Also includes a paragraph by Dean about music. This is a new untouched copy.

VG++ Gonna Hustle You/   without sleeve   MB $3
   Summer Means Fun   *Fun Music!*
   Same as above, but no sleeve. This is really a fun record. Incidentally, the first side was originally banned by Liberty records, so Jan and Dean did Surf City as a second choice! Some months later, they changed the words of Gonna Hustle You, and released it under the revised title, THE NEW GIRL IN SCHOOL!

P++ The New Girl In School/   Lib. F55672   MD $2
    Dead Man's Curve   *The hits!*
    The original hits by the original artists!

G-- Drag City/   Lib. F55641   MB $3
    Schlock Rod   *Best 45?*
    Drag City is one of the tightest J&D songs, and the 45 has the best sound to me. The flip side cannot be beat in terms of comedy.

N+ Summertime, Summertime/   J&D 401   MB $10
   California Lullabye   *Dean!*
   This is what Dean was doing soon after the accident. He designed the label, which is orange! And side 2 is a slow love ballad! And it is the only song I can think of that was written, produced, and sung by Dean alone!

N+ Fiddle Around/   MB $6
   A Surfer's Dream   *Jano & Jilly!*
   Released after their contract with Liberty was expired, Fiddle is a very early cut never intended to be released! Full of bomps, I love it! Side 2 has good ol' Jill Gibson doing the high parts instead of Dean again!

29

N+	Ride the Wild Surf / The Anaheim, Azusa, and Cucamonga Sewing Circle, Book Review, and Timing Association	*Incredible!*	MB $6

There is no way an LP can capture the excitement of this classic 2-sided 45! This is peak, prime J&D. On AACSCABR, Jan's arranging is incredible!

G+ Yellow Balloon / same song backwards   by the Yellow Balloon   *weird...*   MB $3

It is unclear just what and how much involvement Dean had with this 45. The flip side is sure his style... And it was a big hit! Sounds like the 59th St. Bridge Song!

G+ Good Feelin' Time / I've Got A Feelin' For Love   MB $3

This is the follow up by the Yellow Balloon. It is very good, and the flip is co-written by none other than Jill Gibson! Both singles are on the Canterbury label, which is Yellow (what else???).

M The Drag / Running Bear   Reprise 20226   MB $3

These are instrumentals, with no involvement by Jan or Dean. The flip is the old Big Bopper/Johnny Preston song. It is a promo copy, and is much like Duane Eddy. The artist is Rick and the Ric-O-Shays.

G+ Angel My Angel / Never   Carol Conners   Capitol 5152   MB $3

Again, no Jan and Dean involvement. Writing on label from a radio station. Carol is really something!

LP ALBUMS

SEALED Studio Out-Takes   J&D 1001   MB $11

This a new and totally unique item. It was made by Jan's brother, so the story goes. Mono & Stereo, it has Jan and Dean stuff that would normally have never seen the light of day. Included: 4-minute, X-rated version of Dean Man's Curve; Coke commercial; a never released 1961 song; Batman LP music; Jan in the studio learning to sing Three Window Coupe; sixteen unheard-of treats from '61 to '79!

VG- Surf City Stereo   MB $10

This was the first big-budget J&D LP. Lengthy and funny liner notes by Bill Balance, DJ. Included on the LP are Glen Campbell, Hal Blaine, Leon Russell, the Matadors, and others too numerous to mention. Tunes include: Honolulu Lulu, Kansas City, Soul City, Way Down Yonder in New Orleans, and a great take-off on American Bandstand, Philadelphia, PA!

VG Command Performance, Live In Person, Including Songs They Performed on the TAMI Show   MB $10

Mono with a name written on the back cover. The front cover shows Dean with his skateboard, J&D singing on stage, 4 color photos! The back has the two best pictures ever on an LP, singing on a different stage, Dean with his surfer haircut (see photo on back of SM #2). Here is how they sounded live in the mid-'60s. All the hits: Surf City, Dead Man's Curve, Little Old Lady, Sidewalk Surfin', Here They Come--- plus I Get Around, All I Have To Do Is Dream, Little Honda, Rock and Roll Music, Do Wah Diddy, I Should Have Known Better, and Louie, Louie! Hear them kid and joke between songs ("Look on your hand and tell me what's next!"). When Lloyd Thaxton heard them do Dream on his TV show, he exclaimed, "Hey, you guys really can sing!" To which the Duo replied, "Who did 'ja think was makin' all those records?"

N- Filet of Soul   Stereo   MB $11

Check out the story in this issue. Note: the stereo version of this LP has the 45 version of Nor. Wood, but in stereo, and has the non-45, Drag City LP version of Dead Man's Curve (diff. lyrics and music).

VG++ Filet of Soul   Mono   MB $10

Here is the mono version, which has a totally new, live version of Norwegian Wood, and a strange version of Dead Man's Curve-- it is the 45, except no sound effects, no harp, and a strong lead and drums at the end.... Oh yes, Michele is on both versions, but has applause in mono and cheers in stereo?! A name is written on the back cover.

See Folk 'n Roll

Below   Jan is in his cast in this one. The trade ad had Dean telling Jan, "Well, you always said you wanted an original cast album!" There is a lot to tell about this one. I Found A Girl is great! Hang On Sloopy has

SUNSHINE MUSIC 3

JAN AND DEAN / PAPA DOO RUN RUN
DISNEY WORLD
ORLANDO, FLORIDA
FEBRUARY 9, 1980

Where would be the perfect place to put on a concert about California sun, cars, and girls? Fantasyland, of course! And that's exactly where Jan and Dean were.
There were no tables, no chairs, no place to sit, but who really wanted to? There was only us, the music, and all the room in Fantasyland to dance, take pictures, sing, and just go crazy!
The concert started with a thirty minute show at 10:00 pm, another at 11:30, and the final show at 1:00. Each show began with Papa doing some Beach Boys and some originals. Let us not forget though the one and only (thank goodness!) Wipe Out.
Jan and Dean then came on stage to complete the set. The entire audience at all the shows whether old, young, or in-between acted like teenagers again.
We had a summer sun all day and a summer warmth all night! Perfect "Surf City" weather for all of us "California Girls".
At one point during the final show (I'm surprised it took so long;) Dean got on his skateboard and started "Sidewalk Surfin'" all around the stage. It ended when he hit a cord and wiped out!
After the concert I got the chance to talk to Jan and Dean again. It's a great priviledge and a delightful experience. It's really fun to be with them whether talking to them in person or just being at one of their concerts.

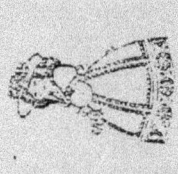

FOR SALE

Color & B&W Pictures of Jan and Dean, and Papa Doo Run Run in Concert at Disney World, Florida, February 9, 1980.
Available: 35 B&W of J&D and Papa
            12 Color of Papa
            33 Color of J&D and Papa

Black & Whites-- $5.00
Color-- $6.00

Please allow 4-5 weeks for delivery. Make checks or money order payable to: Pat Silva/305 Foxfire Dr./Albany, GA 31705

---

them swatting (girl) flies in the studio. It's A Shame To Say Goodbye has Jill G. Where Were You When I Needed You was a year prior to the Grassroots hit 45. A Beginning From An End was a little-known 45. It is the most touching of all J&D songs. It is a variation of Dead Man's Curve, except that it tells of a daughter and a difficult child-birth ("She looks, and acts, and talks the way I remember you--But that doesn't mean I don't miss you..."). I get misty and goose-bumpy every time. On the lighter side, the back has 4 pictures with captions by Dean: "If you are a Beach Boy Fan sit on (rail road) tracks only at night"! Also, Folk City is a take off on Dylan et al, a la Surf City (Folk City, Here We Come!), It Ain't Me Babe and Turn, Turn, Turn have the greatest harmony.

Folk 'n Roll: G+ Stereo   MB $9
               VG- Stereo   MB $10
               G Stereo   MB $9   (name on back cover)
               VG- Mono   MB $10

JAN AND DEAN WITH PAPA DOO RUN RUN/PALACE THEATER/CINCINATI 1-23-80

It was almost too good to be true! Jan and Dean were appearing at the Palace for the second time in five months. They were brought back by popular demand-- which just goes to show how much they've been missed, and how great they still are!

Papa started the show with a mixture of old and new Californian songs. As usual, they were full of energy and really set the crowd wild!

After a short break, Jan and Dean come on stage. They began with New Girl In School and continued to thrill the crowd with such greats as Drag City, Baby Talk, Little Old Lady, Surf City, Sidewalk Surfin', and Deadman's Curve, with a few Beach Boy songs thrown in as well. At one point, Dean asked, as he often does, if anyone had brought a skateboard to the show. No one had, which may have been a good thing since the stage did not appear to have enough room for Dean to do any tricks.

The J&D humor and magic was definitely evident! Even after being called back for an encore, the crowd still cheered for more!

After the show I was allowed backstage briefly. I had met J&D when they were here in August of '79, so this time I was at least able to control my nerves a bit. But I was genuinely impressed with the changes in Jan in only the few intervening months. He continues to become even more great!

By Charlene Copes
New Carlisle, Ohio

SUNSHNE MUSIC 4

Issue 3

SUNSHINE MUSIC

FIRST CLASS MAIL

To:

SUNSHINE MUSIC
c/o Doc Rock
Box 1166
Lawrence, KS 66044

SUNSHINE MUSIC

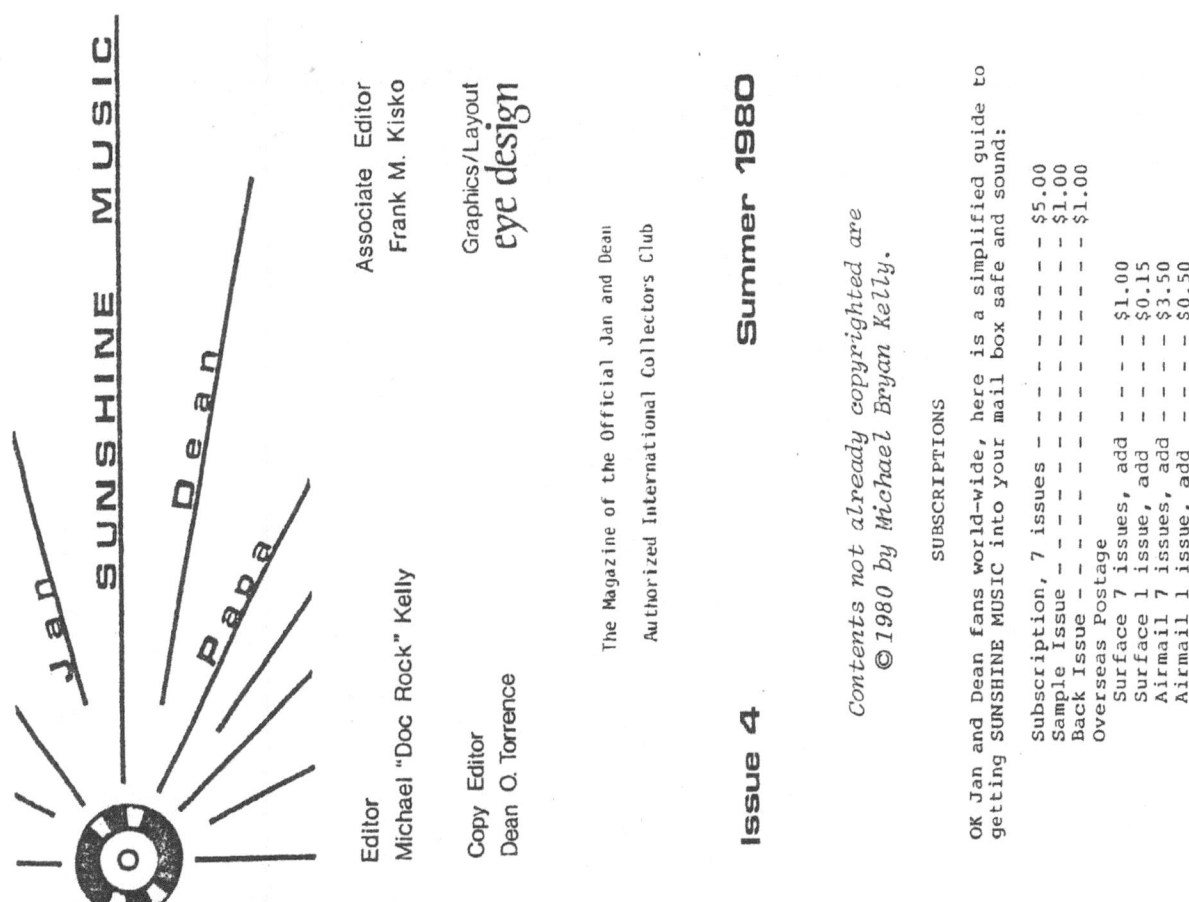

Jan Dean Papa SUNSHINE MUSIC

Editor
Michael "Doc Rock" Kelly

Copy Editor
Dean O. Torrence

Associate Editor
Frank M. Kisko

Graphics/Layout
eye design

The Magazine of the Official Jan and Dean
Authorized International Collectors Club

Issue 4   **Summer 1980**

*Contents not already copyrighted are
© 1980 by Michael Bryan Kelly.*

SUBSCRIPTIONS

OK Jan and Dean fans world-wide, here is a simplified guide to getting SUNSHINE MUSIC into your mail box safe and sound:

```
Subscription, 7 issues - - - - - - - - - - - $5.00
Sample Issue - - - - - - - - - - - - - - - - $1.00
Back Issue - - - - - - - - - - - - - - - - - $1.00
Overseas Postage
    Surface 7 issues, add - - - - $1.00
    Surface 1 issue, add  - - - - $0.15
    Airmail 7 issues, add - - - - $3.50
    Airmail 1 issue, add  - - - - $0.50
Brown Mailing Envelope (6x9)
    7 issues, add - - - - - - - - - - - - - $1.50
    1 issue, add  - - - - - - - - - - - - - $0.25
```

Issue 1 sold out (temporarily?).

Make checks payable to Michael Kelly.

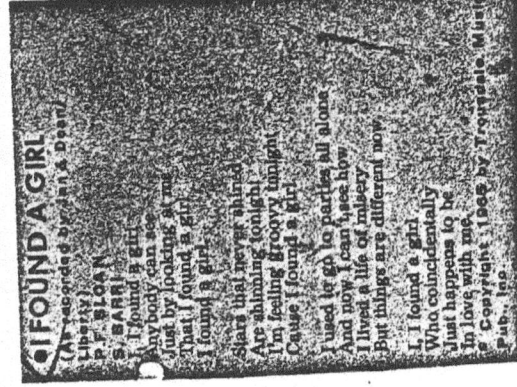

SUNSHINE MUSIC 4

SKELETONS IN CONCERT!!!

A few months ago, I gave the lyrics to Lloyd Hicks of the SKELETONS so that they could do the song in concert. Little did I know how soon I would hear them, or how well they would wear Jan and Dean's Baggy Pants!

Lloyd called me and said that he would be in Lawrence. He was nice enough to put me on the guest list at the box office. My problem was that my two daughters were visiting me from Denver, where they live with my ex. So, I needed a baby sitter. The only one I could find was slated to turn into a pumpkin at the early hour of 9:30, so I flashed down to the Free State Opra House (formerly Red Dog Inn) at 8:30.

I knew the band was late, because they did not have my name at the box office. But when I showed them my Doc Rock card, that got me in anyway. The Skeletons were to start at 9:00, but the heat (17 days over 100 at that point) slowed them down, and they did not actually get underway until 9:20! I was biting my nails! I had to split in ten minutes!

Fortunately, I had a chance to meet them on stage as they were setting up, and explained that I had to leave quickly. They said they would start out with some Jan and Dean material. And did they!

After a warm-up of a smashing Ventures-type instrumental, they went into JENNIE LEE! Lloyd, the drummer, took the bomps, and missed nary a one. The keyboard man sang lead (from a crib sheet, which blew away with the force of a cooling fan after one verse but was retrieved) and sounded better than Arnie (not too hard to do). Well, the crowd went wild. I have seldom seen such a response from a band that was not a top national hit name. Hooting, screaming, clapping, and cheering.

The SKELETONS tore into POPSICLE next. I was astonished at how well they recreated the record! The keyboard and bass guitar did the falsetto parts, sort of double-tracked. The lead guitar did a good job on Glen Campbell's break in the middle. And the keyboard guy (I wish I had made notes of their names and instruments) had a little set of chimes which were dead ringers (no pun planned) for the record!

When the cheering had begun to die down, and the stomping had subsided, they started BAGGY PANTS (READ ALL ABOUT IT IN THE DAILY NEWS). This was not as close to the record as the others, but then Herb Alpert was not on hand to help out. Nevertheless, the strange J&D Dore' tune was as well liked as the rest. I personally could not believe that there, in 1980, I was hearing that J&D 45 done live by anyone, least of all such a great band!

Another Ventures thing was next, and it was 9:30, so I ran out to the car and shot home, listening to Fiddle Around on the tape player. Support the SKELETONS. They deserve it. And never pass up a chance to go see and hear them. You deserve it!

☆ ☆ ☆ ☆ ☆ ☆ ☆ ☆

Let Me Explain

FIRST, let me say that when you write me, please include an SASE. Most of you do, but for the newcomers--SASE, please!

SECOND, when you send money for a subscription, do two things.
A) Make the check payable to Michael B. Kelly.
B) Please indicate which issue you want the 7 issues to begin with. I cannot keep track of which sample issue, if any, you may already have.

THIRD, the most frequently asked question I get is, what is Jan and Dean's tour schedule. You can keep asking, but I usually will not know. This is because, as Dean explains it, they try to schedule as close in advance as possible. They often know only two weeks in advance. Which means that I cannot print a schedule, since it takes well over two weeks to get SM out.

I will print a schedule when I can. And I will answer your SASE's when I can get the info from Dean or Winston or another source.

FOURTH, the other most frequently asked question is about J&D records. For old records, see within. For new ones, I will let you know as soon as and if there is any new J&D material to be released.

LAST, did you see Jan and Dean on the TODAY show Wednesday, July 23, 1980? It was listed in TV GUIDE, and was terrific. If there is enough interest, and if enough of you missed it, I will run a transcript of the interview in the next SM.

Lay-tah!

Word Search (Continued from p. 9)

36 J-D's early manager, producer and longtime friend (last name)
37 Jan is "King of The _____"
38 Cities J-D sang about: _____, _____, _____...
39 "Tryin' to make a livin' as a _____..."
40 Actor who played Dean in 1978 (last name)

SCORING

(right answers are worth one point each. Multi-answer questions are one point if you got all patterns together)

30-40 You're a whiz — practically a J-D clone! Were you there?

20-30 Hey, pretty good on this trivia. Maybe Myke will feature you on his "Doc Rock" radio show!

10-20 Yeah, we know. You picked up your brother in-law's copy of SM and since you had nothing else to do, decided to try the puzzle. Don't call us, we'll call you.

0-10 You're a Led Zeppelin fan, aren't you?

SUNSHINE MUSIC 4

Old Wax and New Waves

About 6 or 7 years ago, record collectors began to take a new and active interest in Jan and Dean records. Suddenly, an old Liberty LP that had been going for 2-3 dollars suddenly had a minimum bid of 9-12 bucks! Suddenly!

Seeing a chance to cash in on the new money-interest in the less common J&D material, somebody came up with the idea of doing a J&D bootleg LP. Now, bootlegs were no new deal at that time. However, they were limited to really big artists, such as the Beatles, the Stones, or Bob Dylan (did you know that Bobby Vee hired Dylan as a piano player and backup singer in the early '60s when the latter's name was still Zimmerman, but fired him almost immediately because he was so bad?). I for one was surprised and pleased to see a J&D boot, even though I already had all the songs on the stereo LP.

OLD WAX AND NEW WAVES has four areas of specialization: Early Arnie and Dore cuts; Liberty cuts that were never on an LP; Jan's post-wreck material; and Dean's post-wreck material.

EARLY ARNIE AND DORE CUTS

Baggy Pants was on a Doré 45, but not on the Doré LP. It is an early, and fantastic comedy song about a guy who crashed a la-ti-dah party and was self-conscious about his wrong-side-of-the-tracks clothing ("I hope nobody saw my baggy pants").

Gee was originally done by the Crows in 1954, and is considered by many to be the first rock and roll record. Jan and Dean added bomps, although they are less dominant than in Baggy Pants. Gee was also a 45 by Barry and the Tamerlanes (I Wonder What She's Doing Tonight) and the Pixies Three (442 Glenwood Ave., Birthday Party), and a remake of New Girl In School, Summertime USA). It took me over a decade of active searching to find the 45 of Gee. I yelled so loud when I found it in a 10¢ box, that everyone in the store stared at me!

I Love Linda is an obscure and rare Jan and Arnie cut most 45's of which are DJ copies. No bomps here, but there is a very unusual rhythm, and if the only Jan and Arnie you have heard is Jennie Lee, then this you gotta hear!

The Beat That Can't Be Beat was the flip of I Love Linda. Dum Dee Dum Dee Dum Dum in Tieu of Bomp!

Such A Good Night For Dreaming (Doré) was not on the early LP, but is probably the love-ballad-J&D at their best. This is a sort of a cross between Angel Baby and To Know Him Is To Love Him, and I love it, especially Dean's second solo.

LIBERTY NON-LP CUTS

Freeway Flyer was the flip side of Here They Come, J&D and quite a surprise. Because, for better or for worse, J&D had pretty much left the drag-sound/sound-effects car songs behind at this point, going for a more simple style. Yet, here was a song complete with police sirens and the old car-crash sound effect! It sounds left over from the Little Old Lady LP sessions, featuring a fine oboe.

Fiddle Around, dredged up from the Liberty files by the execs of that late company, was released after the wreck (and significantly, after J&D's contract had expired) against their wishes, if not without their knowledge. I, for one, am not unhappy. I love this simple throwback to the early '60s bomp sound.

JAN'S POST-WRECK CUTS

Tinsel Town was in some ways a high-water mark for Jan. His third Ode 45, it had much of the complexity of a Drag City, and featured that trademark of Jan's, sound effects. Here, it is freeway traffic and a jet aircraft! Jan did this number alone on Dick Clark's Saturday Action show. He was alone, in the sense that Dean sat it out after he and Jan did Surf City. Jan did have two comely young ladies to help on backgrounds, and a large rubber thumb as a prop (this tune is subtitled Hitch A Ride To Hollywood).

Blue Moon Shuffle, the flip side of Jan's premier post-wreck, Ode 45, will be recognized by the more discerning listener as Tinsel Town without the tinsel! That is, it is an instrumental. (A vocal version of this title was the "A" side of Jan's second Ode release, but was sans the sound effects and some vocal parts. This is not on the boot.)

Mother Earth was in reality the first thing Jan did after the wreck. In the TV Movie, they substituted Little Lovely Lady Linda or whatever. This cut is really beautiful. When I got the 45, I cried. Jan was back, and with a new sensitivity.

Blow Up Music was almost an instrumental, sounds like a partially-completed track, is quite nice to listen to, and was the flip of Tinsel Town.

I Know My Mind was one of the records released by Jan on Warner Brothers under the name Jan and Dean. As far as I know, neither is on this one. It was the flip side of the rare Laurel and Hardy, and is dated in its sound to the psychedelic era. It is of fairly minor interest, except as an insight into Jan's new development. On a scale of one to ten, I give it a seven. It pre-dates Mother Earth, but Jan was not yet doing his own vocals, understandably.

35

SUNSHINE MUSIC 4

So, you think you're the world's greatest Jan & Dean trivia freak, huh? Well, prove it!

DIRECTIONS

READ CLUES THEN SEARCH FOR AND CIRCLE YOUR ANSWER! WORDS MAY BE HORIZONTAL, VERTICAL OR DIAGONAL FRONTWARD OR BACKWARD! LETTERS MAY BE USED MORE THAN ONCE! GOOD LUCK!

1. Jennie Lee was the "_____ Girl."
2. J&D's football team and current T-shirt hit
3. Streets and locations listed in 1963's "Dead Man's Curve" _____ ax _____ to _____ j
4. "I've got a '48 _____ and it's Olive Green..."
5. Name of Jan's present dog
6. Jan's real first name
7. Read all about it in the Daily News.
8. Hometown of Papa Doo Run Run
9. "Sun and fun at _____ Beach."
10. Label of "Move Out Little Mustang" by _____ (last name)
11. Dean's present car
12. Jan's personalized California license plate
13. Doris Day's Legendary Masked Surfer (last name)
14. Dean sang with the Beach Boys to #1 in 1965
15. Some of the record labels Jan, Arnie and Dean have appeared on: _____, _____, _____, _____, _____, _____, _____, _____,
16. J&D's junior high school
17. Dean lives in late movie star _____'s house
18. "Surf City" went top ten there last year
19. Site of Murray the K's June 1978 show in which Jan & Dean performed together (New York)
20. Site of J&D's "reunion" concert, Spring 1978
21. Jan's band, 1977-1978
22. Nicknames of engineers Lindstrot and Howe
23. Actor who played Jan in 1979 TV movie (last name)
24. Who needed together her hair done?
25. Dean's late Graphics Co.
26. Arnie's current occupation
27. Producer of TV's "Dead Man's Curve" (last name)
28. Beach Boy who cameoed in the movie (last names)
29. J&D's 1965 movie that was never completed
30. Monkee who recorded with Jan in 1968
31. Dean won a Grammy in 1972 for their album cover
32. Dr. Vit-A-Min's wretched wife
33. J&D's high school football team
34. Winning horse at the Surf City racetrack
35. Maker of Jan's favorite cookies

Laurel and Hardy were, as you know, the first thing Jan recalls seeing after the wreck, projected on the wall of his hospital room. They were also the "A" side of his second WB 45, and I swear that Dean is on this one. I hear his falsetto, and while he does not recall any specific songs, he says he did in fact go into the studio and do some parts at Jan's request at this time. This is a very enjoyable tribute to the comedy duo J&D emulated quite successfully.

DEAN'S POST-WRECK MATERIAL

Summertime was a hit twice in the early '60s for the Jamies. Featuring a high lead, it was a natural for Dean to do. It was released on two 45's, on Magic Lamp and on J&D records. There is a strong Spector influence here. Overall, an excellent cut.

California Lullabye was called Lullabye in the Rain when it was on the Columbia LP that never was. This is the only thing ever written, produced, and sung by Dean solo. Congratulations, Dean. This is your Mother Earth, fantasti

ODDS AND ENDS, AND I DO MEAN ODDS!

Smile Just Smile was a 45 by a really obscure group the Nortones. Some people say this was really Jan and Dean. They must be deaf.

Tomorrow's Teardrops is a 45 Jan did solo in 1961. The label wa presumably designed by Dean, and named Ripple after J&D's favorite beverage.

It is a lament of impending disaster in love. The flip side of Jan Barry's 45, My Midsummer Night Dream turned up as the flip of most copies of Heart and Soul. This is a totally different recording and a slightly different title.

Well, that is what is on this gem. Eighteen cuts. all but one J&D! Too bad the boys don't get any $ from it. Oh, yes, one other thing. The LP has a white cover with an insert (sometimes green, sometimes off-white). The insert has the title, lists the cuts, and depicts what appears to be a modestly pregnant young woman. Some copies have a bla white label, some colored labels with printing (one side ye the other green). And the name of the label varies from El Wizardo to nothing at all!

The record itself may be black, or it may be marble blue and black: El Strango!

THE ALL-TIME, A-1 JAN & DEAN WORD SEARCH

```
F O L K S A L T E D M A I L L I W E A Z U S A O E
A C P L N T U O E A S H O L L A N D O R E M O G P
N H P A O B A G G Y P A N T S Z O O T U W N N Y T
T E J S I L N I R M R B A B Y S A N J O S E O S H
A V H L T N C P A S A D E N B U I C K T L A N A B
S Y A E R L A D Y Y A T E L I N M G W L O O A E K
T M I R A S U N D S C H W A B S N G A T V I M E I
I M A M W Y F A L L R L A B S E L H R S E E A M T
C S P G D I L D D R E A L R F T C Y N I F P N O T
B C I N D Y N R E O S N L E J & D F E T A S A C Y
P A L L A D I U M O C K B A Z O O M R R M N I Y H
F A I I A B H W G N E Y E S D A H G B A O O S S A
A B B E R R Y A T E N O L P R Y E E R C U R I A W
N R E E E R P K O Y T A A M A S N R O I S A U E K
T A R R A B O N E S H O I O G T Y E T H A B O L I
A B T D W N B U R N E A R B T R I H H P M B L E T
N O Y L A I R E P M I & B D I A N C E A O C L I L
T N S J D E L M O E G M A A O G N L R R S P O S L
O E L O E U A E R L H A N V R O E E S G P M E D I
P N O H R A N R S C T G D Y T B J M L I N D A A J
K O A N R L K S C H S I I J E A A W R S A N H D T
N S N S Y S I O H E E C T O D N N R A C L O A L E
I I D T J E A N E T T E S N S A A V A H L K T E S
T V G O T H A M U C A M O E U H H I R A F I C R N
S A T N I S U R F S U R C S U E E N T O N Y H N U
S D O U L P O L L U T I O N B I I E F T A N E W S
```

SUNSHNE MUSIC 4

FROM THE FILES

In 1958 two blond-haired, blue-eyed suntanned, six-foot tall Los Angeles born guys sat down at a piano and a self-built tape recorder and made what was to be the first of many hit records. "Jennie Lee" led the unbroken string of chart-toppers which includes, "Baby Talk," "Surf City," "Linda," "New Girl In School", "Dead Man's Curve," "Little Old Lady From Pasadena" and "The Anaheim, Azusa And Cucamonga Sewing Circle, Book Review and Timing Association."

HP Editor Don Paulsen, miniature tape-recorder in hand, caught up with the duo backstage at the Paramount Theatre where they were appearing in the WMCA Good Guy show.

DON: This is a rare appearance for the two of you in the New York area. Is there a difference between audiences here in the East and those on the West Coast?
DEAN: Some of the differences are: they're from different places. Really, though, there's no difference.
DON: Surfing and hot rod music began as a fad on the West Coast.
DEAN: They're here to stay. It's like contemporary folk music.
JAN: As long as the records are good they're gonna sell, no matter what they're about.
DON: How did you two get started as recording artists?
DEAN: We met in high school. It started out with four or five guys in a singing group and it kept breaking down until there were just the two of us. We cut a record that we thought was good and took it around and sold it.
DON: Had you always wanted to be a singer?
DEAN: No. At that time I just wanted to continue in school.
DON: You've both managed to combine a singing career and a college education.
DEAN: Yes. Jan's a medical student and I just changed from industrial Design to Fine Arts. Why don't you ask us when we have to go onstage?
DON: Okay. I guess right now you your job is more important than mine. Anyway, it pays more. (After Jan and Dean finished their performance on the Paramount stage, we sneaked out a rear entrance to avoid the mob at the stage door, dashed up to Broadway and caught a cab. As the cab waited for the traffic light to change, a breathless fan came sprinting up and snapped a picture. A few minutes later, in their hotel room, we watched television and continued the interview.)
DON: How would you describe the very distinct sound of a Jan and Dean recording?

JAN: Sudden, expected vocal modulations. Adornments ... like orchestrations ... different types of instruments ... a heavy drum sound. We use two full sets of drums on every session. We use three guitars. A high piercing falsetto voice, and full 4 part harmony.
DON: How would you compare your sound with that of the Beach Boys?
JAN: They have a more natural sound.
DON: What sort of changes have there been in the musical scene since you've been recording?
JAN: There've been a whole lot. Differences in sound ... better orchestration ...
DON: Would you say there was a general trend in pop music toward more sophistication?
JAN: There's nothing more sophisticated while still remaining basic. The feeling is still down-to-earth, I don't like that term "pop" music. I'd say it's a modern sound ... modern music.
DON: Who's your favorite performer?
JAN: Chuck Berry.
DON: When you were starting out as singers did you have any influences?
DEAN: Chuck Berry. The Monotones.
JAN: We started out as a group with a few other guys but they just gradually dropped out.
DON: This was before you had a big record?
JAN: Yes. They got disgusted and never showed up.
DON: Do you think that now they regret dropping out?
DEAN: They probably don't remember us, it was such a long time between their leaving and our first record.
DON: How long was it?
DEAN: Two weeks. No, it was much longer than that.
DON: Who are some of your tv favorites?
DEAN: Ralph Belvederes ... on the Rollex Derby. And I just can't wait to get home and turn on David Brinkley and watch him twiddle his thumbs.

DON: In your travels, is there any one place you enjoyed the most?
DEAN: Hawaii.
DON: Have you written a song about it yet?
DEAN: We did one called "Honolulu Lulu".
JAN: Forget about it. It was a bomb.
DEAN: Top ten to us is a bomb. Top three is okay.
DON: Are there any other activities or hobbies, like surfing and hot rodding, that would make good topics for songs?
DEAN: Skiing tried to make it. Really.
JAN: Telephone-calling. Shaving.
DON: Can you write songs about all this?
JAN: (Sings) I was shaving in my bathroom early one night.
DON: Dean, you're wearing what I guess you'd call a surfer's hairdo, which was common on the West Coast before the Beatles came along. How did the surfers feel when the Beatles came out with a similar hair style?
DEAN: The surfers should be getting residuals. They wont a piece of their action. Actually, surfers have been wearing their hair like the Beatles for three or four years — even longer. Some guys wear it longer than the Rolling Stones.
DON: How did the style originate?
DEAN: When they came out of the water it was like that. In fact, that's how the Beatles got theirs too.
DON: What would you say is the reason for the success of Jan and Dean?
JAN: You're only as good as your records are. We just seem to be able to feel something when we know it's good and be able to record it. We've been around for a long time. We've met a lot of people, which always helps.
DEAN: What we're doing now is following trends. Like, a lot of singers establish their own style and they stay there no matter what happens from then in the world about them. You have to change with the times. If something like the Twist comes along you should do a Twist record, because that's what people want. We didn't. When the Twist came out we refused to do a Twist record and those were about our leanest years. When surfing hit, we loved it, knew what it was and we said, "why shouldn't we sing about it, too.."
DON: What sort of changes, if any has success made in your lives?
DEAN: You never want to think you changed. But it all depends on how you take it. We were talking to George Maharis about a year ago, and he took it about the same way we did. As long as he enjoyed it, it was okay. But as soon as it started to pressure him, he'd get off. He didn't care what it cost him. He would rather be happy than stay in the same groove that he didn't really like.

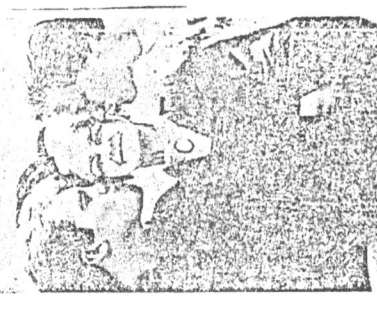

DON: Where is George these days?
DEAN: I don't know. But he's happy wherever he is. When we talked to him a year ago, he wasn't doing anything then either and he didn't really care. He'll come up with the right thing sooner or later. That's the way we feel. As long as we don't have to do it for a living and to eat by, it's okay. We don't have to worry about anything and get ulcers and all that stuff.

(Jan and Dean had to return to the theatre for the next show, so I reluctantly concluded one of the most enjoyable, candid interviews in my job as a Hit Parader editor.)

Hit-making "Granny" gets a kiss.

All of Jan & Dean records including "The Little Old Lady From Pasadena" are now produced and arranged by Jan Berry, who has also collaborated with Brian Wilson and Roger Christian in the writing of the last four hit records.

An interesting side-line to the Jan & Dean story is that throughout their recording and entertainment career, they have continued their education and at present, Dean Torrance is a year away from graduating at the University of Southern California in the field of Industrial Design, and Jan is in his third year of medical school at the California Medical School.

The boys will utilize this coming summer vacation from school to make appearances nationally, including the Dick Clark Tour, Freedomland and the Steel Pier. They have also recently recorded the title tune for the Columbia picture, "Ride The Wild Surf" and their voices will be heard over the titles in the picture.

Letters

Dear Doc Rock,

I want to take this opportunity to tell you how nice Jan and Dean are. I recently attended a Jan and Dean concert in Columbus. It was the third time in a year that I had seen them, and this was by far their best performance.

After the show about 30 of us waited outside for them. We heard that Jan wasn't feeling well (it had been hot and humid all day), but he did walk through the crowd and smile.

When Dean came out, he signed autographs for everyone! He talked to everyone, and didn't get into the car until everyone who had waited was taken care of!

Many stars wouldn't have taken the time Jan and Dean did. Since Jan obviously wasn't feeling well, they both could have left via another exit, or just rushed by into their car, but they knew people had been waiting a long time just to see them, so they took time to visit with their fans.

Jan and Dean are a true "Surfer's Dream."

Sincerely,

D   M
        Cleveland

Lennie Foster, a Science Teacher in her late 20's, saw the same concert and was also waiting outside for Papa and Jan and Dean...

It was certainly worth the wait! Papa Doo Run Run (except for Jim Armstrong) came out fairly early and left quickly, but they did stop for pictures and signing autographs.

A short time later, Jan came out with Jim. One of the guards had mentioned that Jan wasn't feeling well, and as Jan started coming out he looked totally exhausted by the heat. The crowd of fans stepped aside so he could get through, and y also began clapping for him. Then he really began to smile. As he walked through the crowd, he would put out his left hand and grab whoever was close by to help steady himself, because he was so tired. I was standing there smiling and cheering along with everyone else, when Jan stopped and put his hand on my shoulder! I expected him to keep on walking, but he just stood there and held on to me. I could tell he was having a hard time, so I took his hand and he then held on even harder.

He continued holding onto my arm for support, until he got into the car. As he let go of my hand, he shook it. Neither of us had said a word, but in that short span of minutes I felt so much admiration and respect for Jan Berry. I was thrilled that I could have been any help to him at all. It was one of the most magical moments of my entire life!

About 15 minutes later, Dean came out. Even though it was not only hot, but now also very late, Dean very nicely gave out autographs and kisses (WOW!) to all those who wanted them. He was so nice and pleasant, smiling all the while. He, too, made a great impression on all of the fans who were so anxious to meet him.

Lennie

It was so sad when it was all over and we had to go back home. Still, it had been such a fantastic evening all around! Jan and Dean are the GREATEST!

JAN AND DEAN RECORD AUCTION

To participate in this auction, send all bids to : Stephen A.G. Peters
#1705 Bathgate Drive
Ottawa, Ontario, Canada
K1K 3y3

Only winners notified. Payment to be made in American funds. Postage and packing extra, will be added to winners' statements. Only one minimum to note. Bid only what you can afford.

UA 50859	Hang Ten w/PC-- Jennie Lee/Vegetables	M/M
UA REM 402	Remember Jan and Dean EP with PC	M/M
Lib. 55792	Surf City, Honolulu Lulu, Dead Man's Curve, Little Old Lady	
Lib. 55580	You Really Know How To Hurt A Guy PS only, tears	VG
	Surf City/She's My Summer Girl PS only, writing on	VG+
J&D 401	Summertime, Summertime/California Lullaby MB $10	M
Ode 66023	Mother Earth/Blue Moon Shuffle Jan Berry promo	
A&M 1957	Little Queenie/That's The Way It Is Jan Berry	M to M-
Lib. 55724	Ride The Wild Surf/Anaheim Azusa CSCBRAIA	M
Lib. 55833	I Found A Girl/It's A Shame	VG+
		M

WANT: TINSEL TOWN, STOCK OR PROMO COPY

J&D PHOTOS AVAILABLE

Live color photos of Jan and Dean, taken both on and off stage. Other stars also available. Send SASE for details, and be sure to mention SUNSHINE MUSIC. Address: Mrs. Connie Celentano, 4639 Los Feliz Blvd. Hollywood, California 90027.

REGARDING LARRY MELTON

THERE HAVE BEEN A LOT OF PEOPLE WHO HAVE APPARENTLY HAD TROUBLE GETTING RECORDS FROM LARRY MELTON. THAT IS, LARRY TAKES THEIR MONEY, BUT NO LPs EVER ARRIVE. ON THE OTHER HAND, SEVERAL MORE PEOPLE HAVE TOLD ME THAT THEY GOT THEIR LPs IMMEDIATLY. I HAVE SPOKEN WITH LARRY ABOUT THIS. HE SAYS THAT IT IS ALL A BIG MIX-UP. SO HERE IS WHAT WE WILL DO. IF YOU HAVE SENT CASH, A MONEY ORDER, OR A CHECK WHICH HAS BEEN CLEARED BY THE BANK, BUT HAVE NOT GOTTEN ANY RECORD(S), WRITE ME WITH THE DETAILS. I WILL PASS ON THE INFORMATION TO LARRY, AND HE HAS PROMISED TO SATISFY YOU. LET ME KNOW IF HE DOES OR DOES NOT. AND BE SURE TO WRITE ME, EVEN IF YOU HAVE PREVIOUSLY, ABOUT THIS MATTER

SUNSHINE MUSIC

SM Record Auction

Last issue, the first Sunshine Music Jan and Dean Record Auct. was featured, and the response was unexpected! I mean, that was one popular auction. Many of the bids were unexpectedly high, although there were also some real bargains that were had. So, here we go again. No minimums this time, since you seem to know what things are worth to you. I will not be able to accept bids below my costs, however. Postage and insurance and junk like that will be added later. Please enclose an SASE with your bids, and later when checks are written, make them payable to Michael Kelly, even if I tell you not to (inside joke, not funny at all).

Barbara Ann ("Beach Boys") VG
This is the original Capitol release from early '66. As you may know, Dean sang lead on this classic track. Jan was down the hall at the time, but that is another story. Barbara was also on the first J&D Liberty LP single by the Regents. In early '60s, when it was a hit single by the Regents. In reality, when you consider the girl's name and the bomps, you see that this is really just a remake of that all-time #1 Classic Rock and Roll Hit, JENNIE LEE!

Ride the Wild Surf/Anaheim Azusa... VG
I said it now and I am saying it then, these songs just never sound as good on an LP as they do on a 45. When the record spins faster, and the grooves are wider, the sound is better, that is all there is to it. Tangible excitement!

I Found A Girl/It's A Shame To Say Goodbye Mint
At a time when protest songs threatened to wipe out the spirit of rock and roll (what was left of it after the San Francisco acid-rock finished with it), J&D came through with another great sunshine-music hit.

(picture sleeve) Little Old Lady From Pasadena (no record) M-
This is a color sleeve with Jan and Dean wearing each others clothes, and the fit is terrible! Not to mention Deans pants tucked into his (Jan's) socks, and his (Jan's) shirt not tucked into his (Jan's) baggy pants!

Baby Talk/Jeanette Get Your Hair Done G-
The original Jan and Dean 45 on Dore records. The flip side includes Dean as a writer, which probably explains the humor although Jan has the last line, "I'm a-gonna cut your hair off, Chick!"

There's A Girl/My Heart Sings #OL - G
Nice, light, early J&D. Cowritten by Herb Alpert! Plus, Dean sings lead on My Heart Sings, which he didn't do too often in later years.

FOLK 'n ROLL LP   Stereo VG-
                         Mono VG-
This was probably the first LP that featured much humor on the cover. Dean wrote the liner notes, actually captions for four semi-candid photos. For instance, they are standing in a burned house, captioned "Lady Bug Lady Bug Fly Away Home Your House Is On Fire And Jan And Dean Are Having A Cook-In."

OLD WAX AND NEW WAVES BOOTLEG LP Stereo New/Mint
This was sealed, but I opened it to check on the color of the wax. It is black. This LP completes the collection which has GOTTA TAKE THAT ONE LAST RIDE or the ANTHOLOGY LP, because it has 45 flip sides, Arnie material, and other oddities not included on compilations. Includes post-wreck material by both boys (boys?). I doubt that bids under $20 will have a chance, but let your pocketbook be your guide.

FILET OF SOUL LP   Stereo M-
This is the strangest of all J&D LP's, a real hodge-podge of cuts from the 1963 studio to the 1966 stage. Sort of a non-Jan and Dean's non-golden hits volume nothing! And here you get to hear what J&D singing voices sound like when there is a minimum of engineering done. The various live cuts are like having J&D in your living room, as opposed to having them in the studio and your living room in the studio. Also, here is the only live version of Honolulu Lulu ever released!

STUDIO OUT-TAKES BOOTLEG LP Stereo Sealed
This has material unavailable elsewhere. Practice takes, mistakes, out-takes, background demos, the Coke commercial, Batman LP effects rehearsals, a never-released song, 16 tracks of unbridled Jan and Dean. Again, it is doubtful that bids under $20 will be competitive, but bid what it is worth to you.

Bid early, as first-come breaks ties! So does an SASE!!

THANKS TO:

Jan, Dean, Lloyd Hicks, Stephen McParland, Pat Silva, Charlene Copes, Melissa Mauldin, Beth Kreuger, Frank Brockel, Ryuichi Tanaka, Linda Hunter, Suzy Harvey, Steve Peters, and Gary Zenker, to name a few. (P.S. Sorry, Gary that you are last again, even though the list is not even alphabetized!)

SUNSHINE MUSIC 4

SHORT CUTS

The Jan and Dean TV SHOW has been shown in several areas, including, according to reports, Southern California and New Jersey. It was scheduled for my area, but instead, Bonnie and Marie was shown!!!

Special thanks go out to HONOLULU LULU for the J&D WORD SEARCH and other material appearing in this and upcoming issues of SM!

New LP: Excelsior XMP6016 The Best of Jan and Dean has nine cuts by Dean and Papa. It is distributed by Pickwick, International, in LP, cart, and cassette. The best part is the hand painted cover picture of J&D! A must for the cover alone it would seem!!

Brian appeared onstage with J&D Easter week at Disneyland. He played bass and seemed fairly relaxed.

Guess who has a TAMI SHOW poster on his wall. Mr. J. Berry! Envy!

Word is that Jan also has a director's chair from DMC The Movie which says "To Jan Berry From Pat Rooney." More interestingly, it seems that a sequel may not be beyond the realm of possibility!

Jan also has a phone answering machine: "Bvring! Click! (A female voice with "Where's A Girl" in the background) Jan and Dean Enterprises. Neither Jan nor Dean is available right now. Please leave your real or fictitious name after the beep and maybe they'll get back to you shortly. Beep!"

KRLA, the Los Angeles oldies station, ran a year-long poll of favorite artists. On my birthday (July 4), they announced the list. Elvis, #1; Beatles, #2; Beach Bums, #11; Jan and Dean, #36. Not bad, eh?!

The current issue of CALIFORNIA MUSIC (2 Kentwell Ave., Concord 2137, Australia) is called "Surf and Drag Music Novelties and Oddities" and of course features Jan and Dean.

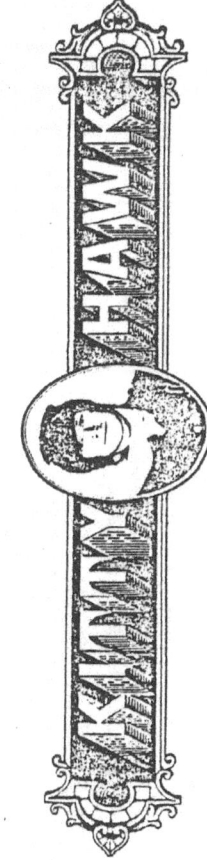

SKELETONS!

Haven't you ever wondered whether or not Jan and Dean have any skeletons in their closets? Well, wonder no more! They do have skeletons--but in the midwest! The Skeletons is a rock band from St. Louis which recognizes rock 'n roll roots. Namely, Jan and You-Know-Who. In fact, it is not unusual for them to slip Gas Money or Baggy Pants into one of their sets! And the crowds love it, natch! Now, the Skeletons have a Jan and ARNIE 45 out. Using the name Bobby Lloyd and the Windfall Prophets (see, J&D humor even before the needle hits the vinyl!), they have put out GA$ MONEY. Same song, same beat, with added verses and added stereo!

But wait, there is more! Now, by special arrangement with SUNSHINE MUSIC, you can get all the Skeletons' records direct from Borrowed Records! These are all the same basic group, although the name on the label varies from release to release.

GA$ MONEY A rocker--the title tells it all! b/w Sleepwalk, an excellent remake of the old Santo and Johnnie #1 Classic! Complete with 2-sided cardboard sleeve-- $2.00.

DRIVING GUITARS A nice rocking version of Jan and Arnie's classic ("Wouldn't it be neat if we could run on surplus wheat?") b/w Crazy Country Hop, the old Johnnie Otis song lives again! --$2.00 Complete with a 2-sided, heavy paper sleeve (he's even wearing a Papa shirt!).

TRANS-AM The first protest-drag song I've ever heard, a fine sound which protests draft registration while singing about cruising! b/w Tell 'Em I'm Gone, an old-time rocker with a new-time sound. Complete with picture sleeve, $2.00.

VERY LAST DAY b/w SOUR SNOW Sorry to say I have not heard this one, but the title of the flip sounds interesting to say the least. No picture sleeve (yet), $1.50.

ORDER FROM: BORROWED RECORDS
Dept. SM
2820 W. State
Springfield, MO 65802

***** Tell 'em DOC ROCK sent you!

Yesteryear Hits

TEN YEARS AGO
January 25, 1964
SINGLES

1 THERE! I'VE SAID IT AGAIN Bobby Vinton (Epic)
2 LOUIE LOUIE Kingsmen (Wand)
3 I WANT TO HOLD YOUR HAND Beatles (Capitol)
4 SURFIN' BIRD Trashmen (Garrett)
5 POPSICLES AND ICICLES Murmaids (Chattahoochee)
6 OUT OF LIMITS Marketts (Warner Bros.)
7 HEY LITTLE COBRA Rip Chords (Columbia)
8 FORGET HIM Bobby Rydell (Cameo)
9 UM, UM, UM, UM, UM, UM Major Lance (Okeh)
10 DRAG CITY Jan & Dean (Liberty)

SUNSHINE MUSIC 4

Kelly
2817 Crawford
Parsons, Ks. 67357

R S I c/o ->
RECORDS & SERVICE INTERNATIONAL
(213) 467-7983

JAN & DEAN AUCTION/SALE #1
BID CLOSING DATE: SEPT. 11, 1982

Thanks to Sunshine Music for letting us get this rather late J&D list inserted in this issue (it was intended to be printed within). We have recently moved all our operation into one location (the warehouse part was previously a couple of miles from the office), and getting resettled was a job. Also, the establishment of a second business name; "Rock-a-Round" which we will start advertising with soon (legal problems with another R.S.I. named business caused magazine advertising to stop some months ago), and a new business member, Gerry Bridges. There are some nice items in this list; all guaranteed to be carefully graded, etc. Space is limited, so postage/U.P.S. charges are not included here; please write or call to reserve anything set sale, and we will bill you. Thanks for now.

GENERAL BIDDING POLICY & INSTRUCTIONS (please read):
(1) All bids must be in writing. Please use numbers on the left, and give part or entire description, and your bid. Either print clearly and dark or type with a good ribbon (your bid sheet will be photo copied and returned with your bill for any winning bids and/or set sale items we bill you for). Please use either 8 1/2"x5 1/2" or 8 1/2"x11" paper size only, and make sure you name and address appear along side your bids/order.
(2) SET SALE ORDERS: U.S. orders should be paid with the order, or phone us for a short term reservation (payment must be sent right away). Make sure to add all additional costs (sales tax for California, postage or U.P.S. charge, etc.); orders that do not include all due costs will be held up until we can send a debit note, and receive the balance due (if you are not sure how much to include, phone us or write with SASE). Money received for items already sold will be refunded immediately, unless; (A) we receive payment by personal check and fill part of the order (if the whole order is not filled, we return customer's original check), (B) you have made bids which are accepted in the auction, in which event we will give you credit against any bids until the auction closing, and then send any due refund or credit you against your auction bill. Overseas & Canada: Send your order without payment; we will send a bill with the amount due, including postage/insurance cost (please specify that you want air mail insured, air mail/no insurance, or surface mail insured, and insurance/customs requirements. If you are also bidding in the auction, we will send one bill for all items available at the time of auction closing, unless requested otherwise (to save you postage expense).
(3) Any bid may be changed or cancelled prior to the posted bid closing date; otherwise you must honor your bids. If you are on a limited budget, we will accept your bids totalling any amount, but you tell us your spending limit amount; we will then make sure you are billed only for items that fit within that limit. If you use this method, you should list your bids in order of interest to you, most important first.
(4) Upon receiving our auction bill, and the amount due is more than you can immediately afford, we will accept a deposit of 20% or more of the bill, and hold the item(s) up to thirty(30) days more for balance payment.
(5) C.O.D. is available only by U.P.S. (which serves only the 48 continental states), with 25% deposit. Upon arrival, C.O.D. packages are payable by money order or cash only; no checks.

```
AUCTION LP's  (note minimum bids)
1LP Batman /Lib. LRP 3444     mono  M-           $20
2LP Ride the Wild Surf /Lib. LST 7368  mono  M-        rare sealed copy  $30
3LP J&D Anthology Album  /U.A. UAS-9961 dbl. DJ emboss M inc. booklet   $15
4LP Jan & Dean with the Soul Surfers /L-J 101      rare edition featuring the four
   Challenge tracks - nice photo on jacket back . mono  M   -6   $15

SET SALE LP's   (note; when two copies, different condition/price are
   listed, they have #### between them)
5LP Folk 'n Roll /Lib. LRP 3431   mono    M   $25   ####   M   -3   $20
6LP Filet of Soul /Lib. LRP 3431  M   --3  $25   ####  M   -3  5   27  $12.50
7LP Popsicle /Lib. LRP 3458   mono  E   -3  27  $18
8LP Surf City /Lib. LRP 331   mono  M   --3  $25
9LP Ride the Wild Surf /Lib. LRP-3368   mono  E   -3  27   $25
10 LP Golden Hits Volume Three /Lib. LST-7640  mono  M-/E-  -27  $35
11LP Very Best of Vol. 2  /U.A. LA515-E    NS 1        $12.50   M   -3  $15
12LP "Heart and Soul" of /Design DLP 181   contains four songs from Challenge
   label singles (other tracks by instrumental group)  M-  -3  -7  27  $5

Auction 45's    (Note minimum bids)
Dore label:
001 Clementine /Dore 539    VG   -16  --8     $3
002 We Go Together /Dore 555     M   $6
003 Baby Talk/ Dore 522  autographed DJ copy (guaranteed real - the pen ink
   for Dean's is definitely aged and faded - Jan used a ballpoint - see
   illustration)    G to F  (it needs a cleaning)          $30
Liberty label:
004 Clementine /Lib. 55860   obscure  M/M-        $12
005 A Beginning From an End /Lib. 55849              pic slv   M   --3  $15
006 Drag City /Lib. 55641   DJ copy   E       --8  27  $6
007 From All Over the World /Lib. 55766       DJ   M/M-  -4  --8  $5
008 Linda /Lib. 55531      rare DJ copy      poor condition
009 The New Girl in School /Lib. 55923   DJ   M   -8   $8
010 Popsicle b/w Norwegian Wood /Lib. 55886   M   $5
011 A Surfer's Dream b/w Fiddle Around /Lib. 55905   M   $5
012 Honolulu Lulu /Lib. 55613      pic slv only   1# below mint   $6
Misc. labels:
013 Yellow Balloon /Columbia 4-44036   E       Columbia sleeve   $15
014 Vejtables b/w Jenny Lee /Lib. 50859        DJ   art slv   E   27   $10
015 LEGENDARY MASKED SURFERS      Gonna Hustle You  b/w Summer Means Fun
   /UA-XW270-W    DJ  pic slv    M   -3   $12
016 Sidealk Surfin' /U.A. XW670-Y19     M   $10

Set Sale 45's
Dore label:
017 Baby Talk       /Dore 522   G+    --8  27   $3
Liberty label:
018 You Really Know How to Hurt a Guy /Lib. 54549      'all time hit' series (60's
   pressing)     M/M-    hair crack 3/8" inch in (no play affect)   $2
Other labels:
019 Wanted One Girl /Challenge 9120   M   $15
020 Heart and Soul b/w Those Words /Challenge 9111       looks F, plays E  16  $5
021 Sidewalk Surfin'  /U.S.A. UA-XW670-Y   19   F   $3

JAN BERRY 45's  Auction:
022 Tomorrow's Teardrops /Ripple 6101   VG/G   27   $8
023 Don't You Just Know It /Ode 66034    DJ  M    $15
024 Skateboard Surfin' U.S.A. /A&M 2020  19  M/M-    $5
025 JAN & ARNIE  Gas Money /Arwin MM 111-45    M   minor lab. tear
```

CONT. OVER

SUNSHINE MUSIC 4

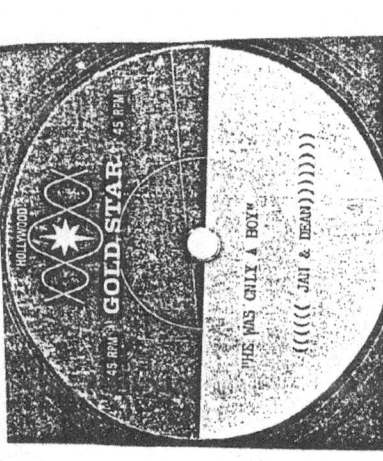

```
JAN BERRY 45's     Set Sale:
026  Mother Earth b/w Blue Moon Shuffle /Ode 66023   M/M- $8
027  Sing Sang a Song /Ode 66120  DJ/19  M  Ode sleeve  $15

Misc. & Related LP's   AUCTION
13LP  BEL-AIRE POPS ORCH.  Jan & Dean's Pop Symphony No. 1 /Lib. LRP-3414
      (1965) JAN BERRY & GEORGE TIPTON arranged and conducted  mono E- 27 -5 -9  $15
14LP  various artists; J&D, VENTURES, JOHNNY RIVERS, DEL SHANNON, T-BONES,
      others "California Gold" /U.A. P26013 (Columbia Record Club) mid-70's
      double collection - obscure                    M  -3       $12
15LP  TONY, VIC AND MANUEL  A Go Go /Reprise RS-6139  also known as the
      Matadors, they sang back-up on J&D sessions - obscure   E  -3  $8

Misc. & Related 45's   AUCTION
028  HAWLEY, DEANE  Queen of the Angels /Liberty 55446  JAN arranged  VG-  $3
029  MATADORS  Perfidia /Colpix CP 698  The Matadors sang back-up on some J&D
      sessions - JAN BERRY produced       E+/E-     $5
030  CURTIS, SONNY (of the Crickets)  So Used to Loving You /Dimension
      1024   this side arranged by Jan - flip side is Beatle novelty song  E  $8

Related 45's   SET SALE
031  PAPA DOO RUN RUN  Be True to Your School b/w Disney Girls  /RCA NB-10404
     M DJ/16 -8  $10
032  various artists; J&D, BEACH BOYS, DICK DALE & GARY USHER  "The Beach
     Years", very limited promo EP (33 1/3) for a six-hour radio program prepared
     by Roger Christian & Jim Pewter, 1975 - inc. music and interviews  $15

Related LP's   SET SALE
16LP  EGAN, WALTER  Not Shy /Col. CJ 35077   feat. Dean back-up vocal one track
      - also feat. STEVIE NICKS       DJ M/M-  --3    $4.50

Reissues / Boots   SET SALE
J&D, plus ROY ORBISON, SHIRELLES, 4 SEASONS  "Things Go Better With Coke"
     (1965) radio spots EP, J&D do two commercials, limited boot)   $8
"oddities" picture disc (17 tracks, obscure 45 sides) M  $25
"Studio Out Takes Vol. 2" LP  $8
"Rarities" /Blue Pacific double LP -rare tracks, unreleased versions, misc.  $12

         *** SUPER SECTION (SPECIAL ITEMS) ***
Rare Test-pressing:  "Save For a Rainy Day" LP, not made by Columbia (there are
      rumoured test pressings on that label), but for the J&D label - test label is
      unmarked and has the pressing plants name "Fidelatone"  M- -21  min. bid $125

Metal dub or accetate:  "He Was Only a Boy" (one sided) /Gold Star Studios
       label, 8" diameter    F     min. bid $25


ABBREVIATIONS FOR RECORD CONDITION
NS   = new, still factory sealed
M    = mint (appears as new/unplayed)
M/M- = overall mint with very minor scuff(s)
E    = excellent (very light wear)
VG   = very good (evident wear, but should
       play satisfactory on any set)
G    = good (more than average wear, but not bad)
F    = fair (excessive wear, still some playability)
DJ   = promotional copy   pic slv = picture sleeve
art slv = art sleeve      undg = underground issue
A/B  refers to 45 side, or jacket front/back
-/+  used for inbetween conditions to above grades
NOTE: when two record condition grades appear like
E/VG, the condition varies one side to another


OTHER CONDITION & SPECIAL DETAIL CODES   -- = very minor (or small)   - = minor (or small)
 1/ cut-out mark in jacket        10/ jacket or sleeve damage       19/ promo copy same song each
 2/ cut-out mark in label         11/ jacket or sleeve tear             side, generally mono/stereo
 3/ jacket or sleeve wear         12/ label tear                    20/ second pressing of 3 or 4
 4/ label wear                    13/ jacket or sleeve stain            label styles - still vintage
 5/ jacket or sleeve repair            or water damage              21/ pressing mark or visual
 6/ jacket corner(s) wear         14/ label stain or water dam.         defect - no play affect
 7/ writing or marking on         15/ sticker on jacket/sleeve      22/ 'DJ' rubber stamp on jacket
    jacket or sleeve              16/ sticker on label (note:       23/ picture/lyric sheet included
 8/ writing or marking on             if DJ sticker, DJ/15 - DJ/16))24/ jacket corner(s) bent
    label                         17/ shop bin wear (sealed LP's    25/ lyric sheet included
 9/ jacket edge(s) wear           18/ warpage (will track)          26/ special promo insert included
                                                                    27/ outstanding visual scuff(s)
                                                                        that do not affect play
```

SUNSHINE MUSIC 5

SUNSHINE MUSIC — Dean Unmasked! — See page 6! — Issue 5

SUNSHINE MUSIC
c/o Doc Rock
Box 1166
Lawrence, KS 66044

To:

Whos is this using Dean's Kittyhawk telephone? See p. 6!!

FIRST CLASS MAIL

SUNSHINE MUSIC

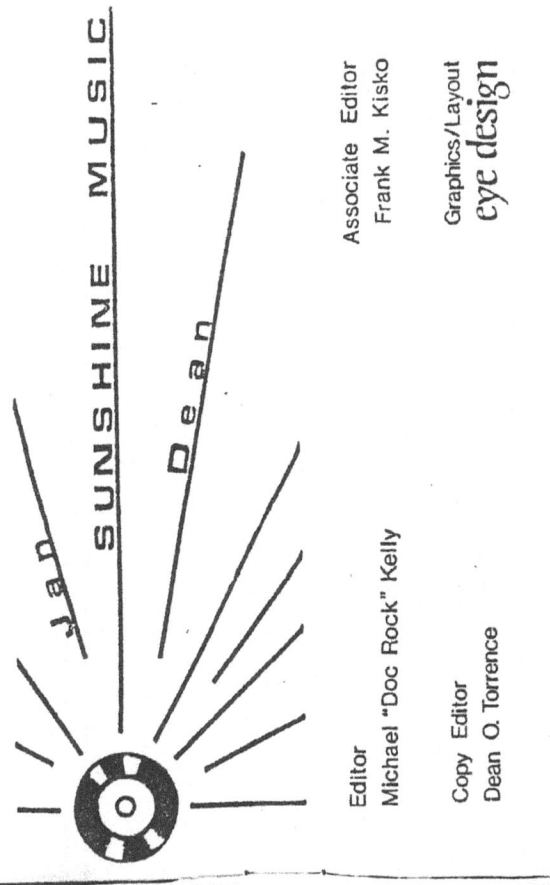

Jan SUNSHINE MUSIC Dean

Editor
Michael "Doc Rock" Kelly

Copy Editor
Dean O. Torrence

Associate Editor
Frank M. Kisko

Graphics/Layout
eye design

Issue 5   **Fall 1980**

THE OFFICIAL JAN AND DEAN
AUTHORIZED COLLECTORS' CLUB

*Contents not already copyrighted are
© 1980 by Michael Bryan Kelly, so there!*

SAMPLE ISSUES of *SUNSHINE MUSIC* are $1.00. Period.
However, seven-issue SUBSCRIPTIONS go as follows:

USA	USA, sent in 6x9 envelope	Non-US Surface	Non-US Air	Surface Envelopes	Air Envelopes
$5	$7	$7	$12	$10	$15

Those are totals, nothing to add. All previous guides
are void. Make checks payable to Michael B. Kelly.

● **HERE THEY COME
(FROM ALL OVER THE
WORLD)**

By Phil Sloan and Steve Barri

Hey, everybody see them arrivin'
The greatest stars you'll ever see
Some are flyin' and some are drivin'
from Liverpool to Tennessee
Chuck Berry's checkin' in from St. Lou
He's gonna sing Maybelline and
Memphis too
There's the Four Seasons from New
York City
And Leslie Gore now sure looks pretty
Here they come from all over the world
Here they come from all over the world
A million guitars swingin', dancin' and
singin'
So come on, come on, come on
Can't you just hear everybody singin'
The biggest sound you ever heard
Clappin' and a-stompin while the
guitars are screamin'
Better go spread the word.
Don't forget the Motor City sound of
the day
The baby lovin' Supremes and Marvin
Gaye
The king of the blues soulful James
Brown
The Beach Boys singin', "I Get
Around"
Yeah, round, round, get around I get
around
(Repeat chorus).
They're comin' from over the world
They're comin' from over the world
Those fab lookin' guys with the moppy
long hair
The Rolling Stones from Liverpool
gotta be gear
Gerry and the Pacemakers, Billy J. too
Are all gonna be there, to sing for you
Here they come from all over the world
Here they come from all over the world
A million guitars swingin', dancin' and
singing
So come on, come on, come on,
From all over the world.
© Copyright 1964 Trousdale Music.

LET ME EXPLAIN

I have heard a number of people express a criticism of SUNSHINE MUSIC, specifically, that my issues come out too infrequently. There are many other 'zines on related topics which do come out more frequently than SM comes out. And, there are some (such as BOMP) which come out even less frequently.

Let me explain.

First, SUNSHINE MUSIC is a club, not a magazine. What does that mean? Well, for one thing it means that I spend more time answering Jan and Dean mail than I spend putting out SM. Recently SM joined the National Association of Fan Clubs. As revealed by this organization, it is standard for fan club publications to come out four times a year. SM, so far, has four seasonal issues per year. However, at some time it may come out more or less than four times a year. That is why a subscription is for seven issues, not for one year.

Parenthetically, our club was originally called a "Fan" club. When Dean told me of his plans to someday revive Jan and Dean's own "Fan" club, I decided to change the name to "Collector's" club. Serendipitously, Dean later came up with the same new name for the club, so with issue number two, the change was made. As a "Collector's" club, SM is the only person or publication authorized to utilize non-current photos of J&D.

A second reason why SM comes out as often as it does is that it is completely a one-man operation in terms of writing. With the exception of a few letters and one historical reprint so far, every word is mine. Other publications may come out more often, but they are full of reprints and material written by other persons. There is nothing wrong with that. It is just a difference which results in my less-frequent publication schedule.

Third, SM is total Jan and Dean. I could come out much more often if I included information on other artists I admire, such as Lesley Gore, Freddie Cannon, Bobby Vee, Lou Christie, Angles, Pixies Three, or the Beach Boys. But SM=J+D.

Any questions?

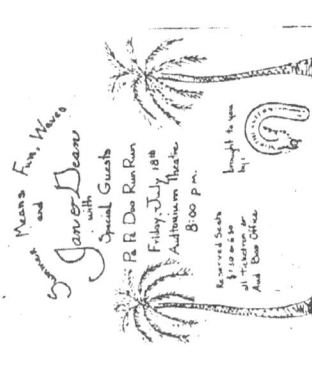

There are a lot of late-breaking developments as SM goes to press.

Flash--Chicago--Now Available, the premier issue of GONNA HUSTLE YOU, a new Jan and Dean fanzine. It will come out six times a year, and include trivia, columns, photos lift-out, a history of Jan and Dean's recordings, interviews, and more. For your copy, write US--Sharon Fox/5742 W. Giddings St/Chicago, IL/60630 Sample:$1.20 Subscriptions:$6.00 yearly
Non-US--Stephen J. McParland/2 Kentwell Av/Concord, 2137 NSW/Australia Sample:$2.00 Subscriptions:$10.00 yearly

Flash--California--The band PAPA has been fired. A new JAN AND DEAN BAND is being formed, and will probably include at least two of PAPA as a core, but reports as to who are conflicting.

Flash--Los Angeles--Jan and Dean and the JAN AND DEAN BAND will spend the first half of October on a tour of Hawaii and Australia. Specific dates and locations have not been released.

Flash--Sepulveda--A new authorized Jan and Dean FAN CLUB (as opposed to Collectors' Club) is organizing. Reportedly, photos, information, and other material will become available. Send an SASE to Jara Beaubien/9029 Columbus Av #30/Sepulveda, CA 91343

Flash--Hollywood--SUNSHINE MUSIC has been contacted by the staff of the syndicated TV show AMERICAN TOP TEN. The producers wish to feature JAN AND DEAN on an upcoming segment. The show has been renewed for a second season. Each show features the top music of the day, from rock to country. A special feature each show is an update on a rock and roll act which started in the '50s or '60s. SM has supplied the shows staff with a full history of Jan and Dean up to the items on this page, plus a multitude of photos from 1958 to 1980. An air date has not been scheduled, but the shows are not taped much in advance, since the music is totally current (except the historical part of the update feature, of course). Besides music and photos, a tape or film clip of the update artist is shown along with the update information. Watch for this! I will notify anyone who wishes about the air date for this show, if you will write me requesting the information, and enclosing a self-addressed, stamped post card or envelope. Note: the film clip shown will not be from the TAMI show!

Flash--Los Angeles--A writer has been working for the last year on a book about the career of Jan and Dean. This will be an excellent book, as it is being done as an inside job, so to speak, not a book written by an outsider.

Flash--Park Avenue South, NY--The Editor, Writer, Publisher, and Janitor of SUNSHINE MUSIC has signed a contract with ARCO/Prentice Hall for a book. Unrelated to records and music, the book is slated for a mid-Winter release. More information in a later issue.

"Dean" Unmasked!

Most people--even most fans--do not realize that, for many years Jan and "Dean" have been placing clues in their songs and on their album covers and picture sleeves. Clues about what? Well, apparently Dean is dead, or at least that is what is inferred by the aforementioned clues!

There is no use my trying to "convince" you. Obviously a double (perhaps Bruce Hatch's cousin?) has been in use for some time now. Bet to explicate the clues, and let you decide for yourself.

Notice how Dean is tugging at his necktie, struggling to get air. This is one of several clues that Dean actually succumbed to suffocation.

Proof!

Look at the cover photo of the first Jan and Dean Liberty LP.

More proof is offered on the Little Old Lady LP cover. Note that Dean is wearing a "Blue Fox" sweatshirt. Haven't you always wondered what the Blue Fox stood for? It is a little known fact that the Blue Fox is the sign of death by suffocation for a ancient Sepulveda Indian tribe, native to Southern California!

The Ride the Wild Surf cover were not cast in this film. Why do you suppose Jan and Dean were not cast in this film. No, not that cock-and-bull story about Frank Sinatra, Jr., being kidnapped. I mean, who would want to kidnap Frank Sinatra, Jr.? No, the producers discovered the truth about "Dean," and refused to go along with the charade.

The Linda LP cover offers some of the strongest proof yet. First, note that Jan has a girl, but Dean does not. How could he, if he were in fact dead? I mean, what kind of a relationship could a girl have with a deceased person? What could she say to open a conversation with a dead man, "Turn me on"? Actually, the more convincing clue on the Linda LP is in the fact that most copies of this LP have a paste-over cover. That is, the original cover said "Jan and Dean Take Linda Surfin'." However, Linda threatened to expose the secret if they kept this title, so the title of the LP as shown on the spine of the cover was modified as a compromise. It was changed to "Mr. Bass Man Takes Linda Surfin'."

Linda apparently demanded that all existing unsold copies be changed. Thus, the great paste-over, putting new spines on thousands of Liberty LPs. Not all of the original Linda spines were covered with the Mr. Bass Man spine. Many have been uncovered on the spines of such other Liberty artists as Vic Dana, Walter Brennan, and the Chipmunks.

Haven't you always wondered why some records say Jan and Arnie, while others say Jan and Dean? Why Arnie was left out of the TV movie? Do I have to paint you a picture?

Listen to Ride the Wild Surf, especially in stereo. Listen with care to the very last note. Hear Dean's voice holding after the other voices have released the last note? "Gotta Take That One Last Ride" is the line just sung, obviously referring to that big surf in the sky. Same reference for the LP reissued lately by the same title, GTTOLR.

As the years went by, a number of people in the business had to discover or be told the truth. This resulted in a number of "Dean Tribute" records being released, several of which became hits. For example, "Ney York's A Lonely Town, when you're the only surfer boy around" was a clear reference to Jan's being withour a partner.

Jack Nitzsche recorded the tribute "The Lonely Surfer." This is but one of the indications that Dean actually drowned, possibly while surfing. The Four Seaon's "No Surfin' Today" is thinly disguised by referring to a female surfer. The same goes for Honolulu Lulu, where "Dean" hollers on the record when Lulu wipes out. And of course, there is the Ventures "Hawaii 5-0,"referring to the police investigation into Dean's demise.

Apparently the strain of all this became too much for Jan in the mid-'60s. His car accident seems now to have been an elaborate cover-up for his building emotional stress, and he called it quits as far as Jan and Dean went, and checked himself into a therapy situation. In the early '70s, he tried it again at the Surfer's Stomp Revival, but the strain was still there, and he quit again, until he finally came out with his own records, under several variations of his own name (Jan, 1 Jan 1, Jan Berry) to show that Dean was long gone. He had tried this in the early '60s as well, as Jan Barry on Ripple records, and even on the Liberty 45"The Universal Coward."

Jan's first Ode 45, "Mother Earth," is a reworking of the old "Ashes to ashes" bit.

SUNSHINE MUSIC 5

It is not clear who replaced Dean on records. It is a fact that Harry Nilsson passed himself off as Dean for a while. Brian Wilson sang Dean's part on some records, including "Don't Ya Just Know It." Side One of the LP GTOLR acknowledges Brian's aid in keeping the secret. Etched in the run-out groove is, in a clever copy of Dean's writing, "Thanks, Brian." Of course, Brian was a close friend, and the strain told even more on him than on Jan. But then Brian's breakdowns over this have been widely documented elsewhere.

You have heard that it is Jan's brother, not Jan himself, pictured on the cover of the Save For A Rainy Day LP? It is hard to tell as the photo has been deliberately obscured, but Dean is not on this cover either. His sister Kathy was used in his stead!

Jill Gibson frequently substituted for Dean on records, such as on "It's As Easy As 1,2,3." Here, the real artist is shown in the run-out groove, on the A-side of the Liberty Golden Hit Series reissue, where it says "Jano & Jilly."

You would think that "A Beginning From An End" referred to a mother's passing away in child birth. For those in the know, this was a veiled reference to Dean's replacement, again referred to as a female to further hide the truth: "(he) looks like you in every way, but that doesn't mean I don't miss you," sings Jan. In fact, if you hold the Folk 'n Roll cover up at a 104 degree angle during an eclipse of the moon in Cancer you can see a skull-less vertebra in the leaves of the tree!

Yet More!

More Proof!

Turning to the 45 picture sleeves, their first, on Dore, has Dean away from the girls, and facing sideways, while Jan faces us straight on and is next to the two girls (for every boy). See, the famous line from "Surf City" refers to the fact that, since Dean is not around, Jan gets his girl as well as his own!

The next sleeve, for "Gee," repeats the pattern of Dean sideways and Jan straight on! While on the actual "Surf City" sleeve, Jan is holding Jill, while Dean is holding a surf board! There is added significance in this. Surf boards are wood, as are coffins. The "woodie" coffin is a frequent reference in Jan and Dean records. ("I've got a '34 wagon and we often referred to is in fact a coffin ("I've got a '34 wagon and we call it a woodie") as in "Surf City." The woodie itself is usually a hearse, as in the Drag City LP song "Surfin' Hearse." The Quads song by the same title is another Dean tribute song.

One cannot ignore the famous line in "Sidewalk Surfin'," "You can do the tricks the surfer's do, just try a Quasinodo or the *coffin, too!*"

Still another Dean-tribute record was recorded by Bob Vaught and the Renegades on GNP Crescendo Records: "Surfin' Tragedy."

LP Heaven!

After Jan's wreck, and after it was clear he was going to be "OK," I was still very sad. Sorry for myself you might say. You see, I thought that my Jan and Dean LP collection was never going to grow. And all I had at that time was my set of all of their Liberty LPs. Well, little did I know the wealth of Jan and Dean LPs which were to be released over the next 14 years!

First, there was the Popsicle LP (6-66). Even though this was old material reissued, it was still a great new treasure. Little, even less, did I know that reissued material would be responsible for the bulk of the many unexpected LPs to come!

Second was GOLDEN HITS VOLUME 3 (8-66). That was an even bigger surprise than VOLUME 2 had been (9-65), but did not have as many hits as that one had had.

That did it for Liberty. The rest of the collection is hard to put in the order I got them, but here goes. I had to go to LA in 1973 to get a copy of their first LP THE SOUND OF JAN AND DEAN (1960) on Dore. I later gave this LP to Dean, who had not even seen a copy since about '64! After, of course, I got another copy for myself!

On the other hand, Dean gave me his (1966) boot-type LP SAVE FOR A RAINY DAY. Numbered J&D 101, this was a demo LP Dean made and which got him his contract with Columbia records, culminating in the hit 45 "Yellow Balloon." There was also a second, studio version of this LP produced, an entirely different recording, but it was never released in the US. Actually, I have heard of two stereo DJ copies turning up without covers!

This latter version was also released as a DJ LP in England. At auction, Dean himself was said to have been outbid by $25 in the late '70s, when a collector got it for $325!!

Meanwhile, two other forms of the same LP became known. For one, the LP was released to the public in Japan. It is rarer than trouts' eyelids, because when a Japanese LP is pulled, all copies are recycled into new LPs, not sold as cutouts. I was very lucky to get a mint quality tape of this LP. We were all lucky when a poor quality bootleg of this Colombia LP was issued on "Last Ride" records a few years back. It is stereo.

There is no need to entirely leave the '60s behind, yet. Dean re-recorded "Yellow Balloon" as The Yellow Balloon, and another LP came out of this. On Canterbury records, this LP has Dean's art on the cover, and his voice, especially notable on the track "Can't Get Enough of Your Love."

The sleeve for the 45 "You Really Know How To Hurt A Guy" should have been obvious in its clues, but was neatly camouflaged by the title itself. On one side, there is a poor unfortunate with, and get this, *a neck iron clearly constricting his breathing*. Dean, quite naturally under the circumstances, has a very empathetic expression on his face. By contrast, Jan appears bemused!

The other side depicts *decapitations!* The head Jan is holding represents Dean's, as can be seen from their expressions, especially "Dean's."

PROOF POSITIVE!!

One of the more dramatic clues is to be found when playing a Jan and Dean record backward on your turntable. At the end of "Drag City," the phrase "yeah, listen to 'em whine" is repeated over and over again. Played backwards, this comes out as Dean saying, "Eniw me ot nestil haey." Which is obviously "Turn me on next life."

Why did Jan and "Dean" plant all of these clues, and more? Was it a stunt to boost record sales? Why not just admit that Dean was gone, if he in fact is?

Write me and tell me your theory. Also, I know that there must be many, many more clues. Write me and tell me of the clues I am sure you have noticed but had no idea what significance should be attached to them.

---

7 AM ② ⑧ **GOOD MORNING AMERICA**
—David Hartman
④ ⑤ **TODAY**—Tom Brokaw
Sixties rock stars Jan (Berry) and Dean (Torrance) discuss their comeback. (2 hrs.)
⑪ ⑬ **WEDNESDAY MORNING**
—Bob Schieffer
⑭ **RAY RAYNER**—Children
⑯ **HAZEL**—Comedy
㉖ **NATURE OF HUMAN CONFLICT**
㉜ **STAR TREK**—Cartoon

AFTERNOON

Noon ③ **JAN AND DEAN**—Music
⑤ **ZOOM**—Children
⑨ **STAR TREK**—Science Fiction
⑪ ⑬ **SESAME STREET**
—Children
㉖ **NEWS**
㉗ **CARTOONS**
㉚ **THREE STOOGES**
㊵ **BIBLE BOWL**
12:15 ⑫ **TO BE ANNOUNCED**
12:30 ⑪ **ENGLISH CHANNEL**
1. The dangers of polyurethane upholstery are examined in "Armchair Inferno." 2. "Beginnings," a film study of ballet. 3. "Lady Policemen." (2 hrs.)

SUNSHINE MUSIC 5

A subsidiary of Liberty, Sunset, put out an LP called JAN AND DEAN (1966). Featuring a variation of the photo used on the "Honolulu Lulu" 45 cover, it features old Liberty LP cuts. The pressing is of poor quality.

In terms of chronological order, the first real thrill came when Dean put out the ANTHOLOGY ALBUM on the label which took over Liberty, United Artists (12-66).

This was really a history of Jan and Dean, both in music and text. This was Dean's project, in more ways than one. When it came time to design the graphics for the LP, UA asked Dean if he had any photos. They asked him as though he were just an artist, not an Artist. He ended up designing the entire LP, not to mention trade ads and other LPs in the Legendary Masters Series, which included double LPs by Ricky Nelson, Eddie Cochran, and Fats Domino. Still available, and one of the best compilations for any artist, the newer issues have done away with the special label Dean designed.

Not much later came GOTTA TAKE THAT ONE LAST RIDE, another 2-LP set on UA. With any kind of promotion at all by UA, this should have hit the charts like the highly promoted set by the Beach Boys. Dean even did a poster insert (their first LP on Dore had a poster, too!). Since Dean is not a fan of stereo (see upcoming SM interview), all tracks are in mono, but sound very clean. The DJ version has a self-stick insert, but the limited "liners" Dean wrote for the jacket are great enough: IT IS EXPRESSLE FORBIDDEN TO SUCK OR SMOKE THIS RECORDING IN ANY MANNER OR FORM. IF ACCIDENTLY SWALLOWED TAKE TWO HOTDOGS AND A COLD SHOWER WITH A FRIEND.

As a bonus, we got the first post-wreck photo of Dean and Jan on the back cover!!

Into the '70s. At the start of the decade, interest was low, and so were prices for J&D collectables! Then, as we who were active at that early time began bidding against one another, the price for rare singles rose fast. The result: bootlegs of old and obscure cuts.

The first boot was OLD WAX AND NEW WAVES, described last issue. Around this same time, UA began a series of VERY BEST OF... LPs, covering the multitude of artists now owned by this conglomerate label. THE VERY BEST OF JAN AND DEAN VOLUMES ONE AND TWO were a treat, since they featured cuts long unavailable. You see, Liberty never cut out a Jan and Dean LP. But when UA took over, all the old LPs were pulled like fast. Thus, any cut not on the ANTHOLOGY or GTTOLR was just not commercially available. Until THE BEST, which featured things like "Batman," "We Go Together," and the classic "You Really Know How To Hurt A Guy" (missing from the 2-LP sets because Dean has other favorites).

Taking care of UA, we jump up to 1980, and UA 999. Dean was in charge of the cover of DEADMAN's CURVE, and the cuts sound good in this re-mix on modern equipment.

Back to 1974, a little-know Warner Brothers LP called THE FORCE had a real surprise. The ultra-rare "Laurel and Hardy" was included on this sampler, one of the songs Jan did very soon after the wreck!

The next year, UA did a very nice compilation of Surf 'n Drag music. Although the artwork is sexist, the music is tops, with many different artists included. Even Annette and Frankie Avalon, not authentic, being movie-types, get on. Jan and Dean do "Surf City," "Honolulu Lulu," "Sidewalk Surfin'," and "Ride the Wild Surf!"

Next we come to K-Tel. They started selling shortened oldie packages on TV around 1972. They started by doing shortened versions of hits, with a verse or two cut out of each song! Irritating, but probably meant they had to pay less royalties to the original labels. They ended this practice in a few years, and in 1976 came out with TWENTY GREATEST HITS/GREATEST STARS. Including our heroes. And the old favorite photo which is Dean's favorite (see RIDE THE WILD SURF LP cover; et all). The songs on the 45 label on J&D Record Co. releases; et all. The songs here were original and uncut: "Surf City" and "Little Old Lady."

However, K-Tel had a plan. Why, they figured, pay those old record companies anything for their old masters? I mean, if the artist still has vocal chords, lets fly'em up here and redo the hits. Original hits by original artists, just not original recordings.

Chubby Checker, The Angels, Frankie Ford, Gary Lewis, Bobby Vee, you name 'em. Some are very good. Many are bad. Some had lost their voices (Gary Lewis). A few were very tight. Dean and Papa, for instance. Nice little re-makes. Minus Jan, Lanky, Bones, and Lou, they were still good.

So, in 1977, we had HERE COMES SUMMER. A period of transition for K-Tel, since "Ride..." is the Liberty version, but "Sidewalk Surfin" is a remake. As if that is not weird enough, we have "I Get Around" by "Jan and Dean" (Dean and Papa). This is the only case I know of where K-Tel has an original hit by a non-original artist. Although Dean is probably on the bB "I Get Around," after all.

Another surprise on the same LP is a pair of songs by (?) The Surfers (?). Probably Papa without Dean, The Sunrays' "I Live For The Sun" and the Rivieras' "California Sun" turn up, another strange move for K-Tel.

One may note at this point that up until 1978, the J&D songs most identified with them were "Surf City" and "Little Old Lady." Then came the TV movie. From now on, "Dead Man's Curve," re-dubbed "Deadman's Curve," will turn up a lot!

50

SUNSHINE MUSIC 5

And, that just about was all she wrote for US releases after the wreck. My LP collection looks much different that I thought it would by 1980. The 15 Liberty LPs are now side by side with some 15 releases since then.

Last issue, I told of the new Excelsior LP. This has all ten of the cuts Dean and Papa did for K-Tel, and is a part of a big series of oldie issues, most featuring "various artists" including J&D. The cover art is stunning, and not unlike Dean's style. The portraits are taken from, of all things, the cover photo from the original Dore LP!

This issue, I can announce a new bootleg LP. It is called LEGENDARY MASKED SURFERS, but has no connection with Dean's project by that monniker. Brand new, it has these cuts:

SIDE ONE
Gotta Getta Date
Gas Money
I Love Linda (preceding all Jan and Arnie)
Baggy Pants
Those Words
She's Still Talking Baby Talk
Frosty, the Snowman
Freeway Flyer
Fiddle Around

SIDE TWO
Hawaii
Tijuana (Old Lady remake)
Love and Hate
Fan Tan
Summertime
California Lullaby
Like a Summer Rain
Louisiana Man
Yellow Balloon

SIDE THREE
Taste of Rain
Love and Hate (diff. version)
Only a Boy
Laurel and Hardy
I Know My Mind
Don't You Just Know It
Tinsel Town (new version)
Sidewalk Surfin' ('70s version)

SIDE FOUR
Ride the Wild Surf (minus viol
Here They Come (diff. version)
Summertime, Summertime
Summer Means Fun
Fin City (diff. version)
Sing Sang A Song (")
Little Queenie (")

Literally hundreds of dollars worth of rare stuff all on one boot LP. Some of these were only released on DJ copies, others are versions that were never released at all!

LP HEAVEN!

WORD SEARCH ANSWERS

So, you went crazy trying to unscramble Honolulu Lulu's Jan and Dean, A-#1 Word Search? Well, I'll take pity on you! ANSWERS:

1. Bazoom Girl
2. Bel-Air Bandits
3. Sunset, Vine, La Brea
   Schwabs, Crescent
   Heights, Doheny
4. Buick
5. Lady
6. William!
7. Baggy Pants
8. San Jose
9. Malibu
10. Imperial
11. Porsche
12. Jan OK
13. Melcher
14. Barbara Ann
15. Arwin, Dore, Challenge
    Liberty, J&D, Magic Lamp,
    Sunset, B'r'er Bird, Warner
    Brothers, Ode, A&M, UA, Ripple
    (Left out Columbia, White Whale)
16. Emerson
17. Bogart
18. Holland
19. Palladium
20. USC
21. Aloha
22. Lanky; Bones
23. Hatch
24. Jeanette
25. Kittyhawk
26. Graphics Artist
27. Rooney
28. Johnston; Love
29. Easy Come, Easy Go
30. Davy Jones
31. Pollution
32. Hypo
33. Barons
34. Stinkpot
35. Famous Amos
36. Adler
37. Bomps
38. Surf, Drag, Folk, Gotham, Detroit
38. Louisiana Man
40. Davison

Collectors Notice:

SOMETHING OLD, SOMETHING NEW, NOTHING BORROWED, NOTHING BLUE

Here is your chance to add to your Jan and Dean collection. Make checks payable to Michael B. Kelly.

1. SET SALE The new, four-sided LEGENDARY MASKED SURFERS LP. New and mint, $13 post paid. For insurance, add 50¢. For First Class postage, add $1.00.

2. BID Rolling Stone Magazine, Sept. 12, 1974. This has on the cover, "The Tragic History of Jan and Dean." Inside is lengthy article about Jan and Dean by Paul Morantz, Jan's lawyer. This article formed the basis for the TV MOVIE.

3. BID Phonograph Record Magazine, July, 1975. The 10x13 color cover photo is of Dean, a blonde beach bunny (or at least a California girl) and a youngster (a Dean clone?) sitting on a park bench made of a surf board. Inside are articles pronouncing THE BEACH IS BACK, with articles about Jan and Dean, the Beach Boys, Johnny Rivers, and others!

SHORT CUTS

****They tell me that Dean, who skateboards on stage every night, "tried a spinner but his wax didn't hold." He hurt his back in the fall, but not badly.

****J & D played LA's prestigious GREEK THEATER on June 30th. The GREEK is an outdoor amphitheater which hosts such acts as Neil Diamond, Joni Mitchel, or Barry Manilow (whoever they are). Widely promoted on KRLA and posters all over town, the show was a virtual sellout! The crowd loved J & D, and this is quite a coup for an act that played the GOLDEN BEAR in Hunnington only last year! Special Guests of J & D at the GREEK: Jeff Baxter (formerly with Steely Dan), and the Dooby Brothers. Guests at the party afterwards: Flo and Eddie (of the Turtles), Richard Hatch, the Rams Cheerleaders, and Sterling Smith (of the beach boys' band).

****Another last-minute update on the tour. J & D will be in Australia 10-16-80 to 11-14-80. I'll try to get the specific dates.

****A new single is rumored but unconfirmed.

**** Jan has shelved his own single since he is so busy touring with pard Dean. His 45, "Hot Cookie," aka "Hot Shot," aka "Hot Lookin' Lady," features the great Hal Blaine. The instrumental track was laid down a year ago January, and by October Jan had completed the background vocals. The flip is/was slated to be "Blue Moon," and the whole thing is said to have a slight disco feel. A single on the charts is Jan's dream, justifiably. "It's been 14 years," friends have heard him say wistfully.

Jan & Dean On 1260 KYA

J: Bomp-bomp-bomp (opening to Jennie Lee)...

D: Cut! Cut! Good, good! What's your name, fella?

J: Ah-- Dean! No, ah, JAN!

D: Hi, Jan! My name is Dean, and I'm here to tell you that you are listening to the Bay area's Golden Gate Greats. How do you like it so far, Jan?

J: Well, I don't know yet...

D: OK. Good-bye.

Announcer: Have you guys ever surfed?

D: Well, bath tubs, hot tubs, nowadays it's hot tubs. We haven't surfed since, (Ed.: Good song title!). First time in a long time, it was out at Waikiki.

J: Well, now don't kid him! It's been quite a while since we have gone surfing!

D: OK, I'll have to admit Jan just watched. Watched all the girls, that is, getting wet!

A: (laughs all through this)

D: No, shoot, we had boards way back in the early '50s. We'd be out a Malibu, and on a big day, there'd be maybe five people! And we felt that was really crowded!

J: Yeah, it was great then!

A: Well, on an interview with the Beach Boys, they may have been kidding, but they said that they had never been surfing! You're very good friends with the Beach Boys, right?

J: Oh, yes, sure....

D: ...the Beach...what, who?

J: Oh, come on, knock it off Dean!

D: Oh, yeah. That copy group, I remember them, I think.

A: That's the one, the guys that copied you two. Anyway, they said they hardly had surfed at all. So I was curious about you... Or how about sidewalk surfing? Been on a lot of skateboards?

D: Sure! As a matter of fact, we've been skateboarding

Jan & Dean hold crowd

By Jean Marie Balaty
Bulletin Correspondent

LOS ANGELES — Crossing the age gap, Jan and Dean swept into the Greek Theater last week for a one-night stand, backed by Papa Doo Run Run.

After a 45-minute warmup by Papa, etc., for an audience that didn't need one, teen-age fans who were turned onto the surf sounds of the '50s by the TV movie about the 1966 highway tragedy that almost wiped out Jan, "Deadman's Curve," and their parents who were teens when the duo hit the big time some twenty years ago, the headliners appeared.

Jan (Berry) and Dean (Torrence) thoroughly pleased their audience that greeted the end of each song with ever more thunderous applause, screams and dancing in the aisles.

The team offered some of their early hits, recorded with the Beach Boys, including, "Jenny Lee" and "Baby Talk", "Drag City", "Little Deuce Coupe" and "Linda".

In spite of its classical appearance, the Greek adapted well to the surfin' sounds.

SUNSHINE MUSIC 5

on stage almost every single night for the last three or four months. Not that we want to!

You see, the Beach Boys were very busy. They worked basically every single night of their lives, while we went to school five days a week and did rock and roll just when we felt like it. (Ed.: The BB were busy? I mean, going to graduate and medical school, doing TV shows, the TAMI show, concerts on weekends, recording on week nights, writing songs and producing other artists, AND LOTS OF FREE TIME FOR SURFING! SHEEEEE!!!)

So, we had more free time to do some of the things that we all were supposedly doing, like surfing!

A: I've got one for you: Who is the Little Old Lady From Pasedena?

D: Well, we'll have to admit that the Little Old Lady was really from Oxnard, but Oxnard didn't rhyme with anything, soo.....

J: Nowww, Dean...

D: Actually, there really was a little old lady that was in a Southern California car commercial. She drove a dodge and in the series of commercials she would blow off people. (Ed.: Shut them down, so to speak. And, her real name was Kathryn Miner. She appeared in many TV shows in her "Little Old Lady" costume, including Tonight and Man From Uncle.)

She was just a character in a Dodge commercial. But, WE thought it was a NATIONAL commercial, and figured she was getting national exposure. Why not write a song about the famous little old lady?

We wrote the song, it came out, and only then did we learn that it was just a local commercial! The record was a hit anyway, even though no one had ever heard of her before, so I suppose, what difference did it make?

A: Tell us a little about what Jan and Dean have been doing lately. Dean, don't you do graphics?

D: Yes, I have a graphics company in LA where I do a lot of music-related business, like LP covers.

A: Talk about yourselves. What are your favorite foods, TV shows, your favorite current artists... Tell us ANYthing!

J: (laughs)

D: Jan's favorite food is--

J: Hummm, let me see... CHOCOLATE CHIP COOKIES!

D: Yes, Famous Amos can be found on Jan's training table every morning, along with Twinkies and Slurpies!

J: Yes, that's right!

D: Jan's favorite TV show. Talk quick, Jan, this is Top 40 radio!

J: Hey, wait. Slurpies are awfully good!

D: Yes, Slurpies, so if any of you out there have any Slurpies, bring them tonight and we'll get you in free!

A: Ha! They'll hold you to that!

D: Oh, NO! I forgot about radio. Oh, well... Favorite TV shows. I don't know.

J: It's fun to figure out these things.

D: Oh, it isn't so much fun! Mostly I watch sports. Jan is too busy watching ladies!

A: You guys still live in Southern California?

D: Oh, yes! We are old Southern California boys, probably will never move.

J: RIGHT!

D: We were talking before with you about the KYA Teenage Fairs. We used to do a lot of things with that at the Cow Palace. Those were a lot of fun back in the '60s.

A: Can you recall who appeared with you in those days?

D: Yeah, the Hell's Angels!

A: They are still around here.

D: I heard!

A: They are still together.

D: That group has a better PR department than we do.!

They're in the news a lot. As for the Cow Palace, most of the time we were by ourselves. But we did one, not connected with the Teenage Fair, with the Beach Boys, Bruce and Terry, Phil Spector and his band, the Ronnettes...who knows who else. That's too far back. We have "Surfer's Senility," where we cannot remember two weeks ago!

A: Is it true that you have a second-generation audience now?

J: That is very true.

53

FROM THE FILES

D: That is what really makes it satisfying for us. It is because of the film demographics of DEADMAN'S CURVE. It was shown once on a Tuesday night during Easter vacation, and once on a Friday. Both not school nights. A lot of kids were home, these were TV nights. No school the next day. So possibly all these parents were saying, "Hew, we remember these guys! You kids are gonna sit down and watch something for a change that Mom and Dad want to see."

These eleven to fifteen year olds say, "Nayh, we wanna watch something exciting like Donnie and Marie!" But, as soon as they saw what it was about, skateboarding and surfing, the same stuff they are doing now, they quickly related to it. And since most stations had been playing Jan and Dean records all along, it gave them something, some identity to go with those songs they had been exposed to for the last couple of years.

Now, these kids are coming to our concerts. Usually we have a very young audience as a result.

A: One quick question: Where is Surf City?!

D: Jan, you wrote the song, where the heck is Surf City?

J: We never could find out!!

A: It was mythical?

D: Well, as soon as we find out, we'll let you know!

(Ed.: Autumn LP #101 is titled AYA'S MEMORIES OF THE COW PALACE. Recorded live Sept. 28, 1963, it has the following artists: George and Teddy, a local act, Dionne Warwick, the Righteous Brothers, the Drifters, Betty Harris, Bobby Freeman, the Ronnettes, Dee Dee Sharp, Freddy Cannon, and JAN AND DEAN!!!

-FI

Pat Silva -FI

Once-Troubled Jan and Dean Back From 'Dead Man's Curve'

By SCOTT CAIN

In advance, there was no way of knowing how the Jan and Dean appearance would turn out.

For all practical purposes, they had been away from performing for more than a decade. Jan Berry's injuries in an automobile accident were supposed to be dreadful. Conventional wisdom held that he could not perform again.

When it was announced that Jan and Dean would sing with the Beach Boys at an Omni concert, many people were incredulous. Numerous callers asked whether the announcement could possibly be correct.

It was, but there was a certain sense of foreboding about the event. After all, the Beach Boys have problems of their own, what with Brian Wilson's unpredictable behavior and Dean Wilson's frequently surly temperament.

The logical fear going into the show was that it would be grotesque and embarrassing. Happily, this was not the case. Jan and Dean's performance was terrific. Jan's spunkiness and livelinees won the heart of everybody there. He didn't ask any special favors.

The way it happened was this: A slot for the Jan and Dean act was inserted in the middle of the Beach Boys' set. Numerous members of the huge Beach Boys' band, including singers Mike Love, the principal singer, provided backup for the two guests.

Jan and Dean performed three songs: "Surf City," "Dead Man's Curve" and "The Little Old Lady From Pasadena." Jan sang the lead vocals. The lyrics are intricate and certainly pose a considerable hurdle to anyone with Jan's physical problems. He never missed a word. He never missed a beat. He was never off-key. He picked up immediately on stage antics. He also did all the talking for Jan and Dean, and was completely charming.

Jan has some difficulty in movement. His right side is not fully mobile, but he waits without any assistance and even joined in little dance routines that the other musicians were doing, although his movements were not as expansive as theirs.

Jan, who was extremely handsome in his youth, still looks nice. His face has filled out and he has lost the hard appearance that he used to have. His eyes have a merry twinkle and he smiles easily. He has let his hair grow to shoulder length, but it is well kept and looks good.

Dean Torrance, his partner, looks much the same as he did a dozen years ago, still full of mischief and giving the impression that he would dearly love a day at the beach.

After Jan and Dean performed their short set, they left the stage, but they rejoined the Beach Boys later during an encore. This was a merry occasion, in which even Brian Wilson lurched around the stage, doing awkward choreography.

The show could not have been a happier occasion. The Beach Boys performed a selection of their greatest hits, guaranteed to bring down the house. The basic five-man band had such a large number of backup musicians that individuals could leave the stage for a long time without being missed. Mike Love, the principal singer, dominated the show as usual.

It was he who pointed out ecstatically as they made their way onto the stage that this was a sentimental gesture on the audience's part, of course. The important thing is that Jan and Dean also got a standing ovation when they made their exit, and it was one they had earned.

LETTERS

Editor
Michael "Doc Rock" Kelly

Associate Editor
Frank M. Kisko

AUG 28, 1980

DEAR MIKE,
IN LOOKING OVER THE LATEST ISSUE OF S.M., I NOTICE IN THE S.M. RECORD AUCTION, THAT YOU HAVE A SEALED COPY OF STUDIO OUTAKES LP. YOU ALSO STATE THAT "BIDS UNDER $20 ARE LIKE PISS-ING AGAINST THE WIND" BEING INVOLVED WITH J & D AS MUCH AS YOU ARE, YOU AND BOTH KNOW THAT EVERY-BODY CAN GET THIS LP FROM BOMP RECORDS FOR A CASH PRICE OF $8 PLUS $1.50 P & I. WHY MILK CLUB MEMBERS FOR ATLEAST $10.50 MORE THAN THE LP IS WORTH? IF THE CLUB IS HURTING FOR BUCKS, MAKE IT A CLUB PROJECT TO SELL THE LP AT A RESONALBE PROFIT, BUT NOT 100 PERCENT. IF YOU DIDN'T KNOW ABOUT BOMP, I'M SORRY. BUT I KNOW YOU DO, SO I GUESS I'M NOT. I DO HOPE THAT THIS CLUB IS NOT HEADING INTO MARK PLUMMER TACTICS. I ALSO HOPE YOU ARE BIG ENOUGH TO PRINT THIS LETTER IN S.M. #5   THANKS,

Les M. Kabn

GREG SHAW, BOMP RECORDS, P.O. BOX 7112, BURBANK, CA, 91510. I GET ALOT OF NICE, INNOCENT, PEOPLE LOOKING FOR J&D STUFF, HELP OK?

Dear Les—

Thank you for your letter. I may or may not answer it in print. But in any event, I thought I would not make you wait until the next issue to reply.

When Shaw came out with the Outakes in his list, I ordered two (one of my). Then, I tried to order more, and he sent me a card saying that he was out, and could not get any more.

On the chance that he was just bulling me, I had friends in other states order for me in thier names, and he told them all that he was out, and could get no more.

Finally, I found a place in Hawaii that had it (but not for a mere $3). I ordered several, got back a few with a refund check for the balance, and slipped in the plastic on the bottom copy was a notice "last copy in stock."

As for SM needing funds, I operate in the red, not counting my time. I spend over 100 hours per issue, including correspondence. Believe me, I am not getting rich by ripping off SM members.

Feel free to obtain from bidding. And anyone can feel free to bid as low as they want for anything I offer. I hope they win. I did not put a minimum of $20 on Outtkaes. I just informed interested parties that they will be courting disappoint- ment if theyexpect to be a winner for less than that.

Thanks again for your feedback. Keep in touch.

DOC ROCK   P.O. Box 1166   Lawrence, KS 66044

Dear Michael,

I just had to write and tell you that we have been finding some very interesting records in the most unusual places! We have spent a lot of time at flea markets and junk stores as you suggested. We went back to the same place where we found Baby Talk last week, and believe it or not the man had gotten a copy of Jennie Lee and was holding it behind the counter for us! For $2.00! What a steal!

Then at a flea market we got an original Liberty Little Old Lady for 20¢. At another flea market we got Yellow Balloon for another 20¢. Each of these is in excellent condition, no skips. We come out dirty and grimy because the records are stacked 30 high with no covers, but is it worth it!

At record conventions these records go for $15 to $20 each. We get a lot of funny looks from people, on our hands and knees crawling through albums at Goodwill, but that's where we found a great Pop Symphony for 25¢! Now we just laugh when people look at us!

I hope you don't mind my writing to you, but I just like to let you know that you advice has really paid off, and to keep encouraging peo- ple to dig through dirty old records. In two weeks we got 4 obscure 45s and 2 obscure albums. At times when our hands are filthy and it is hot, we say there can't be anything here, and then we say, but Doc Rock says you'd be surprised what you'd find, and we have found a lot!

Also, thanks for the info about concert info. We both sent a letter requesting tour information. We asked about the fan club but hope to get our information without joining as we are very happy with you, and what you have done, and we feel that it would be very, very hard to beat your fan club. Thanks again for all your hard work on this fan club as I know the time it must take. You are appreciated by all Jan and Dean fans.

Sincerely, Diane

Dear Dianne,

THANKS, and congratulations on your finds!

Doc Rock

Subscribe to SUNSHINE MUSIC!

SUNSHINE MUSIC 6

SUNSHINE MUSIC
c/o Doc Rock
Box 1166
Lawrence, KS 66044

To:

FIRST CLASS MAIL

SUNSHINE MUSIC 6

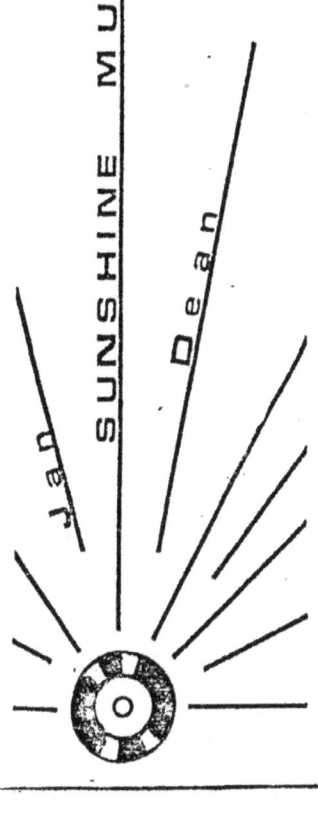

Editor
Michael "Doc Rock" Kelly

Copy Editor
Dean O. Torrence

Associate Editor
Frank M. Kisko

Graphics/Layout
eye design

The Magazine of the Official Jan and Dean
Authorized International Collectors Club

Issue 6   Winter 1981

*Contents not already copyrighted are
© 1981 by Michael Bryan Kelly.*

SUBSCRIPTIONS

OK Jan and Dean fans world-wide, here is a simplified guide to
getting SUNSHINE MUSIC into your mail box safe and sound:

```
Subscription, 7 issues  - - - - - - - - - - - $5.00
Sample Issue  - - - - - - - - - - - - - - - - $1.00
Back Issue  - - - - - - - - - - - - - - - - - $1.00
Overseas Postage
   Surface 7 issues, add - - - - - -  $1.00
   Surface 1 issue, add  - - - - - -  $0.15
   Airmail 7 issues, add - - - - - -  $3.50
   Airmail 1 issue, add  - - - - - -  $0.50
Brown Mailing Envelope (6x9)
   7 issues, add - - - - - - - - - - - - - - - $1.50
   1 issue, add  - - - - - - - - - - - - - - - $0.25
```

Make checks payable to Michael Kelly.

●POPSICLE

(As recorded by Jan & Dean/Liberty)
BOBBY RUSSELL
BUZZ CASON

My phys. ed. teacher's got me working
    too hard
Relax at the school sitting out in the yard
Just me and my baby
I'm holding her hand
Then pop ding-a-ling
Here comes that popsicle man
Orange, lemon, cherry and lime fudge
Then tutti-frutti and a grape that's
    fine
Buy one for me and one for chicks my
A lot of good eating on a popsicle stick
Popsicle, popsicle
If you want to keep cool it does the
    trick
And it comes on a stick
Some people buy popsicles just for
    kicks
Buy me and my baby we save the sticks
To keep brother and sis as quiet as a
    mouse
We give them popsicle sticks to build
    a popsicle house
Popsicle, popsicle
But If you want to keep cool it does the
    trick
And it comes on a stick
So when you hear the bell go ding-a-ling
That's the popsicle man and he's the
    goody king
Save popsicle wrappers and before long
You'll win a phonograph to play this
    record on
Popsicle, popsicle, popsicle, popsicle,
popsicle, popsicle Ad infinitum
● Copyright 1962 by Lowery Music,
Inc.

57

Jan & Dean at Harrah's

by Dee LeClair

Between early May and late August, 1980, I had seen Jan and Dean in concert on six different occasions. The first was at the Dixon (California) May Fair when, as a reporter for a local newspaper, I was sent to cover their concert and ended up "flipping" as I hadn't since listening to their music as a teenager in the 60s. The last was in Portland, Oregon, a 600-mile trip that I made gladly for another chance to see them perform—not realizing it would be Christmas time before I saw them again.

Needless to say, both of these concerts, as well as the ones in-between, were terrific (so much for professional objectivity!) and, when I heard they would be appearing at Harrahs, a casino cabaret in Stateline, Nevada (dates were Dec. 15-28, 1980) that was only about a two-hour drive from my home, I knew I had to see them again.

In the four intervening months between the Portland concert and the Harrah's gig, Papa Do Run Run, or at least three of their number, had come to a parting of the ways with Jan and Dean because, as Dean told me, they had different goals and different ideas about where they wanted to perform. Mark and Jimmy D. stayed with Jan and Dean and three new musicians, Chris Farmer on bass, Hal Rappleyea on drums and Sterling Smith on keyboard, were added to form a group that is tentatively being called "Surf Brothers." (the quotes are Dean's.)

I managed to secure an assignment to review the show for my paper and was off on the next bus to Tahoe! For those who may have worried that the departure of Papa may have meant a change or a lessening to Jan and Dean, I think I can safely tell you to relax. It is, as it always has been, very much J & D's show and the new musicians do an excellent job of backing them up, unobtrusively taking the spotlight for a few of the lead vocals, but leaving most of the work to our favorite dynamic duo!

Rock singer offers words of hope to paralyzed miner

By BILL SMITH
Globe-Democrat Staff Writer

The music done, the theater seats empty, the blond rock 'n' roll singer put his left arm around the young man in the wheelchair.

"Take it easy," the singer said. "One day you'll get there."

"It's hell," said the young man, straining to make himself understood.

"I know," said the singer. "It's rough. Just keep up the good energy."

THERE WAS nothing particularly spectacular about this meeting. Simple, quick, even but awkward perhaps. An autograph. A photograph.

But for 21-year-old Mark Pieszchalski, an Ashley, Ill., coal miner, it was an important step in his struggle to become whole again.

"It gives me hope," he said.

It was Pieszchalski's sister, Marcia Bequette of Ballwin, who decided to try to arrange a backstage meeting between her brother and 36-year-old Jan Berry, half of the popular 1960s duo Jan and Dean who appeared here Sunday night.

Fourteen years ago this month, Berry lost control of his Stingray and slammed into a parked truck. That accident, which left him in a coma for nearly a year, was similar to the one three years ago that left Pieszchalski crippled.

WHEN BERRY came out of his coma, he had to learn again how to talk, walk, read and write. Today, he continues to take speech therapy.

As Berry knelt beside the wheelchair, Pieszchalski's wife, Debbe, stood at her husband's side.

The Sunday night meeting at the Kiel Opera House, Mrs. Bequette hoped, would bolster her brother's strength, toughen his determination to leave the wheelchair eventually and make his way back onto the mines that had been his life.

Pieszchalski and his wife had been high school sweethearts. For the first five months after they were married in the spring of 1977, "they were typical happy newlyweds. The couple was living comfortably on the money that came from the mines."

THEN, ON OCT. 24, 1977, Pieszchalski's car ran into a farm tractor on a rural stretch of road near Ashley. For six months, he was unconscious, with a 1-in-10 chance of surviving his head injury.

"I just knew he wouldn't die," said his wife, who for the first three months slept in the hospital's waiting room.

"For six months he just lay there," she said. Eventually he regained consciousness, but for several more months his communication was limited to blinking, moving his eyebrows, squeezing his wife's hand.

The recovery process since then has been frustratingly slow, but the progress is definite.

Pieszchalski communicates in rough, guttural words now. Gradually, he is learning to feed himself, even to drive a car.

THERE IS HOPE he may eventually walk again.

"I've come this far," he likes to say. "Why stop now?"

Sometimes, though, his wife said, he gets down on himself.

"He doesn't understand why it had to happen to him; why it's taking so long for him to come back."

In 1977, as Pieszchalski lay unconscious in his hospital bed, the television story of Jan Berry's accident and his recovery was shown.

"It was very, very hard watching it," said Mrs. Bequette.

"There was the same humiliation; the same frustration that we've seen in Mark," said Mrs. Pieszchalski.

There were no miracles here Sunday night. Nobody had expected there would be.

As the burly stagehands rolled sound equipment off the stage, musicians in jeans and shining blue jackets hustled playing cards at each other.

Nobody paid much attention as the singer squeezed the young man's hand, smiled and jumped off across the stage.

Jan Berry, left, of the Jan and Dean singing group, gives words of encouragement to Mark Pieszchalski of Ashley, Ill., who suffered an accident similar to the one Berry was in several years ago.

—Globe-Democrat Photo by Rick Stonkoven

Circa 1978...

NOT an ad

Some may talk about Jan and Dean in past tense, but they're alive, well

MUSIC REVIEW

By MARC ZAKEM
Courier-Journal Contributing Critic

Rock encyclopedias and reference books published as recently as last year refer to Jan and Dean in only the past tense. You'll read, but as singers, the duo no longer exists.

A packed crowd at Simpsonville's Beef and Boards Dinner Theater learned differently last night, Jan and Dean and their backup band, Papa Doo Run Run, brought the house down by once again staging their brand of surf music. And they did it with less nostalgic overtones than anyone would have a right to expect.

Nowadays when an act once is invited to hear a group harkening from the '60s, it is well advised to expect massive personnel changes, as in the case of the Association and the Grass Roots, two bands that have recently played Louisville.

Yet, there they were, the two and only Jan and Dean — a band that has had to overcome more than its share to be singing together still.

Jan Berry, the writer of the band's hits, was in a near-fatal car crash in Los Angeles in 1966. The accident left him severely handicapped and, at 36, Berry had to learn to arise and talk again. He just came through on therapy, and Dean

Torrence attempted a solo career. They made an appearance together in 1973, which was blasted critically, and for a while after, Dean carried on as "Jan and Dean Show" without his former partner.

That's all behind Jan and Dean now. After CBS aired a television movie, "Deadman's Curve" (the name of one of the group's hit records), a whole new generation renewed its interest in the band.

On stage, Jan still limps, and from takes care of most of the talking and joking around, but when they play music, it still sounds fresh and exciting. Much of the credit for that goes to the vocalist' backup band Papa Doo Run Run opened the show last night with some West Coast classics, "California Sun" and a couple of Beach Boys tunes.

The vocals were much tighter than the Beach Boys' own concert work of recent years, and a version of "Why Do Fools Fall In Love" was updated with more guitar fills and power chords. They filled the dinner theater with the loudest volume of

any recent musical guest, but the crowd, ranging in age from 14 to 40, didn't seem to mind.

Jan and Dean don't like to think of themselves as an oldies group, and they refer to their recent activity as a "second phase," rather than a comeback. But, of course, an oldies group is still what they are. The music was pure mid-60s and pure surf city.

They performed their own "Little Old Lady from Pasadena" and "Baby Talk" as well as the Beach Boys' "Fun, Fun, Fun" and "Good Vibrations." But it's a trick they can get away with because Barry and Beach Boy Brian Wilson often shared writing credit, and the two groups guested on each others' songs.

Still, the songs are successful because the band has wisely updated the music. "Good Vibrations," like "Wipeout," was pure punch, with new drums and guitar parts. Likewise, the other songs rocked as well as rolled.

For their encore of "Barbara Ann," Jan and Dean were joined on stage by two members of the Fifth Dimension, who will be appearing at Beef and Boards Saturday evening. Along with Maxine Andrews, the groups are part of Jim Ed Brown and Helen Cornelius and Jim Perry's four-night concert series at the theater. Last night, Jan and Dean made sure the series got off on the right foot.

The format of the show, although of necessity it was of shorter length in the cabaret than a full-length concert would be, is virtually unchanged from other shows I have seen and our favorite J & D songs are still very much present in the musical line-up. Songs performed at the show I saw included: Honolulu Lulu, Jennie Lee, Linda, the traditional hot rod set (Drag City, Deuce Coupe and Shut Down), Baby Talk, California Girls, Ride the Wild Surf and, of course, Deadman's Curve and Surf City. The only new song I noticed in the repertoire was the Lennon-McCartney "You've Got To Hide Your Love Away," on which Jan did a superb job with the lead vocals. He gets better every time I hear him.

The audience, lacking in teenagers because of the cabaret setting, was energetic and enthusiastic--Jan and Dean truly do have a universal appeal that transcends age groups.

'Tis rumored they'll be on a tour circuit this coming summer that will be similar to last summer's. If they do get anywhere near where you live, I strongly recommend that you take whatever steps are necessary to catch the wave--er, show.

THE DIXON (CALIFORNIA) TRIBUNE—THURSDAY, DECEMBER 25, 1980—PAGE 13

Surf's up at Stateline

by DEE LECLAIR

A Jan and Dean concert is far more than a couple of singers entertaining an audience. It is, to borrow a phrase from the psychedelic 60s, a be-in, a love-in, an outpouring of affection from enthusiastic, dedicated fans to a couple of guys who have done more to make music "fun" than any other entertainers in the 22 years since "Jennie Lee" first zoomed up the charts.

The duo's first public appearances in nearly four months are being warmly received by audiences in Harrah's Stateline Cabaret.

It's a slightly new sound with the departure of Papa Doo Run Run, the band that has played backup for the act since they first joined forces for the 1978 TV movie, "Deadman's Curve," which chronicled the duo's early career.

According to Dean, three members of "Papa," have gone their separate ways because they had different career goals and different ideas about the places they wanted to play. The two who remain, Mark Ward and Jimmy D. Armstrong, have been supplemented by three new musicians — Chris Farmer on bass, Hal Rappleyea on drums and Sterling Smith on keyboard — and the sound, while slightly different from "Papa," is rich and full.

Although the teenage screams that usually characterize a Jan and Dean concert are missing from the cabaret setting, the 20-to-40-year-olds who come close to filling the room create a fair amount of their own screaming, lending credence to my oft-stated belief that Jan and Dean's audience appeal is a universal one that transcends age groups.

The hour length of the cabaret show isn't nearly enough to showcase all the favorite songs. Within the time limit though, they do a good job of conveying the spirit of a full-length concert, not only with a selection of the well-loved songs, but with the famous Jan and Dean humor that once earned the duo the nickname "Laurel and Hardy of the surf crowd."

The old favorites are there — "Honolulu Lulu" with Dean's wonderful hand gestures, "Linda" with the new background group "Surf Brothers" providing a strong in-

JAN AND DEAN

strumental assist and the always-popular hot rod set ("Drag City," "Little Deuce Coupe" and "Shut Down").

Jan, whose near-fatal 1966 accident was foretold in that penultimate of rock tragedy songs, "Deadman's Curve," gets stronger in his vocal leads with every show I've seen him in Friday night he did a superb job with the Lennon-McCartney "You've Got to Hide Your Love Away," in addition to handling lead vocals for "Ride the Wild Surf" and several other songs he wrote 20 years ago.

There may not be any snow at Tahoe this coming holiday weekend, but the surf's up and the trip to catch that one perfect wave is definitely worth it. Jan and Dean remain in the Stateline Cabaret with twice-nightly performances through Dec. 28. For information about show times, call (toll free) 800-648-3773.

Hooking helps

A song without a "hook" is like a banana split without the banana.

"You live and die on those hooks," says Dean Torrance of the singing team of Jan & Dean, which had 25 consecutive hits with hooks during the late '50s and early '60s.

After a hiatus of 12 years, Jan Berry and Torrance got back together two years ago, and they're now appearing in Harrah's Tahoe lounge through Dec. 28.

Torrance says his favorite hooks are "Go Granny, Go Granny, Go Granny Go" from "The Little Old Lady from Pasadena" and "You Won't Come Back from Deadman's Curve," from the song of the same name.

Before they developed their own distinctive "California music" sound, Torrance says the duo's early recordings "were an amalgamation of many, many people, like Dion and the Belmonts, The Drifters and The Coasters. Those were the groups we grew up with."

Their first studio was Berry's garage, where the singers recorded a few "pretty primitive" songs before having a hit with "Jenny Lee."

Among the songs that followed were "Baby Talk," "Linda," "Surf City," "Sidewalk Surfin'," "Honolulu LuLu" and "New Girl in School."

According to Torrance, the "California music" of the Beach Boys and Jan & Dean replaced the "teen-age idol" songs of the '50s "because it had full harmonies (ranging from super-deep bass to falsetto) and really danceable tunes."

"We were stacking vocal parts," recalls Torrance, "doubling and tripling stuff. On 'Deadman's Curve' we had something like twenty-four actual voice parts, and we only had four tracks to work with and only three or four voices doing the parts."

If they're given the opportunity, says the tall, blond singer, Jan & Dean would like to return to the record business: "There are plenty of good tunes out there," he notes.

Hook 'em, fella.

SUNSHINE MUSIC 6

The Jan & Dean Criss-Cross

Now that you've recovered from the Word Search, it's time to hear your hair out over the Jan and Dean Song Title Criss-Cross! This is a two-step puzzle, created on three different levels.

Level One is for the new or casual J+D fan, one who never misses them when they're in town. You're the one singing along with them for two hard, loving every minute of it.

Level Two is for those who have a few J+D albums lying around that were donated by an older brother or sister or purchased with hard-earned babysitting or lawn-mowing money in 1964.

Level Three is for the hardcore J+D freaks who have memorized the B-side sales statistics of J+D records, who own anything remotely related to the duo or listen to them daily on tape or turntable.

Directions: On a separate piece of paper, write the answers to the clues, all of which are song titles or portions of titles (except when otherwise indicated). One title has been given to start you off. For example, "F" is given. Look through your answer list for an eight letter title with "F" as the fourth letter.

If you're a Level One fan, don't worry! You can complete your portion of the puzzle easily — if you know the answers.

Level One

1. Haint surfing, fishing in the ? fjord and no liquid medium in Nanaimo
2. Jan and Dean's pre-Surf City biggie in 1962
3. Jan and mate of Pasadena senior citizen said _____
4. Plastic frippery is identified in _____
5. A J+D salute to some Ladies and the mountains of its dramatic success (acquire)
6. Mythical predator
7. What will keep brother/sister girls in a noose?
8. A number of the Donna Reed Show was peripherally involved with this LP and its namesake film
9. The "big game flippin'" over whom?
10. Where do "the cheaters ring your ears"?
11. They couldn't record this in 1963, it was too racy
12. Jan's fantastic welcome to Los Angeles, '70s involved with this LP
13. Hawaiian wave rider of the female gender

Level Two

14. Jan moaned flatly about a blockhead in _____
15. Chauffeur of school-age type persons, first name
16. Jean and Dean left Malibu as their forwarding address to the postal service in "_____"
17. In which pile did J-D "stop at the sugar shack for chow and some jivin'"?
18. Little Old Ladies Seldom Power _____
19. Seven grand awaits the winner in "_____"
20. Jill sang background with Jan on _____
21. Where would (1964's) topless granny be banned?
22. Picasso to a jawline
23. Sneaky dude in tights who keeps "evil at bay"
24. In 1962, J+D left California and found a girl where?
25. While there, what did they find in a barn and shell out five bucks for? (different song)
26. _____ easy as 1-2-3
27. What did the Titanic Twosome first in this Sloan Barri piece?

Level Three

28. Dedicated to Dick Clark
29. Girl's name is the title on "_____"
30. In which garage was this Falcon born?
31. Released on Almond Dean _____ records
32. Hideous athletic footgear worn by Ivy League girl
33. "Gubby Kysell"
34. A possible permanent position was hinted at in _____
35. "I'm a gonna cut yo' hair off _____"
36. No surf in this 1962 seasonal release!
37. Dean sang about something his native California doesn't have in _____
38. Again ode to a cowlady
39. A purely romantic culmination by J+D for what funeral rite?
40. J+D covered the Vees
41. 1960's tracks were lost again in 1965—else 1960 wasn't totally awful, leaving a bizarre jumble
42. The "wind and sea" was responsible for
43. Newspapers, firearms and glass are mentioned in _____
44. What do Jan and Jamie folks get?
45. Remix (Beatles? Trinidad?) Abstracts?
46. He pay F says for lack of this substance has Jan from _____
47. Horne gripes about a bad habit of Jan in _____

SUNSHINE MUSIC 6

JAN AND DEAN

JAN AND DEAN: A REASSESSMENT

BY MICHAEL SMITT

In many a cursory history of rock and roll, Jan and Dean are written off by the ignorant as a footnote to the Beach Boys, seen as purveyors of a music singlehandedly created by and totally original to Brian Wilson. There are three main reasons why this view is wrong. First, Jan and Dean had their first hit record, written and produced by themselves, as early as 1958, four years before the Beach Boys released Surfin'. Secondly, their distinctive style, formulated over this period with a succession of records, was admired by Brian whose first songs are clearly reminiscent of Jan and Dean's with the bomps and high falsettos and the interaction of high and low voiced lead vocals. Thirdly and most importantly, the reason why Jan and Dean remained highly original in the era of surf music was the excellence of their record productions.

With no record company to finance them, with no studio facilities, Jan and Dean recorded Jennie Lee on two home tape recorders in Jan's garage, creating an echo effect by using the tape delay that appeared in transferring the recording from one tape to the other. Even on this early song, the production techniques that made their records so sophisticated were there in genesis. The fact that they enjoyed experimenting with the limited technology at their disposal, that they spent hours and hours until the sound was right, the fact that there being just two of them caused them to discover and utilise vocal overdubbing. The Beach Boys' records for many years were far more natural sounding than Jan and Dean's for the simple reason that they as a five piece band could sing and play their songs more or less directly onto tape. For Jan and Dean, the full harmonies and depth of their sound had to be built up layer by layer, and so they developped a highly original studio sound that was to reach its peak in productions like Jan's Dead Man's Curve

Drag City and Anaheim, Azusa... and Dean's Vegetables, with an incredible 54 vocal overdubs. Their records are highly distinctive because of the innovative production techniques used and between 1963 and 1965 it is superiority of production that separates their records from the Beach Boys' although musically and lyrically there are many similarities.

Listening to Jan and Dean and Beach Boys' records through this period illustrates the distinction I am trying to make between the two approaches. The Beach Boys' records are basically the group singing and playing straight, occasionally augmented by additional instruments. Production is generally limited to enhancing this natural sound, by a careful balance of background and lead vocals and of lead instruments. The studio techniques employed are vocal overdubbing and echo, devices already well explored by Jan and Dean, the sustaining of notes electronically, and sometimes the speeding up of a tape to raise a song's key and give it more vitality. Jan and Dean alone could never simply sing and play onto tape. They had to use studio musicians and production to create their records, and they used the very best. Rather than simply having a studio backing group, they employed the best session musicians available, those also to be used by Phil Spector and, interestingly, to be used by Brian on Pet Sounds. And Jan, recognising the possibilities of the studio went for a big wall of sound, two full sets of drums on every session, three guitars, a full horn section, orchestration. There is always a very tight rhythm section led by Hal Blaine's brilliant drumming, backed with a swirling depth of echoed sound, piano, percussion, horns, strings, on top of which comes the overdubbed four-part harmony, over which again comes the lead and counterpointed falsetto vocals. Were this not enough, many records also include added sound effects. The aim was not simply to enhance a natural sound but to create a sound in the studio. It is for this reason that covers and live versions of Jan and Dean songs were never as successful as those of Beach Boys' songs. Jan and Dean's own live performances were and are so great

because they recognised it was impossible to reproduce their recorded sound and concentrated instead on their other genius, satire and lunatic comedy, mainly Dean inspired, and the resulting idea of never taking themselves or their songs seriously - which was how it should be.

It is not my intention to devalue or deny Brian Wilson's genius, merely to redress the balance and perspective that sees Jan and Dean as mere imitators of his sound. Jan Berry was a highly innovative producer and arranger who created unique and distinctive surf and hot rod records, the most sophisticated and adventurous records of the genre. Brian's special talents only reached their peak once those trends had passed and by which time Jan had been put out of action by his accident. It would be unwise to speculate on quite how Jan and Dean would have developed beyond this point or quite how their music would have compared with the Beach Boys', but it is interesting to note that Roger Christian who worked with both and who called Jan a "master producer", said that were it not for the accident, he "without a doubt would be producing hit records today." Historians and critics of rock and roll please note.

****

Table of Contributors

Frank Brockel	page	4
Dee LeClair		5
Dean O. Torrence		6
Timothy Kelly		7
Dee LeClair		8
Dee LeClair		9
Honolulu Lulu		10
Dean O. Torrence		12
Mike Smitt		14
Doc Rock	most everything else	

Biography

8-63

LIBERTY RECORDS
6920 Sunset Boulevard
Los Angeles 28, California

J A N & D E A N

In 1958 when experts were predicting a quick fade of rock & roll music as well as the record stars of that year, Jan & Dean, the tall, blond, sunburned high school students who were riding the charts with "Jennie Lee" and "Baby Talk", were undoubtedly included.

Well it's 1963 and rock & roll is still here. Jan & Dean, now college students, taller and even more suntanned are not only still on the charts, but are more successful then ever.

Since their first recording dates in the family garage, with manager-producer Lou Adler five years ago, Jan Berry and Dean Torrence have developed into one of the best selling and most exciting acts in the business.

In the first six months of 1963 they accounted for over a million single record sales, ("Linda" and "Surf City") and two smash albums, ("Jan & Dean Take Linda Surfing" and "Surf City".)

An unusual sidelight to the Jan & Dean story is the educational part of their lives. Both boys throughout their

- more -

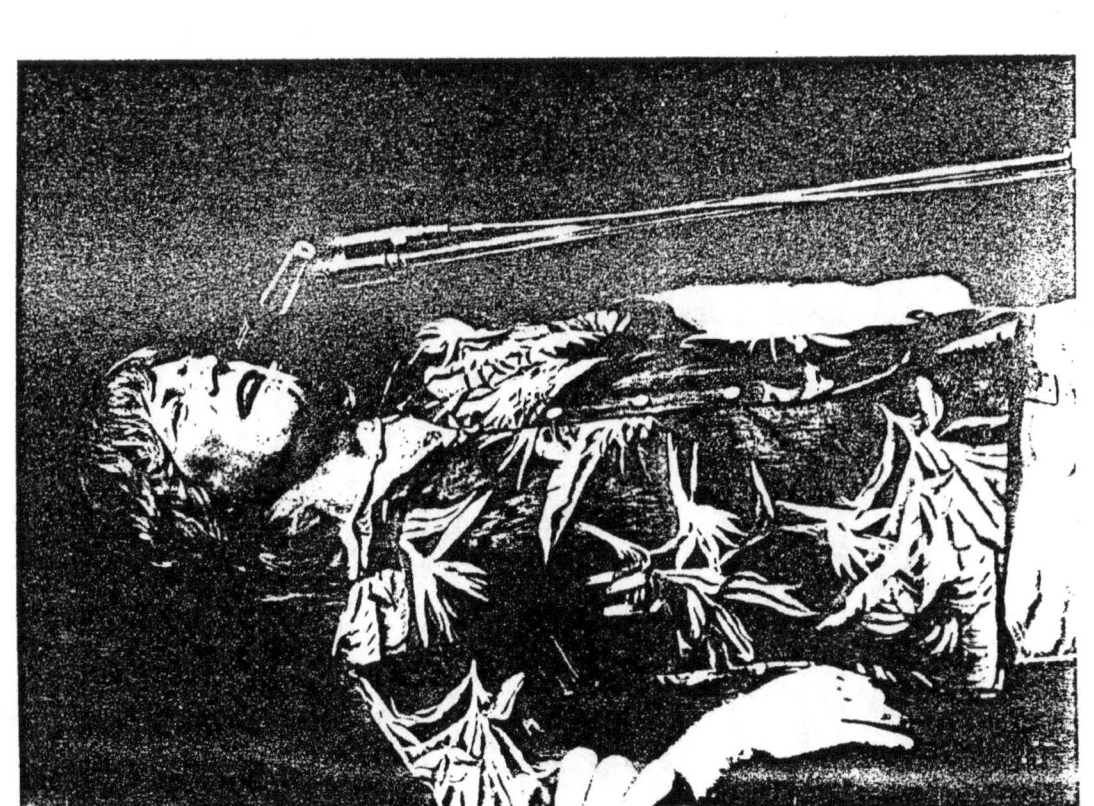

SUNSHINE MUSIC 6

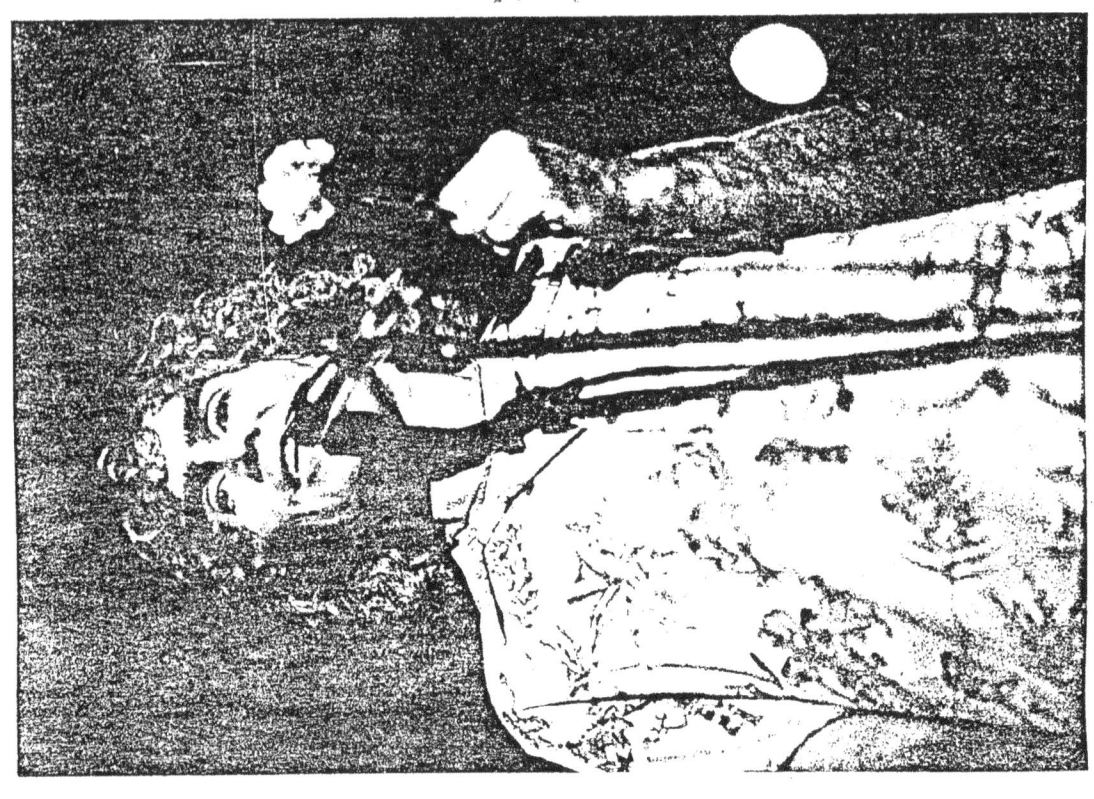

Jan & Dean
Page Two

careers have diligently continued their studies. Recently Jan was graduated from the University of California at Los Angeles having completed pre-medicine. Standing joke on the campus, was that he may become the first rock & roll doctor. Simultaneously Dean has completed two years at the University of Southern California, majoring in Art and Mechanical Design.

Jan & Dean now record under an agreement with Screen Gems Music Production Company, a subsidiary of Columbia Pictures, supervised by Executive Vice-President Don Kirshner. The records are released exclusively by Liberty Records. All recording sessions and activities are still directed by Lou Adler, now a Vice-President for Columbia Pictures music and record department. Jan who has developed into a top arranger & producer serves as both on all Jan & Dean sessions.

Now it looks like television and movies are in the offing for the handsome duo from West Los Angeles.

All in all, for a group whose career was supposed to fade quickly, Jan & Dean continue to fool the experts by displaying talent and enthusiasm on a daily basis:

##

PERSONAL MANAGEMENT:
Lou Adler
Screen Gems - Columbia Music Inc.
HO 6-5188 HO 2-3111

SUNSHINE MUSIC 6

SHORT CUTS...

■■■ I am assured that Jan and Dean will be on AMERICAN TOP 10.... Someday. They were supposed to have been on the week ending 11-16, but they weren't. Maybe by the time you get this, they will have been on.

■■■ The new Jan and Dean band has been formed. The members and instruments are described elsewhere in this issue. They have been rehearsing in the same garage in which Jennie Lee was done, and using the same trap set!

■■■ Marny is no longer offering tapes, and she has moved, so please save yourself trouble and do not send orders to her.

■■■ Thank you to everyone who has sent nice letters. Also thanks for contributions of written material as well as photos. I can use anything you can send, including newspaper clippings about J&D. However, I cannot guarantee just when I will be able to print them.

■■■ The limited pressing of the Legendary Masked Surfers Rarities LP offered in the last issue is totally sold out at the source.

■■■ A reader sent to the Mike Douglas Show asking about J&D, sometimes guests on that show. All she got back was a recipe. "Is that a clue?"

■■■ A "new" J&D LP is out. It lists for some $10, and has...the ten K-Tel cuts. The gimmick here is that the discs were made from the master recording tapes, so the fidelity should be superior---if you have a $2,000 stereo outfit. Save your money.

■■■ Pat Akin, 22 Ratho Close, Glenrothes, FIFE KY6, 2GG, Scotland, UK (whew) would like a pen pal. She is 23, works as a bank clerk, likes TV, movies, SF, ELO, ABBA, etc.

■■■ The Mayor of Los Angeles proclaimed June 20, 1980, as "Jan and Dean Day." Pretty good, huh?

■■■ A mid-February concert by Jan and Dean and the "Surf Brothers" had to be cancelled because of the number of ticket sales. It seems that there were requests for tickets exceeding the capacity of the auditorium by a factor of three! They will be rescheduling the show when they can get J&D for several consecutive nights.

■■■ Australia has not yet been rescheduled.

■■■ Last New Year's Eve the Beach Boys had their 20th Anniversary concert. Their premier concert was New Year's Eve 1961, so this kicks off their 20th year. All six "original" Beach Boys showed up, and oldies never done in concerts these days, such as "Surfin'," were featured. The encore was a real show stopper, since it featured Messrs. Berry and Torrence on stage doing "Barbara Ann" and "Fun, Fun, Fun," complete with lots of goofing off and special lyrics.

■■■ In '81 Jan and Dean will be touring the nation. There is occasional studio activity, but no label has offered an acceptable contract. In the studio Jan is his old self, singing all the vocal and instrumental parts, writing music on the spot, and transposing parts from one instrument to the next, all at the speed of light. Yea, Jan!

■■■ Last issue featured the cover story "Dean Unmasked," with a cover photo of Jan and Dean singing "Batman" on the Lloyd Thaxton TV show. In the photo Dean has a Dean, the Boy Blunder mask around his neck. Of course, the article was a satire of the "Paul is Dead" craze of the late '60s. Due to the tragic assassination of John, the follow-up to that story is being back-burnered.

■■■ When you write SUNSHINE MUSIC, always enclose an S.A.S.E. This includes letters, orders, queries, bids, and anonymous threats. The volume of mail is such that I must have an S.A.S.E. to reply, even if it is only to return your check on a sold-out item. Thanks.

■■■ New subscribers, please specify the issue number you want your subscription to start with! Otherwise, you are liable to get a duplicate with your sample issue, or miss out on an issue in between your sample issue and the first issue of your subscription.

■■■ Frequently asked: Do I still offer my 11-page discography of Jan and Dean? Sure, still $2. Tells dates, label #'s, flip sides, version variations, boots, and some data on appearances on TV, other people's records, and the likes. Emphasis, however, is on Jan and Dean records, per se.

■■■ After several delays and postponments, AMERICAN TOP 10 with Casey Casem finally showed the Jan and Dean Update. The good news is that they returned the photos, sleeves, and other material I sent them for the segment. The bad news is that neither station in my area that carries the show showed it that week, so I never got to see it!

■■■ All back issues are now available, #'s 1 to 5, at $1 each. Airmail overseas, add $.50 per issue.

67

SUNSHINE MUSIC 7

SUNSHINE MUSIC

issue 7

SUNSHINE MUSIC
c/o Doc Rock
Box 1166
Lawrence, KS 66044

To:

Roland Coover, Jr.   8
1537 E. Strasburg Rd.
West Chester, PA 19380

FIRST CLASS MAIL

Here's a deal... Send me a snapshot (3½ x 5 max) of you with Jan and/or Dean, and find yourself on the back cover of SM, like Troy Hammond, Ohio U!

SUNSHINE MUSIC 7

Jan & Dean SUNSHINE MUSIC

Editor
Michael "Doc Rock" Kelly

Copy Editor
Dean O. Torrence

Associate Editor
Frank M. Kisko

Graphics/Layout
eye design

Issue 7 — Spring 1981

The Magazine of the Official Jan and Dean Authorized International Collectors Club

SAMPLE COPIES of SM are $1 in the US and surface overseas. Airmail, $2. SUBSCRIPTIONS are good for six (6) issues, at the rates indicated below.

	USA, mailed in envelope	Non-US Surface	Non-US Air	Surface Envelopes	Air Envelopes
USA $5	$7	$7	$12	$10	$15

Envelope Charge is for Postage

CHECK THE NUMBER ON YOUR ADDRESS LABEL. THE NUMBER THERE IS THE NUMBER OF THE LAST ISSUE OF YOUR SUBSCRIPTION. IF THERE IS NO NUMBER, LUCKY YOU!!!!

Make checks payable to Michael Kelly.

© 1981 by Michael Bryan Kelly unless already copyrighted.

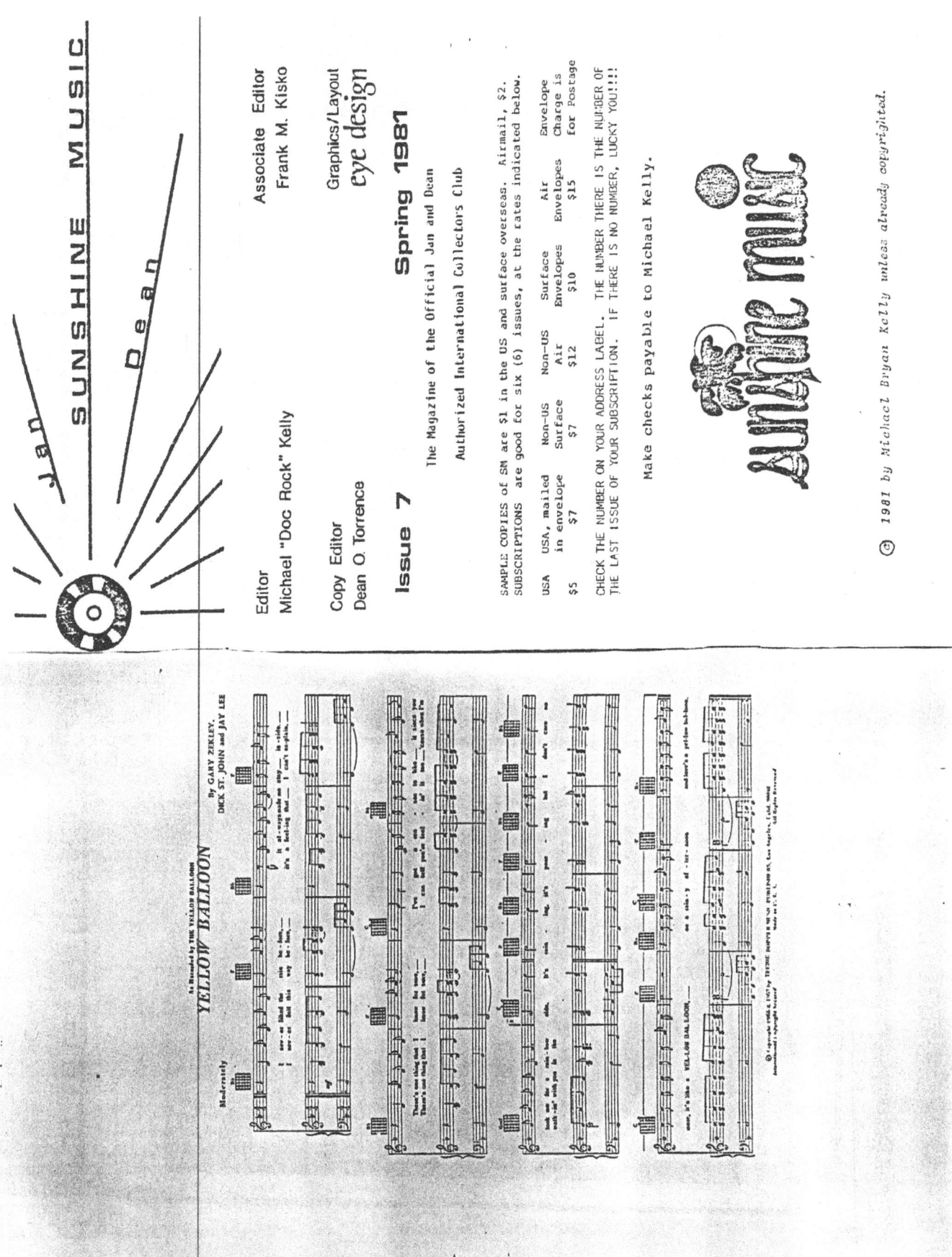

YELLOW BALLOON — As Recorded by THE YELLOW BALLOON — By GARY ZEKLEY, DICK ST. JOHN and JAY LEE

SUNSHINE MUSIC 7

LET ME EXPLAIN

This is a good time to answer, or at least address, some of the most frequently-asked questions I get in the mail. "Where will Jan and Dean be appearing?" I wish I knew. Repeat calls to California looking agents and such have turned up little. Here is what I have at this time:
Daytona Beach, March 25/Lake Tahoe, May 4-17/Reno, May 19-31

"What are Jan and Dean's birthdays?" March 10, Dean; April 3, Jan.

"Why don't Jan and Dean put out any new records?" SEE NEXT ISSUE!

"Why was the song 'Yellow Balloon' done by two groups, and who was on what version?" SEE THIS ISSUE!!

Starting with this issue, a new feature: THE JAN AND DEAN PRESSBOOK. Each Sunshine Music will include material from the official publicity files. Including, this issue, the new official J&D photo!

As always, thanks for all of your great letters. Thanks especially for the beautiful Christmas cards, and for the SASE's!!

Oh, yes, the bad news. Due to increased postage and printing costs, a slight price increase goes into effect with this issue. Inflation. Sorry. Actually, the increase is less than the combined rates of inflation, including postage, printing, and paper. Incredible, isn't it...

SHORT CUTS

Jan and Dean Free Concert presented to you by Budweiser, March 25, Daytona Beach, Fla., on the beach!!!

In September, 1980, Jan and Dean put together a new band. It is called THE JAN AND DEAN BAND, not the SURF BROTHERS as reported several places. Yes, Dean referred to them as the S.B., but it was a joke, (Dean has a million of 'em). Besides, Dean added to the joke, "They'll have to earn the name."

What became of Papa? Well, Mark Ward and Jim Armstrong wanted to keep playing music on the road, and didn't mind traveling a great deal of the time. The other members wanted to stay closer to home. All are still pals. Any other stories of the breakup are false.

The sound of Jan and Dean is still heard--just listen to radio jingles and TV commercials. Their surf harmony is still around, and dominates the airwaves.

...and, maybe Jan and Dean did some of the vocals you hear--if you have heard Ocean Pacific Sunwear ads lately--does something sound familiar...stay tuned!

:::::JAN AND DEAN HAVE SIGNED WITH ICM AGENCY, AND NOW RUB SKATEBOARDS WITH THE LIKES OF ABBA, KENNY LOGGINS, THE KINKS, LINDA RONDSTADT, KENNY ROGERS, JAMES TAYLOR, ROBIN WILLIAMS, LITTLE RIVER BAND, AND FOLKS LIKE THAT!!!

...AND NOW A WORD...

Last issue I mentioned a person who wanted pen pals. This issue I am listing Troy Hammond, 125 Washington Hall, Ohio University, Athens, Ohio, 45701. Troy has a slightly used copy of Jan's "Skateboard Surfin' USA," 45 copy, featuring Dean on falsetto. Released April, 1978, Troy wants to trade or sell this item.

Since there is an interest in individuals corresponding and dealing one amongst the other, I am going to try something (which may help to underwrite the cost of SM). If you want a certain record, or have an extra to offer, or want to correspond with someone of common interests, or whatever, send me the info and $1. I will print the item here in SM.

Regular advertisers, note: The rate is $5 for one-half page.

E. B. Krueger offers to make tapes for people. Beth lives at the following address: Tuttle Road, Piffard, NY, 14533. Write first for availability, and SASE her. (Has many of Marny's tapes.)

The same offer is made by Barb Sweigart, 432 S. 9th ST., Akron, PA, 17501. She says she will tape her records, or your records, and can use your cassette tapes, or supply them for you at a low rate.

Daine Moehring, 1343 3rd Gladys, Lakewood, OH, 44107, makes this friendly offer. She has good luck at locating J&D records at good prices locally. If you want to write her, she may have, or be able to get for you, specified records you need. SASE her for details.

Here is a strange one. My book, THE FITNESS FACTOR: Practical Body Building for Health, a non-sexist fitness book, is coming out in May. Now, I wouldn't ask you to buy it. However, feel free to, if you want to. Regardless, I was daydreaming the other day, thinking of ways to be sure the book gets attention from bookstores. Imagine with me. What if everyone reading this called their local bookstore and special ordered a copy now, before it is released. Then, all the bookstores and distributors would be familiar with the title when it was released. No one who ordered it would have to buy it, because it hasn't been released yet! [If a bookstore asked for a deposit, then it would be better to skip the whole deal.] The publisher is ARCO. But, it's just a daydream... Good book. Lotsa pictures...

SUNSHINE MUSIC 7

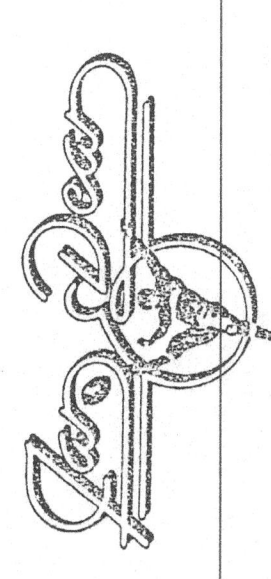

PHASE ONE BIOGRAPHY
(1958-1966)

Both Jan Berry and Dean Torrence attended Emerson Jr. High School in West Los Angeles. After graduation they also both attended University High School (also in West Los Angeles). Not until their senior year in high school did they really become close friends, when they both made the varsity football team and by chance happened to get team lockers next to one another....It wasn't long before a bunch of guys on the team discovered that the sound in the shower was the best echo around.

Group songs were popular that year, so it was just a matter of time before Jan, Dean and some of the other guys started singing the songs of the day in the University High shower room.

The football season ended, and that meant that the showers were to be used by the baseball team. So the group, by now called the "Barons," had to start practicing in the boys' restrooms during lunch, but the teachers began to complain. It wasn't long before the Barons had their first big break: they were asked to sing at the school assembly. This meant that they'd have to really get their first sound together. Jan had two tape recorders but no microphone, so Jan offered to steal the assembly microphone from the auditorium during lunch one day. (Jan was a master thief); he got it! After securing the mike, the Barons began a meeting at Jan's house where they'd practice their songs on Jan's tape recorders. They used two tape recorders so they could make a tape delay by going from one machine to the other creating an echo effect—it was almost as good as the shower room!

At that point there were six guys in the group: Chuck Steele was lead singer because he was black, Arnie Ginsberg was first tenor because he was Jewish, Wally Yagi was second tenor because he was a Jap, John "Sagi" Saligman was also second tenor because Wally didn't sing very loud, Jan Berry was the bass singer because he was the biggest, and Dean sang all the high stuff because he was the only one who could. All they needed was a band. Bruce Johnston, a neighbor of Jan's, wanted to play piano; so he did. Sandy Nelson, a neighbor of Dean's, wanted to play drums; so he did. A friend of Sandy's played saxophone. The big day came and went, but everybody did say the Barons sounded just like the real records.

Jan said they should keep on practicing after school, even though there was no real good reason to. They all made it to practice for a few weeks, but then more important things began to take the place of practicing for nothing. Wally bought a '57 Chevy so he had to work on his car after school; Arnie met a girl at the Frostee Freeze so he hung out in the parking lot until she got off; John's mother wanted him to be an accountant, just like his father, so he couldn't come to practice. Chuck lowered his Buick so low that he couldn't drive it down Jan's driveway (and besides he said he had a better offer to be lead singer of the Del Vikings or the Coasters or something like that).

... She was a stripper, Swear to God!

This left Jan and Dean. They had one original song they'd both written. They called it "Sally She Lived Upon The Hill." One night while they were trying to figure out the words to "She Say" by the Diamonds, Arnie came by and told them that he'd broken up with the girl at the Frostee Freeze. But he had found a girl he liked better....she was a stripper. Swear to God! And she had two of the biggest "you-know-whats" that you've ever seen. He thought they should all drive to downtown L.A. to see for themselves. Since they weren't doing too well figuring out the words to "She Say," they all agreed. All the way downtown Dean thought seeing any size "you-know-whats" were bigger than he'd ever seen.

As they arrived at the Follies Burlesque, they saw a huge sign that read "Jenny Lee, the Bazoom Girl—Park Free After Six." Upon sitting down (as far back as they could get), the show started. Jenny came out dancing and ever Jan said: "She has the two biggest 'you-know-whats' I have ever seen." Dean commented "I thought I had seen some big ones in my day but without a doubt these were the biggest."

It was a hot night and yet all the old men were carrying coats and making strange noises. As Jenny Lee bounced, the old men would accentuate the bounces by chanting "bomp bomp, bomp bomp" etc. Later that evening, while driving home in the car, Jan, Arnie and Dean started the "bomp bomp" chant and added some lyrics reflecting Arnie's love for the future Mrs. Ginsberg, and the song "Jenny Lee" was born.

"Half a pie was more than a third"

Four months later, it was the number 3 record in the nation. Yes "Jenny Lee" by Jan & Arnie was a smash....but "where was Dean" you're asking? That's what Jan wanted to know, when he found out that the tape Jan, Arnie and Dean had made in his (Jan's) garage was going to be released by a real record company. Jan called Dean's mom to ask her where he was. She told Jan not to bother Dean because he was in the army doing his duty and that he'd be out in six months. She suggested that maybe when Dean got out he could start going to practice again, unless, of course, he got the best job in the neighborhood at Dick Martin's Chevron. It was rumored that Johnny Jameson had to get married and would probably be leaving his position at the gas station as a result of the impending scandal. By all rights Dean was expected to fill his shoes and a few tanks while he was at it. Jan wished Dean's mom good luck for him and said Arnie had mentioned something about "half a pie was more than a third." Dean's mom said she would be glad to send it to Dean the next time he sent him his vitamins.

One Sunday, a couple of weeks after Dean got out of the army, he attended the weekly Barons vs. Counts football game at Palisades High School. After the game (the Barons won 24-14) Jan asked if he wanted to go up to his garage and work on some songs. Dean was wondering where Arnie was. Jan said that Arnie and Jenny were working on a new act together, or he went in the navy... he couldn't remember. So Dean agreed that it was indeed time for Arnie to retire. A short time later, Jan acquired a song from Jan & Dean's future producer, manager and friend, Lou Adler. They worked on "Baby Talk" for about two months. Yes, you might say two months seems like a long time to work on a song, especially when it was only 2 min. & 17 sec. long. But as Dean remembers, "We would sing about 4 bars at a time (which wasn't that unheard of) but between those bars we would go to the beach, play some volley ball, or go down the street and violate some girls or maybe even cruise Goodie, Goodies, a popular local drive-in." Once they finished putting on their voices and the piano, Lou Adler had his friend, Herb Alpert, do the arrangements. Then they went into the studio and combined the rhythm section with the vocal tape—that's all there was to it. Three months later "Baby Talk" was #7 in the nation.

The follow-up to "Baby Talk" was a song written by Herb Alpert and Lou Adler titled "There's A Girl." It made the charts but that's all it did. Next came "Clementine" which was also recorded slightly differently by Bobby Darin at right about the same time. Jan & Dean were amazed when their "Clementine" jumped on the charts from nowhere to #40 (it was especially amazing as their record had only been out six days and nobody particularly liked it). Next week the error was corrected and Bobby Darin's version was added to the title "Clementine" and Jan & Dean were taken off. Eventually, it did make the charts, but again, that's about all it did. Then followed a few stiffs.

The next chart record they had was a song that had already been a hit some years before. "We Go Together" was recorded originally by the Moonglows in 1957. More stiffs followed: such greats as "Baggy Pants," "White Tennis Sneakers That Are Black" were among them. All the tunes up to that point were on Dore Records during the years 1959-1960, except "Jenny Lee," which had been on Arwin Records in 1958.

In 1961, Jan & Dean were determined to sign with a major company and never to deal anymore with record companies that carried on business out of a tent in an empty lot. So they cut a song that would certainly be worthy of the attentions of a major record company. The song was "Heart & Soul" and it was released on, yes folks, Challenge Records. Well, at least they didn't carry on business out of a tent. They had an almost new camper with decals of trout on the sides and Challenge Records painted on the door.

A short time after "Heart & Soul" had reached its final reward, trout season opened and it was time to look for a new company once again.

Coming into summer

This time Jan & Dean wouldn't compromise. Only the best... after being turned down by all the best, they signed with Liberty Records.

Jan & Dean were excited about their first release on a top 10 record. The first release came and went; and summer came and went. The follow-up was produced in desperation by Liberty's hot producer, Snuff Garret. The song was "Tennessee."

S U M M E R T I M E   K I C K S

SUNSHINE MUSIC 7

Attention !

Jan & Dean collectors.
A black & white, 3¼ by 5½ postcard of an original painting of Jan & Dean by Joseph P.M. Trapani.

Limited edition of 100 will be signed, dated and numbered. Send a $2.00 money order and self-addressed stamped envelope to :

Joseph P.M. Trapani
7 Belleview Ct. Apt. 7D
Belleville, New Jersey
07109

First 100, all others returned.

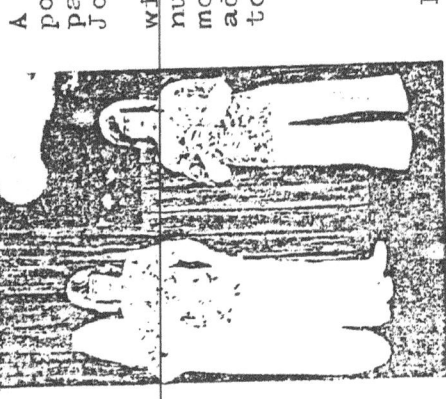

After "Tennessee" peaked on the charts, in the 70's somewhere, nobody had any new ideas; so it was decided that they would do a golden hits album. (In the music industry, that does make sense.) Liberty would get the rights to some of the old Jan & Dean hit records on the other labels and Jan & Dean would fill the rest of the album with old hit songs by other people. Since they hadn't made much money for Liberty, they wouldn't give Jan & Dean much of a budget to work with. This meant they would have to do all of the background vocals themselves. One of the relics they did for this album was "Barbara Ann" (originally done by the Regents).

Jan & Dean sang all the background parts and Dean sang the lead, all in falsetto — high voice stuff. Once they finished and listened, they liked what they heard, a new sound kinda. They then looked for another song, preferably about a girl, that lent itself to a falsetto lead and some good vocal background parts. The old standard "Linda" had what they were looking for. They cut it and it made it.

Jan & Dean's new sound was a success. Because "Linda" was a hit record, they were allowed to do another album using "Linda" as the title song. Surfing music had just arrived via The Beach Boys and Dick Dale, so Jan & Dean, being physically involved in surfing, figured it was just natural that they should become involved with this generic California music.

"Two girls for every boy"

They had done some hops with The Beach Boys and had sung live with them on numerous occasions. So it was just natural that, on their next album, they do Jan & Dean versions of "Surfin'" and "Surfin' Safari" and maybe they would con the Beach Boys into cutting the instrumental tracks and also helping out on vocals.

They conned 'em. After the session was over, Brian Wilson asked Jan & Dean if they wanted to hear The Beach Boys' new single and Jan & Dean, of course, said they would. He sat at the piano and started playing "Sweet Little Sixteen" by Chuck Berry, but wait just a minute, the words weren't the same. He called it "Surfin' USA." Jan & Dean tried to talk Brian into giving the song to them, but he said he had another song that wasn't finished, but if they wanted to finish it they could have it. He played the intro on the piano, "Two Girls For Every Boy." Jan & Dean took it. "Surf City" was #1 in the nation and top 10 in almost every foreign market in the world.

The next song Jan & Dean put out was entitled "Honolulu Lulu," on which was written on a napkin in a drive-in. Next was the start of the car song era, "Drag City" of course. One of the songs on the "Drag City" album was a return of The Beach Boys and Jan & Dean together. "Little Deuce Coupe". "Surf City" and Love helped Dean sing lead and on which Glen Campbell played some incredible guitar licks.

The song that followed "Drag City" was one of Jan & Dean's all time personal favorites. Dean says "I liked everything about it: the melody, the vocal parts, the tracks and the lyrics (also the premise). This, I think was our most obvious satirical record". This opened a whole new area for Jan & Dean, singing about things that were never sung about before and probably will never, ever, be sung about again. The subject matter included a drag racing old lady, a board with skates on it, a topless grandmother, a popsicle, some vegetables, a senior citizen car club, and even a taco wagon. Anyway, the song they were originally talking about was "Deadman's Curve." On the other side, which was also a hit, was "The New Girl In School." This song was originally titled "When Summer Comes, Gonna Hustle You" which was written by Brian Wilson and was given to Jan & Dean at the same session he gave them "Surf City".

They recorded it before "Surf City" but when they played it for people, adult types, they would exclaim: "You can't say 'hustle you' on the radio!" "Bust Your Buns", "yes, but not 'hustle you'"...well, Jan & Dean didn't know what the hell they were talking about, so rather than argue, they finished "Surf City" and rewrote "Gonna Hustle You" so that it became "The New Girl In School." "Gonna Hustle You" can be found in its original form on an album entitled "Filet of Sole" that was put out a few years after "The New Girl In School" and a short time after "Satisfaction" by The Stones.

"The Little Old Lady From Pasadena" was next. It was written about a real little old lady who was doing local Dodge TV commercials in Southern California and writing a song about her just seemed to be an obvious thing for Jan & Dean to do at the time.

The longest title of the year was bestowed upon their next song: "The Anaheim Azusa and Cucamonga Sewing Circle Book Review and Timing Association." It also wins the award for the most diversified influences, a certain Bach Chorale linked quite smoothly with "I Get Around" by the Beach Boys.

Following "Little Old Lady" came "Ride The Wild Surf," which actually was the title song from the movie of the same name. Jan & Dean were supposed to be in this epic — their film debut costarring with Fabian. But right about the same time, a close friend of Dean's kidnapped Frank Sinatra Jr., so the movie people kicked Dean out of the film.

...to be continued

WANTED-- All J&D Fans, to join the Kim and Jara Jan and Dean Fan Club, memberships free for how ever long you want to join will get newsletters, information, articles & photos if interested contact Jara Beaubien/#30/9029 Columbus AV/Sepulveda, CA 91343.

...from page 22

Mike,

A check is enclosed for issues 2-5. If all the issues are like the sample you sent, they'll all be good. Most clubs send out one page typed, for a whole lot more money!

Thanks,
Vikki Lewis

To The Reader from Doc Rock--

OK, so we have conclusive proof that Dean-is-Dead clues were planted all over the famous Jan and Dean records. The only question is, why? Publicity stunt? Could they have been as popular without this bit? What do you think was the point of planting all those clues. What was the motivation?

???

Sting Ray

by Jorge Cubria
& Doc Rock

Concurrent with the release of "Surf City" in Spring, 1963, an instrumental was released on Warner Brothers by a group called The Routers (Roo-ters). The song: "Sting Ray."

In November of the same year, one of the best Jan and Dean albums, Drag City, was released. On this LP: "Sting Ray." But with a difference!

For one thing, there is clapping moving from one speaker to the other, progressively aggressively. But, more interestingly, there is some dude—excuse me, hombre—talking about Jan and Dean's Sting Rays, IN SPANISH.

1. "Que suave caminan los Sting Rays de Jan y Dean."
2. "Mire Farita que suave el Sting Ray -upa-."
3. "De vuelta farita, echele a andar."
4. "Mira como toma las vueltas el Sting Ray."
5. "Que curiosoita la pulga."
6. "Entrele Jan y Dean."
7. "Me dicen que el Sting Ray de Dean."
8. "Camina mejor que el de Jan..."
9. "Porque el de Jan es mas viejo."

EN INGLES.

1. "How great do Jan and Dean's Sting Rays go (or run or walk)."
   "Que suave" is Mexican slang for "Great." In Mexico, Jan is not pronounced like it is here, not "Jan," but "Yan." "Han" is more like Spain Spanish. But, "Suave" is Mexican slang, Southern Mexico, probably Mexico City One.
2. "Look, pal, how great the Sting Ray is -giddy-up-."
   "Farito" here means something like buddy, fellow, or man, but would usually never be used this way. "Faro" means light, or headlights. "Ito" suffix indicates love or something small, diminuitive, so "Farito" means little light on a car—can also be a nickname.
3. "Again, man, make it go!"
   "De vuelta" means again. "Echelo a andar" equals make it go, or turn it on.
4. "Look how the Sting Ray takes the curves."
5. "How curious is the little flea."
   This is a 100% Mexican expression-curiosita is diminuitive of curious. Flea means a little car.
6. "Come on Jan and Dean."
7. "They tell me that Dean's Sting Ray..."
8. "Runs better than Jan's."
   "El de Jan" is a correct grammatical form.
   "El del Jan" is a familiar form, but grammatically incorrect.
9. "Because Jan's is older."

[Then, in English, he says "That means Dean's Sting Ray's faster than Jan's."]

Tape List

Interviews:

Dean & Bill Lee (1973) 3hours C/G+ 24 min. $1.20
Brian talks about J&D and Jan (1974) ½hour (Brian's side) G 22 $1.10
Dean & Steve McFarland (2/25/79) ½hour VG 30 $1.50
Dean on WXRT, Chicago (2/8/78) F/G/phone 40 $2.00

Conversations: (Made on portable cassette recorder; fair to good quality)

Jan, Tom Sumner, Mark Flummer (4/76) Mom's apt. Fuzz in beg. 60 $3.00
Jan at home with Mark Flummer (4/77) 30 $1.05
Kathy Torrence & Mark Flummer (4/77) Dean's sister 60 $3.00
Papa Doo Run Run & Mark Flummer, Vancouver (10/22/77) 60 $3.00
Papa Doo Run Run & Mark Flummer, Seattle (11/11-12/77) 45 $2.25
Dean, Marny Koch, Alexandra Lee (11/23/77) Dean's office 45 $2.25
Dean's parents, Mark Flummer, Marny Koch (3/24/78) 28 $1.40
Papa Doo Run Run, Mark Flummer, Marny Koch (8/24/78) Disneyland 25 $1.25
J&D, Papa, et. al. (8/23/79) Backstage Palo Alto 45 $2.25
Jan, Diane Osborne, Mark Flummer (12/9/79) Jan's apt. 60 $3.00

"Review" - Michael Kelly on Jan's Topeka concert (3/79) 18 $.90

Concerts:

Jan at Palomino Club (11/14/76) VG 45 $2.25
Papa Doo Run Run (Summer 1977) VG/E 43 $2.15
Jan in Topeka (3/14/79) F/G 71 $3.55
Jan at Macon County Light Co. (3/16/79) G 19 $1.75
J&D at Palladium, NYC (7/15/78) F/F 35 $1.95
J&D and Papa in Palo Alto (9/23/78) F/G 2 shows 97 $4.85
J&D and Papa in Palo Alto (2/23/79) G 2 shows 110 $5.50

Incomplete concerts:

J&D and Papa, My Father's Place, NYC (5/10/79) G 70 $3.50
(Gap in the Papa's portion)
J&D and Papa, Auditorium Theatre, Rochester, NY (7/19/80) G 85 $4.25
(Last ¼ of concert missing—never trust your sister-in-law!)

J&D Albums and Singles available; $2.00 for LP, $.20 each for 45, plus cost of blank cassette. Write for list; include SASE please.

Blank cassettes: TDK-D 90 min. $2.00 each
                  TDK-AD 60 " 3.25
                  TDK-AD 90 " 4.90
High bias or other brands available on request
OR - send your own tape.

Postage: $.50 per cassette (1st class)
         2.00 int'l. air (each)

Beth Krueger
Tuttle Road
Tifford, New York 14533

CALIFORNIA MUSIC HAS THE FACTS AND INFORMATION ON JAN & DEAN, THE BEACH BOYS AND ALL OTHER SURF MUSIC RELATED GROUPS AND SUBJECTS. IF YOU WISH TO KNOW MORE, CONTACT:

AMERICAN OFFICE: (US Subscribers ONLY)
SHAGGIN R. FOX
5742 N.GIDDINGS ST. CHICAGO, IL. 60630
($10 for 6 issues, $20 for 12 issues

HEAD OFFICE: (All other subscribers)
STEPHEN J MCFARLAND
2 KENWELL AVENUE, CONCORD, 2137,
NEW SOUTH WALES, AUSTRALIA

SUNSHINE MUSIC 7

PHOTOGRAPHY: NORMAN SEEFF

Sunshine Music... ...on a Rainy Afternoon

In April of 1967, a great song hit the Billboard charts. It followed in the tradition of a good many other songs, in that the title of the song and the artists name were the same (The Busters, "Bust Out," B. Bumble, "Bumble Boogie," Kool and the Gang, "Kool and the Gang," (I know this last one came after '67--skip the details)Paul and Paula, "Hey Paula," to name a few.).

Generally, records of this type are one-shot affairs, with the group put together for that one song, albiet with a few minor follow-ups. But that is not the point here. The point is, who the heck was the Yellow Brlloon, and why?

Moreover, why write about it in a Jan and Dean mag? The answer is that, just prior to the release of "Yellow Balloon" by the Yellow Balloon, the same song was released by---Jan and Dean!

(In point of fact, Jan was not on the record. He was still recovering from the car wreck. This is a fairly minor point, since there were many "Jan and Dean" records Dean was not on, including "Easy As 1,2,3," "You Really Know How To Hurt A Guy," "A Surfer's Dream," and "I Found A Girl." At the time of the tragic accident, the recording contract with Liberty was up, and the duo needed a new label. One choice was J&D Records. Another was Dunhill. As it happens, Dean went with Colombia. This was the best way he knew to keep Jan and Dean's name alive and options open, so that, if possible, they could resume their career when Jan was better.)

Having two versions of the same song out at the same time was nothing new. Witness: "He's So Fine," Chiffons and Angels, "Butterfly," Charlie Gracie and Andy Williams, "Heart and Soul," Cleftones and Jan and Dean, "Hot Rod Lincoln," Johnny Bond and Charlie Ryan, "Young Love," Crewcuts, Tab Hunter, Sonny James. But the mystery here grew from the facts that everyone knew Jan was laid up, and no one knew who was in the group The Yellow Balloon.

Here in Kansas, the mix-up was documented. On KEWI, Jan and Dean's version was the pick of the week. On WREN, Jan and Dean's version was listed, then when the program direstor saw that Billboard was charting the Yellow Balloon's version, switched artists in mid-survey. Meanwhile, cooletheads prevailed at WHB, and both versions were charted together!

Just to make sure things got good and confused, the flip side of the Yellow Balloon's 45 was the same song, played backwards! The label came two ways, spelled backwards, and mirror-imaged!

Then of course, there was the LP by the Yellow Balloon, called-- YELLOW BALLOON! But, what happened to SAVE FOR A RAINY DAY, the Jan and Dean LP containing "Yellow Balloon"? It was never released, due to interpersonal difficulties summed up well in the movie DEADMAN'S CURVE.

(SAVE FOR A RAINY DAY copies have turned up here and there. I have heard of two stereo DJ copies in the US. I have been told of at least one stereo DJ copy in a white jacket released on CBS in England. And in Japan, the LP was just plain released, by CBS/Sony. Unfortunatly, in Japan records are not stockpiled. When they quit selling, they are recycled. So, there are no "cut-out" copies of the LP drifting around Japan.)

A final complication: Dean recorded a demo LP which contained a totally different recording of "Yellow Balloon," and had it pressed. This was in mono only.

MK Now that all of the facts are before you, the best way to clear up the controvesy once and for all is to ask Dean.

MK Tell me about the mono SFARD album on J&D.

DT It's a terrible album! I recorded it in a garage. The Columbia album was really nice, I reerecorded and remixed everything. I went through a whole lot of generations on that thing (the J&D LP), which robbed all the fidelity from it. It was more or less a very elaborate demo record.

MK The J&D LP was recorded before the Columbia "Yellow Balloon" 45?

DT Yeah, that got me the Columbia deal. Even the song "Yellow Balloon" is not the same recording.As a matter of fact, this one, on J&D, is much closer to the other one. Did you ever hear the other version, by the Yellow Balloon?

MK Sure, I have it, and their album. Who are they?

DT The same people, just about.

MK Huh??

DT I cut it different ways. The first way, the J&D demo, was kind of the standard way, and similar to the one that came out on Columbia. Something of a Beach-Boys-type sound.

Then after I listened to it for a while, I began to hear more possibilitie in it. "Happy Together" by the Turtles had just come out, I liked the feel on that. "The 59th Street Bridge Song [Feelin' Groovy]" had just come out by the Harper's Bazaar. With its changes of tempo....

MK Speaking of the Turtles, "She'd Rather Be With Me" always reminded me of the Jan and Dean stuff, the harmonies, the horns, the modified "bomps." Especially the ending.

DT Yeah, I was on that.

MK You were!! I've gotta go refile that under Jan and Dean in my collection

DT The Turtles picked up a lot of their style from us, and I was involved with a lot of their designing, singles sleeves and all that jazz. And I sang on pretty many of those records.

MK Do any titles come to mind?

DT Umm. "She'd Rather Be With Me." "She's My Girl," I think I sang on.

MK What about the BATTLE OF THE BANDS lp. Any of those songs?

DT Yes, a couple of those, but I don't even remember which ones.

MK "Surfer Dan"?

SUNSHINE MUSIC 7

DT No, I didn't sing on that one, of all cuts! I really don't remember specific songs. What I'd do is go down and be talkin' to them about concept on cover art and so on, and they'd say, "Hey, we need some voices." They wouldn't even mention a title, just ask me to sing a part. But they had some really fine songs.

"Elenore" I nearly got for myself! They decided that they didn't like it after they had finished it. I knew that was a hit record. But they had gotten another song that they liked better from Harry Nilsson called "The Story of Rock and Roll," or something like that.

The Turtles said, "Boy, this Nilsson song is really gonna be a hit." I said, "'Elenore' is the hit!" So about every other day I'd see them and ask if they were gonna release "Elenore." I'd even already designed the trade ad for them for "Elenore" and they hadn't even decided to release it yet! When I told them that, they said that was the only reason I wanted them to put it out--so I could get paid for the art!

Finally, I told them that if they didn't like the song, they should give it to me. They wrote it, they'd still get the royalties.

MK Were you going to cut it the same way?

DT EXACTLY the same way. I was even going to talk them into giving me the track, and I would just put on my lead voice or whatever it needed. And even split it with them, or something, anything just to get that good song out.

The Nilsson song came out, and it stiffed. They followed it right up with "Elenore," which went to number one here (MK note: #6 nationally).

MK Not to change the subject, but...who sang on the Yellow Balloon "Yellow Balloon"?

DT Oh, yeah! Well, approximately the same people.

MK But, on the Jan and Dean version, it sounds to me like about all of the voices are you...

DT Yes, they were. Oh, I see, then how could the same people... I meant this J&D record, demo version. This is more like the non-Jan and Dean version.

My demo LP version was closer to their version. When I changed it, I didn't even tell the writer. Gary Zekely wrote the song for me. He liked the way I did it, and when I mentioned that I was going to change it, he said, "Oh, no!" He thought it was really good the way it was already done.

I told him I wanted to change it..., but if he liked this way better, we will do it that way, but for somebody else. And he said, "OK."

MK What did Columbia do with all of the copies of their SPARD LP that they must have had on hand when it was decided not to release it?

DT It probably wasn't pressed.

*Elenore is being worked on as a possible J&D song at this very moment.
12 March 1981

MK But it was listed in all of the record catalogs.

DT I'm sure that only the numbers got released, 'cause--but, man, I don't know, because I get checks for it. I actually get checks with the, well, I'm sure it's the LP number! It's not a whole lot of money, but it does have the LP number. Still, when I call, everytime, they tell me that they never really released that LP. Yet, I get checks. I can't figure it out. Maybe they pressed it, but never fabricated it, put covers on it. (MK note: Perhaps the checks were for overseas release royalties.) (DT note: Good point.)

MK Maybe there is a whole warehouse of them somewhere with no covers...

DT If I could find out, I might try to get them. It is a lot better LP than the J&D version. That demo had bad generation loss. All I had to work with was two four-track recorders.

MK I know what you mean. When I record, by the time I do some background parts, then a lead or two, the background is gone, and I have to do it over.

DT Yes, that's the exact same situation. But, all it was was a demo.

So, dear SM reader, that is the story. Dean cut the demo, released only on the mono, private release LP J&D 101. Then, he had second thoughts about style, and changed it for the Columbia 45 release. Then, to please the composer, he also did a version, much like his original version, and with the same personnel, with a "group" called The Yellow Balloon.

It has recently come to light that Don "My Three Sons" Grady was in The Yellow Balloon. Dean's voice, in fact, is all but missing from the YB single by YB. However, for all those who still doubt that Dean was in fact The Yellow Balloon, I offer evidence. (DT note: Hope statute of limitations is up!)

*** The term "yellow balloon" refers to the sun. A primary motif in Dean's artistic style is heavenly bodies, primarily the planets and the moon, but also the sun.

*** The color featured most often in Dean's art of the period was yellow.

*** The back cover art has the sun and flowers, pure Torrence.

*** The credits are full of Dean's kind of humor and style. The heading is "Cast of Characters." When I asked Dean if he and Jan played instruments, he replied, sure, I play the pillow and Jan plays the paper triangle. The "Cast" includes the following persons playing, among others, the following "instruments: Frosty Green, organ, piano, clavinet, ashtray; Frisby Forestep, banjo.

*** Don Altfeld (where have we heard THAT name before!!) is listed as "Consulting Physician." The "Producer" is Yodar Critch, just the kind of name Dean would make up.

*** Dean can be clearly heard singing backup bomps and falsetto on "How Can I Be Down," and falsetto on "Can't Get Enough of Your Love," among other cuts.

*** Having heard tapes of the Colombia LP, there are many stylistic similarities between it and the YB LP on Canterbury.

76

Letters

HI, Doc--

Are you sure Dean didn't write "'Dean' Unmasked?" It's like his style!

Thanks, Becky Shugart

Dear Beckey,

Asking if Dean wrote that is like asking Paul McCartney if he is dead. Sort of. In a way. I think.

Thanks to you, Doc Rock

Myke,

Dean is definitely dead!!! Gotta Take... was the last album "he" wrote liners for, & the warning not to smoke or swallow was the last clue. Dean had obviously obtained a copy of the "Fire" tapes from SMILE and was listening to them while eating hot dogs. His house caught fire & he ran into the shower & turned it on to avoid being burned but the smoke he inhaled killed him. Another clue in the same album is the fact that Vegetables was on it(?) this was written by the same people who write SMILE, & Brian is the "friend" (to take the cold shower with & who wrote both songs).

Thanks, Todd Vittum

Dear Michael--

Of course there are other clues that Dean is dead. Jan didn't really have a broken leg, he just used those crutches to give "Dean" a few well-placed bomps on the noggin [to keep him in line]. "Dean" is smiling on the Filet of Soul cover, but don't let that fool you, check out the Golden Hits Vol. III cover, "Dean" is obviously grimacing in pain because of one of Jan's direct hits!

Also on GHVIII, the graffiti say "Jan and Dean," but George Harrison's name is right under "Dean," proving that this Beatle was another "Dean" for a time, singing all those Beatle songs Jan did, as well as a few falsette leads with a rubber band around his (sic.).

Why did Jan make "Dean" climb the Watts Tower (in the middle of the riots, no doubt)? What were the songs "Eve of Destruction" and "Only A Boy" really about? Other methods for killing off this "Cat" - "Dean" - who certainly proved harder than Rasputin to Kill.

Another graffiti on GHVIII "Galindo" is clearly a reference to the hit man hired to get Dean.

*** The address for Canterbury records is not far from Kittyhawk.

*** Composer credits for cuts on the YB YB LP include such J&D vets as Jill Gibson, Don Altfeld, and Gary Zekely. (Also, a "Grady.")

*** Gary Zekely and Dean recut "The Restless Surfer" in 1965 as "Other Towns, Other Girls."

Discography

Demo LP	SAVE FOR A RAINY DAY MONO	J&D 101	
45	Yellow Balloon/Taste of Rain	Colombia 4-44036	3/67
45	Yellow Balloon/Noolab Wolley	Canterbury 508	4/67
LP	The Yellow Balloon	Canterbury CLPM/CLPS 1502	
LP	SAVE FOR A RAINY DAY (unreleased)	Colombia 2661/9461	
	(bootleg version Last Ride LR33-7802 stereo only)		
45	Good Feelin' Time/I've Got A Feelin For Love	Canterbury 513	
45	Can't Get Enough of Your Love/Stained Glass Window	Canterbury 516	
LP RUMORED FOR RELEASE IN 1981, A BRITISH STEREO LP SAVE FOR A RAINY DAY!!!			

* * * * * *

□□□□□□

CHECK THE NUMBER ON YOUR ADDRESS LABEL! THE NUMBER THERE IS THE NUMBER OF THE LAST ISSUE OF YOUR SUBSCRIPTION. IF THERE IS NO NUMBER, LUCKY YOU!!!!

BEACH BUMS

FOR SALE--The Fall, 1979, issue of NUTSHELL MAGAZINE Featuring a multi-page, illustrated article about the Beach Boys. Bonus: Theatrical-sized (21½ x 31½) color poster of Bette Midler starring in THE ROSE. $2, postage included. Make checks payable to Michael B. Kelly, mail to Sunshine Music.

"NEXT SUMMER COMES GONNA HUSTLE YOU"

THE JAN & DEAN MAG
Published 6x a year
$6 for 6. US/AUST.
US fans contact:
SHARON A. FOX, 5742
W. Giddings Street,
Chicago, Ill 60630

ISSUE 1 SOLD OUT

All other countries $10 for 6 issues
to Head Office - Stephen J McFarland
2 Kentwell Avenue, Concord 2137, NSW
AUSTRALIA. Each subscriber receives
a Jan & Dean supporter's card/photo.

SUNSHINE MUSIC 7

the fact that he is wearing a black shirt but NOT black shoes!

The background on this cover is significant. This is a record tribute. On the back, note Dean has the everpresent skateboard, while only Jan is without a hat!

What is not so obvious is that Jan has been replaced in later years, as well! On the back of the Little Old Lady LP, the death-symbol lady is smashing both of them, but Dean has his feet way back because he is long gone, while Jan is about to go at that precise moment.

Only the gypsie, when she cried, foresaw this event!

In light of this, re-listen to "Who Put the Bomp." At the end, Dean seems to be asfixiated by a "bomb" of toxic gas, while with Jan it was a bomp in the ear!

It was clear before 1966 that they were both replaced. On the Popsicle LP Jan has on a dark jacket. And, "Dean" is LAUGHING, happy that Jan has rejoined him. Note the two black ribbons.

Read Jan's testament: "the mouse (Jan) ran up the stick (of life) one stopped at the rapper cause he was scared to death. Read between the lines! Jan was gone, but would return to us. To put it in Jan's own words, "because After Godfrey was on at the same time," then he said he would return: "But afterwards I used to do out and watch ants". See? From "up there" everyone looks like ants!

Being in heaven is a great experience. The youngster on the cover meant that the duo would achieve childhood again, be reborn. The popsicle has two sticks, one for each guy, surrounded by the cold of death, but with the sucking of a warm, innocent, pretty little blond they would be reborn again, as predicted by the red background of the second DMN/NGIC cover.

On the back, of course Jan wears shades to hide his tear-rimmed eyes. Of course, the band dedicated to redoing J&D hits calls itself the Skeletons. Still, on The Very Best Vol. II, we see them being reborn from a pair of empty bottles. The back is almost without colors which means death, but the frame means old memories and the flower symbolizes new life. Not just any kind of flower, but a paper flower, which means: life, but not just any kind of life, but artificial life, meaning a reborning life.

So, Jan and Dean were reborn in 1976. Could there be any more evidence?

Yours, Jorge Cubria, Mexico

Another clue—Jan didn't change "Hot Shot" to "Hot Cookie" just because Someone else had a hit by that title. He just didn't want to be too obvious. But, why did "Dean" eat the transistorized C.C. Cookie on the Batman LP? No wonder it didn't taste good-- it was poisoned! Also, on the Last Ride LP the outgrooves message says "The last ride may be the best ride"-- maybe getting rid of Dean for good.

Beth Kruger

AND, WHY ARE THOSE SURFERS MASKED???

Dear Doc,

I KNEW IT ALL THE TIME!! Dean was indeed dead. That Dean was dead was so obvious that I never thought that anyone would ever doubt it.

The album "DMC/NGIS" the cover was done two ways. One had red with the guys wearing white shirts while the other was balck with the guys in purple. I understand that black was first, and black is the color of mourning, while purple is the color they use to cover the alters in the Catholic Church during the Holy Week in which Christ died. This is an obvious mourning tribute.

The side "Dean" is on says "Dead Man's Curve." (Too much coincidence, isn't it?). And, the words over Jan are in red, indicating that Jan was still alive at this time. However, on the back if you observe well enough you will see the words "Bucket T" on Dean's side, the "T" representing a cross over a grave. Then, in the Linda LP the two surf boards are in the form of a corss, with Dean in their midst! (Another "coincidence"?)

Have you noticed that on this LP they do the song "The Best Friend I Ever Had" (this is just too much) and then comes "The Gypsie Cried" (Who did she cry for?) and then "When I Learn How To Cry" (don't you think this is too much crying and weeping for a Jan and Dean album, something, something was going wrong at this time).

Then on Command Performance "Dean" is holding an empty instrument case, very much the symbol for a coffin, and the skate board inside representative of the means of conducting Dean to the next life! Besides, what else could the words on their sweatshirts mean, if not a trip to the other life? "Go Go" (Go where? To Heaven.)

Then in GI/VI, Jan holds a hat in his hand, and men always remove their hats at funerals. Jan is wearing flowers which represent life, while DEan is wearing none. Plus, they are kissing an old lady who is wearing BLACK GLOVES! Literally kissing the symbol of death!

Jan's shirt is blue and white, while Dean's is BLACK AND WHITE, the colors of Death. They are riding a skate board tandem, but Dean is in front, in the front of the vehicle which will transport us all someday. Dean is on front, naturally. He has on black sneakers, showing he was gone, but Jan, only mourning at this point, as shown by

SUNSHINE MUSIC 7

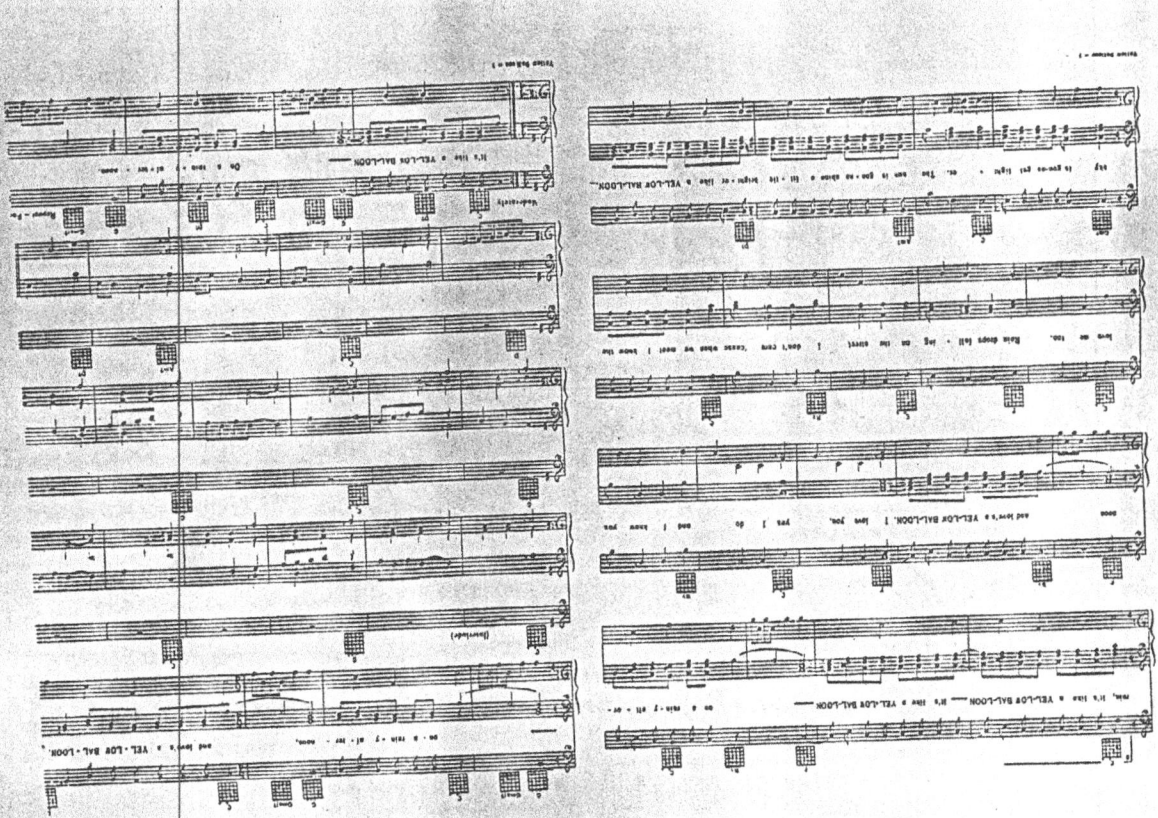

Hi Mike!

    Just a short, but vital addition to the "Dean is Dead" school of thought. Jan and "Dean" apparently patterened the hints after the much publicized "McCartney is dead" scandal. The most obvious reference is, in my opinion, the covering of McCartney's "Norwegian Wood," What could be more direct than "this bird has flown?"

    "Dean" later turns up flying Kittyhawk.

    Morefurtherovers in the second place "Dean" and "Dead" are identical except for the <u>last letter</u>. Early versions of the movie theme were rumored to have been titled "Deadman's Curve."

    Morefurtherover in the third place, Phil Sloan penned the ultimate (penultimate?) tribute song about Dean's funeral, namely "From All Over The World," referring to all the rock 'n' roll stars who came to pay respects.

    Well, gotta go-go.

Best Always, Steve Peters, Canada

Dear Steve,

    Who patterened hints after whom...? Ringo was still just a little Dick when Dean's hints began appearing!

Doc Rock

[Interesting to note that the club head is a doctor...]

Hi,

    Another clue has surfaced. On the OUTTAKES album, "Dean" lets us know he has supposedly died, by yelling during "Dead Man's Curve," "I'm being burned by the fire!" That's enough proof for anybody.

I Rest My Case,
Todd Vittum

Mike,

    Just got issue #5. I'm excited. Please send me all back issues. The girl on the POPSICLE cover is making a face that indicates death. (Dean must be dead.) Note the shape of my check-must be another clue!

Thank you,
Mark Hoffman

Mike,

    I just hope it's true!

Arnie Ginsburg

...continued page 9

SUNSHINE MUSIC
c/o Doc Rock
Box 1166
Lawrence, KS 66044-0154

To:

FIRST CLASS MAIL

Sharon Fox with ½ of the Wright Brothers!

SUNSHINE MUSIC 8

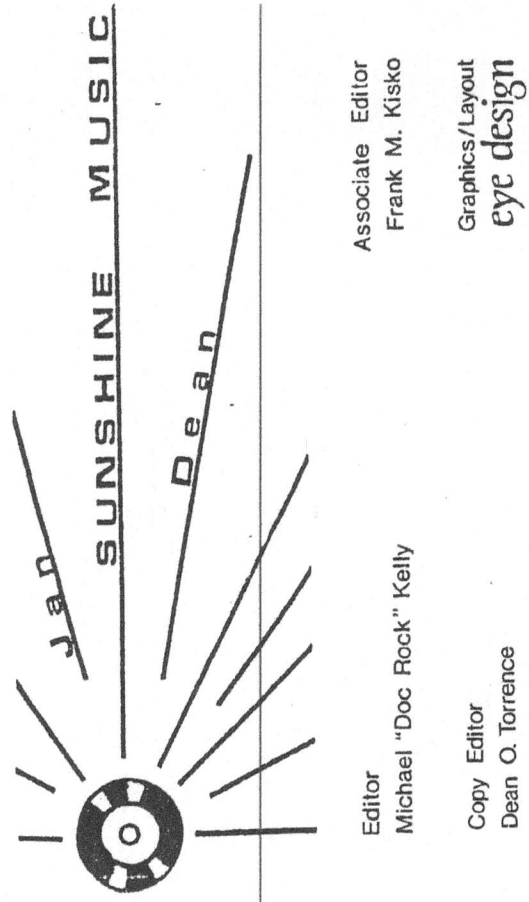

Jan and Dean SUNSHINE MUSIC

Editor
Michael "Doc Rock" Kelly

Copy Editor
Dean O. Torrence

Associate Editor
Frank M. Kisko

Graphics/Layout
eye design

The Magazine of the Official Jan and Dean
Authorized International Collectors Club

Issue 8   **Summer 1981**

Contents not already copyrighted are
© *1981 by Michael Bryan Kelly.*

SUBSCRIPTIONS

OK Jan and Dean fans world-wide, here is a simplified guide to getting SUNSHINE MUSIC into your mail box safe and sound:

SAMPLE COPIES of SM are $1 in the US and surface overseas. Airmail, $2.
SUBSCRIPTIONS are good for six (6) issues, at the rates indicated below.

USA, mailed in envelope	Non-US Surface	Non-US Air	Surface Envelopes	Air Envelopes	Envelope Charge is for Postage
$5	$7	$12	$10	$15	

USA $7

★★ CHECK THE NUMBER ON YOUR ADDRESS LABEL. THE NUMBER THERE IS THE NUMBER OF
THE LAST ISSUE OF YOUR SUBSCRIPTION. IF THERE IS NO NUMBER, LUCKY YOU!!!! ★★

FEB.-MAR., 1962

★ **POOR LITTLE PUPPET**
HOWARD GREENFIELD   JACK KELLER

Once he had a mind of his own
He used to be a man amongst men
Ev'rything was swell till he met that Jezabel
And he hasn't been the same since then
And I doubt if he ever will again
Poor little puppet, she's got him tied to a string
That poor little thing, he does what she wants
Ev'ry time she moves her finger, poor little puppet
He's a fool, an ordinary fool
He can't tell the evil from the good
I tell him ev'ry day
That he should break away
But he never seems to listen when he should
I guess it's 'cause his head is made of wood
Hurts me so to see him pushed around
How I wish that I could set him free
Time and time again I'm broken hearted
When I look into the mirror and I see
That little puppet looking back at me.
© Copyright 1961 by Aldon Music, Inc. Nevins-Kirshner Associates, Inc.

New SUNSHINE MUSIC Logo described by the artist herself, Honolulu tulu:

*A gentle sense of timelessness
As evoked by the timeless tunes of
Jan and Dean's endless harmonies
and all that stuff.*

*Music drifting up to the sun
It's been there forever
And it will always be there or so it seems
at least I'd hope so!*

SUNSHINE MUSIC 8

PHASE ONE BIOGRAPHY
(1958-1966)

"Bust your buns"

All of a sudden the boys found it was time to return to the magic of Brian Wilson. Taking one of his songs off of an old BB album, "To Catch A Wave", Jan & Dean rewrote it and called it "Sidewalk Surfing". To get a recording of a skateboard, they put a long extension on a microphone so they could record out in front of the recording studio on the sidewalk. Jan said he was better at crashing (he said he was better at everything), so they recorded him doing his famous wipe-out act and that's how the record starts.

Dean came up with "Bust Your Buns" and, of course, the rest is record biz history.

Next there was a few contrived songs that were lacking the Jan & Dean humor. Next came (holy moly contrived) "Batman" which was the last single record that Jan & Dean recorded together and also was the last single record they did for Liberty Records.

During the first phase of their career, Jan and Dean were more than just singers. Known as the "Laurel and Hardy of the Rock and Roll" they were complete entertainers whose music was simply the most visible phase of their talents.

Jan and Dean were the hosts of the now-legendary "T.A.M.I. Show", featuring the Rolling Stones, James Brown, The Beach Boys, Diana Ross and other rock greats.

They were to be the stars of a movie called "Easy Come, Easy Go" (a title later used for an Elvis Presley film that was unrelated), co-starring Terry Thomas and featuring a newcomer named Mel Brooks, in his first screen role. On the first day of shooting there was a train wreck involving two locomotives and a flat-bed car that were part of a scene, and more than thirty cast and crew members. Jan broke his leg in the wreck. The cast Jan is wearing on the cover of "Folk and Roll" is the result of that wreck. Filming was suspended.

All the while that Jan and Dean were recording stars and were flying around the country playing concerts on the weekends, they were both full-time college students, Dean in the school of architecture at the University of Southern California where he earned a bachelor degree in fine arts, and Jan at U.C.L.A. where he was pre-med and upon graduation he was accepted in medical school.

"It just wasn't the same"

When Jan received a notice to report to his draft board in April of 1966, he didn't think twice about it, knowing that his status as a medical student would get him a certain deferment. To Jan's surprise and horror, he was told (in error) that he was eligible to be drafted. Getting into his Corvette, Jan pressed down the accelerator, trying to scatter his misfortune in the convertible's wind. On Whittier Drive in Beverly Hills, Jan pulled out to pass a slow-moving vehicle and slammed full-speed into a truck that was unexpectedly parked at the curb. Jan's Corvette was a twisted pile of junk and Jan was smashed apart so badly that he wasn't expected to live. He remained in a coma for months and when he finally awoke, he discovered that he'd sustained severe brain damage and couldn't walk, move or speak. The doctors told Jan's family that he'd never be a fully functioning human again.

As quickly as it had begun, Jan and Dean's career as a duo was over. Dean tried to continue on his own, making a deal with a major record label for some songs-in-progress that were to have been Jan & Dean's next record. But, as Dean has often said, "It just wasn't the same."

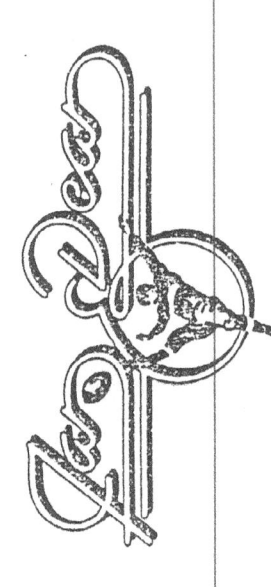

PHASE TWO BIOGRAPHY
(1977-1981)

A few weeks following the debut showing of the successful movie made for television "Deadman's Curve" (the Jan & Dean story), Mike Love of The Beach Boys was jogging on a beach some place in the South. Two young boys, one thirteen and one fourteen, caught up with Mike and jogged with him for a while. After introducing themselves the first question they asked Mike was: "do you know Jan & Dean?"

Mike was very surprised since these kids hadn't been born during the time Jan & Dean were recording hit records. Mike asked "how do you know about Jan & Dean?" and they responded that they had seen the film "Deadman's Curve" and would love to see the real Jan & Dean in concert someday. Mike told them he would call Jan & Dean when he got back to Los Angeles. The two boys thanked Mike for his time and jogged off.

A couple of days later, Mike returned to his home in Santa Barbara, California. Mike called Dean and they met at Mike's house. Mike asked Dean if he would be interested in becoming involved with his new special projects band Celebration. They were working on sound track music for a movie entitled Almost Summer. They were also going to be heavily involved in the promotion of the film as well. Mike Love and Celebration were going to play free street concerts in all the major cities in which the movie was to open and he asked Dean to be a special guest.

Dean quickly accepted Mike's offer and rehearsals were set up with Celebration. The debut concert was set for April 28th, 1978 at Dean's alma mater, the University of Southern California. The event started with a lunch for band members at the Alpha Chi Sorority. Hearing of a free lunch, two other Beach Boys and one other Jan & Dean showed up, Brian and Carl Wilson and Jan Berry. It was like Summer 64 had never ended.

The concert started with Mike Love and Celebration playing all the music from the sound track plus their new single, the title track from the movie of the same name "Almost Summer." Then Mike introduced Brian, Carl and Jan & Dean and the concert became a full blown event. The audience was treated to an afternoon filled with all the major classic summertime songs ever done by the two most important summertime groups in pop music, The Beach Boys and Jan & Dean.

There were to be only two more of the Mike Love and Celebration concerts. The money that had been promised for the promotion of the film was put on hold and the project came to an abrupt halt. But the magic had already happened, people were really gettin' off on seeing even just some of The Beach Boys and Jan & Dean together.

Surfin' Deja Vu

Mike and Dean got together again and put together "The Beach Boys/Jan & Dean Surfin Deja Vu Tour 1978". August 25th everyone met at the Los Angeles International Airport and boarded a lush private jet and headed for Grand Haven, Michigan, site of their first concert together in fourteen years. The tour ran from August 25th through September 2nd. Half way through the tour they were joined by ex-Beach Boys and ex-Jan & Dean band member Bruce Johnston.

Returning to Los Angeles after the very successful tour, Jan & Dean started making plans to put together their own touring band.

Dean had been managing/producing the locally based, second generation surf band, Papa Doo Run Run, and Dean had performed with Papa Doo Run Run on many occasions during the five years they had been associated. It seemed natural for Jan & Dean to reenter the music was backed by Papa Doo Run Run.

SUMMERTIME KICKS

SUNSHINE MUSIC 8

The first day on the road was an outdoor concert at Fresno State University. The school expected 3,000 to 5,000, but over 12,000 paying customers showed up to rock and roll in the California sun.

The next stop was Busch Gardens in Williamsburg, Va. where 6,000 teenagers and pre-teens were there to see their first Jan & Dean concert. The balance of the five week tour was spent working the rock & roll circuit clubs and, when it was over, the highlight dates were still the first two, Fresno St. and Busch Gardens.

Jan & Dean now went to work on their first television special "Jan & Dean's California Special." Some footage had already been shot at the Fresno State Concert and there also was some very rare footage of Jan & Dean from the Sixties that had surfaced. A special one night concert was arranged at the Coconut Grove in Los Angeles with Glen Campbell who was once Jan & Dean's guitar player, as host of a tribute to Jan & Dean, co-starring Richard Hatch who had played Jan Berry, and Bruce Davison who had played Dean Torrence in the TV movie "Deadman's Curve", along with Beach Boy Bruce Johnston as a special guest.

This concert was filmed and became part of the television special. Once the television special was finished, Jan & Dean played Christmas week through New Year's Eve at Harrahs in Tahoe where they broke all house records. Three weeks later they headed out for their second national tour. The first night out, middle of January, Jan & Dean drew 12,000 plus to Old Chicago Amusement Park, 80% of whom were under 18 years of age. In the next two weeks, Jan & Dean packed theaters in Illinois, Indiana, Ohio, Michigan, Pennsylvania, Georgia, Virginia, New York and Florida.

A breath of fresh air

The second tour's success confirmed what had been apparent since the first date at Fresno State, that Jan & Dean had been catapulted to stardom again, thanks to a TV movie and their own infectious music and humor. Where the first tour might have been thought to have succeeded as a result of curiosity aroused by the movie, the larger success of the second tour, many stops of which were in the same places as the first, confirmed that it was the special chemistry of Jan Berry and Dean Torrence together onstage that charms audiences.

In a business that has chosen to take itself so seriously over the past decade that many have forgotten that rock and roll started out as a way for kids to laugh, dance and have fun, Jan & Dean's return to full-time performing is just the breath of fresh air audiences seem to be clamoring for.

DEADMAN'S CURVE MOVIE BIOGRAPHY
(1969-1979)

It was Easter week 1969 when Paul Morantz, a young law student at the University of Southern California, met Jan Berry at a resort motel in Palm Springs, California. Paul and Jan became instant friends. After listening to some of Jan's stories, Paul who dabbled in freelance writing, decided to write a feature story about Jan and his struggle against all odds.

The story first appeared in the University of Southern California Daily Trojan in a short-edited form. Later Paul spent many months re-writing the article for a California magazine called "West." Just about the time he was putting the finishing touches on the story "West" stopped publishing.

By this time Morantz had graduated from law school and was busy practicing law. The story was shelved.

A couple of years later, Paul got itchy to write again. He dug out Jan's story and re-read it. Paul realized that the story could easily be expanded to include the whole Jan & Dean story. At this point, Paul called Dean and they got together to discuss what had begun to take on the proportions of a larger project.

After many regular meetings and major rewriting Paul and Dean submitted the re-written story to Rolling Stone, after it had first been turned down by all of the major general interest magazines on the ground that not enough people would remember Jan & Dean to justify its publication.

Rolling Stone accepted the story with tremendous enthusiasm, scheduling Jan & Dean to appear on their cover with the article given a major spread within. The publication date was September 12, 1974. But a funny thing happened on the way to the press, Nixon resigned and Nixon's picture pushed Jan & Dean's off the cover. But the story ran and was very well received. There seemed to be a renewed interest in Jan & Dean. Being the naive guys they were, Dean and Paul now decided that the story had all the elements of a feature film, so they started writing a treatment/screen play and started shopping the property all over town.

After two years of rejections a deal was finally made with CBS to make the movie for television. The production of the film "Deadman's Curve" starring Richard Hatch ("Streets of San Francisco", "Battlestar Galactica"), Bruce Davison and guest-starring Dick Clark, Wolfman Jack, Mike Love and Bruce Johnston of The Beach Boys was started in late 1977.

The real Jan and Dean consulted daily on the set, ensuring the accuracy of facts and projecting a more subtle hovering presence that carried through Hatch and Davison's characterizations.

The film aired February 1978 and again in April 1979. The mail started pouring in, average age, fourteen! Yes, you can come back from Deadman's Curve.

SHOW	SHARES				
FEBRUARY 3, 1978	9:00-9:30	9:30-10:00	10:00-10:30	10:30-11:00
CBS Deadman's Curve	28	28	31	33
NBC Rockford Files	32	32		
NBC Quincy			31	32
ABC Cruise Into Terror	29	29	30	31

SUNSHINE MUSIC 8

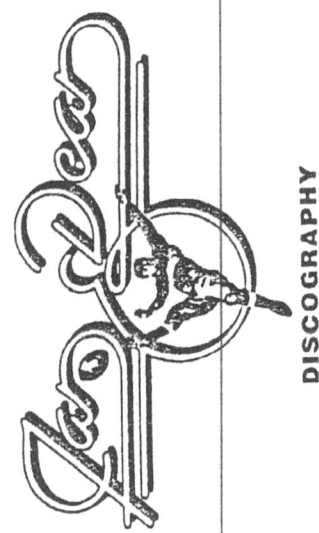

DISCOGRAPHY

SINGLES:

Date	Title	Cat#
4/58	JENNY LEE/JAN & ARNIE*	A108
7/58	GAS MONEY/JAN & ARNIE*	A111
11/58	I LOVE LINDA/JAN & ARNIE	A113
7/59	BABY TALK/JAN & DEAN**	D522
10/59	THERE'S A GIRL/JAN & DEAN**	D539
1/60	CLEMENTINE/JAN & DEAN**	D548
4/60	WHITE TENNIS SNEAKERS/JAN & DEAN**	D555
7/60	WE GO TOGETHER/JAN & DEAN**	D576
10/60	GEE/JAN & DEAN**	D583
1/61	BAGGY PANTS/JAN & DEAN	D610
7/61	DON'T FLY AWAY/JAN & DEAN**	C9111
9/61	HEART & SOUL/JAN & DEAN**	L55397
12/61	WANTED, ONE GIRL/JAN & DEAN**	L55454
4/62	SUNDAY KIND OF LOVE/JAN & DEAN**	L55496
7/62	TENNESSEE/JAN & DEAN**	L55522
10/62	MY FAVORITE DREAM/JAN & DEAN**	L55531
1/63	FROSTY THE SNOWMAN/JAN & DEAN	L55580
4/63	LINDA/JAN & DEAN**	L55613
7/63	SURF CITY/JAN & DEAN*	L55641
10/63	HONOLULU LULU/JAN & DEAN**	L55672
2/64	DRAG CITY/JAN & DEAN*	L55672
2/64	DEADMAN'S CURVE/JAN & DEAN*	L55704
5/64	NEW GIRL IN SCHOOL/JAN & DEAN**	L55724
8/64	LITTLE OLD LADY/JAN & DEAN*	L55727
10/64	RIDE THE WILD SURF/JAN & DEAN**	L55766
2/65	SIDEWALK SURFIN'/JAN & DEAN**	L55792
4/65	FROM ALL OVER THE WORLD/JAN & DEAN**	L55833
9/65	HOW TO HURT A GUY/JAN & DEAN**	L55845
11/65	I FOUND A GIRL/JAN & DEAN**	L55849
12/65	UNIVERSAL COWARD/JAN BERRY	L55860
1/66	BEGINNING FROM AN END/JAN & DEAN	L55886
5/66	BATMAN/JAN & DEAN**	L55905
8/66	POPSICLE/JAN & DEAN**	L55923
11/66	FIDDLE AROUND/JAN & DEAN**	M401
11/66	SCHOOL DAY/JAN & DEAN	CO44036
3/67	SUMMERTIME, SUMMERTIME/JAN & DEAN	WW261
11/67	YELLOW BALLOON/JAN & DEAN	WB7151
11/67	VEGETABLES/LAUGHING GRAVY (DEAN)	WB7219
6/68	ONLY A BOY/JAN & DEAN (JAN)	WB7240
9/68	LAUREL & HARDY/JAN & DEAN (JAN)	U50859
12/72	STILL OF THE NIGHT/JAN & DEAN (JAN)	UXW270
4/73	VEGETABLES/JAN & DEAN (DEAN)	UXW670
6/75	GONNA HUSTLE YOU/JAN & DEAN (DEAN)	O66023
9/75	SIDEWALK SURFIN'/JAN & DEAN (DEAN)*	O66120
3/76	FUN CITY/JAN & DEAN	
	SING SANG A SONG/JAN BERRY	

DISCOGRAPHY

ALBUMS:

Date	Title	Cat#
4/60	JAN & DEAN SOUND**	D101
2/62	GOLDEN HITS/VOLUME 1**	L7248
5/63	TAKE LINDA SURFING**	L7294
6/63	SURF CITY*	L7314
11/63	DRAG CITY*	L7339
5/64	DEADMAN'S CURVE*	L7361
8/64	RIDE THE WILD SURF**	L7368
10/64	LITTLE OLD LADY FROM PASADENA*	L7377
1/65	COMMAND PERFORMANCE*	L7403
9/65	GOLDEN HITS/VOLUME 2**	L7417
11/65	FOLK 'N' ROLL**	L7431
1/66	POP SYMPHONY	L7444
3/66	BATMAN**	L7441
5/66	FILET OF SOUL**	L7458
6/66	POPSICLE**	L7460
8/66	GOLDEN HITS/VOLUME 3**	U9961
12/72	ANTHOLOGY ALBUM**	U341-H2
11/74	GOTTA TAKE THAT ONE LAST RIDE	U-EA443
5/75	VERY BEST OF JAN & DEAN/VOLUME 1	U-EA515
8/75	VERY BEST OF JAN & DEAN/VOLUME 2	L-999
11/79	DEADMAN'S CURVE**	

*TOP TEN RECORD
**TOP ONE HUNDRED

A/Arwin
D/Dora
C/Challenge
CO/CBS
L/Liberty
O/Ode
U/United Artists
WB/Warner Bros.
WW/White Whale

JAN & DEAN RELATED

ALLEY OOP/DANTE & THE EVERGREENS
I GOTTA DRIVE/THE MATADORS
MOVE OUT LITTLE MUSTANG/RALLY PACKS
SUMMER MEANS FUN/THE FANTASTIC BAGGIES
TOPLESS BATHINGSUIT/THE FANTASTIC BAGGIES
SLOOP JOHN B/THE BEACH BOYS (DEAN)
FUN, FUN, FUN/THE BEACH BOYS (DEAN)
RHONDA/THE BEACH BOYS (DEAN)
BARBARA ANN/THE BEACH BOYS (DEAN)
ELENORE/THE TURTLES (DEAN)
BUY MY ALBUM/NILSSON (DEAN)
BE TRUE TO YOUR SCHOOL/PAPA DOO RUN RUN
SHE'S SO TOUGH/WALTER EGAN (DEAN)
PACIFIC OCEAN BLUE/DENNIS WILSON (DEAN)
GIRL IN THE BLUE T-BIRD/WALTER EGAN (DEAN)
MY BABY CAME BACK/WALTER EGAN (DEAN)

Teen Screen

EXCLUSIVE PERSONALITY ARTICLES
Elvis Asks: "Are You The Girl I Need?" ... 13
(12 COLOR PICS OF ELVIS)
Annette's R-E-al Love ... 39
Jan and Dean: Why They Spin Up, Win They Re-United ... 42
(12 COLOR PICS OF JAN AND DEAN)
Buzz Clifford Asks Your Help! ... 22

FABULOUS NEW CONTEST!
Win A Date With Bobby Vee! ... 37

BANDSTAND BOOK (A Swingin' Special Section)
FULL COLOR pictures of 22 of THE REGULARS ... 26
Myrna Horowitz News and Gossip Column ... 25
Meet Norman Kerr ... 53
Fan Clubs For Norman Kerr ... 30

FUN AND IDEAS
Pet Pals ... Over 340 With Loads of Pictures ... 34
Fan Clubs ... 55 Clubs Listed With Gossip by Shirley Gee ... 45
Records At Random ... News and Reviews ... by Lois Epson ... 49
Show Biz Quiz ... Test Your knowledge ... 8
You Asked ... The Things You Want To Know ... by Nancy Stratford ... 9
Hollywood Young Set ... The Latest News and Gossip ... 12
by Linda Lee Walery
Teen Problem Clinic ... The News In Pictures ... 16
Your Problems Answered ... by Elizabeth Carson ... 60

FULL COLOR PORTRAITS!
SUPER LARGE PIN UP OF ROY DONAHUE ... 24 & 35
ELVIS ... by ... JAN ... 42 ... DEAN ... 43

SPECIAL COLOR BONUS!
12 FULL COLOR PICTURES OF THE REGULARS ... 24 & 27

FASHION BONUS SUPPLEMENT!
The ABC's of Back To School Fashions ... by Jean Lacy ... 50
LATEST FASHIONS IN FULL COLOR!

SPECIAL ATTRACTIONS
Real Readers ... Our Reader To Vote ... 6
Reviews Of The New Movies ... Review and Recommended ... 48
Top Winner ... Your Letters To Teen Screen! ... 61

NEXT MONTH
The Teen Photo Gab That Change Robin Rebelled's Life (with a full page Full Color pin-up Exclusive!) & Another New Contest, Featuring All Your Favorites In Full Color!

KITTYHAWK GRAPHICS BIOGRAPHY
(1967-1981)

With Jan and Dean's career over as a result of Jan's accident, Dean turned his attention to design, which he'd been studying at U.S.C. during Jan and Dean's recording career.

Sticking to the business he knew best, Dean opened KITTYHAWK GRAPHICS, a graphics design firm specializing in music industry design and packaging.

In 1967, less than one year after Jan's accident, Kittyhawk was sharing office space with an enterprising young producer named James William Guercio, who came to Dean with a design project. Guercio wanted Dean to help design a logo for a new group Guercio was producing, called "Chicago Transit Authority." Using elements of the Coca-Cola logo design, Jan and Dean came up with a basic concept which was then given to a lettering expert to refine and complete. That logo, later shortened along with the group's name to "Chicago," was Kittyhawk's first major project.

In early 1968 Dean designed the first of over two hundred album packages to follow, "The Turtles Golden Hits."

In 1969 Dean designed the first of nine covers for The Nitty Gritty Dirt Band, a relationship that continues to this day and has resulted in three Grammy Award nominations for "Best Album Cover of the Year."

In addition to those nominations, Dean won a Grammy in 1972 for "Best Album Cover of the Year" for the album "Pollution" by the group of the same name.

Some of the album covers designed by Dean O. Torrence are:

NITTY GRITTY DIRT BAND
- Alive
- Uncle Charlie
- All the Good Times
- Will the Circle Be Unbroken
- Stars and Stripes Forever
- Dirt, Silver & Gold
- Dream
- The Dirt Band
- Let's Make a Little Magic

THE BEACH BOYS
- 15 Big Ones
- Beach Boys 69
- M.I.U. Album
- Love You

NILSSON
- Harry
- Nilsson Sings Newman
- The Point
- Scatalogue

LINDA RONSTADT
- Linda Ronstadt

ANNE MURRAY
- Annie

JAN & DEAN
- Anthology Album
- Very Best of Jan & Dean
- Gotta Take That One Last Ride
- Deadman's Curve

WALTER EGAN
- Not Shy

STEVE MARTIN
- Let's Get Small
- Wild and Crazy Guy
- Comedy is Not Pretty

SUNSHINE MUSIC 8

ALWAYS PICKING UP JAN & DEAN
FOR YOU!

WHAT DO YOU NEED? SEND YOUR WANT LIST AND SASE.
I'LL FILE YOUR NEEDS ON A "FIRST-COME" BASIS AND GET
BACK TO YOU—OF COURSE, NO OBLIGATION...AND IF YOU
DON'T KNOW WHAT YOU NEED, DOC ROCK PUTS OUT A SUPER
DISCOGRAPHY FOR ONLY $2!

SPECIALIZING IN
:::JAN AND DEAN
:::BEACH BOYS
:::SURF MUSIC
:::BUT WE GET IT
 ALL FROM FOLK
 TO CLASSICAL

LET ME "GET AROUND" FOR YOU!

DIANE MOEHRING VOSTEEN
1343-3RD GLADYS
LAKEWOOD, OH 44107

JAN & DEAN
60 PAGE BOOKLET

ONLY
4.98 EACH
PLUS 1.25
FOR POSTAGE
AND HANDLING
OVERSEAS
AIRMAIL — 2.60

ORDER NOW
ONLY 500 PRINTED
COMES WITH A 2
COLOR COVER ON
GLOSSY PAPER

RARE JAN & DEAN MEMORABILIA

SEND CHECK OR MONEY ORDER TO:
ALAN LUNGSTRUM
P.O. BOX 1062
WEST COVINA, CALIF. 91793

---

the air. The more things to occupy the hours of the day, the better.

This is the reason that Jan decided to continue singing as a single when Dean found it too rough to mix tunes and text books. Jan then cut a single on the Dore label and his manager released it in the Southern California area to see what the fan reaction would be. Although the sales were adequate, the mail wasn't.

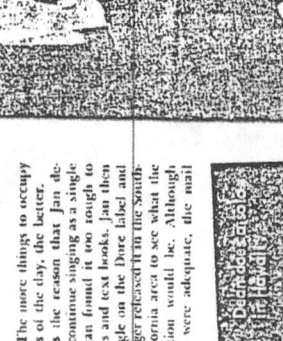

The boys' fans were upset beyond reason. They did not want to divide their loyalties and begged the fellows to return being a team. One young lady went on a starvation diet, which fortunately only lasted two days, but at least she proved her point.

As all this was taking place, Jan and Dean began realizing how much they missed being together as an act. Always good pals socially, they sincerely enjoy working as a duo.

A meeting was held with their manager, Lou Adler, and a plan devised whereby the youthful entertainers can sing together and still continue all of their schooling.

They will only travel during the summer months when there is no school. They will make local personal appearances or cut records only on the weekends when neither of them has any homework. This will enable them to fully benefit from all their interests and, at the same time, satisfy their listening public.

Both gentlemen, at one time or another, have considered giving up school for a permanent singing career, but after much thought have agreed that the entertainment industry doesn't offer as much security as the other professional occupations they have in mind. This is why they are giving college a whirl in a most serious manner. There is still a chance they will quit before graduating, concentrating only on music, but then it might easily be the other way around.

I asked Jan, who seems to constantly have rhythm bottled up inside himself, how he could ever be happy giving up music.

"Oh, I'd just have rock 'n roll piped into all the operating rooms at the hospital and have a real swingin' medical center going before," He was joking — but I knew just by the twinkle in his eye.

Dean, whose ultimate dream is to be an industrial designer of automobiles, told me he'd design cars with special radios that just play rock 'n roll stations. He was joking, too — but it wouldn't surprise me.

Individually, they are treating complete, mature and suggest from their parents. It wasn't always this way, however. Their parents frankly objected to a singing career for either of them—that is, until they had thrown their first record. Now the older folks are as hip to the music scene that Jan and Dean feel they should give up their jobs to become song writers or artist managers.

Jan and Dean not only look like each other (even though they aren't related), but share many things in common. Both are extremely athletic and dig the beach, sailing, bowling, horseback riding—or any other outdoor activities.

They often double date and this is where one of their basic differences takes place. Dean likes quiet, conservative girls and Jan prefers them to be just a bit wild and unpredictable.

Most recently Dean has been dating Roberta Shore and Trudy Love-joy (Frank's daughter). Jan has been dating Sherri Jackson, Annette Funicello, and Shelley Fabares.

END

Jan and Dean live it up with Connie Francis.

SUNSHINE MUSIC 8

SUNSHINE MUSIC SUBSCRIBERS' PAGE

Subscribers may list services, items, records, whatever they may have for sale or trade here for just a buck.

**** I have two records for sale, $2.00 each. One is Dead Man's Curve/Drag City, slight crack but plays well. Other is Sidewalk Surfin'/Honolulu Lulu in excellent condition, both moneyback guaranteed. Paula Moore, 33 Short Rd, Westfalls, NY 14170

**** THE PICTURE SLEEVE GUIDE by Jim Cates, 2nd Edition, lists 99.99% of all of the 45 rpm picture sleeves released in the '50s and '60s, including Ban and Spleen, of course. Send $7.95 to Words and Music GUIDE-2 4014 W. 21st St., Topeka, KS 66604.

**** Want J&D pen pals, and pix. Love to write letters, about William Jan Berry and Dean Ormsby Torrence. Paula Moore, 33 Short Rd, Westfield, NY 14170

**** Poster from the 3-25-81 Free Concert on the Beach for auction or trade: SASE w/ replies to Todd Vittum, 412 Quadrant RD, N. Palm Beach, FL 33408

**** JAN AND DEAN FANS--Subscribe to "Surf City," the Jan and Dean fan club. For $2.40 a subscription. Also join the fan club for free. Write for info. at the Jan and Dean Fan Club, P. O. Box 117, Arma, KS 66712.

**** I had many letters from people wanting a copy of the new J&D publicity photo that was in the centerfold of the last SM. So, I got a negative made of the original 8 x 10 glossy, and am offering to get prints made right here on this page! Be the first on your block to have an 8 x 10 glossy of our own beloved Span & Gleen. Merely send $3.50 (overseas add $.50 surface, $1.50 air) and them be patient a few weeks while the prints are being made. Just sent it in to ol' box 1166, & I'll do the rest! Why not, I always say?

LET ME EXPLAIN!!!

The rumors run rampant! Doc Rock died! Mike Kelly is no longer authorized to issue Sunshine Music! Michael is too spaced out on drugs to carry on...

Admittedly, it has been a long while between issues. I could mention that since the last issue, my book came out. Or I could tell about how my kids visited from California where they live with my ex. I suppose it might be worth mentioning that I moved this summer. Or tell of how the tornado that totalled our K-Mart (thank goodness) also hit the place we just moved into. Then there was the disruptive influence of the collapse of the walkways in that Kansas City hotel. My parents were there, it was my idea that they go, and I almost went with them. They tried to help the dying for over an hour before enough help came. My parents were themselves missed by just inches.

You know, I never announced any schedule for SM issues. True, one might reasonable expect the next issue (this issue) to be the summer, 1981 issue. Don't forget, the last day of summer is September 21st!

My real reason for putting off the summer issue was so that I could include a special bit story on the Jan and Dean show that I went to in July, my first ever, including Backstage with the Bel-Air Bandits. And that was written. Now the catch. Part of my authorization is that Dean goes over each issue before it gets printed, makes corrections, adds information, gives me feedback. He doesn't require this, but he did ask me real nicely, and I consider it an honor and a privilege, and it keeps SM up-to-date.

But the catch is, now that J&D tour so much, it takes a long time for Dean to get a chance to answer all the mail that builds up while he is on tour. Obviously, I need to plan ahead better and get the stuff for an issue mailed to him way ahead of time.

To wrap this up, The present issue you now have is a special issue I have put together in place of the one I planned and sent to Dean. It contains material of the type which does not need any significant input, especially the bio, which Dean wrote anyway! The material I planned for this summer issue, number 8, will instead appear in issue 9. OK?

Now, in theory, issue 9 should come out fairly quickly, since it is already written and in Dean's mailbox if not his hands. On the other hand, I hate to make promises. I just interviewed for a new job several hundred miles away from Lawrence...

One nice thing about being late foops, did I just admit something?) with an issue: it generates a lot of mail, cards and letters with gentle reminders of new addresses and old subscriptions that didn't yet run out...

NOTICE. THE NUMBER IN THE UPPER RIGHT-HAND CORNER OF YOUR MAILING ADDRESS LABEL IS THE NUMBER YOUR SUBSCRIPTION ENDS WITH. GOT THAT?

WHEN SUMMER COMES **GONNA HUSTLE YOU** THE JAN & DEAN MAG
Published 6x a year
$6 for 6. US/AUST.
US fans contact:
SHARON R.FOX, 5742 W.Giddings Street, Chicago, Ill 60630
All other countries $10 for 6 issue to Head Office - Stephen J McParland 2 Kentwell Avenue, Concord 2137, NS AUSTRALIA. Each subscriber receives a Jan & Dean supporter's card/photo

AMERICAN OFFICE: (US Subscribers ONLY)
SHARON R. FOX
5742 W.GIDDINGS ST. CHICAGO, ILL, 60630
($10 for 6 issues, $20 for 12 issues)

HEAD OFFICE: (All other subscribers)
STEPHEN J MCPARLAND
2 KENTWELL AVENUE, CONCORD, 2137,
NEW SOUTH WALES, AUSTRALIA

CALIFORNIA MUSIC HAS THE FACTS AND INFORMATION ON JAN&DEAN,THE BEACH BOYS AND ALL OTHER SURF MUSIC RELATED GROUPS AND SUB-JECTS. IF YOU WISH TO KNOW MORE, CONTACT:

SUNSHINE MUSIC 8

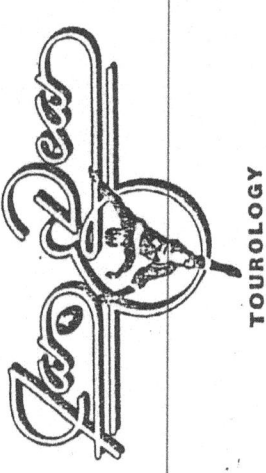

EDITORIAL

There is a new bootleg out. It is called OUTTAKES VOLUME 2. This is the second time Billy Berry, Jan's brother, has released material from the 2-inch Liberty sub-master tapes he has. This one has early alternate versions of "Little Old Lady," "Ride the Wild Surf," "Skateboarding," and "Sidewalk Surfin'," among other things.

There are three ways to look at this new LP. First, it is not well organized. It is as if no planning went into it at all, nor is it coordinated with Volume 1. Second, it is WRONG to release studio practice sessions, early takes, and bloopers. This is private material which J&D never intended to have released. It would be like putting out a compilation of first-draft pages from my book THE FITNESS FACTOR along with photos that were just meant as jokes, or which were rejected because they were not acceptable for some reason. I would hate it, and it would be an embarrassment. A bootleg of rare songs, out-of-print 45's, even finished alternate versions is one thing, but just scraps of studio work?

Third, looking at it as a J&D devotee, I love the two OUTTAKES lps. Getting a glimpse at the early stages of songs, variations in music and lyric, even errors and joking around, is an incomparable treat. After all these years of playing the records at home alone, I now feel as if I had actually been there in the studio at one time. I can personally thrilled to get to hear this stuff!

What do you think? Incidently, Volume 2 also has a fantastic excerpt from the PILOT, a song "Tick-Tock" which is so simple, yet one of Jan's greatest products. It is said that Billy may soon offer color video tapes of the pilot...

A V A I L A B L E   N O W   F R O M - -
C R Y S T A L   B A L L   R E C O R D S !

A Japanese LP called Jan and Dean "Oddities" on Magic Carpet Records! The cover is in color, and there are photos, both rare and not-so-rare...

Seventeen Tracks, including: TOMORROW'S TEARDROPS, early '60s by Jan//FROSTY THE SNOWMAN, SHE'S STILL TALKING BABY TALK, COKE 90" by Jan and Dean//and thirteen of Jan's post-wreck productions, featuring SING SANG A SONG, MOTHER EARTH, TOTALLY WILD, FAN TAN, and the legendary GIRL, YOU'RE BLOWING MY MIND!!

PLUS**A flexible, one-sided 45 of "Surf Bunky," not by Jan and Dean. Crystal Ball Records % Ed Engle
45-10 Kissena Blvd.
Flushing, NY 11355

TOUROLOGY

1979

FEBRUARY
- Keystone Club, Palo Alto, Cal.
- Keystone Club, Berkeley, Cal.

MARCH
- The Roxy, Hollywood, Cal.
- The City Yard, San Clemente, Cal.
- Cerritos College, Cerritos, Cal.
- Golden Bear, Huntington Beach, Cal.

APRIL
- Sweetwater, Redondo Beach, Cal.
- Dinah Shore Show
- The Roxy, San Diego, Cal.
- Chico Slate, Chico, Cal.
- Fresno Slate, Fresno, Cal

MAY
- Cellar Door, Washington, D.C.
- Busch Gardens, Williamsburg, Va.
- Bottom Line, New York
- Hard Rock Cafe, Hartford, Conn.
- My Fathers Place, Long Island, N.Y.
- Stars, Philadelphia, Pa.
- Paradise Ballroom, Boston, Mass.
- Great S.E. Music Hall, Atlanta, Ga.
- Coconut Grove, Los Angeles, Cal.
- Old Waldorf, San Francisco, Cal.
- Civic Center, Redding, Cal.

JUNE
- The Roxy, Hollywood, Cal.
- Golden Bear, Huntington Beach, Cal.

AUGUST
- Auditorium, Bend, Ore.
- Armory, Pendleton, Ore.
- Brown Stadium, Pasco, Wash.
- Armory, Salem, Ore.
- Armory, Astoria, Ore.
- Carowinds, Charlotte, N.C.
- Harrahs, Tahoe
- Old Chicago, Chicago, Ill.
- Palace Theatre, Cincinnati, Ohio
- Front Row Theatre, Cleveland, Ohio
- Dutchess County Fair, Rhinebeck, N.Y.
- Auditorium Theatre, Rochester, N.Y.
- Temple Music Festival, Philadelphia, Pa.
- The Bayou, Washington, D.C.
- Palace Theatre, Greensburgh, Pa.
- My Fathers Place, Long Island

SEPTEMBER
- Disneyland, Anaheim, Cal.
- Big Surf, Phoenix, Ariz.

- Fairgrounds, Anderson, Cal.
- Old Waldorf, San Francisco, Cal.
- Fairgrounds, Tulare, Cal.
- Sports Arena, San Diego, Cal.

OCTOBER
- Mill Run, Chicago, Ill.
- Harrahs, Tahoe
- Civic Center, Medford, Ore.

NOVEMBER
- Paramount Theatre, Portland, Ore.
- Paramount Theatre, Seattle, Wash.
- Cerritos College, Cerritos, Cal.
- Circle Star, San Mateo, Cal.
- Laguna Bowl, Laguna Beach, Cal.

DECEMBER
- Midnight Special
- Harrahs, Tahoe

1980

JANUARY
- Park West, Chicago, Ill.
- Old Chicago, Chicago, Ill.
- Holiday Star Theatre, Merrillville, Ind.
- Palace Theatre, Cincinnati, Ohio
- Beef & Board, Simpsonville, Ky.
- Front Row Theatre, Cleveland, Ohio
- Palace Theatre, Greensburgh, Pa.
- Agora, Youngstown, Ohio
- Center Stage, Detroit, Mich.

FEBRUARY
- Geo. Washington University, Washington
- Rogues, Virginia Beach, Va.
- Agora, Atlanta, Ga.
- Disneyworld, Orlando, Fla.
- Sunrise Theatre, Ft. Lauderdale, Fla.
- NEC Convention, Washington, D.C.

MARCH
- Fairgrounds, Colusa, Cal.
- La Posada, Phoenix, Ariz.
- Imperial Fair, El Centro, Cal.

APRIL
- Disneyland, Anaheim, Cal.
- Shrine Mosque, Peoria, Ill.
- Masonic Hall, Toledo, Ohio
- War Memorial, Nashville, Tenn.
- Kiel Opera House, St. Louis, Mo.

MAY
- Fairgrounds, Dixon, Cal.
- Harrahs, Tahoe
- Circle Star Theatre, San Mateo, Cal.

JUNE
- Greek Theatre, Los Angeles, Cal.

JULY
- Carowinds, Charlotte, N.C.
- Beef & Board, Simpsonville, Ky.
- Ontario Place, Toronto, Canada
- Meadowbrook Music Festival, Rochester
- Ohio Theatre, Columbus, Ohio
- Kings Dominion, Richmond, Va.
- Temple Music Festival, Ambler, Pa.
- Auditorium Theatre, Rochester, N.Y.
- Central Park, New York, N.Y.
- Rogues, Virginia Beach, Va.
- Westbury Music Fair, Westbury, N.Y.
- Fairgrounds, Central Point, Ore.
- Fairgrounds, Salem, Ore.
- Sunrise Theatre, Ft. Lauderdale

AUGUST
- Bay Front Aud. St. Petersburg, Fla.
- Lakeland Civic, Lakeland, Fla.
- Plantation Music Park, New Bern, N.C.
- Playpen, Wildwood, N.J.
- Orchestra Hall, Minneapolis, Mn.
- Plantation Theatre, St. Louis, Mo.
- Mill Run Theatre, Chicago, Ill.
- Holiday Star Theatre, Merrillville, Ind.
- Wolf Trap Park, Vienna, Va.
- Garden State Art Center, Holmdel, N.J.
- Hol Tin Roof, Edgartown, Mass.
- Paradise, Boston, Mass.
- Riverside Park, Agawam, Mass.
- Idaho St. Fair, Boise, Idaho
- Paramount Theatre, Portland, Ore
- Paramount Theatre, Seattle, Wash.

SEPTEMBER
- Disneyland, Anaheim, Cal.
- Fresno Fair, Fresno, Cal.

DECFMRFR

SUNSHINE MUSIC 8

LETTERS

Dear Michael,
I still think Dean isn't dead. Yes, I noticed his long hair, but it couldn't be Kathy because--you know, she isn't filled out.... I was in an accident a few years ago, seriously, and spent 1½ years in a wheelchair, until I saw DEADMAN'S CURVE on TV. That movie got me off my buns and now I'm walking again! So Jan saved me!
Paula

P.S. If you were riding downhill on a bike and your beddle fell off, how many frogs are in your oven?

Michael,
Do you suppose if everyone wrote to America's Top 10, Box 1019, Hollywood, 90028, they might rerun the J&D update?
Cindy

Dear Michael,
Is Kittyhawk closed for good? Are J&D married (not to each other)? Let me say that SM is much cooler than most J&D or BB mags--for one thing, it is always on time.
Laura

Dear Laura-- Dean cannot do design work on tour, but nothing is forever except the SURF! J&D were married but got divorced--Jan couldn't stand Dean's cooking. ḥemit oN Michael

Doc,
I think I know why all the clues about "Dean's Death" were planted. Reason 1: Keep It Simple--Dean never died. He was only critically injured. Dr. Jan kept bringing him back. Good Practice.

Reason 2: Think Big--The New Girl In School to Cosmic Cowboy OR What Do You Want To Be When You Grow Up? Finding clues to prove that Dean is Dead was fun but when he asked why they are there, dear Doc Rock made the game serious. But isn't that what Jan and Dean are all about? Fun, yet serious, simple, yet complex. They only reflect what is in us also: the comic-cosmic tradition contradiction: the tragicomedy that is life.

Likewise, people see things from their own perspectives, like the blind man feeling the elephant. Why would someone even think to look for clues? People expend a great deal of time and energy building ivory towers, yet a few well-placed explosive charges bring them down in seconds. We tend to do the same with people.

The triumph-over-adversity theme is replayed over and over, and so it is with the D is D clues. The clues are repeated over and over, yet never fully accomplished. Did Jan the singer want to get rid of Dean, yet Jan the med student want to bring him back? Is it Dr. Frankenstein and the love-hate relationship with the monster he created? Wanting him dead, yet wanting him alive? But, these clues are there only if you want them there. Jan and Dean are as simple or as complex as the listener wants them to be. Are they frivolous fluff or cosmic cowboys? Yes.
Beth

Dear Mike,
I have a Holland 45 of "Yellow Balloon" by the yellow Balloon's (sic). Did Dean design this?
Les

Dear Les-- Do trout have eye lids? Michael

Dear Michael,
Keep up the good work! Seems the new SM always turns up after a horrible day at work as the light at the end of my very long tunnel--SUNSHINE MUSIC!
Nancy

Dear Nancy, Will you marry me? Anon.

Dear Michael,
At the end of "Freeway Flyer" it is obvious what they are depicting--hear Dean scream? And recall that "big black and white job"? Hearses are usually black or white, and there were always "Surfin' Hearses..."
Laura

Hi Mike!
Do you know of any J&D video tapes?
Denise

Dear Denise: The legendary PILOT (see issue 1), the surrealistic adventures of Or & Wil is rumored to be a VTR boot soon! MK

Dear Doc:
What is "Coke Jingle" and "Pop Symphony?"
Jeff

Dear Jeff: In the mid-sixties, many top artists were recorded doing the coke jingle. J&D were among the very first. ALL of the songs were soundalikes to current hits (such as Oh! Pretty Woman and Paper Tiger, Roy Orbison and Sue Thompson). All were by the orig. artists. These were as well done, one, by the Supremes, actually made the Top 40 of one station. J&D's sounded not just like any one song, sort of a cross between TAMI, Freeway Flyer, and Old Lady. They did 4 versions, 90 sec, 60 sec, 30 sec, and 10 sec. The 50 is a short version of the 90. The 30 is great, and the 10 is brief. All four were released to radio stations on a J&D Coke LP. The two longer ones were released on an EP, which also includes Roy Orbison, Shirelles, and Four Seasons.

TYPICAL FAN LETTER

Dear Jan,

This is a for real, genuine, honest to goodness fan letter to some really great guys from a teenager in love.

You see all summer long this California Girl has been dreaming of some fun, fun, fun, in your little deuce coupe.

Don't worry Baby, I'm not a little old lady from Pasadena. I'm a surfer girl who's looking for good Vibrations in Surf City. So let's go surfin U.S.A. and not wipe out on Deadman's Curve.

At the hop I'm gonna hussle you and don't worry Baby I get around.

Now don't back down when I race your little honda at Drag City because I'll shit you don't On Graduation Day, let's go sidewalk surfin to Hawaii.

So Sail on Sailor,
Barbara Ann

P.S. Linda wants you to surf on into her life!

The EP, according to a letter from Peter C. (thanks, Peter), is available, apparently as a bootleg, for $10 + $2 postage from Disques Du Monde/Box 836/Madison Square Station/NY NY 10010. If you order, tell them Sunshine Music sent you and ask them to send me a copy in exchange for this free add!

As for the Pop Symphony, you might call it Jan and Dean's Greatest Hits with a Twist. Or, as Jan called it, a Pop Symphony in 12 Hit Movements. Jan arranged 12 hits from Baby Talk to you-name-it for full orchestra and Hal on the trap set. It is great, with good liners by Jan, photos of the sessions, and it is usually found only in stereo.

I would say this was a project close to Jan--he called it "Pop Symphony #1!"

Dick Clark rolled into town with his annual show at the Hollywood Bowl. Just the day before the big event I was at the 'Leading Man' shop on the Sunset Strip with Jan & Dean as they had to pick up special outfits made for the Clark Show. The outfits were light-Blue toreador suits and they certainly looked sharp.

Then Jan & Dean invited me to join them at the Bowl rehearsals the following afternoon. Since I had already promised to spend the afternoon with Eve Johnson (Troy Donahue's younger sister) I accepted for the both of us. Eve and I got to the Bowl early and the rehearsals turned into somewhat of a picnic. Sandwiches, cakes, coffee, and sodas were served between numbers being smoothed out.

I was with Jan and Dean when they picked up their outfits for the Dick Clark Hollywood Bowl show.

SUNSHINE MUSIC 9

SUNSHINE MUSIC
c/o Doc Rock
2708 Crawford
Parsons, KS 67357

To:

FIRST CLASS MAIL

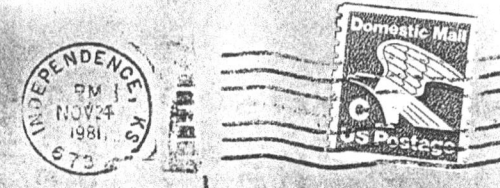

Roberta Shore watches Jan Barry roll for a strike. He made it.

SUNSHINE MUSIC 9

THE MAGAZINE OF THE OFFICIAL JAN AND DEAN AUTHORIZED INTERNATIONAL COLLECTORS' CLUB

Editor
Michael "Doc Rock" Kelly

Associate Editor
Frank M. Kisko

Copy Editor
Dean O. Torrence

Artwork
Honolulu Lulu

issue 9   fall 1981

Contents not already copyrighted are © 1981 by Michael Bryan Kelly.

SUBSCRIPTIONS

OK Jan and Dean fans world-wide, here is a simplified guide to getting SUNSHINE MUSIC into your mailbox safe and sound:

SAMPLE COPIES of SM are $1 in the US and surface overseas. Airmail, $2. SUBSCRIPTIONS are good for six (6) issues, at the rates indicated below:

	USA, mailed in envelope	non-US Surface	Non-US Air	Surface Envelopes	Air Envelopes
$5	$7	$7	$12	$10	$15 Envelope Charge is for Postage

Please enclose S.A.S.E. (self-addressed stamped envelope) with all letters.

★ *CHECK THE NUMBER ON YOUR ADDRESS LABEL. THE NUMBER THERE IS THE NUMBER OF* ★
★ *THE LAST ISSUE OF YOUR SUBSCRIPTION. IF THERE IS NO NUMBER, LUCKY YOU!!!!* ★

● DRAG CITY
By Roger Christian, Jan Berry and Brian Wilson

Just tuned my car and *now* mm she really peels, *a-lookin'*
~~Looks~~ real tough with chrome re-versed wheels
My ~~waxes~~ blue coral wax job, ~~she~~ sure looks pretty
Gonna get my chuck and make it ~~quick~~ out to Drag City
Gonna Drag City and *takin' on my* ~~wheels~~ *Run to them now*
Gonna Drag City, my ~~chicks are really singin'~~ *that'll she Jo*
Better yet gonna miss now
The deejays sayin on my favorite station *that*
Drag city races are the fastest in the nation
The rails are the wildest and the ~~rods~~
~~customs~~ cars are pretty
Get your doll, and make it now to Drag City *get some heavy gas*
It's at a city sprints a
Burning rubber, thick exhaust really fills the air.
Final tunes tacked-up ~~engine~~ and action everywhere
Checkered flags and wheels stands

Cover photo by Dee LeClair

Let Me Explain

Boy, I sure expected to get this issue out sooner than this. But you see, I got another great story to tell. Yep, we moved again. This time clear across the state, to Parsons, Kansas. I got a job here in October, and between moving and starting on a new job, well, you know the old story. Now my problem is finding a place to "print" SM for me. So far, the only place I can find here wants to charge me 3 to 4 times what the place in Lawrence charged. NOTE THE NEW ADDRESS FOR ALL SUNSHINE MUSIC CORRESPONDENCE ON THE BACK COVER!! IN CASE THE POST OFFICE TORE THE BACK COVER OFF YOUR COPY, HERE IT IS AGAIN: 2708 Crawford, Parsons, KS, 67357.

This is issue number nine (9). If there is a number 9 on your address label, then you'd better renew your subscription if you want to stay my friend!

Short Cuts

Guess what just ran out? The three-year performance contract that Jan and Dean have been operating under for, well, three years. One assumes that a new contract will be signed soon, but until one is, there is no Jan AND Dean, at least not officially!

The Bel-Air Bandits have gone the way of Papa, Aloha, and all the rest. A new band is being organized which will have all new members, no holdovers from previous organizations.

The Jan and Dean single "Ocean Park Angel" b/w "Blue Moon" (Holy Bomps!!) was going to be released, but will not now. "Angel" is really a wonderful record, sort of the story of Honolulu Lulu, 1981. Maybe someday...

DEAN TORRENCE PHASE II is a Japanese LP of songs which would have been used in the movie had the film company not decided to lease the Liberty originals. They were cut by Dean Jim Armstrong, Mark Ward, Gary Griffin, Chris Farmer, Bruce Johnston, and Hal Rippleyea, between '77 and '81.

The back cover has color photos of Jan, of the girl on the cover of the Jan and Dean press book, and of Dean throwing Oreos at himself, among other photos. The songs include ..l City, Drag City, Ride the Wild Surf, Sidewalk Surfin', Surfin' USA, W... ut, Barbara Ann, and Pipeline.

Notable in its absence is Dead Man's Curve. Noteworthy is Barbara Ann. You know, at the end of the LP version of Barbara Ann by Dean and the Beach Boys, Carl can be heard thanking Dean for suggesting and singing lead on that worldwide favorite. Well, on this LP Dino returns the thanks!

Perhaps the treat of treats on this LP is four new songs. New, sort of. Remember in the movie when J&D are playing the car radio while they are out parked. Did you ever notice that that is Dean on the car radio, singing the oldies Get A Job, A Teenager In Love, One Summer Night, and I Only Have Eyes For You (Silhouettes, Dion and the Belmonts, Danleers, the Flamingos). Well, here at last we have Dean doing these impressive tunes on a stereo, superior fidelity LP. I mean, you have to hear these songs to believe them. This is Dean at his peak, or one of them anyway. I was doubly surprised when I heard them, because these are different takes of these four songs than the ones that I am used to hearing for the last few years. The main differences are in the introductions and in the lead vocals. Anyway, thank your lucky turntables that these puppies

BACK STAGE WITH THE BEL-AIR BANDITS

The ultimate experience for any Jan and Dean fan is to get backstage at a J&D concert. Obviously, only very few can ever get to go backstage, and not just because backstages are so tiny. After X-thousand concerts in 23 years, think how many people would have been backstage at all of concerts combined even if only the most dedicated, mature fans were allowed back each time!

Besides, backstage is a time for relaxation, winding down (or up as the case may be), cooling off (or warming up...), going to the bathroom (yes, J&D are human like the rest of us), and like that.

On the other hand, in 23 years, how many originators and heads of Official Jan and Dean Clubs have there been? No more than a handfull, even if you count Dean's sister Kathy.

So, SUNSHINE MUSIC now takes all the fans BACKSTAGE AT TOUR '81:

Last Winter, Dean sent me the publicity material I mentioned last issue. With it was a note, "Michael, see you this summer." Since seeing me means coming to Kansas City, I was thrilled, if not surprised, when my program director at the radio station, Mr. Lee, told me last spring that J&D would be at KC's Worlds of Fun theme park, come July.

So, July 10, 1981, I headed for KC with my wife Buzzie and my daughters Corina (Ray Peterson) and Marlena Jeanette (Four Seasons, J&D) who were visiting from California where they live with my ex-wife. Aged 9 and 6, they know the album cuts and flip sides better than I do--I mean every lyric and background part.

We arrived at Worlds of Fun early, but not early enough. The outdoor theater was already half full. The first show was to run from 8 to 9. At 2 minutes 'til 8, J&D and the Bel-Air Bandits pulled up in limos, and the show started on the dot. It ran a fantastic ½-hour overtime!

After the first show, I went to the gate leading to the backstage area and joined the mass trying to con the guards into letting such great dedicated fans backstage. The guards refused all requests, as they should. But, Dean had written to me, "See you this summer." My problem was, how to convince the guards that I should get backstage?

I tried to get a guard to take my card back to Dean, but he, she, and they wouldn't even consider it. I was glad for J&D, but upset for me and SUNSHINE MUSIC. Who should turn up then but Mr. Lee, my program director. He did get a guard to take his card backstage to a DJ who was MCing the show. The DJ came out, and took my card BACKSTAGE to J&D's illustrious manager, Winston Simone. WS came out and rescued me from the clutches of the guards. So, through the magical gate I went, accompanied by: Buzzie, who said she'd leave me if I got backstage and didn't get her back, too; my kids, who told me they'd become Beach Bum fans if I left them out; Mr. Lee, who told me I'd get fired from the radio station if he got left behind; Mrs. Lee, who told me nothing but no doubt told Mr. Lee something; and the hoots and jeers of the other fans who asked me to get them autographs.

SUNSHINE MUSIC 9

At Worlds of Fun, backstage is an air-conditioned mobil home. At the door to the mobil home, my entourage was cut off, and I went in alone. Probably the most _____ (fill in with whatever you think is right) moment of my life. There are two rooms. The one I am in has the Bandits and Jan. No one seems to notice me. I peer into the far room. There is Dean. (Funny, you don't look dead.)

DEAN!!! My heart races, my knees knock (for real), as I casually stroll over stick out my hand, and nonchalantly stammer, "Hi, D-d-d-ean!"

He shakes my hand, "Hi, Michael, how 'ya doin'?"

Cardiac arrest. It's really DEAN, Burmuda shorts and no shirt (like, Kansas in July is sorta hot). Here I am, doing like Don Knots, and what does Dean, the perfectionist say next? "How was the show?"

MK   Only great! Actually, even better than a lot of the older shows people have sent me tapes of. All of the singing is great, and the new band is really good! Too bad you couldn't have done "Linda," tho'.

DT   Glad you liked it. I think the new band is really super.

MK   I'll tell you, it wasn't easy getting backstage here! They have good security for you. You can feel safe. Even when I tell people how I got here, you'll still be secure, because it takes a radio station program director and a fan-club head combined to make it!

At this point, there was small talk about they're coming to KC, and then someone came in, saw my camera, and asked if I wanted him to take my picture with Dean...

MK   You talked me into it! Uh, Dean, could you please hunker down? I'm 5-9, but next to you I always look like I am standing in a hole or something!

So, Dean did bend his knees and descend to my level!! Great guy! Later...

MK   Dean, my two daughters just sang along with the whole show-- they are right outside, and would love to meet you. Is it OK if I bring them in?

DT   ...well, sure, why not!

So, I went to the door, and called the kids in. Buzzie, Mr. Lee and Mrs. Lee gave me dirty looks as I closed the door on them...

MK   Dean, this is Corina...

DT   (Sings as he kisses 9-year-old Corina's hand) Corina, Corina...

Corina blushes, rolls eyes, and generally dies on the spot, overwhelmed!

MK   ..and this is Marlena.

DT   Hi, Marlena, how are you?

Marlena is stunned. Dean, in person. She bites her 6-year-old lower lip and freezes up. Then comes an awkward silence. I suddenly recall that Buzzie has a copy of the new mag (see elsewhere in this issue), so I tell Dean to hold on a sec while I go get it -- and her. This time, Mr. and Mrs. Lee are sure they will never get in when I close the door on them.

MK   Dean, have you ever seen this book? No? Well, look, it has all kinds of old photos--oops, that's Arnie, let's skip that page! But look at these old pictures, articles, pictures, and trade ads.

At this point Dean really gets into the book, then some officials from Worlds of Fun come in and distract him. Suddenly, up walks JAN!

JB   Hi! What's happening?

MK   Hey, Jan, look at this book. Here you are with no shirt on, and in this book is a picture of you and Arnie singing in the shower with no nothin's on!

JB   Yeah! Boy, these are good pictures. Look at this one. This is the best picture of me, because my mouth is like this (makes a face like the one on page 23, which is pretty good since there are over 90 pictures in the book).

Jan flips through the book, laughing, pointing, and commenting about the various pictures...

JB   (On page 13) That's Shelly!

MK   Shelly Fabares?

JB   Yes!

MK   Jan, these are my girls. They love you, could they get their picture with you?

JB   Well, that would be just great.

So, Jan sat on a chair and put my girls on his lap for a few shots! After that, I wander in to talk to the band. These guys have just finished a fruit bowl provided by the management, and have apparently just turned into fruits! I mean they are off the wall. I started off by tossing them copies of SUNSHINE MUSIC six and seven. Winston grabbed at them, blurting, "Oh, new issues of SUNSHINE MUSIC! No, I have this one..yes, this one I don't have! Oh, Boy!" I tell ya, it does a publisher good to hear that! Then, the fun began!

WS   (Winston Simone) Hey, Michael, do you know the band?

MK   No, introduce them to me, but let's tape it!

WS   (Into the recorder) Hi, this is Winston Simone from WWIN, BACKSTAGE with Jan and Dean and their band of Bel-Air Bandits. We're going to go around the horn here and have everyone introduce themselves, and like that!

JB   My name's Dean... (Big laugh from the band!!)

WS OK, I'll do the rest, Mark Ward, rhythm guitar, Chris Farmer, bass. Danny Behart on drums, Gary Griffin on ...
JB (Grabbing the recorder) Hey, all you SM readers, HAVE FUN! Can you dig it!!
WS Now, Jan, nothing off-color now...
JB Ban and Jean!
WS (Mouthfull of fruit) Gary Griffin, keyboards, Jim Armstrong, lead guitar. The rest of our entourage is filled out by Carl Grossman, Rober Stout, and Rick Knowls. I, of course, am Winston Simone.
B-AB (Bel-Air Bandit) Alan Shapiro left us yesterday.
JB Well, how did you like that, people?
WS You have to be there--all the time there is laughing, hooting, and interrupting. Jan walks across the couch, it all reminds me of the "interview" on page 24 of the new book.
WS As you can see, spirits are running kind of high here backstage. Uh, I think we're gonna sign off now...
B-AB How do you spell relief, Mr. Berry?
JB Whats that, one more time...
WS NO! We're gonna sign off right now...no, we're going to have some words from Gary Griffin. This will of course be printed transcript-style in the next issue of SUNSHINE MUSIC. Gary...
GG (Voicco Basso Profundo) Thank you, Winny, thank you very much!
WS Yeah, sure, Gary, what is it like, playing with Jan and Dean? What's it like being on the road?
GG Why, it's a honor, one heck on an honor. You know, when I was just a kid a-growing up in Cincinatti, I never thought...ha-ha-ha...that, I NEVER thought I'd ever hit the bigtime, but by golly I did it and I'm darn proud. (All of this in an exaggerated, joking tone. In fact, GG always talked in an exaggerated, joking tone!)
WS Did you listen to Jan and Dean records when you were young?
GG Oh, yeah! Yes. Uh-huh. Sure. Yep. That's right. Sure did!
WS OK. Now, Mark Ward. Mark, how long have you been a Jan and Dean Fan? Oops, Mark just left. All right, we'll talk to Rober Stout. Rober is Jan's personal secretary. How long have you worked for Jan?
RS TOOOO LOOONG!
MK Where's his tuxedo?
WS We retired him tonight.
B-AB For one night only--he's taking a sabbatical.

JB And Rober is a great announcer.
B-AB And, Mr. Simone, how long have you been Jan and Dean's manager?
WS Well, I've been with Dan and Jean, er, ah, Jan and Dean...
JB and the B-AB's (All hoot and jeer!)
WS ...we go back, well, since the '60s... (Note: WS is a young man.)
B-AB Have you been along that long?
WS Why, sure, I started managing them when I was seven years old.

At this point, I took pity on Mr. Lee (that's his air-name--his real name is Bill Lee) and Mrs. Lee (that's not her air name, but no one knows her real name) outside, so since they had been out there over one-half hour, since he did make it possible for me to get a message backstage, and since he would fire me from the station if I didn't, I opened the door and invited him in. I was clearly power-mad at this point. Forgive me, Dean, it won't happen again!

MK Jan, I'd like you to meet my boss from the station, Mr. Lee and his wife.
JB Bill, hi. You're his wife? Hi.
B-AB There really are radio people here?!?
WS Oh, Mark Ward is coming into the room now!
JB Bill, you know, when I recovered from the accident, I still had some problems. Tonight I was a little off on some songs--but there is still the second show!!!
WS Back to Gary, Gary, you were with the Beach Boys organization. How would you compare the Beach Boys organization with the Jan and Dean organization?
GG Beach Boys...Jan and Dean...er...ah...gol...err...Beach Boys? GAG!
WS OK, that's it for the Beach Boys organization. Now, how is life playing with Jan and Dean? What's that like, compared to the Beach Boys?
GG It is much smoother, playing with Jan and Dean. We have a new road manager, Mr. Salvol.
WS What happened to the old road manager?
GG Six-feet under...
WS And what is your favorite magazine?
GG My favorite magazine? Why, SUNSHINE MUSIC, of course! I have evry ish!
WS Rober, what is your favorite publication?

I left Dean with the recorder because I needed to go take some pictures of the band. Fortunately, Dean did not do the promos as I had written them--straight. He did them with that incomparable Dino humor! Here is what I found on the tape when I played it back later...

DT What is "ABC's?"

BG (Buzzie Gentry) "ABC's." He doesn't type real well. You read SUNSHINE MUSIC even before it is printed, you should know that by now!

DT Oh, thanks, right. "You're learning your rock 'n' roll ABC's with DOC ROCK, and "J" stands for JUST the two of us, Dan and Jean--er, ah--Jan and Dean, excuse me!"

BG Ha!

DT "Hi there! This is Dean Torrence of Jan and Dean telling you that you've got Doc Rock on your radio on Lawrence radio KLWN!"

"You're getting a rock and roll education on the way to your boogie-woogie degree with Doc Rock and Dan and Jean, Jan and Dean, 'cuse me."

"In the rock 'n' roll ABC's, "D" stands for me and my Dad, Dean Torrence, Jr. and Sr."

"Summer means Fun with Doc Rock and Jan and Dean, and a record, or something like that!" (Then, in his Spleen voice) an' I think that's jus' plenty!

When I came back, Dean was done with the promos and back reading the book again! So, I took it and autographed it. Turn about is fair-play, I always say! Dean didn't look too happy after I had defaced the cover, though, so Dean, feel free to order as many copies as you want from the ad herein. You know, as good as that booklet is, I kinda resent it, because a lot of the stuff in it I was planning to run in future issues of SM. Oh, well.

Now, at the concerts, one can purchase a "Summer Kicks" or a "Bel-Air Bandits '81" T-Shirt. But backstage, I had on my old "Bel-Air Bandits '69" T-Shirt. Not that I wanted to. I just hadn't brought along enough cash--no one warned me about the T-Shirts, unfortunately.

Back backstage, my T-Shirt caught Jan's eye...

JB Hey, Dean, look at his old shirt. Like I told you before, it's "Bel-Air Bandits," not "The Bel-Air Bandits."

At this point, I am ready to explode with excitment. Here are Dean and Jan, poking their fingers into my chest and debating good-naturedly about my old T-Shirt!

DT Yeah but...

ML (Mister Lee) No, it's "Jan and Dean's Bel-Air Bandits."

JB But all you're doing...

DT Listen to him, he's saying if you take "Jan and Dean's" off, it'd be "The Bel-Air Bandits," like it'd be the "Oakland Raiders"...

Papa/Bandit and Winston reading their favorite magazine, SUNSHINE MUSIC!

RS PLAYGIRL!

WS And your second favorite?

RS GQ.

WS Well, we're checking off here backstage. We look forward to sayin' hello to all of you SUNSHINE MUSIC READERS ALL ACROSS THE NATION and we're going to close out now with a little bit of a song. A little something we like to call "Goodnight Sweetheart."

At this point, the Bandits sang, acapella. I wonder if I could bootleg that?

One of my goals was to get some promos for Doc Rock on the Radio, so now that the tape recorder was free, I went back to where Dean was. I had to be tactful, however. I mean, you can't just stick a tape recorder into Dean's face and say, here, promote my show. Not if you want to get backstage again someday. So, noting how interested he still seemed to be in the new J&D booklet...

MK Dean, tell you what I'm gonna do. I will give you this book if you will cut some promos. I have got them written out here for you.

DT OK, I think you've made yourself a deal!

JA (Jim Armstrong) Hey, Dean, let me look at the book while you do the promos!

I'll tell you, folks. Congratulations go out to Alan Clark and Mike Lungstrum on that book. It was so popular backstage that if I'd had a dozen copies instead of just one (a gift from Honolulu Lulu--if I didn't thank you now, I'm thanking you then), I think I could have gotten the whole crew to come do a show at my house!

BEACH BANDIT

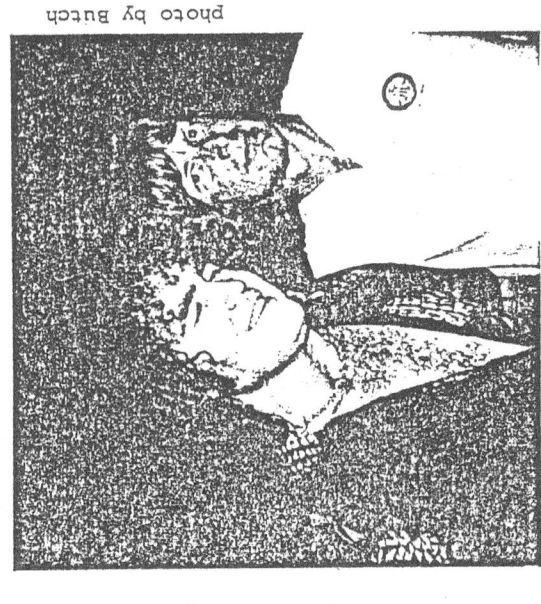

photo by Butch

Dot with Doc in the original "69" shirt.

JB   I know that, but this is much better, it sounds better. "Bel-Air Bandits," that's how I think it should be.

DT   Well, I know how you think, kinda like a broken toaster.

JB: Well, it's OK to be different if you wanna be.

MK   At Beach Boy concerts I wear it inside out. (Dean tried to ignore this jest of mine, so I jabbed him gently in the ribs and repeated it)

DT   They can't read anyway!

ML   You go to Beach Boy concerts?!?

JB   You know, that's interesting. "69!" That's amazing! Really, how did you get that shirt?

DT   Dean's sister Kathy sent it to me back in 1967.

JB   Oh, really!

MK   Yes, when you were still in the hospital.

DT   Yeah, that was one of our real shirts, one of our football shirts. Well, in the book (note: page 34) Jan shows off his shirt, his number was zero.

JB   It's like you said, Mr. Lee, but there still is no "the."

DT   Yeah, see, that's the way they really were.

Apparently neither Jan nor Dean had ever seen this article before. It has always been one of my favorites, since it shows Jan at the piano, Dean playing his guitar, the football jersey, the cast and crutches, a great profile of Jan, not to mention his apartment. If I'd known, I'd have run it in SM already!

MK   Dean, is it true that you know Jackie DeShannon personally?
     Oh, no, that's Bobby Vee! (Bobby Vee and Jackie starred in a movie, Jackie toured the US in 1964 with the Beatles, and this week I interviewed Bobby. He knew Jackie even before the movie they did.)

ML   No, he doesn't know Jackie DeShannon, but he met all of Mike Love's wives...

DT   Before he did!

JB   Back to the shirt, you still have that shirt after all these years! Fantastic!

MSL (Mrs. Lee) Wait, you got it in '67, why does it say '69?

MK & DT All of the shirts from the '60s said '69. Then, after that they always had the year of the tour, like '81.

MSL Jan, would you like to autograph a really old LP for me?

JB   Well, I'll check it out! That's from a loong time ago--about 1965. There you go!

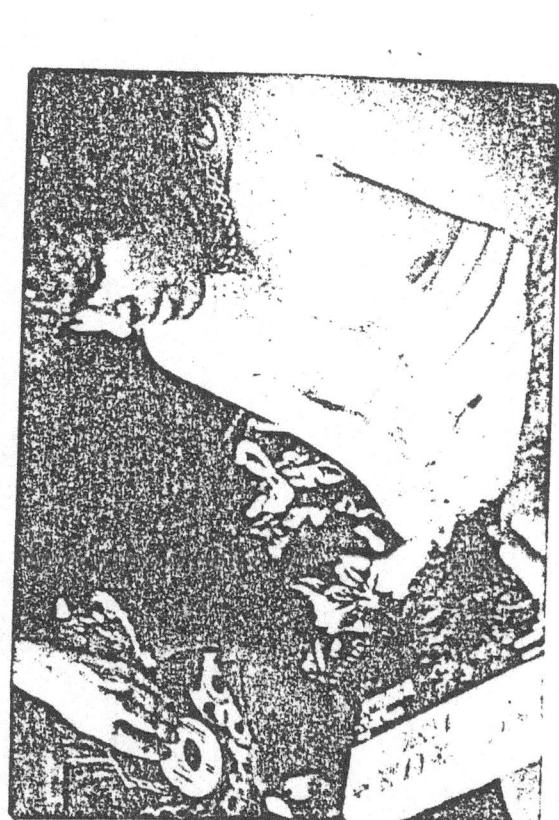

VOICE: Fifteen minutes to showtime!!

MSL Thanks. Now, this 45 is for my husband, Mr. Lee. It's older!

JB   (Sings) We go together...(coughs, picks up the everpresent Perrier)...wait a second...(sings again)...we go together, la la lalala.

MK & JB (Get this, singing with Jan) Let's go steady, ooh, you are my first love, oh oh oh oh ooh! (Followed by general applause and laughter.)

MK   I sang with Jan!

BG   You got your dream!

JB   That song was nice. I didn't think they were going to release that.

ML   Obviously, they did!

MK   Well, Jan, we'd all letter go so you can get ready for the next show.

JB   Oh, yeah, I'm just hot & tired...

MK   Thanks a lot for letting us back. It was a great first show.

JB   Hey, really, it's tremendous to see you wearing the old-time shirt, it's amazing.

MK   Thanks. You know, the last concert you did back in 1966, before the wreck, was here in Kansas City! Did you know that?

JB   It was, WHAT?

MK   Your last show was here just before your accident!

JB   No kidding?

MK   That's right, and two weeks later, you were coming to my town, just an hour away, so I didn't come to see the Kansas City show. But you never made it because of the wreck, so this is the first time I have ever seen you together in concert! I've been waiting 15 years for you to come back so I could see you!

JB   Wow! Wow! Well, you made it!

MK   Yes, because Jan came back!

JB   Well, Jan and Dean and the team Jan and Dean and the Bel-Air Bandits might do it again, I don't know...

MK   You mean, another hit record?

JB   Well, that's a long way to go, but...

MK   Buzzie and I love "Sing Sang A Song," and "Totally Wild!" Good records!

SUNSHINE MUSIC 9

had brought a tape along of a song he liked but Dean wasn't thrilled with. He asked the DJ to play the tape, and see what the listeners thought. The song: "Only a B...." That was ironic, since it is a song of real tragedy.

Less than a month later, word came out that J&D would be in Kansas City one weekend, and here in Lawrence the next. There were wild and kookie promos done by J&D on KC radio for that show. But I passed it up. I was a senior, but had no car and little cash. So, my plan was to cover the local motels and when they came to Lawrence, I'd meet them!

Instead, during the week between KC and Lawrence, my Dad called me over to see a story in our local paper. That was one of the worst days of my life, and not because I wouldn't get to see them.

Obviously, I should have gone to KC to see them. Imagine, J&D in person in 1966, with a 16-member band, horns and all, doing the current hit "Batman!" Judging from how they hoked up the DNC recitation in those days, you can imagine what they did to "Batman!"

Last month, I was talking to an aquaintance about J&D. It turns out he, too, was a senior in '66, in KC. His class trip was, you guessed it, to go see the J&D concert. He said it was incredible. Everyone was falling out of their seats, literally, laughing so hard. He said that it was not so much the songs, but all the cutting up. He said he has never forgotten it, or seen another show anywhere as good.

I asked him if he knew if that was their last show. He said, yes, it was. He knew, because the next week in class, there was an announcement that Jan had just wrecked, and that KC was the last show.

KOMA kept playing that tape of "Only A Boy." I learned it, and never thought it would be a hit. In the interview on KOMA, Dean had given his home address as the new fan club address. I wrote him, and that was how we became friends, later on. But, a few days after the concert that never was, I listened to KOMA while parked in the dark with a date. Suddenly, the DJ said, "We have Dean Torrence of Jan and Dean on the phone. Dean, how is Jan."

This was how I learned how really bad off Jan was, still in a coma. The DJ ended the call by thanking Dean for taking time out of his busy schedule to talk to him. Dean answered, "well...you know, I'm not really so busy...there isn't much to do anymore...not now..."

My date asked me why I was crying...

WANTED--by Doc Rock--RCA LP by John D. Loudermilk; tapes of oldie radio programs, especially Dick Biondi (WCFL Chicago?) and from the West Coast, Art Laboe--got lots to trade, too. Don't forget the new Doc Rock/Myke/SM address: 2708 Crawford, Parsons, KS 67357.

HEY! Like, if your address label has the number 9 (nine) on it, it is time to resubscribe unless you wanna be a stinker & quit!

JB   Yeah, well, those records are in the can, but there is a bootleg.

BG   We like 'em anyway!

JB   Ha-ha! I think if we take it slow, we might make it. But, we'll see.

MK   OK, thanks again. Dean, do you remember when we talked at Kittyhawk in 1973 about how your last show was at Municipal Auditorium in KC?

DT   I thought it was Oklahoma City?

MK   Oklahoma City, Kansas City, one of the two. Anyway, we better get goin', I guess.

DT   OK, you going back out for the second show?

MK   Yes! Thanks a lot!

DT   Nice to meet all you guys!

MK   Have a good show, Bandits, so long, and have a good vacation later in the week.

B-AB Thanks!

WS   Thanks a lot, Michael! So long!

MK   Thank you, Winston!

So, we went out for the second show. The first show had had several hundred people who had to stand because all the seats were taken. The second show was almost as bad (or good, as the case may be), in terms of seating. On stage, it was great!

Since the first show had run 90 minutes instead of 60, the second show had to start at 10:30 instead of 10:00 so that there could still be an hour between shows. Good thing, too, since I had been BACKSTAGE between shows! The second show went even better than the first had! Jan and Dean and the band were really up. The music was faster paced. The crowd was cheering constantly, instead of just between songs. Several songs had to be cut in order to finish in time for the park to close, but one song was added that was missing the first time around..."LINDA." THANKS, DEAN!!!

While I have your attention, Dean, I'd like to clear up the question of which city hosted the last Jan and Dean show of the First Phase.

In the spring of '66, a neighbor asked if I would babysit. Well, it had been years since I had sat on a baby, but they were desperate, so I agreed to do it. The last thing they told me before they left for the evening was that I should not fiddle with the hi-fi at all. The first thing I did after they had pulled out of the driveway was to put KOMA, the Oklahoma Giant, on the hi-fi. The very first thing the DJ said was, get this, "We'll be replaying that visit by Jan and Dean, who are appearing here tonight, again in a few minutes!" In shock, I stayed tuned and heard the interview twice. It was wild and kookie, but all I really remember now was that Jan

100

SUNSHIME MUSIC 9

LETTERS

Dear Mike,

Well, I see it's that time. Here is my $5 for another round! Someone asked about video tapes. I found a place through GOLDMINE called Video Heaven, Box 144C, Holland, MI, 49423, that sells the TAMI SHOW, JAN AND DEAN'S TV SPECIAL, and JAN AND DEAN AT THE FORUM. About $55 a shot, or 2 for $100. Why was issue 8 in a yellow cover? A cryptic reference to the song "Yellow Balloon"? A pun on the name SUNSHINE MUSIC? Symbolism of the last golden days of summer? And finally, here is a postcard with a picture of SURF CITY--at last we all know where it REALLY is--Rehobeth, Delaware!!

Kathy D.

Dear Kathy,

Delaware? Anyway, #8 had three different covers. Some were the usual pink, officially called Cherry. Also, a few were really pink, a paler shade than Cherry. But most were glorious yellow. Why? Well, I found out at the last minute that if I wanted Cherry, or even pink, I would have to wait a week! So, I went for yellow. No, I have no idea what color (colors) number nine will be!

Mike

Dear Mike,

For one dollar (refundable) you can get a video-tape catalog from Ron P. Wood, RM 1116, 6253 Hollywood Blvd., Hollywood, CA, 90028. He has a lot of good J&D tapes.

Louise T.

Dear Myke,

Here's my $5. I guess you know Mike Love got married today! His guests included the other Beach Boys, Jan and Dean, Dick Clark, and the service was done by Wolfman Jack who is an ordained minister!

Jim D.

SUBSCRIBERS' ADS

For Auction: Jan and Dean "Yellow Balloon" (Zip 936) 12-inch single on clear vinyl! Numbered, only 100 pressed! Will trade for Jan Berry Carnival of Sound LP. Ronald Coover, 1537 East Strasburg Rd., West Chester, PA, 19380

Wanted--Tapes of Jan and Dean concerts, and pen pals. Write Debbie Hash, RR3, Bloomfield, Ind., Box 250, 47424

Wanted to Buy: Liberty LPs TAKE LINDA SURFIN', GOLDEN HITS, POPSICLE, BATMAN, and 45s, non-Liberty releases, bootlegs, Yellow Balloon on Canterbury. Kevin Sprague, 491 Prospect, East Longmeadow, Mass., 01028.

CALIFORNIA MUSIC HAS THE FACTS AND INFORMATION ON JAN & DEAN, THE BEACH BOYS AND ALL OTHER SURF MUSIC RELATED GROUPS AND SUBJECTS. IF YOU WISH TO KNOW MORE, CONTACT:

AMERICAN OFFICE: (US Subscribers only)
SHARON M. FOX
5757 W. CLEMENS ST, CHICAGO, IL, 60630
($10 for 6 issues, $20 for 12 issues)
HEAD OFFICE: (All other subscribers)
STEPHEN J. MCFARLAND
2 MERIWELL AVENUE, CUMBERLAND, 2137,
NEW SOUTH WALES, AUSTRALIA

The Jan & Dean Criss Cross

ERK! Last time, ol' Doc plumb forgot to print the answers to the JAN AND DEAN CRISSCROSS! So...

Level One of the Criss Cross was for people with the answers to the recently issued Jan and Dean LPs containing old and new material.

Level Two was for those fans who have the more popular of the Liberty LPs, like Drag City, Little Old Lady, Ride the Wild Surf, and like that.

Finally, Level Three was for the freaks, or as Dean calls them (us?), the CRAZIES!!

Level One 1-13 Level Two 14-27 Level Three 28-47
1. Sidewalk Surfin' 2. Linda 3. Red Dodge 4. Baby Talk 5. AACSC-BRTASSN 6. Surf City 7. Popsicle 8. New Girl 9. Ride the Wild Surf 10. Drag City 11. Hustle 12. Tinsel Town 13. H. Lulu 14. Poor Little Puppet 15. Horace 16. Tell 'Em I'm Surfin' 17. Surf Route 101 18. Shift 19. I Gotta Drive 20. When It's Over 21. Boston 22. My Mighty GTO 23. Batman 24. Tennessee 25. Bucket T 26. It's As 27. A Girl 28. Philly PA 29. Julie 30. Leon's 31. Fan Tan 32. Black 33. Something A Little Bit Different 34. Wanted, One Girl 35. Chick 36. Frosty 37. Like A Summer Rain 38. Bonnie Lou 39. Coke 40. Gee 41. Tijuana 42. Cindy 43. Baggy Pants 44. A Date 45. Louisiana Man 46. Rain 47. Gas Money

LET DEAN EXPLAIN

SM Dean, two of the most frequently asked questions are, "Is Kittyhawk still open," and "Why haven't Jan and Dean been able to get a record company to release some new material?"

DT Well, let's take Kittyhawk first.

SM OK. I imagine that touring and designing on a schedule isn't easy. Your address has recently changed. Does this mean that Kittyhawk has been shut down, or is it sort of on standby now.

DT Actually Kittyhawk has been on standby for about 10 years! So that is nothing new. But it is still in operation.

SM Which means...

DT Well, the only thing I am not doing is taking on new work, per se. I'm still working with my previous or current clients, but if my clients do not have any projects, I am not actively going out pursuing new business.

SM Then you are slowing down, more or less?

DT Not at all. In fact, I'm moving my office to get bigger space.

SM How do you keep Kittyhawk so active when you are on the road so much?

DT I have an associate, and I will probably end up getting more associates.

SM Very interesting. Now, what about getting some record company to put out a new LP or 45?

DT There is a very good reason for that. And it goes back to the early article you did about J&D LP's.

SM In other words, there's record companies, and then there are record companies?

DT Exactly. Even within one company, there are ups and downs. They might be asleep one month, but with Liberty/UA, they were always known for not selling albums.

MK Really?

DT We could have a record like "Surf City," #1, and barely do any business selling albums. Now that is not our fault. You cannot sit there and decide that, creatively, this or that is why an album didn't sell. That is bull, it is not relevant. That company couldn't sell records, they never could. That's why artists learned that they might take Liberty or UA when they could get on it, but as soon as they could get off, they were gone!

MK Amazing. I was never aware of that at all.

DT ELO used to complain about that. They would be in the Top 10, and half of the LP's would be returned by the distributors, unsold!

Meanwhile, their friends who were also on the Top 10, but on other labels, were selling over twice as many albums! That was just the company's fault. It wasn't ELO's fault creatively or artistically.

SM Boy, that is a totally new perspective for me, one that I never imagined. But it is very enlightening.

DT That is why record album charts are crazy, they as often as not will reflect trends within a record company as much as anything. Liberty would be in good shape at one point in time, then they would go into a down cycle for a couple of months. Say they fired two or three key people, in a mid-stream management upheavel just when you have a record come out! That record is not going to do well, no matter who or what is on it!

SM That seems unprofessional.

DT Another thing, you should never have a record come out during a convention of people in the record-company business, because they all lose it! They are off in Hawaii for two weeks, they lose track of the record, then when they come back they feel lazy, all of their enthusiasm is gone, and the poor group suffers. That's the way it is, it is a dumb business. For all of the millions and billions of dollars these people can make, it is run very shoddily, by people who are not creative or just don't care.

SM You are speaking of things that went on, happened to you before. How is it today?

DT Well, better. They have learned to care, because the record business is down 40%! That is why, well, EMI has bought Liberty, Capitol and UA. So now we have the same company for our old stuff that the Beach Boys have. Yet, our reissues will not get the media push, the TV publicity that the Beach Boys got because they no longer have the money to spend that they used to have. So our compilations unfortunately will not get the attention the Boys' did.

SM So when ALL SUMMER LONG was issued, old Beach Boys tracks, and sold so well, it wasn't just luck or the innate worth of old Boys' tracks?

DT When you spend $250,000.00 on television..

SM I saw those ads all the time for the Boys' albums.

DT ... a quarter of a million dollars, strong early '70s dollars, just on television--K-Tel knows this, but it is expensive. Now, major record companies don't like to put big bucks into TV ads. Know why?

SM I have no idea.

DT Because if they do it for one act, then they are gonna have to do it for every other act. K-Tel can do it, because they have one

SM Then you have been able to interest labels in Jan and Dean.

DT I haven't had to try. I am running a probing offense. If they make a down and out, I'll take it. We have had many companies showing an interest, but why get involved with a label that does not have it financially or creatively? If they want to guarantee distribution and promotion, will finance a fan club, and all the rest, OK. Otherwise, why go to the trouble?

SM No argument here. As much as I like new material, from a professional standpoint you're clearly on the only logical track.

SM Readers who are interested in records from Japan, I can help you. 1. Dean Torrence Phase II LP $12. 2. Other J&D Japanese pressings (5 reissues of original LPs, 2 Japanese unique LPs) mostly $10. 3. Fantastic Baggys LP (stereo, original cuts plus three singles never on LP before) $10. 4. Super Stocks School Is A Drag (stereo, special limited issues) 2 copies only, $20, overbids welcome. RYUICHI TANAKA, 3-17-23 Kugenuma-Sakuragaoka, Fujisawa, 251, JAPAN. (Note from Doc Rock: I vouch for Ryuichi. We have been writing for years, and trading and selling each other records. He is prompt, honest, and packs records very, very carefully. Also, Japanese LPs are packaged fantastically, and have superb fidelity as well as lyric sheets most of the time.)

"There's No Surf In Cleveland" but we have lots of Jan & Dean at reasonable prices. Free lists or send us your wants. Let the little old lady get around for you. She has the time cause there's no surf in Cleveland.

DIANE VOSTEEN
1343-3 GLADYS
LAKEWOOD, OHIO
44107

THE MASKED GRANDMA

---

project that comes out every couple of months, they spend the money, but they don't have any acts signed to the label. All they do is lease the master tapes or make new ones. This way, no acts can complain. On Capitol, Glen Campbell would complain, "I have a new LP coming out, look, I just saw a commercial for the Beach Boys", and you won't do one for me." So if they do it for Glen, then Rondstadt wants one, the fighting never ends. With 50 groups on a label, you open a can of worms if you start that whole thing. They have told me as much.

SM Seems like a shame that one act can't get the ads, "just because."

DT You got the picture! I have often suggested that they do it by levels. The artists could attain these varying levels by sales and by longevity at the label. Being at each successive level would justify or authorize a certain greater amount of money spent in whatever medium. That way when an artist complains, it can be shown why he doesn't get what another act might get. Yet, he knows that he can earn his way to the higher levels by working at it. You get a number one hit, they push your LP, especially if you have been around a few years. That takes it out of the area of whim, or of who has the pushiest manager.

SM The way it is now, the squeaky wheel gets the oil?

DT Whenever a label person says, "I hate so-and-so's manager," that meant that that manager was pushing, but I also noticed that that artist always got a lot. A good manager with a different approach, not pushy, wouldn't make it. The company moves only when it is kicked.

SM This obviously relates to your selection of a label to go on in the '80s?

DT Sure who wants a label that you have to kick? Or one that won't distribute? People don't realize that "Baby Talk" was a national #1, the charts don't reflect that. Yet the song was #1 when it was first released in LA, then by the time that popularity passed, say about three months, it physically reached the rest of the country, those key West Coast markets were lost, and if a record is #1 everyplace, but not at the same time—it never makes national #1.

SM Reminds me of your UA remake of "Sidewalk Surfin'" in 1973.

DT A good example. It was released in California, and made #1 or 2 in San Diego. UA was owned by TransAmerica, who gave them their operating money. One month, TransAmerica pulls in the purse strings and says your not getting as much money this month, UA, because TransAmerica in general is not doing well right now. So, the record company has no budget that month, and an act with a new record gets cut off. All of this has no bearing on quality of records, so chart position is irrelevant overall. Yet, with this record, it was a hit in San Diego, but didn't get distributed in San Diego were also Top 5 nationally, my record was not heard or seen outside that city.

103

Louise Texler (tiptoes)
Dean Torrence (kneeling)

sunshine music

THE MAGAZINE OF THE OFFICIAL JAN AND DEAN
AUTHORIZED INTERNATIONAL COLLECTORS' CLUB

Editor
Michael "Doc Rock" Kelly

Associate Editor
Frank M. Kisko

Copy Editor
Dean O. Torrence

Artwork
Honolulu Lulu

issue 10   winter 1982

*Contents not already copyrighted are
© 1982 by Michael Bryan Kelly.*

SUBSCRIPTIONS

OK Jan and Dean fans world-wide, here is a simplified guide to getting SUNSHINE MUSIC into your mailbox safe and sound:

SAMPLE COPIES of SM are $1 in the US and surface overseas. Airmail, $2. SUBSCRIPTIONS are good for six (6) issues, at the rates indicated below:

```
USA, mailed    non-US    Non-US    Surface      Air
USA  in envelope  Surface    Air    Envelopes  Envelopes  Charge is
$5      $7        $7       $12      $10         $15     for Postage
```

Please enclose S.A.S.E. (self-addressed stamped envelope) with all letters.

★ *CHECK THE NUMBER ON YOUR ADDRESS LABEL. THE NUMBER THERE IS THE NUMBER OF*
★ *THE LAST ISSUE OF YOUR SUBSCRIPTION. IF THERE IS NO NUMBER, LUCKY YOU!!!!*

OCEAN PARK ANGEL

EVERY DAY THE SUN COMES, SHE GOES TO PLAY
  SHE RIDES A BIKE DOWN TO THE BEACH WHERE SHE'D LAY   -(JAN)-
WATCHING SURFERS WAITING FOR WAVES, HEY HEY HEY

SHE LOOKS SO GOOD, SHE LOOKS SO FINE
  THAT LITTLE OCEAN PARK ANGEL OF MINE
SHE LOOKS SO GOOD, SHE'S SO DEVINE,
  THAT LITTLE OCEAN PARK ANGEL OF MINE

IT'S THE KIND OF DAY, NOTHING CAN SPOIL   -(DEAN)-
  THE SMELL OF PALM TREES AND COCONUT OIL
WATCHING THE SURFERS WAITING FOR WAVES, HEY HEY HEY

SHE LOOKS SO GOOD, SHE LOOKS SO FINE
  THAT LITTLE OCEAN PARK ANGEL OF MINE
SHE LOOKS SO GOOD, SHE'S SO DEVINE
  THAT LITTLE OCEAN PARK ANGEL OF MINE

(BREAK--PIANO AND FEMALE CHORUS)

SHE LOOKS SO GOOD, SHE LOOKS SO FINE
  THAT LITTLE OCEAN PARK ANGEL OF MINE
SHE LOOKS SO GOOD, SHE'S SO DEVINE
  THAT LITTLE OCEAN PARK ANGEL OF MINE

SHE LOOKS SO GOOD, SHE LOOKS SO FINE
  THAT LITTLE OCEAN PARK ANGEL OF MINE
SHE LOOKS SO GOOD, SHE'S SO DEVINE
  THAT LITTLE OCEAN PARK ANGEL OF MINE

produced by Don Altfeld with Jan Berry/flip, Blue Moon (Holy Bompa!)

Cover Photo: Donna A. Stamatin

SUNSHINE MUSIC 10

LETTERS

Dear Mike,
   Please renew my subscription to SM! I have enclosed a money order for $7. Please send my copies in envelopes.
   Keep up the good work. I enjoy SM very much.
   Thanks for the article on DEAN TORRENCE PHASE II! I saw it listed in GOLDMINE and wondered what it contained. By the way, it was listed for $50.00! Thanks for directing me to Ryuichi Tanaka!
                                    Hang Ten,
                                    Linda M.

Dear Mike,
   How about doing a big article on Dean's graphic work? I can help you with some of the obscure LP covers he did!
                                    That's all!
                                    Lees B.

Dear Lees,
   I am working on such a project–at this very time! I am looking at issue 11 or 12 for a major story on Dean's stuff! OK? I'd love your input!
                                    Myke

SUBSCRIBER ADS!!

Hey! I print J&D T-Shirts. You can have it say anything about J&D that you like! Also SURF CITY, BEL-AIR BANDITS, etc. Write: Paula Moore, 33 Short RD, West Falls, NY 14170

AUCTION: A Jan and Dean BUTTON from the 1980 Dr. Pepper Central Park Music Festival. Has a red and white pic of J&D, the same photo as on the new DMC LP. Bids to: Louise Texler, 2825 W. 12th, Brooklyn, NY 11224

THE JAN AND DEAN ILLUSTRATED WORLDWIDE DISCOGRAPHY has just been released by Goran Tannfelt. The cover is color, and has three rare photos of J&D and the Little Old Lady herself! This has long lists for some 18 countries and lots of interesting facts. Like, did you know that all J&D '60s 45's were released in both black and red plastic in Japan? Or that their first LP in that country was JAN AND DEAN'S BEST HIT PARADE and was 10 inches in diameter? Or that their first 45 on that island country was THE GYPSY CRIED b/w LET'S TURKEY TROT'! Many sleeves and LP covers from all over are also shown. $6 will get you an airmail copy from the author, Goran Tannfelt, Lilla Nygatan 16, 111 28 Stockholm, SWEDEN. Nice job, Goran, a loyal SMer!

Send in your subscriber ad with $1, & wait by your mailbox!

SHORT CUTS

SMer Cathy out in Concord, CA, reports that Papa has a new single! It's on Blue Pacific Records and the song is LADY LOVE. The flip is SLOW DOWN.

Meanwhile, Jan is taking OCEAN PARK ANGEL b/w BLUE MOON around to see what kinds of deals might be possible.

Still waiting for word on whether the duo will be legally a team again in the near future or not. Some might wonder, why wouldn't they just naturally sign another three-year contract. Well, keep in mind that there are other things in life besides one-nighters. Like KITTY-HAWK GRAPHICS, and other business ventures.

Jan's telephone answering machine had a bright and cheery Christmas Message for any caller who happened to dial the right number in late December. You never know what you will hear on Jan's end of the line anymore!

Don't forget to check the number on your address label to see if this issue might be your last!

LATE FLASH!!! Word has just reached SUNSHINE MUSIC from California that Jan and Dean will have the new record out soon. Furthermore, a new Jan-Dean contract has been signed. Finally, Jan and Dean have a new manager.

Let Me Explain

Today is the 7th day of the 2nd month of the 2nd year of the '80s.. So, it is too late to go see Richard Hatch in the "Glass Menagerie." Sorry. After 10 issues, I see why pro-'zines are published on a schedule that has a Christmas issue written in July and released in October!

The reviews of "Glass Menagerie" were mixed, but personal reactions agreed that the actors did a dynamic job and that the overall production was excellent.

Next issue of SM will tell about a new J&D SM Sweepstakes; Wedding-Bell news; and the musical answer to the age-old question, "Who Put the Bomp in the Bomp, Bomp, Bomp!"

Oh, yes, the next LET ME EXPLAIN will probably be longer. Just keep those cards and letters coming, plus SASE's and subscription renewals!

106

SUNSHINE MUASIC 10

FROM OUT OF THE PAST COMES THE SOUND OF... DORE RECORDS!!!!!

Now, most of us tend to assume that DORE records is a thing of the past, as the Shirelles once sang. But, here in January, 1982, I got a package from DORE!

Actually, it was an LP, and it was sent to me by one John Greek, who is associated with DORE. Lew Bedell, owns DORE, and his cousin owns ERA. Thus the explanation of why some DORE singles (not by Jan and Dean) were released at the same time on ERA, and why Baby Talk was put out on the Golden ERA Series some years back.

What DORE LP did Mr. Greek send SUNSHINE MUSIC? No, it was not DORE 101, THE JAN AND DEAN DORE SOUND. Rather, it was DORE 401, COLLECTORS DELIGHT VOL. 1-VARIOUS ARTISTS-THE "ORIGINAL" CUTS.

Side 1	Side 2
Jan and Dean	Deane Hawley
Baggy Pants	Look For a Star
Such A Good Night For Dreaming	Like A Fool
Julie	Rainbow
The Zanies	Rita and the Tiaras
The Blob	Gone With the Wind Is My Love
I Don't Wanta Get Involved	Ronnie Height
Tony Casanova	Come Softly To Me
Boogie Woogie Feeling	Billy Joe and the Checkmates
Mike Gordon and the Agates	Percolator
Rumble at Newport Beach	Summertime In Venice
The Teddy Bears	L. J. Bugerbee
Wonderful, Loveable You	I Bought My Little Brother A Chemistry Set

Now, the reason that John sent me the LP was for my opinion, feedback on the LP and the concept. He asked me about the three cuts by J&D. He said that these were not on the K-Tel LPs which feature the DORE LP cuts and some other DORE tracks. (DORE sold K-Tel these they were chosen for this reason. Sorry, John, but Julie (also known as Oh! Julie) WAS on the original LP. Nice try, but the song you wanted was Judy's An Angel. Yes, this song was on the DORE LP 101, too, but on DORE 45 583, an entirely different version was released 21 years ago this month. And a much better version than has appeared since on the boot of LP 101 or on the K-Tel LPs which feature the DORE LP cuts and some other DORE tracks. (DORE sold K-Tel these cuts, just as Liberty sold K-Tel their tracks. It is amazing how much interest K-Tel has shown in J&D, between recording the songs and buying or leasing all the old stuff)

Now, Baggy Pants has the most superior fidelity I have ever heard! It beats boots, 45s, and LP 101 by miles! Thanks, John Greek and Lew Bedell!!

On the OTHER hand, the other 2 J&D cuts leave much to be desired! "The sound quality is questionable on 2/3 J&D cuts, but I guess these were cut in the garage." Gee, I wish Jan had never mentioned doing Jennie Lee practice sessions in a garage back in '58. Whoever that reporter was, he/she ran with it. I have even seen claims that Little Old Lady and Drag City were cut in a garage, which is absurd! Well, John, as you asked, I listened to those cuts, and the sound quality is more than questionable. It is appalling. DORE must have stored those master tapes next to a microwave or something. Since I have the 45s of those two songs, I can tell you that any problem in the new LP's fidelity on those two songs is not due to primitive recording in 1959!

So, in terms of J&D, the LP has problems. One incorrect cut, and two sound like hell. You have to hear it to believe. Let me offer Lew the loan of my mint DORE 45s for the next pressing (which John said might be in blue or clear plastic!).*

Moving on, John asked me if the photo of J&D on the cover of the LP was rare enough to insert as an 8x10 glossy. Well, I have that as an 8x10 glossy, autographed three times over the years, so the photo is not the rarest. I'd say, go for a really rare one from the DORE photo-session outtakes, if possible. John mentioned doing the photo as a poster. Well, I suggest reprinting the poster that originally came in the LP in 1959 (which I also offer to loan to DORE). When I called John Greek in California after getting the LP, he said that apparently that poster was only in the radio-station copies of the LP. Now THAT would be a rare photo!

John said that they were considering making the LP slicks available as "wallpaper," and enclosed several. Not a bad idea. SMers, write me and let me know what you think, and I will pass on the verdict!

The cover also has a photo of the Teddybears, but the cutline has Phil Spector and Marshal Lieb switched. John says that a second pressing (the first is not out as of this writing) would feature several changes besides the possible photo insert, the colored plastic, and the change of J&D tracks (1). For one, the photo credits would be fixed. For two, the cover might go multi-color, instead of white and DORE-Blue. Three, the back-cover listings would include the overlooked tracks (which are listed on the label) by Billy Joe.

What the LP needs most of all is LINER NOTES! I mean, for collectors to be tempted, they need to be--well--tempted. For instance, the BEATLES' RARITIES LP would sound normal to an average listener, especially to one who was unborn when the non-rare original 45s were hits. But the liner notes point out the small details that make the BEATLE'S RARITIES rare!

So, for John Greek, for Lew Bedell, for Jan and Dean, and for SUNSHINE MUSIC readers all over the world, here are some home-spun LINER NOTES for LP 401. LEW: I'D LOVE TO SEE THESE ON THE NEW VERSION OF THE LP!!

Besides, Lew, just think! By putting out the new version, the first becomes a collectors' item for real, and all us J&D freaks gotta buy both! Double your sales!!

*Late word from Associate Editor: Clear version has been released!

107

COLLECTORS DELIGHTS VOL. 1

All right, class, welcome to the Doc Rock School of Musical Cool! You know, it takes a Rock 'n' Roll education to get your Boogie-Woogie Degree. I know it took a whole lot of joyfull music to get my Rock 'n' Roll Ph.D. So c'mon, and dig DORE RECORDS COLLECTORS DELIGHTS!

For you Freshmen, let me mention that DORE was one of the myriad small labels that were the backbone of Rock 'n' Roll in the '50s and early '60s. In those Golden Days of Rock 'n' Roll, many of the big record labels did not yet take teen pop music seriously, and so small, independent labels like DORE flourished, providing many of the biggest hits and most interesting tracks ever cut into black plastic.

SIDE ONE

BAGGY PANTS--Jan and Dean

The initial three cuts on LP 401 are by Jan and Dean. After a year on ARWIN records in an earlier incarnation called Jan and ARNIE, Jan and DEAN came to DORE in 1959. One attraction of the label for J&D was the fact that their friend Phil Spector was at the label (see Teddybears, below). J&D's premier release for DORE was Baby Talk. Originally a local LA record by the Laurels on SPRING records, Baby Talk was a number one hit, a fact not reflected by most national charts because of the slow spread of the hit across the US in 1959.

After Baby Talk hit, J&D cut an LP for DORE titled THE SOUND OF JAN AND DEAN. That sound is represented here by three obscure J&D tracks which were not on that original LP! First comes the delightful Baggy Pants.! Subtitle on the 45: (Read All About It). Release # and Date: 583, January 1961. Composer: Bob Roberts. The humor which J&D would make their trademark in the later '60s, with songs such as The Little Old Lady (subtitled From Pasedena) and Popsicle was foreshadowed here!

Such A Good Night For Dreaming--Jan and Dean

Cut two's as much un-like the typical J&D cut as cut one is typical. Here we have that rarest of all rarities, a J&D love ballad! DORE release # and date: 576, October 1960. Composer: Hank Hunt and Barry Mann Released before Baggy Pants, Such A Good Night For Dreaming was on the last DORE 45 by J&D to make the national charts. The co-composer, Barry Mann, wrote many more famous tunes, including Who Put the Bomp, Come Back Silly Girl, Only In America, On Broadway, You've Lost That Lovin' Feeling, and Uptown.

Judy's An Angel--Jan and Dean

Actually, it was the flip side of this record, called Gee, that made the charts. Originally recorded by the black group the Crows, Gee is considered by many to be the very first Rock 'n' Roll record!

This song was the flip, "A"-side of Baggy Pants. Written by Jan, Dean, and Don Altfeld, it is a typical 1961 rocker. It even has a mid-tune recitation by Jan! And alternate version, without the recitation, was included on the J&D 1960 DORE LP. Who is Don Altfeld? Well, he was a close pal and song writer for J&D for many years. At this writing in 1982, J&D have a new, as-yet unreleased single just recorded. It is called Ocean Park Angel, and was produced by--Don Altfeld!

ALTERNATE LINER NOTES:

Oh! JULIE--by Jan and Dean

This unpretentious little tune was on the last J&D 45 issued by DORE, as well as on the J&D DORE LP. Flip Side: Don't Fly Away. Release # and Date: 610, July, 1961. Composers: Ball and Moffat. Often titled Just Julie, this song was a hit around Christmastime of 1957 by The Crescendos, a one-shot artist on the tiny NASCO record label out of Nashville.

THE BLOB--The Zanies

Horror-flick fans of the '50s know all about the movie "The Blob," in which a pulsing, sticky mass engulfs half a city and a third of Steve McQueen. Biggie label Columbia came out with a song called The Blob by the imaginatively-named group, the Five Blobs. The Five Blobs sneaked onto the Top 40 in late '58. The Zanies version was a regional cover with little national success, but a better sound! Record # and Release Date: ___

I Don't Wanna Get Involved--The Zanies

John Greek, still associated with DORE records, arranged this strange little cut. A member of the Wailers rock group, in the winter of 1957-58 John Greek appeared on the same stage with Jan and Arnie! Released more than once on DORE, original # and Date: Composers: ___

Boogie Woogie Feeling--Tony Casanova

This was probably not Tony's real last name, but the DORE records' records are incomplete. Record # and Date: ___. Composer: ___. This record sounds more like a variation on Jailhouse Rock than it does like Baggy Pants or The Blob. DORE was diversified!

Rumble At Newport Beach--Mike Gordon and the Agates

Rumble is the first instrumental on COLLECTORS DELIGHTS. Composers: Mike Gordon and Scott Engel. Release # and Date: 681, 1962. This was a colorful record, featuring as it did police whistles, sirens, et al. Not only that, unlike 99% of DORE records, it was on a yellow record label!

However, the real surprise from Mike Gordon was the flip side, Last Call for Dinner. Although supposedly composed by Gordon and Saraceno, this was actually an instrumental version of the Jan and Dean DORE hit, Baby Talk, composed by Melvyn Schwartz. Last Call had its own colorful sound--a train whistle!

WONDERFUL, LOVEABLE YOU--The TEDDY BEARS

DORE's biggest selling 45 of all times was To Know Him Is To Love Him by this group, The Teddy Bears. The force behind the Bears was Phil Sector. Songs he later wrote, arranged, or produced include Corina, Corina; Pretty Little Angel Eyes, I Love How You Love Me, Da Do Ron Ron, You've Lost That Lovin' Feelin, Deep Purple, Walking In the Rain, and some songs by a British group called the Beatles.

Composer: Phillip Spector. Record # and Date: 520, February, 1959. Flip side: Till You'll Be Mine, composed by Spector. Wonderful,

SUNSHINE MUSIC 10

COME SOFTLY TO ME—RONNIE HEIGHT

Teen-friends Barbara and Gretchen were doing some home recording, just for fun, back in 1959. They invited their boy friend, Gary, over to play a trumpet part with them. Instead of trumpet, he began doing a Jan-and-Dean-type "Dum-DEE-Do-DUM." Well, the girls liked it, and Gary dug it, so they took it around. Soon, the whole country was going "Dum-DEE-Do-DUM" with the Fleetwoods' #1 hit record. Unusually, the song was released on three labels at the same time. It was on DOLPHIN #1; this was changed to DOLTON #1; and simultaneously, the DOLPHIN parent-label, LIBERTY, put out the record. Country-great Bonnie Guitar arranged the tune.

Meanwhile, back at DORE Records, youngster Ronnie Height came out with a "DUM-DUM-DUM" of his own. DORE and Ronnie had a Top-40 hit in many parts of the country with Come Softly To Me. DORE Record # and Date: 516, March 1959. Composers: Gary Troxel, Gretchen Christopher, and Barbara Ellis. Even die-hard collectors will find this DORE hit version a new delight!

PERCOLATOR—Billy Joe and the Checkmates

In the early '60s, there was a popular, or at least well-known and widely-run Maxwell House Coffee commercial on TV. The trademark of the commercials was a musical beat built around the supposed sound of coffee percolating.

Today, most coffee is either instant or drip. But, with the nostalgia wave of the '70s still rampant, Maxwell House has recently revived the old percolator beat.

Late in '61, DORE came across Billy Joe and his band and their song called, are you ready, Percolator. Took that coffee beat right off the TV and into the Top 101. Since it was 1962 when the record came out, and the Twist was big, DORE bought some insurance and subtitled this record Percolator (Twist) on the original DORE 451.

Record # and Date: 620, January, 1962. Flip side: A suspicious instrumental, get this, Round & Round & Round, written by "D. Jay!"

SUMMERTIME IN VENICE—BILLY JOE AND THE CHECKMATES

Another instrumental effort by Billy Joe and company. This was a trademark of DORE, instrumentals. Many DORE 45s had flip sides that had a title, then below, in place of the artists name, just the word "INSTRUMENTAL" in large print. Venice referred to Venice, California, not the one in Italy!

I BOUGHT MY LITTLE BROTHER A CHEMISTRY SET—L. J. BUGERBE

DORE Record # and Date: _____. Composer: _____.
Not to be believed, worth the price of the entire LP, a Chipmunk-type novelty tune. See, there was this guy, and he bought his brother this chemistry set. Such sets were big in the '50s and '60s, when the US was afraid that Russia was going to corner the market on scientists (and thus A-bombs) some day. Anyway, the brother mixes stuff together and the first brother drinks it and turns into a bug, or a bee—Bugerbee, see... A true COLLECTORS DELIGHT!!

So, class, do you agree that COLLECTORS DELIGHTS VOL. 1 is Rock 'n' Roll Education at its best? I hope so, since this LP offers rarities and delights which cannot be gotten anywhere this side of a time machine, or, possibly COLLECTORS DELIGHTS VOL. 2, which will feature The Whispers, The Superbs, The Debonairs, The Fidels, The Jades, and The EntertainersIV! Enroll NOW!

Loveable You was DORE's, Phil Spector's, and The Teddy Bears' follow up to To Know Him Is To Love Him. Not a big success, this 45 has become very rare, a true Collectors Delight!

SIDE TWO

LOOK FOR A STAR—DEANE HAWLEY

After the mid-'60s, a hit was a hit. That is, when the Beatles sang Eight Days A Week or Jan and Dean sang Dead Man's Curve, they had exclusivity on those songs. If anyone else had come out with competing versions of the song, either for national or regional release, they would have had an ice cubes' chance in July of selling any copies.

But in the earlier years of Rock 'n' Roll, simultaneous versions of the same song were often big hits. Little Darlin', Alley Oop, Blue Suede Shoes, Earth Angel, Young Love, and Lollipop each was popular by more than one artist at the same time.

Well, Look For A Star was the star of all multiple-artist hit records. It was popular by FOUR (count 'em: 4!) artists, all at the same time! Garry Mills hit on Imperial records; Garry Miles made it on Liberty records (which later bought Imperial); Billy Vaughn did his version on Dot records (which rereleased Jan and Arnie at one point!); and, of course, Deane Hawley on DORE records.

Look For A Star had a boost for its popularity. It was featured in another horror flick, "Circus of Horrors." Then there was the flip side, Bossman. Remember Johnny Burnette (You're 16, Little Boy Sad, Dreamin') who died in a coating accident in the '60s and his brother Dorsey (Tall Oak Tree, the first ecology hit)? Well, the Dorsey brothers wrote a lot of hits, like It's Late and Just A Little Too Much for Ricky Nelson. Also, Dorsey Burnette wrote Bossman, Deane Hawleys' flip side! Now we all know why Tall Oak Tree was originally released on an ERA 451.

DORE # and Date: 554, June, 1960. Composer: _____.

LIKE A FOOL—DEANE HAWLEY

I don't know ZIP about this record, I am ashamed to write!

RAINBOW—DEANE HAWLEY

In the Summer of '57, a guy named Russ Hamilton made it big in England. He had a hit record on ORIOLE records, a big hit record, called We Will Make Love. In those days, "make love" meant nothing more than holding hands and kissing. But Russ Hamilton did more than "make love." He made big waves, all the way across the Atlantic, clear to the USA, where the FLIP side of Make Love, a song called Rainbow, became a big hit.

Deane Hawley of DORE liked the song, and did regional business with it. Record # and Date: _____. Composer: R. Hulme.

GONE WITH THE WIND IS MY LOVE—RITA AND THE TIARAS

No one at DORE, or anywhere else in LA, has any recollection of who the heck Rita was. For DORE, the song was a late release. Record # and Date: 787, _____. Composer: _____. The song is a delightful Chicano-Motown-Teen Pop blend, with as they say, a good beat!

SUNSHINE MUSIC 10

110

RETROSPECT: WITH RICHARD HATCH
By Lauri Klobas

It's been four years since "Deadman's Curve," the TV biography of Jan and Dean was filmed. The movie, in its initial showing on CBS in 1978 and again in 1979, coupled with syndicated reruns, has continued to garner fans for Jan and Dean and their songs as well as stars of "Curve," Richard Hatch and Bruce Davison. Despite the passage of time since the filming, the role of Jan Berry has remained a special one for actor Richard Hatch.

I recently met with Richard for a brief interview in Hollywood where he was in rehearsal for a stage production of Tennessee Williams' classic, "The Glass Menagerie." We talked during a luncheon break, sitting on a grassy sidewalk strip on Melrose Avenue after a quick jaunt to a health food store.

Richard grew up in Santa Monica and attended Washington High School. It was there he began acting in an effort to overcome his shyness, a problem he admits he still wrestles with. He was aware and familiar with Jan and Dean at the time, a factor that contributed to his interest in "Deadman's Curve." "I was a surfer back in school. I listened to (Jan and Dean) so I was intrigued that way. I love the music... I didn't know what had happened to them."

After high school, he went to Harbor College in San Pedro. He, joined a theatre repertory company in LA and remained with them when they struck out for New York. The company managed to survive and perform. One production, "Exercise," was directed by Richard. He remained in New York when the company was invited to Rome, a fortuitous decision as he was cast shortly thereafter as Phillip Brent in the popular TV soap, "All My Children." He kept the role for over two years. In 1972, after more study and appearances in off-Broadway plays, he returned home to the West Coast. He guested on numerous television dramas such as "Medical Center," "Cannon," "Barnaby Jones," "The Waltons" and "Hawaii Five-O" among others. In 1977, he was cast as Jan Berry in "Deadman's Curve."

He worked closely with Jan in preparation for the part. "I was fortunate because Jan was there, everyday. I spent hours talking to him...I set up my own meeting with him through a friend that knew him. He didn't know I was doing his movie. I just went and had dinner with him and spent a whole evening with him, talking to him

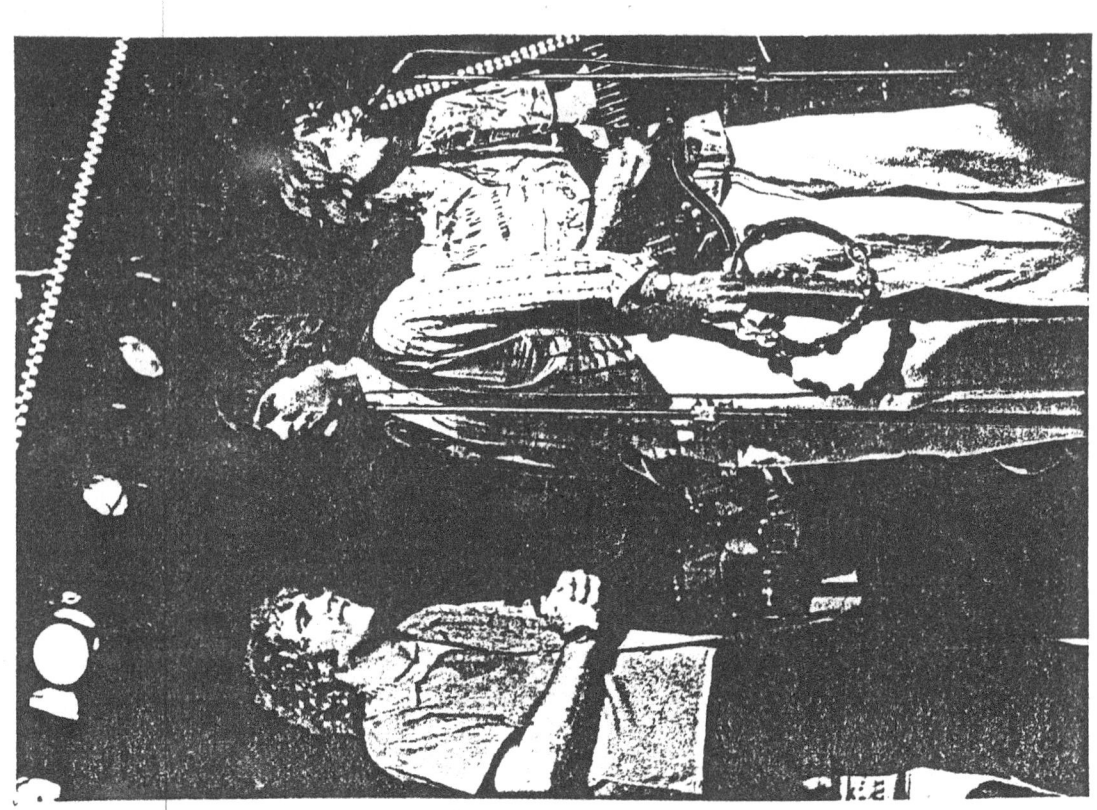

Photographer: DEE LECLAIR

and asking a million questions...he was talking about this movie that was going to be made about him and how excited he was about that. He didn't even know it was me! And so, I got some insights there and then. He was there every single day so I had lunch with him, I talked with him, I watched him move, I watched him walk. I followed him around the set, behind him--he didn't even know I was there...just picking up on everything about him. I was fortunate in having him there all the time and really being able to interact with him." Richard admitted that at the outset, Jan's presence on the set was inhibiting but he overcame that quickly. "(Jan and Dean) were always listening to our scenes off-camera. And it was very strange to depict two people, their relationship on-camera when they're right off-camera, watching the whole thing. They were very affected by the scenes sometimes, y'know, they couldn't stay and watch, they had to leave...I identified with (Jan) in each scene; so did he because he was reliving his past so both could kind of come together after a scene and it was like we shared a common moment...so we had a more special relationship during that filming that made it much more--I think--easy for me to portray that kind of a character." He told me he found it easier to play Jan after the accident than before, primarily because of lack of information on Jan before the crash. "People wouldn't tell me much about what he's really like. They gave me very general kinds of information...even in the reviews they said it was a little muddy in the first half of the movie then after the accident, it became very crystal clear and that was true. I had a much better handle after the accident than before."

He found it a challenge to depict a person who was alive and well and on the set everyday. A little confusion arose in the beginning with having the real-life people around. Richard laughingly recalled having trouble telling Dean Torrence apart from his looks-like-they-could-be-brothers co-star Bruce Davison. "I never used to be able to tell Dean from Bruce because their hair was the same length, they looked very similar and because I didn't know Dean that well. I was always making the mistake when I came up...During the first week of rehearsal, I'd come up and say 'Hi Dean, Hi Bruce,' and if I said 'Dean,' it was Bruce or 'Bruce' was Dean. I was always making the mistake...I think Dean and Bruce looked more alike than anybody. (Bruce) has a real funny personality just like Dean does, similar personality. They have a similar essence about them."

I was curious as to if, while portraying Jan, he'd thought of the problems Jan had faced.

"Yeah," he replied without hesitation. "The idea of that happening to me, yeah, really weirded me out. To comprehend something that drastic altering your life. You know, one minute everything's normal and the next minute you're fighting through a haze...I found it almost incomprehensible, the concept of that happening to me."

The role still remains special to Richard and is listed in his press bio as the one he is most proud of. He speaks of Jan and Dean with respect and affection. And even after all this time, he still indicates frustration regarding script and filming.

"We had problems because the script was overwritten." I did not understand what he meant by this and he explained. "They had three hours of script; that was supposed to be a two hour movie. If (you have) time, (you) rewrite...before you start filming...and make it tight. But if you haven't done that by the time you start filming, you have too much script. You don't have writers working on it. They'll cut a scene in half. They'll people slicing it. They'll cut a scene in half. They'll throw half of a scene and another half of a scene together and it won't make sense." A great deal of the script had to be junked, scenes that dealt with Jan and Dean's college careers and parts showing their partnership and friendship's brighter side. All that was revealed on the screen seemed, for the most part, negative. "A lot of things that I learned about Jan and Dean would have made wonderful copy and would have been very interesting to see...Towards the end of the filming, they only had so much money...I did my best to work what was there and to tie those things together that were thrown together."

The part in "Deadman's Curve" garnered him and Bruce Davison a large legion of fans. It also introduced Jan and Dean and their music to a whole new group of appreciative supporters. Many of Southern California's J&D concertgoers have been lucky enough to catch performances at Disneyland where Richard and Bruce have joined the duo onstage (see cover of SM #9). I asked how that got started.

"They just asked us to come," he replied. "We didn't expect to get up there, we just came. They said, 'Come see us' and we came. They yelled us up out of the audience and then it became a kind of little thing with us. It gave me a chance to get up onstage and sing songs and have fun." Richard indicated this had been something he'd long wanted to do. "It's a rush to get out there in front of a thousand kids, perform and have them yelling and screaming and singing with you. It's great!" he enthused.

I questioned him regarding rumors I'd heard about a possible sequel being made to the film.

"Sequel?" he frowned. He'd not heard this. "You know, whenever I look at the thing, a sequel doesn't bother me at all. If I read a script that's wonderfully written, that touches me, challenges me in some way, then I'll do that."

He told me his portrayal of Jan, "was the most fulfilling role for me because it was closer to me than most people would believe." His own sensitivity helped him with the part. "I empathize with people a lot," he confided. "I can feel people...sense people. Half the trouble I used to get into in life was that I took on on other people's feelings and burdens, not realizing it was theirs and not mine; so it was easy--it's easy sometimes with certain characters." Richard's own struggles with his intense shyness made it difficult, he told me, to communicate his feelings with people. He "felt very cut off from everybody, locked away from everybody," but learned to manage after years of work. In this sense, he empathized with Jan's difficulty to express himself. "I identified very strongly with him because of that."

He keeps in contact with Jan, catching up with him every now and then. He kept in contact with Bruce for a while after the film, "but the last couple years, he's kinda gone off, he was doing plays and he's been all over the country so I haven't seen him very much...For a while, we'd get together sometimes and appear with Jan and Dean at Disneyland."

His lunch break ended and we walked back to the rehearsal studio, saying goodbye as Richard closed up his bag of whole wheat pretzels. He headed back in to his "Glass Menagerie" rehearsal; the show opened January 2nd at the Callboard Theatre and will continue running until February 7th at the Fountain Theatre in Los Angeles.

Richard's plans for the future? "Hopefully, I'd like to do another play." Was the transition difficult, I asked, going from film back to stage performing? "No, because I'm basically a stage actor. I prepare that way, I work that way so therefore, it's not like shifting gears for me." He likes both mediums to perform in for different reasons and does not prefer one over the other.

He's interested in finding a property he can produce and act in as well. "I've got to create my own opportunities to do the things I want to do." And, as his press bio states, "Richard would also like to perform at the Roxy doing his own music and run the quarter mile in record time and learn to fly a single engine plane and do stand-up comedy and direct a play and a movie, etc., etc., etc., etc....."

Richard greets Jan onstage at Disneyland, May 2, 1981

photo by Nancia Attwood

Photographer: DEE LECLAIR

JAN & DEAN
P.G.P.S. SALE...
PRICING
GRADING
PACKING
SHIPPING
THAT YOU'LL LIKE
FREE LISTS...
DIANE VOSTEEN
1343 GLADYS 3RD
LAKEWOOD, OHIO,
44107 / 216·631·8444

sunshine music

J&D, Beach Boys, and all CALIFORNIA MUSIC can be read about with a sub. (sample issue $3 airmail) Stephen McParland, 2 Kentwell AV Concord, 2137 NSW AUSTRALIA. OK?

NEW! FROM THE MAN WHO BRINGS YOU *SUNSHINE MUSIC*!!

The Fitness Factor

16 Chapters, 65 photos, 256 pages,
just released by ARCO/PRENTICE-HALL!!!
THE COMPLETE BOOK OF BODY BUILDING FOR MEN AND WOMEN!

Available from your local bookstore, or send:
$7.95 paperback, $11.95 hardback,
PLUS $1.00 postage and your copy will arrive
PERSONALLY AUTOGRAPHED by mail!
2708 Crawford, Parsons, Kansas 67357

Michael Bryan Kelly, M.A., PH.D,
author of:

'The Fitness Factor'

SUNSHINE MUSIC 11

SUNSHINE MUSIC
c/o Doc Rock
2817 Crawford
Parsons, KS 67357

To:

FIRST CLASS MAIL

JAN BERRY AND
ILENE DIAMOND

Send your photo
w/ J or D for
display here!!

sunshine music

THE MAGAZINE OF THE OFFICIAL JAN AND DEAN
AUTHORIZED INTERNATIONAL COLLECTORS' CLUB

Editor
Michael "Doc Rock" Kelly

Copy Editor
Dean O. Torrence

Associate Editor
Frank M. Kisko

Artwork
Honolulu Lulu

issue 11   spring 1982

Contents not already copyrighted are
© *1982 by Michael Bryan Kelly.*

SUBSCRIPTIONS

OK Jan and Dean fans world-wide, here is a simplified guide to getting SUNSHINE MUSIC into your mailbox safe and sound:

SAMPLE COPIES of SM are $1 in the US and surface overseas. Airmail, $2. SUBSCRIPTIONS are good for six (6) issues, at the rates indicated below:

	USA, mailed in envelope	non-US Surface	Non-US Air	Surface Envelopes	Air Envelopes
	$5	$7	$12	$10	$15

Charge is $ for Postage

Please enclose S.A.S.E. (self-addressed stamped envelope) with all letters.

★ *CHECK THE NUMBER ON YOUR ADDRESS LABEL. THE NUMBER THERE IS THE NUMBER OF*
★ *THE LAST ISSUE OF YOUR SUBSCRIPTION. IF THERE IS NO NUMBER, LUCKY YOU!!!*

YOU REALLY KNOW HOW TO HURT A GUY
(As recorded by Jan & Dean/Liberty)
CHRISTIAN
BERRY
GIBSON

We've been going steady now for such
 a long time
And up until now everything was just
 fine
You say that you love me, but it's not
 the same
It's so plain to see that you're playin'
 a game
You really know how to hurt a guy
You really know how to make me cry
So don't be afraid to say goodbye.

Everytime you hurt me it seems like
 you planned it
I've talked to your friends but they don't
 understand it
When did we lose it, what did I do wrong
We can't break it up now it lasted so long
You really know how to hurt a guy
You really know how to make me cry
So don't be afraid to say goodbye.

If you look at me you'll see tears in
 my eyes
And they'll begin when you're looking
 at other guys
The ones that you look at really catch
 your eye
I know that they're not your kind of guy
You really know how to hurt a guy
You really know how to make me cry
You really know how to hurt a guy
So don't be afraid to say goodbye.
You really know how to hurt a guy
You really know how to make me cry
So don't be afraid to say goodbye.

 Copyright 1965 by Screen Gems-Columbia Music, Inc.

SUNSHINE MUSIC 11

WHO DID PUT THE BOMP IN THE BOMP, BOMP, BOMP??

Once upon a time, quite some time ago, there was a kid who wrote a fan letter to his idol, Dean Torrence. One of the questions he asked in the letter was, "Who really put the bomp in the bomp, bomp, bomp?

The answer surprised him. Quote: ?

So, it seemed that even Dean didn't know. Many years passed. The kid grew older, went to rock and roll high school, on to college, and finally earned his Rock 'n' Roll Ph.D. At last, he had the knowledge he'd always needed to answer the question, "Who..."

Now, there have always been songs with nonsense lyrics. Bass singers in barbershop quartets, street-corner acapella groups, jazz improvizationists, even Bing Crosby have at one time or another sung lyrics which might be spelled something like "Bomp," or "Bop," or "Ba," or "Pa." What we want to examine here is teenage popular music beginning in the mid-fifties, where "Bomp" was a major, identifiable part of the record--of HIT records. We have to overlook flip sides, LP cuts, and stiffs, records that no one ever heard and could not have had much of an impact on teen rock 'n' roll of the original Golden Decade of Rock 'n' Roll, the mid-fifties thru the mid-sixties.

1958

The way I scope it out, the year 1958 marked the beginning of the Bomp. The record, Jennie Lee. The legend, that a stripper of the same name had an enthusiastic audience, including Jan Berry and company, who kept time to her exotic act by chanting "Bomp!" The artist, Jan and Arnie, or Jan Berry, or The Barons, or Jan and Dean and Arnie. It is a moot point.

The important fact is that this record was a huge success, and influenced a lot of later records. Following Jan and Arnie, as the artist was billed on the label, came a slew of other artists with similar names: Danny and Gwen (The Submarine Races),

Let Me Explain

There have been a lot of changes and a lot of confusion in the world of Jan and Dean lately. For instance, just as last issue was going to press, I got calls from several parts of the country from people who had heard rumors that either Jan or Dean was getting married! Now that I have had a chance to check, it turns out that the rumors were just that--rumors.

Coming in future issues of SM--A compilation of Dean's design work, the J&D Sweepstakes, tour schedules, and some special offers to SM subscribers!

SHORT CUTS

THERE'S GOOD NEWS THESE DAYS!!! JAN AND DEAN HAVE *NOT MADE PLANS TO TOUR AND RECORD TOGETHER IN 1982!!!*

Now, how could this be good news? Well, ever heard of double-your-pleasure, double-your-fun? Well, Jan and Dean will be appearing, but not together.

First, Dean, As well documented elsewhere in this issue, Dean is doing concerts with Mike Love of the Beach Boys. However, more frequently he is doing shows with the New Bel-Air Bandits which will probably continue to include elements of Papa.

Second, Jan. Watch the pages of SUNSHINE MUSIC for big news and complete schedules for JAN AND THE ALOHA BAND SURF CITY WORLD TOUR '82!!!

Jan Berry and his new manager/old friend, Keith Ward, have handpicked the New Aloha band, five super-talented rock 'n' roll musicians with 15 or 16 years of experience each who can sight-read and play ANYthing.

Guitar, Dave Loe. Drums, David Hodges. Keyboard, Frank Jansen. Bass, Mike Montessi. Rhythm Guitar, Bruce Sorenson. Starting June 1, *Jan and this group will start a tour tentatively including Kansas and Japan!* More news on that next issue!!

What about "Ocean Park Angel" and "Blue Moon"? Well, dig this! Jan and Keith have gotten together with DON ALTFELD and ROGER CHRISTIAN! The result? A new HIT song for Jan, to be released soon with a flip side, Jan and Aloha on a great new recording of "SURF CITY!"

Then, planned for this Fall, a JAN BERRY LP including: The New Hit, "Surf City," "Ocean Park Angel," "Blue Moon," plus *previously unreleased Jan Berry written and produced material from the golden days of Jan and Dean, the mid-sixties!!!*

Meanwhile, the material being prepared for the Tour includes the J&D and BB5 standards, some classic Chuck Berry, as well as Jan favorites such as "Hide Your Love Away."

DIDN'T I TELL YOU THERE WAS GOOD NEWS THESE DAYS!!!!

Ain't It A Shame was recorded by Fats in 1955, and was a hit on black stations. Pat Boone recorded a cover version for the white teen audience at the same time, and had a big hit as well.

Ain't It A Shame could have been covered for the pop field in 1966 by Frank Sinatra or by Peggy Lee, but it wasn't.

Ain't (That) A Shame was recorded by the Four Seasons in 1963, and was a hit. It was not *covered* by the Seasons, just revived and made a hit again.

Why go into all of this? Well, as far as I know, all of the rock 'n' roll cover versions of the '50s were black originals covered by white artists. (Little Darlin, Tutti-Fruitti, Butterfly, Shake, Rattle, and Roll, and so forth.)

EXCEPT for one: Jennie Lee. When Jennie Lee came out on ARWIN records, it sounded black. There was an artist known as Billy Ward and his Dominoes. Their style was very black-mellow. Their first hit was St. Therese of the Roses on Decca in 1956, not exactly a rock 'n' roll classic. Then they hit on, of all labels, LIBERTY(!) with more mellow sounds in 1957, with revivals of the old songs Stardust and Deep Purple (each revived again in the early '60s by Nino Tempo and April Stevens, brother and sister act).

Their last chart record was a true cover version, their close copy of ARWIN'S tune Jennie Lee. Far from being in the mellow style associated with Billy Ward and his Dominoes, this cover for the black audience was if anything more rocking and raunchy than ARWIN'S.

Myke: I was surprised when I found out that Billy Ward had covered Jennie Lee. True, theirs made only a small splash nationally, whereas yours hit the top of the chart. But...a black artist covering a white record???

Dean: Well, they figured it was the other way around. They thought we were stealing the black sound, so they felt it was OK for the black artist to cover the white artist's song.

In 1965, an interviewer asked Jan who influenced him musically. His answer? The Monotones! They weren't Bompers, but their hit Book of Love was highlighted by a bass part taken from the old commercial, "You'll wonder where the yellow went when you brush your teeth with Pepsodent."

One other source of inspiration for the Bomp has been suggested here and there; a record by the Diamonds called She Say (Oom Dooby Doom). According to Joel Whitburn's RECORD RESEARCH, She Say debuted on Billboard in February of 1959, nine months after Jennie Lee debuted. So much for that as an influence.

So getting back on track, The Bomp was put in The Bomp Bomp Bomp by Jennie Lee! In a white original version and a black cover version!

Where did the Bomp turn up next? Well, you may be familiar with a little number called Baby Talk. In the LA area, a group called The Laurels on Spring records released this song, but Jan and Dean did a slightly later version and topped the charts nationally in late 1959.

After this point, it began to look as if the Bomp was just about dead, to paraphrase Dean. Until the Spring of 1961, when a B I G popular record called Blue Moon was released by the Marcels. Blue Moon had been a standard ballad for decades, but when the Marcels applied Jan Berry's Bomp to it, it took on a whole new image as a song.

Ernie Maresca was no dummy. He was a song writer. He wrote many hit records for Dion DiMuci, including Runaround Sue, and he wrote and sang a hit of his own, Shout! Shout! (Knock Yourself Out). When Ernie heard the Marcels' record, he knew there was more gold to be had out of them there Bomps. So, he wrote a song which was simply full of Bomps.

Now, Ernie was no dummy, as I said, and he knew that the Bomps had originated with Jan. So, he copied the title of Jennie Lee & came up with another two-name chick, Barbara Ann.

He even had a demonstration record of Barbara Ann cut. Much to his surprise, the demo record was actually released in spite of poor fidelity. It was released as being recorded by the Regents, and the composer credits were listed as Fred Fassert. Somewhere, Ernie was lost in the shuffle. Oh, well.

Jennie Lee (twice), then Baby Talk, later Blue Moon, followed rapidly by Barbara Ann.

Jan Berry knew that those Bomps were his, so he got back into the act in a big way. In the Summer of '61, he took the recent hit of Blue Moon and said, hummm, Bomps and old songs, eh?

First thing Dean knew, Jan had come up with a song that the Larry Clinton band had recorded, in September of 1938 and with Bea Wain as singer, had made a hit that Winter. Heart and Soul, Bomp-style, was the result!

Next it was the Regents' turn again. Their follow-up to Barbara Ann was watered down in terms of Bomps, but still had a lot: Runaround.

Exit the Regents.

Enter Barry Mann. Barry wrote a lot of songs, both with and without his wife, Cynthia Weil. These include: She Say (Oom Dooby Doom), Blame It On the Bossa Nova, Sweet Little You, I Love How You Love Me, Come Back Silly Girl, Patches, I GOTTA DRIVE, Uptown, He's Sure the Boy I Love, On Broadway, You've Lost that Lovin' Feelin', and many more.

He had one big early rock 'n' roll hit as a singer-- a song he wrote called Who Put The Bomp (In the Bomp, Bomp, Bomp)? Jan and Dean answered this question on an early Liberty flip side and an LP, with lyrics stating "We put the Bomp in the Bomp, Bomp, Bomp"!

The Marcels' huge success with Blue Moon, not to mention Jan's upbeat Heart and Soul led to another old standard's being revived with Bomps. Heartaches has been overshadowed into oblivion by Blue Moon, yet Heartaches, the Marcels' second record made the top 10 late in 1961.

Quick as a Bomp, the Marcels did another follow up, another revival with Bomps, My Melancholy Baby. Now, Melancholy has long been a song supposedly always requested by drunk bar flies. So, the Marcels began their version with the same Bomps as in Blue Moon. Then, a harsh, intoxicated voice interrupts: "Ah, not that again! Sing Melancholy Baby." "All right, we will!" answer the Marcels in unison! And they do! Almost made the top 40!

Exit the Marcels.

Enter the Beach Boys. (We used to call them the BB5, sort of a take-off on the Dave Clark Five-DC5.)

The Beach Boys had been Jan and Dean friends/fans for many years. So it should not have been a surprise when the first hit by the BB5 in early '62 was a close variation on Baby Talk. Same Bomps, same structure to the song, just singing about surfing is all. This always puzzled me, since all my reading has indicated that only the BB5 drummer what's-his-name ever surfed...

Don and Juan (What's Your Name), Dean and Mark, Travis and Bob, and Bud and Travis (Tell Him No), Bruce and Terry (Summer Means Fun), Tony and Joe (The Freeze, July 1958), and Dean and Jean (Tra La La Suzy, HeyJean, Hey Dean! both 1963). To name a few.

Now, you gotta keep in mind that 1958 was still the very early days of rock 'n' roll. You heard it on maybe one or two local stations, but few people had a chance to see artists either live or on TV. I mean, Jennie Lee was such an early record that it was released on both 45 (invented at RCA) and on 78!

As a result, many people, never seeing Jan and Dean and/or Arnie, thought they should be black to sing like that. Moreover, at least one artist put its music where its mouth was.

Ever heard the term "cover version"? These days the term is loosely and irresponsibly used to indicate that a song on a single or an LP was previously recorded, probably as a hit 45, by another artist.

The real meaning of "cover version" is when an artist who sings to one audience records a song which another artist who sings to a different audience has already recorded and made a current hit.

The best example of a cover version can be seen with Fats and Pats. See, Fats Domino had a lot of hits, even back in the '40s before rock 'n' roll. But in the '50s, white radio stations were not about to play Fats' records like Ain't It A Shame on the airwaves! So, nice-guy Pat Boone (descendant of Daniel) came along and recorded the same songs, "covering" them for the white audiences. Pat did not steal any sales from Fats. Pat's records were heard by an audience who would never in a million years have listened to or bought Fats' records.

Recently, Fats was performing in New Orleans, when he spotted Pat in the audience. He brought Pat up on stage and thanked Pat for making such big hits with Fats' own songs. Without the white cover versions, said Fats, my songs would never have become the classics they did. At that point, Pat and Fats sang a series of duets of the old hits together!

Blueberry Hill was originally a hit in 1940, sung by Ray Eberly with the Glen Miller Orchestra. Fats recorded the song in 1956 and had a bit hit, but not a cover hit-- the song was no longer a hit with Swing fans when the black audiences made Fats' version a hit.

SUNSHINE MUSIC 11

Surf City USA Concert Slated

"Surf City, USA Concert," featuring Dean Torrence of the duo Jan and Dean and Mike Love of Beach Boys fame, is certain to attract a good portion of the 100,000 students expected to converge on South Padre Island during Spring Break 1982.

The free concert is slated for Thursday, March 18 from 1 to 3:30 p.m. at the Island cabana beach area north of the Pavilion. In case of bad weather, the concert will be postponed to March 19 and 20.

Many of the students who grew up with Jan and Dean and Beach Boys tunes will recall the surprising duo that burst upon the 1958 music scene, tragically disappeared in 1966 and then reappeared miraculously in 1978.

The surprising group recorded their first hit about a friend's stripper girlfriend on a home tape recorder in their family garage. The song, "Jenny Lee," hit number one in most markets and Jan Berry and Dean Torrence were on their way to rock 'n roll stardom while they still attended college.

Between 1958 and 1966, Jan and Dean obtained top chart status for 25 songs, with seven of them in the Top 10. But their skyrocketing careers were abruptly halted when Jan was involved in a near-fatal accident. Jan's unfortunate twist of fate left him in a state of aphasia where he had to learn to read, write, walk and talk again at the age of 26.

During Jan's long recovery, Dean turned his attention to design, which he had studied at U.S.C. and began a very successful graphics company, Kittyhawk Graphics, which specialized in music industry packaging, advertising and merchandising. He has designed album covers for The Beach Boys, Steve Martin, Nitty Gritty Dirt Band, Nilsson, Anne Murray, Linda Ronstadt and Walter Egan. Four of his albums have been nominated for Grammys, with one winning the best album of the year honor.

Jan and Dean reappeared as a group in 1978, after a 12-year absence, just about as surprisingly as they started: in a feature television film, "Deadman's Curve," which told the story of Jan and Dean to millions. This reappearance is what Dean terms, "the Second Phase," and the band still spreads the same musical magic that they produced so well for so long. Dean says the music cannot be "oldies," or go through a "revival," because the tunes have stood on their own throughout the 12-year absence of Jan and Dean.

"People want to hear sunshine music in summer and winter," Dean explains. "It is not always seasonal. The music of Jan and Dean is pretty much timeless and evokes a happy response from people. It doesn't seem to matter who does these tunes, it just seems to work."

The current Jan and Dean following of young people in their late teens and early twenties bears him out. "They don't attend the concerts out of nostalgia," he says. "They come because the music is good rock 'n roll."

Since the television special, "Deadman's Curve," Jan and Dean have toured with The Beach Boys band and on their own, with the Papa Doo Run Run band. They recently performed at the Band Shell in Daytona, Fl.

According to Dean, Texas has proven to be one of the strongest areas of followship for Jan and Dean music. "In the Sixties, we spent a lot of time in Texas," he says, although this will be his first trip to the island.

"I've heard stories of Spring Break on South Padre Island and I'm looking forward to being there," he said.

The concert will also mark the first time Torrence and Love will "officially" combine their musical styles on the stage, although they have worked with each other on numerous occasions.

"This will be the first time we'll just kind of combine them," he said. "It's going to be quite exciting for us."

Mike Love has been featured as the leader of The Beach Boys band since its inception in the early 1960s. Not only has he serviced as the band's leading singer and spokesman, but he has also contributed to

(Continued On Page 19)

...*actually p. 21*...

MIKE & DEAN

The Beach Boys' Mike Love

Jan and Dean's Dean Torrence

Speaking of Jan and Dean, Jennie Lee came back to haunt the airwaves in the Spring of 1962 just like Baby Talk did. But whereas Baby Talk came back as Surfin', Jennie Lee came back as Tennessee!

Tennessee is clearly the champion Bomp song of all. Even though it was not Jan and Dean's best-known Bomper, it certainly kept the field open for the next record in the Bomp sweepstakes, by a black group calling themselves the Rivingtons!

The Rivingtons were on a good record label--LIBERTY! They had three records that made the airwaves. One will be discussed later. One was Kicka-Poo Joy Juice, apparently the stuff sometimes consumed by the characters in LI'L ABNER. Another was Mama-Oom-Mow-Mow, which recalled the days of She Say. In terms of hits and Bomps, though, the Fall of '62 heard an incredibly wild record called Papa-Oom-Mow-Mow. "Pa-pa-pa-pa-pa-who-mow-mow-mow-mow-mow" sang the Rivingtons. For my taste, they went maybe a little too far, but for an old Bomp fan like me, it sounded pretty good--as it did to old Bomp fans the BB5. They did Papa on their mid-'60s live LP.

Another newcomer to the Bomps hit a few months later. Like Barry Mann's Who Put the Bomp, Johnny Cymbal's Mr. Bass Man put the Bomps out in front and discussed them in the lyrics. Before Mr. Bass Man, Johnny had stiffed with a song on VeeJay records called Bachelor Man, which went "Hom-in-ah-nom" instead of Bomp. In the later '60s Johnny changed his name to Derek and had a famous record called Cinnamon ("Let me in, Cinnamon, I won't go away").

To tie Johnny Cymbal in with Jan and Dean: the follow-up to Mr. Bass Man was called Dum-Dum-Dee-Dum, and its flip was called Surfin' At Tiajuana!

(On their second Liberty LP, Jan and Dean of course did Mr. Bass Man as an LP cut, not as a cover version!)

Exit Johnny Cymbal.

Enter the Bird.

The early '60s was the era of the dance records. Dee Dee Sharp was the Queen of the Bird with her Spring hit called Do the Bird. The guys at Liberty records were paying attention. The Rivingtons came out that Spring with their only other hit, The Bird's the Word. I have to say that this is my favorite Rivingtons' side, although it was not their biggest seller. More about this song later!

Remember Barry Mann? Most hit songs of the early '60s seemed to be written by him, Jan Berry, Brian Wilson, or Ellie Greenwich. Ellie wrote a lot of songs, many with

...*to page 15*...

SUNSHNE MUSIC 11

MORE BOMPS... from page 10...

her hubby Jeff Barry. For years, I didn't look closely enough and thought that E. Greenwich and J. Barry in small print under a song title meant that Jan was working with someone named Ernie Greenwich!

Anyway, Ellie's songs include I've Had It, Maybe I Know, Don't Ever Leave Me, Hanky Panky, Da Do Ron Ron, and Chapel Of Love. Jeff and his new wife, Nancy are still at it, writing girl-group-type songs like One Day At A Time!

After many years of writing songs for other artists, in 1963 Ellie and Jeff decided to form their own group, called the Raindrops. Ellie did all the parts except-- you guessed it, the Bomps! Those were handled by Jeff, who had one of the lowest voices in rock 'n' roll!

In the Summer of '63, the year of the girl groups, the Raindrops dripped onto the charts with What A Guy. When they toured, Jeff refused to go, so he was replaced by another singer on stage. And since Ellie had used her own voice recorded over and over with itself on the records, she was joined in live appearances by her sister!

(Almost a Bomp record was a follow-up to What A Guy, called That Boy John. However, the song was pulled off the market shortly after it was released because of the shooting death of that president John, Kennedy.)

The next Bomp song was a rarity in rock 'n' roll, a science-fiction Bomp-dance record! I still remember that August afternoon in 1963 when my DJ said "Stay tuned for a crazy new record!" He was right. The Ran-Dells Bomp entry was called The Martian Hop. If you never heard this record, try to imagine the Chipmunks on the bridge of the Enterprise singing Tennessee to Mr. Spock...

I personally have always loved The Martian Hop. And the flip side, Forgive Me Darling, is a tender slow song full of near-Bomps!

Another memory was the December day in 1963 when my DJ played a record, and then exclaimed, "What is this world coming to?!?" He was referring to a new Bomp song, what might be called one of the first Punk records!

From the Great Lakes area, more or less, came The Trashmen. They were well-named. Their record was trash. Called Surfin' Bird, it was deeply rooted in Jan and Dean as well as the Rivingtons' The Bird's the Word.

Beach rocker discusses career

Dean turns South Padre into 'surf city'

by Roger Kelm
Staff Reporter

Anheuser-Busch, Incorporated, is sponsoring what they call "the world's biggest beach party" on South Padre Island over spring break.

The celebration, which began last Sunday and continues until March 19, features free concerts and dances, volleyball and mud wrestling competitions and appearances by the Budweiser Clydesdales and Playboy Playmate Sandy Cagle.

It culminates with a free "Surf City, USA" concert by Mike Love of the Beach Boys and Dean Torrence of Jan and Dean, 1 p.m. March 18 at the Cabanas Beach area, north of the Pavillion.

Torrence talked about the concert, his work and his musical career with partner Jan Berry over lemonade and a "Santiago Skillet" at JoJo's in Austin.

"I'm looking forward to the concert. I hear South Padre's pretty radical," Torrence explained. They held a similar concert at Daytona last year, and plan to play both Daytona and Padre this year.

Torrence said he thought the college crowd, even though many of them were very young during the surf music heyday, would still be familiar with the music.

"Fans of beach music certainly have been aware of who we were and what we contributed," he said. "So those people, if they want to see a freebee, are the ones we really expect to be there."

Jan and Dean first came into prominence in 1958 with their hit single "Jenny Lee," recorded on a tape recorder in a garage. "It was a bunch of high school guys all getting around just experimenting with doing music. All of the sudden they had a song," said Torrence.

The pair was commercially successfull for the next few years, stringing together 25 hit songs, seven of them in the top 10.

In 1966, though, Jan Berry was involved in an automobile accident which seriously impaired his language comprehension and motor skills.

The musical careers of Jan and Dean were to be cut short for a few years following the accident. Torrence took his design degree and formed Kittyhawk Graphics. Since he had already established a number of connections in the music business, that is where he ended up.

DEAN TORRENCE

He has designed and packaged albums for the Beach Boys, Harry Nilsson, Anne Murray, Linda Ronstadt and Steve Martin.

In 1974 a surf music revival concert was sponsored in Los Angeles. Jan and Dean were scheduled to appear, but since they were not truly prepared financially to put together a real band,

The University Star - March 11, 1982

2-62	Colpix	624	Marcels	My Melancholy Baby
2-62	Candix	331	Beach Boys	Surfin'
5-62	Liberty	454	*Jan and Dean	Tennessee
8-62	Liberty	427	Rivingtons	Papa Oom Mow Mow
2-63	Kapp	503	Johnny Cymbal	Mr. Bass Man
3-63	Liberty	553	Rivingtons	The Bird's the Word
4-63	Jubilee	444	Raindrops	What A Guy
8-63	Chairman	403	Ran-Dells	Martian Hop
12-63	Garret	002	Trashmen	Surfin' Bird
3-64	Liberty	672	*Jan and Dean	New Girl In School
1-66	Capitol	561	Beach Boys	Barbara Ann
6-66	Liberty	886	*Jan and Dean	Popsicle Truck

SHOW YOUR 'K'

In the early 1960s, Jan and Dean's songs filled the radio airwaves. Today they're still popular at nostalgia concerts. Here, Jan and Dean "Show Their K!" after a recent performance.

Photography by John Hritzko

Yep, Surfin' Bird was really just the Rivingtons' record revived and reduced to almost nothing but Bomps. Like the Rivingtons had done on the earlier Papa, the Trashmen went too far, and although a big hit, Surfin' Bird really was a terrible record. Their LP, which pictured them hanging off of a sanitation truck, shows how poorly they really played and sung, and their follow-up, Bird Dance Beat, was a pale imitation of Surfin' Bird and got little attention. (A punk group revived Surfin' Bird, doing it even worse, in the late '70s.)

The Trashmen were a late-'63 group. Jan came through again early in 1964 with one of the top Bomps songs of all. The New Girl In School was considered the "A" side of the record by Liberty, but while J&D liked the song, it was the flip, Dead Man's Curve, that they believed in. As luck--no, make that talent--as luck would have it, both sides were smashes, and the Bomps that Jan originated with Jennie Lee proved to be continuingly viable in the face of the British Invasion.

But it was Dean who pulled the next Bomp, in 1966. He had always liked Barbara Ann, Ernie Maresca's ripoff of Jennie Lee, having sung it on the first Liberty J&D LP. So, he suggested that the BB5 do the song on their Party LP. Fun to sing, neither Dean nor Brian and the Beards expected the song to see the 45 racks at the record stores. But Capitol records lifted the track from the LP and made it a world-wide number one seller!

Dean, of course, went unsung even tho' he'd sung the lead on Barbara Ann. But at this point, he had bigger fish to worry over. Jan was in the hospital and Liberty was in the vaults planning the next J&D 45, a Beatle tune. Dean didn't like the version he and Jan had cut just for a trial, so he talked Liberty into putting a classic Bomp LP cut, Popsicle Truck, on the flip side. It worked, and Popsicle Truck, with the word "truck" dropped from the title, closed out the era of the Bomp in the Golden Decade of Original Rock 'n' Roll!

BOMP DISCOGRAPHY

5-58	Arwin	108	*Jan and	Jennie Lee
5-58	Liberty	136	Billy Ward & his Dominoes	Jennie Lee
8-59	Dore	522	*Jan and Dean	Baby Talk
3-61	Colpix	186	Marcels	Blue Moon
5-61	Gee	1065	Regents	Barbara Ann
7-61	Challenge	9411	*Jan and Dean	Heart and Soul
8-61	Gee	1071	Regents	Runaround
8-61	ABC	237	Barry Mann	Who Put the Bomp?
10-61	Colpix	612	Marcels	Heartaches
1-62	Liberty	397	*Jan and Dean	Sunday Kind of Love (Honorable Mention)

SUNSHINE MUSIC 11

SUBSCRIBERS ADS

A JAN AND DEAN and Beach Boy Convention is being planned for this summer in the Cleveland area. Send an SASE for information on attending, displaying, or selling J&D or BB5 items. Addresses: LINDA HUNTER, 5008 Kirk RD, Youngstown, OH 44515 or Lennie Foster, 3521 Tuttle AV, Cleveland, OH 44111.

WANTED TO Buy: Photos of Richard Hatch appearing on stage with Jan and Dean or alone (also address or autograph if possible). Write: Sue Brunot, RD #1, Box 801, Green Hills Park, Greesburg, PA 15601

FOR SALE: Razor Point fat marker pens inscribed with (red print on white) -- "JAN AND DEAN-DEAN AND JAN Two Swingin' Guys for every Honey, Gonna Have Some Fun with Torrence and Berry-Surf City USA" & "Have A Sunny Day" (in metallics on pen cap). Send only $1.50 for each to: LINDA THOMPSON, 1040 N. Laurel AV #8, West Hollywood, CA 90046

LETTERS

DEAR MYKE

HERE IS $5 FOR AS LONG AS THAT WILL GET. (I'M NO STINKER!) I JUST GOT FUNDAMENTAL ROLL BY WALTER EGAN. DEAN SINGS ON "SHE'S SO TOUGH," AT LEAST IT SOUNDS LIKE HIM. SEEMS LIKE, WITH EVEN CHUBBY CHECKER (AND DEL SHANNON AND SO MANY OLD SONGS RE-DONE) HAVING HITS AGAIN, J&D CAN'T MISS. THEY'VE GOTTA PUT SOMETHING OUT, MAYBE A TWO-RECORD DEAL LIKE THE ONE WITH CHALLENGE RECORDS?
TODD V.

P.S. THE PAYBEATS HAVE REDONE "B¹ GAS RICKSHAW" (PVC RECORDS) ON THEIR GUITAR HEROES LP.

Dear Myke,
Please find enclosed $12 for my airmail renewal. I think the magazine continues at a really high standard-- I especially like the inclusion of lyrics. I also wonder if there are enough members to warrent having a Jan and Dean button (badge as we call it here in England). It's hard to advertise your interest to strangers. Anyway, looking forward to the next issue, keep up the good work!
Mike S.

Hi Mike!
Here's my new address.. Moving again, the gypsies got nothin' on me! Good news! In Texas, the Guys (Dean & Mark & Jimmie D., etc.) drew 10,000 people, and have 4 shows coming up at the Pomona fair grounds! Great, huh?!
Becky S.

Dear Myke,
I cannot continue without a renewal to SM starting with issue 10. Hoping thereby to regain your friendwhip!
John L.

Hi Mike!
Can you tell me anything about the J&D fan club in Arma, KS, that advertised in Issue 8 of SM. I didn't send any money, but I did write to them a while back. Are they for real?
Becky

Dear Becky-- Since they placed that ad, I haven't heard a peep!
Mike

Dear Mike,
Just thought I'd tell you of a record that has seemd to go much unnoticed as a J&D collectable. It is Liberty 55446 by Deane Hawley, "Queen of the Angels" b/w "You Conquered Me." Both sides are arranged and conducted by none other than Jan Berry, produced by Lou Adler!

I mention this because of yout DORE 401 story with the 3 Hawley singles. This particular 45 is not listed in any book I've found. However, Hawley's Liberty 55359 "Pocket Full of Rainbows" b/w "That Dream Culd" is, but since I don't have it, I don't know if Jan was involved. Maybe some SM reader would tell us?
Les. K

Myke,
How goes it? Recently I added some new records to my collection:

1. Holland import SUMMER MEANS FUN, CALIFORNIA MUSIC 1962-1974. It includes "Dead Man's Curve," "Ride the Wild Surf," and "Surf City." From the legenday Masked Surfers it has "Gonna Hustle You" and "Summertime, Summertime." Also 4 Beach Boys, 2 Fantastic Baggies, 1 each Mar-Kets, Sharon Marie, Honeys, and Survivors.
2. Malibooz-Malibooz Rule (Rhino Records RNLP 100). '80s Cal. Surf Music with Rock Superstars Dean Torrence and Lindsay Buckingham. Includes their version of "Gonna Hustle You." Dean does mostly background vocals. Has a few pics of him on the back cover, and Jan if I am not mistaken, although he is uncredited.
3. Beach Boys/Jan and Dean Realistic Cat. #51-7010 Capitol Special Market SL 8149, sold at Radio Shack. (Since the old Capitol and Liberty are now both owned by the same parent comapny.) it includes 5 original hits from each artist! Many stores sold out fast, but you can order it. Take care!
Frank B.

SOUTH PADRE, continued...

skips, crackles and the actual sound of the needle hitting the record, and they would lip-synch along with it.

They thought the older audience would find it funny.

Torrence said when he looked into the audience and did not see anyone over 20, he realized the joke would probably not go over. And it did not. Although the local music critics appreciated it as a joke, the audience was not amused.

When the story was retold in the 1978 movie "Deadman's Curve," it had them going on to sing live that night, but Torrence said that really did not happen. "We wanted to, but there was really no way we could."

Since the release of the television movie, Jan and Dean have enjoyed a renewed popularity; so much so that they recently completed a successful five-month concert tour.

Beach Boys/Jan And Dean
4.49 LP
Cassette 4.98

"Surfin' USA", "Surf City", "Deadman's Curve", "Fun, Fun, Fun", "Get Around", "Little Deuce Coup", "Drag City", "Little Old Lady from Pasadena" and more!

only at Radio Shack stores
LP. 51-7010 .... 4.49
Cassette. 51-9010 .... 4.98

SUNSHINE MUSIC 11

...from page 11...
Concert

the group's success and popularity by writing or co-writing such hits as "Good Vibrations," "California Girl," "Fun, Fun, Fun," and "Do It Again."

With such wide ranging talents, it's no surprise that Love has ventured out on his own to develop his versatile skills.

Mike has completed his first solo album project, "Looking Back With Love," and is performing on tour with his "Endless Summer Beach Band," although he still plays an important role in the present Beach Boys band.

In addition, perhaps because he was a trandsetter in the Sixties, Mike is now becoming increasingly involved in the video spectrum of rock 'n roll entertainment. He was creator and executive producer of

"The Spirit of America Spectacular" television and FM stereo broadcast in July of 1981, which attracted the largest nationwide audience for a live simulcast in history.

Mike credits his ability to withstand the pressures of touring and changing music scenes with daily Transcendental Meditation, and TM-Sidhi sessions and a regular routine of aerobic exercise and Nautilus workouts.

Although he's seen a kaleidoscope of changes in the entertainment world over the last twenty years, Mike is challenged by what he has experienced.

"I think the future will be even more exciting," he says. "I'm looking forward to making movies and their soundtracks and to enjoying the promotional and performing aspects of the entertainment business, while trying to do the best job I can so I can look back with pride on what I've accomplished."

K-Top Big Picks of the Week

Charlie Christian 6-8
Honolulu Lulu — Jan & Dean

Bob Barber 8-12
Busted — Ray Charles

Tom Grimes 12-4
Blue Bayou — Roy Orbison

Bob Harris 4-7
What Does a Girl Do — Shirelles

David Axton 7-9
I Can't Stay Mad At You — Skeeter Davis

Rick Douglass 9-Midnight
Nightlife — Rusty Draper

Prof. J. Gizmo Bop 12-6
Two Tickets To Paradise — Brooke Benton

Certified K-TOP 40
Silver Dollar Survey
Monday

RECORDS INTRODUCED AND HEARD FIRST ON K-TOP

Week of September 9, 1963

1.	Blue Velvet	Bobby Vinton
2.	Tips of My Fingers	Roy Clark
3.	Mockingbird	Inez Foxx
4.	If I Had A Hammer	Trini Lopez
5.	Part Time Love	Johnny Taylor
6.	When a Boy Falls In Love	Mel Carter
7.	Heat Wave	Martha & Vandellas
8.	Mickey's Monkey	Miracles
9.	Hey, Girl	Freddy Scott
10.	Sally Go 'Round the Roses	Jaynetts
11.	It's Too Late	Wilson Pickett
12.	Blowin' In The Wind	Peter Paul & Mary
13.	Martian Hop	Randells
14.	Only In America	Jay & Americans
15.	Ooby Dooby	Matt Lucas
16.	Six Days On the Road	Dave Dudley
17.	Monkey Time	Major Lance
18.	That Sunday, That Summer	Nat King Cole
19.	Hello Mudda, Hello Fadda	Allen Sherman
20.	Little Deuce Coupe/Surfer Girl	Beach Boys
21.	Fingertips	Stevie Wonder
22.	Green, Green	New Christy Minstrel
23.	Hey There, Lonely Boy	Ruby & Romantics
24.	Kind of Boy You Can't Forget	Raindrops
25.	Wham	Lonnie Mack
26.	Be My Baby	Ronettes
27.	Straighten Up Your Heart	Barbara Lewis
28.	Walkin' Miracle	Essex
29.	Devil in Disguise	Elvis Presley
30.	Treat My Baby Good	Bobby Darin
31.	This Is All I Ask	Tony Bennett
32.	Wonderful, Wonderful	Tymes
33.	Then He Kissed Me	Crystals
34.	China Nights	Kyu Sakamoto
35.	My Boyfriend's Back	Angeles
36.	Memphis	Lonnie Mack
37.	Cry Baby	Garnett Mimms
38.	Painted Tainted Rose	Al Martino
39.	Hello Heartache Goodbye Love	Peggy March
40.	Sooner or Later	Johnny Mathis

Pick Album — Elvis Golden Hits Vol. #3
Elvis Presley --------- R.C.A. Victor

FROM THE FILES

4-66

Miss Kathy Torrence
Friends of Jan & Dean
2145 Benecia Avenue
Los Angeles, California
90025

Hello,

I am writing to ask you to join the Jan and Dean Fan Club... My name is Kathy, and I am Dean's sister. I think I can make this fan club the best in the nation, but I need members!

I am asking $ 2.00 for a membership. This includes: newsletters, two 8" x 10" photos (autographed especially to you), a membership card and a wallet size photo.

Jan and Dean have promised to personally call a member of their fan club in whatever town they happen to be touring. The first tour begins in March! You may hear from either Jan or Dean very soon.

If enough fans would like, I will print their names in the newsletter for pen pals. There will definitely be contests where you may win Jan and Dean's newest album or one of their own surfer shirts (a clean one!).

Jan and Dean will be appearing very soon on a national T.V. series, so watch for them, OK?

Sincerely,

Kathy

KATHY

P.S.

Foreign Members ---
Please send 20 international reply coupons, which may be purchased at your local post office.

Please send me the following information with your membership dues.

New LP —
DEAN TORRENCE MUSIC PHASE II 1977-1981 —
DEAN, BRUCE JOHNSTON, JIM ARMSTRONG, ETC..
IMPORT $20.00 POSTPAID U.S.

New EP —
ROCK SHOPPE — THE BEACH YEARS — BEACH BOYS, JAN AND DEAN, ETC. HISTORICAL NARRATIVE AND MUSIC.
ROGER CHRISTIAN PRODUCTION $11.00 POSTPAID U.S.

NEW LISTS —
JAN AND DEAN — FREE
WRITE DIANE VOSTEEN
5007 DETROIT
CLEVELAND, OHIO, 44102
216-631-8444

SUNSHINE MUSIC 12 - 13

SUNSHINE MUSIC 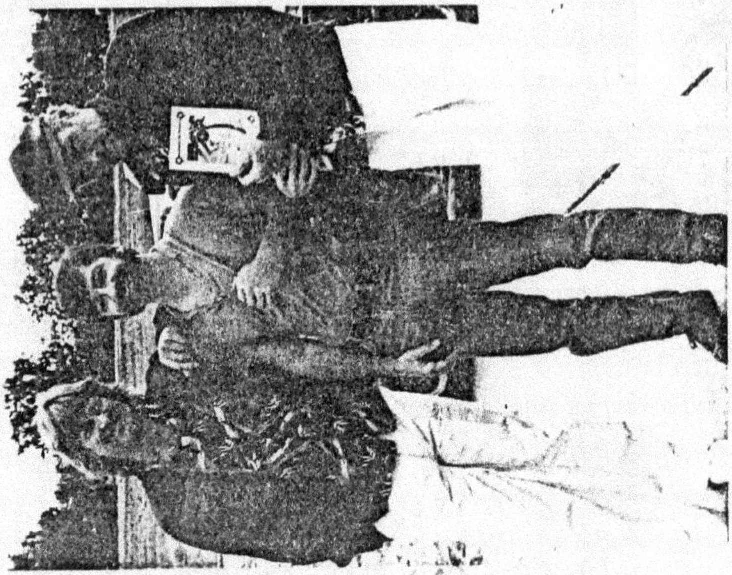
Issue 12-13

SUNSHINE MUSIC
c/o Doc Rock
2817 Crawford
Parsons, KS 67357

FIRST CLASS MAIL

This issue can be the start of your subscription, or a sample issue for which you owe me $2.00! ok?

THOMAS DeTOMASO

Send your photo w/ J or D for display here!!

SUNSHINE MUSIC 12 - 13

sunshine music

THE MAGAZINE OF THE OFFICIAL JAN AND DEAN
AUTHORIZED INTERNATIONAL COLLECTORS' CLUB

EDITOR
Michael Bryan Kelly

COPY EDITOR
Dean O. Torrence

EAST COAST REP
Frank M. Kisko

WEST COAST REP
Honolulu Lulu

Issue 12-13   Summer-Fall '82

*Contents not already copyrighted are
© 1982 by Michael Bryan Kelly*

SUBSCRIPTIONS

OK Jan and Dean fans world-wide, here is a simplified guide to getting SUNSHINE MUSIC into your mailbox safe and sound:

SAMPLE COPIES of SM are $1 in the US and surface overseas. Airmail, $2. SUBSCRIPTIONS are good for six (6) issues, at the rates indicated below:

USA	USA, mailed in envelope	non-US Surface	Non-US Air	Surface Envelope	Air Envelopes Charge is
$5	$7	$7	$12	$10	$15 for Postage

Please enclose S.A.S.E. (self-addressed stamped envelope) with all letters.

★ *CHECK THE NUMBER ON YOUR ADDRESS LABEL. THE NUMBER THERE IS THE NUMBER OF THE LAST ISSUE OF YOUR SUBSCRIPTION. IF THERE IS NO NUMBER, LUCKY YOU!!!!*

★★ MAKE ALL CHECKS PAYABLE TO MICHAEL B. KELLY-----
-----NEW SUBSCRIBERS, PLEASE INDICATE THE NUMBER ON YOUR SAMPLE ISSUE OR THE NUMBER YOU WANT YOUR SUBSCRIPTION TO START WITH, OR ELSE!!-----

● THIS IS A SPECIAL, DOUBLE ISSUE OF SUNSHINE MUSIC!! IT COUNTS AS TWO ISSUES ON SUBSCRIPTIONS. PLEASE CHECK THE NUMBER ON YOUR ADDRESS LABEL. IF THE NUMBER IS EITHER 12 OR 13, THEN IT IS TIME FOR YOU TO RENEW!!

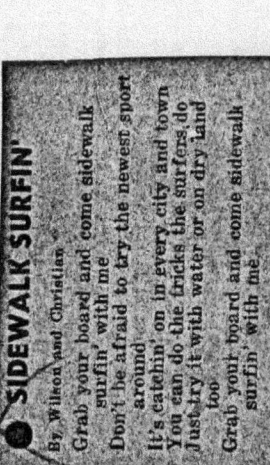

SIDEWALK SURFIN'
By Wilson and Christian

Grab your board and come sidewalk
  surfin' with me
Don't be afraid to try the newest sport
  around
It's catchin' on in every city and town
You can do the tricks the surfers do
Just try it with water or on dry land
  too
Grab your board and come sidewalk
  surfin' with me

You'll probably wipe-out when you
  first try to shoot the curb
Just a fast little push takes a lot of
  nerve
You can hop right over them
  pedestrians too
But keep shufflin' and bustin' down and
  speed right on through
Grab your board and go sidewalk surfin'
  with me

You can do the tricks the surfers do
Just try it with water or on dry land
  too
Grab your board and go sidewalk
  surfin' with me
So get your girl and take her
  tandum down the street
Surfin' on the asphalt is real neat
Before you go let me give you a tip
'Cause if the sidewalk splits
You better pull out quick
Grab your board and go sidewalk
  surfin' with me
Grab your board and go sidewalk
  surfin' with me

© Copyright 1964 by Sea Of Tunes Publishing Co.

● *Cover photo: Mike, Myke, and Dean. Mike is holding SM #11. Photo by Buzzie.*

SHORT CUTS

OFFICIAL WORD FROM THE BERRY CAMP

Jan is busy rehearsing for the tour, he "can't wait" to get started. He did the arrangements for the Aloha Band.

Jan's show will consist of the hits, Beach Boys' songs and Beatles offerings. There are plans for new Jan/Aloha Band originals for the future.

Jan has had four different shows in the Los Angeles area, "practice runs" with little advertisement (more about that in this issue). He's played to small but enthusiastic crowds.

"Ocean Park Angel" is reportedly in negotiation right now. Jan's new single (no name yet) has been suspended for the duration of the tour.

There's already been a change in Aloha Band personnel. Mike Montessi has left and turned bass chores over to Jeff Todd. Jeff plays excellent figures with drive and enthusiasm...rhythm guitarist, Red-haired Bruce Sorensen appears to be "the quiet type"...lead guitarist Dave Loe handles Dean's vocal parts...occasional lead vocalist is drummer David Hodgen...Keyboard player Frank Jansen does not sing but his fingers do the talking in dazzling style on the keys.

Guests at Jan's birthday party in April included Hal Blaine and Jan's new favorite rock group, The Go-Go's!

OFFICIAL WORD FROM DEAN TORRENCE:

As of June 17, resulting from a ceremony in Mount Washington, Maryland, a former Anheuser-Busch executive in charge of P.R., named Ms. Susan Vogelberger has become Mrs.-----Dean------Torrence----!!

Seen on D.O.T.'s left hand---a gold wedding band. Well, there's still Jan....

Dean has been performing with The Bel Air Bandits around the country. The gang has released a 5 song EP (extended play) on 12 inch vinyl called "The Bel Air Bandits With Dean Torrence." Issued on Permanent Records, the disc should soon be available in your local record store. The line-up of songs is "She Loves The Radio," featuring Chris Farmer; "Oh Susannah," with Gary Griffin; "I Don't Want To Lose The Feeling," with Mark Ward and Jim Armstrong;

"I'm Ready, Willing And Able," again featuring Gary; and "Good Vibrations," with Jim Armstrong. Dean is not vocally evident on the record. All songs were recorded live at My Father's Place in Rosslyn, New York, except "She Loves The Radio" which was done in the studio and is slated for single release. The Bandits can be reached at: Surfscouts, P.O. Box 240, Rosalyn, New York, 11576.

...more on p. 47...

Let Me Explain

I reported in SM #11 that Jan's new manager was Keith Ward. This month I was going to tell you that Jan is being managed through National Creative Management. But... say the wild and wacky world of rock 'n roll is hectic to say the least! Keith has left the show to take on another assignment. Tour manager David Fiumano is handling the show right now!

When questioned before leaving about what fans will see when they buy a ticket for Jan's show, Keith answered, "Fans are in for a real surprise. This is one hot show!"

Dates for Jan's show are unavailable at press time, due to the inavoidable delays and crazy rock 'n roll type problems with which the business is fraught. Keith had tentatively planned dates for Japan, Europe and Australia as well as the U.S. It is not known at this time if the agency will follow that format or not.

AVAILABLE FROM JAPAN--Thanks to reliable SMer Ryuichi Tanaka, SM readers may get a new release, new picture sleeve included. "Surf City" b/w "Little Old Lady" on King 7020. The sleeve is similar to the cover of the last SM. Send $6 CASH ONLY and Ryuichi will send your copy airmail. Isn't he a nice guy?

AVAILABLE FROM AUSTRALIA--Thanks to one Chris Ferrell, SM readers may now prove once and for all to their Beach-Boy friends how great Jan and Dean were/are. Sure, Brian wrote/helped write some J&D hits, but it was the genius of Jan that made NEW GIRL IN SCHOOL a hit and the unlimited gifts of Dean that produced the UA track GONNA HUSTLE YOU. And now you can get proof, on the new J&D bootleg! CALIFORNIA COLLECTORS' SERIES VOL. III, LIMITED NUMBERED EDITION OF 500 EP WITH PICTURE SLEEVE AND LINER NOTES! SIDE ONE: GONNA HUSTLE YOU 1962 DEMO FROM BRIAN; DON'T YOU JUST KNOW IT BY BRIAN; AND HIDE YOUR LOVE AWAY BY JAN PRE-ACCIDENT. SIDE TWO: (WHY MUST I BE) A TEENAGE BAT SESSION OUTTAKES WITH STUDIO TALK FROM JAN BERRY. SEND $10 PER COPY (20% DISCOUNT FOR 5 OR MORE COPIES, ADD $3 IF PAYING BY CHECK TO COVER BANK CHARGES)---SEND TO: WEST COAST SERVICES/ P.O. BOX 699/ BLACKTOWN 2148/ AUSTRALIA.

AVAILABLE FROM CHICAGO--Thanks to loyal J&Der Sharon Fox, you can now get the legendary J&D concert booklet from the '60s, designed by Dean, of course! Like, this is the real McCoy gang, full of photos of J&D as kids, in recording sessions, etc! Best of all, the proceeds from the sale actually go to Jan Berry! So, send your $15 for one copy to: SHARON FOX/ 5742 W. GIDDINGS/ CHICAGO, IL/ 60630.

AVAILABLE FROM SWEDEN--Thanks to Goren Tannfelt, SM readers can still get copies of THE JAN AND DEAN ILLUSTRATED WORLDWIDE DISCOGRAPHY, soon to become a collectors' item, I suppose. Read all about it in the daily news, aka SM #10. Or, send $6 for airmail delivery from Goren Tannfelt/ Lilla Nygatan 16/ 111 28 Stockholm/ Sweden.

OCEANS OF FUN AT SURF CITY WITH HONOLULU LULU!!

Back in 1972, the Midwest got one of its first theme parks, WORLDS OF FUN. At that time, hope that I might, the last thing I really ever expected was Phase II of Jan and Dean.

Then, last Summer, as reported in *SUNSHINE MUSIC*, I experienced a glorious Phase II concert at no place other than Worlds of Fun.

On our way to Worlds of Fun last year, we saw a sign--"Future Site of Oceans of Fun." We were too excited to give it more than a moments notice. But the real excitment came when I got a letter from Dean in Spring, '82, announcing a Mike and Dean show at--you guessed it, Oceans of Fun, May 22, 1982!

This was the opening day of Oceans of Fun. Oceans is connected with World of Fun, but admission is separate. And, while Worlds has a concert almost every night, Oceans was having only ONE show all Summer, on grand-opening day, with Mike Love and Dean Torrence!

We arrived early. It was a cold, overcast day, with a chance of severe weather, even tornadoes. This was bad, since Oceans of Fun is really a Mid-Western psuedo-Pacific-coast beach. There is a pool the size of a football field with a wave machine for surfing. This attraction is called--SURF CITY! There is also a pool 300-foot water slide called--HONOLULU LULU!!

I thought I had died and gone to Jan-and-Dean Heaven!!!

The band set up on the edge of a irregularly shaped "pool" with sand in place of cement and a beach with more sand. And what a band it was! Jim Studer on keyboard, with Gary Griffin back on piano (see Gary's photo on page 13 of SM #9). The guitars were manned by Jeff Noskett and Adrian Baker. The backup was handled by Chris Farmer on bass and Mike Kowalski.

The cold weather may have kept some people out of the water, but the band and the audience were great! Soon after we arrived on the beach, the band did their sound check. A great rendition of IN MY ROOM got a great response from the crowd sitting around in the sand. When CATCH A WAVE followed a moment later, the cheers were tremendous.

The comments of the people sitting around us were interesting. It reminded me of the time I saw Jan in Topeka in 1978. Everyone was talking about Jan's health and Dean's absence, and I took it on myself to explain. But at Oceans, the comments went like this:

"Which one is Dean?" (Mike and Dean have not shown up yet at all!)
"That one, I think..."
"You know, Dean used to be a Beach Boy but was kicked out."
"Yeah, so was Jan!"
"Are any of those guys original Beach Boys?"
"Naw...they are all too old to play now. They all quit long ago."

I considered explaining, but then I spotted Dean arriving in a Limo!

It was wonderful seeing Dean again. We chatted about things, like, weddings and stuff. "Well, it's nice to have a change every once in a while," he explained! Soon, Mike Love walked over. Though I have seen the Beach Boys twice, I had never met them. Mike turned out to be one of the nicest people I ever met. I gave him a copy of the latest issue of SM, and I'll be darned if he didn't read it, hold it up for the cover photo when I told him it would be on the front of this issue, and then perform the show with the issue's pink cover sticking out of his jacket pocket!

We went back "stage" with them, actually just some picnic tables set up behind the band. Until a performance on Mike Douglas a couple of years ago, the BB had never performed on a beach. Now, Mike Love was standing up to his ankles in sand, as he and Dean got ready to begin the show!

One more memory--driving in my car in the Summer of '68 and hearing a new surf record on the car radio, DO IT AGAIN. The crowd roared this Spring of '82 as the Mike and Dean band began to play DO IT AGAIN and introduced Mike Love and Dean Torrence!

DO IT AGAIN was followed immediately by SLOOP JOHN B. This band was so good, so tight, that even without Mike and Dean, they sounded as much like the records as ANY band ever could. Then, when Dean or Mike would begin singing too, those magical voices transformed ideal music into perfection itself!

A highlight of this show was the interplay between Mike and Dean. Mike did most of the talking and lead singing, while Dean layed back and harassed him! Dean looked comfortable in his old role, and the comedic effect was grand. The next song started off as CATCH A WAVE. CATCH is thought of today as a Beach Boy hit, partly because it was included on many Greatest Hit Anthologies of the Beach Boys. In fact, it was just an LP cut on the SURFER GIRL album. Of course, when people hear CATCH now, they mistake it for the J&D hit SIDEWALK SURFIN', and that is why it sounds familiar.

Well, this time, it was a new version:

Mike: So take a lesson from a top-notch surfer boy...
Dean: ...then she'll know you're an asphalt athlete!

SUNSHINE MUSIC 12 - 13

Mike: Any one wanna go back to California with us? (Cheers.) Well, we may have a little transportation problem...

Dean: But that's OK, we'll pick you all up after the show!

CALIFORNIA GIRLS.

Dean: This next one is for all you good-looking ladies out there... and for all the marginal ones, too!

DARLIN'. HELP ME RHONDA.

Dean: Looks like we got a lotta little Surfer Girls out there in this bunch! OK; this goes out...wait, I see Gary has picked out his favorite Surfer Girl. He'll probably take her on his next trip to Mozambique! So, you may as well pack your bags!

SURFER GIRL. Then, a new version of an old hit, with Dean playing harmonica! SURFIN' BLUES led to a medly, SURFIN' SAFARI, SURF CITY, AND SURFIN' USA!

That ended the show's first phase. It looked like there would have to be a second phase, but I was curious. Jan and Dean's traditional encore is Dean's BARBARA ANN, while the BB's is FUN FUN FUN. Which would they do today? BARBARA ANN and FUN FUN FUN!!

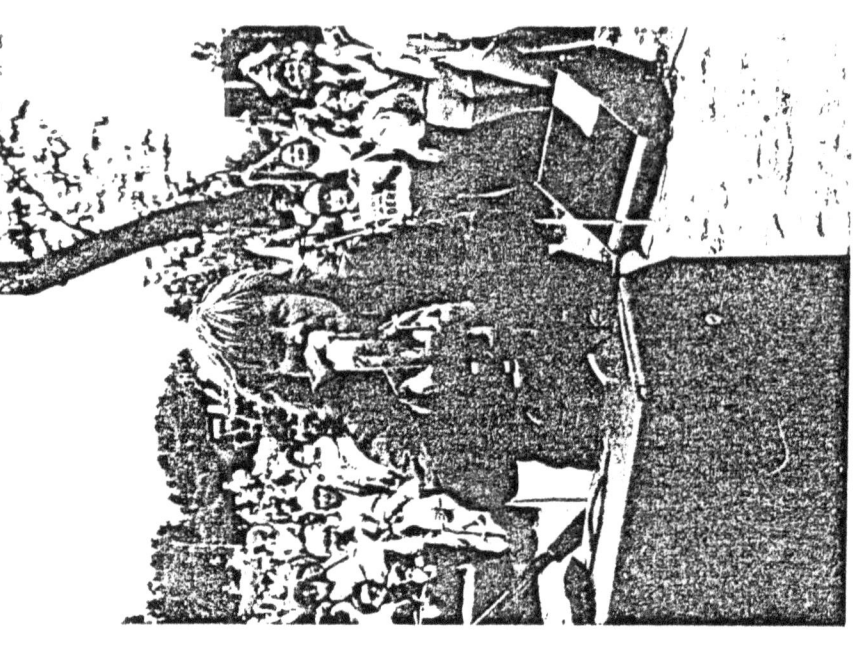

Mrs. Rock with Mike & Dean!

As the music ended, the crowd surged into the picnic-table area-- I mean, the backstage area. The security, dressed in white Bermuda shorts, safari shirts, and pith helmets, tried in vain to hold them back, but gave up when Mike and Dean began signing autographs. This went on for over half an hour, until everyone who wanted an autograph had gotten one.

So, this is Phase III. So far, so good! If you have a chance, don't miss the Dean and Mike show (also known as Mike and Dean...).

* * *

SUNSHINE MUSIC 12 - 13

AND NOW, IT'S TIME FOR THE FIRST (AND PROBABLY LAST) SUNSHINE MUSIC SUMMER SPECTACULAR, RIP-ROARIN' BESTEST EVER, BITCHIN'

JAN AND DEAN SWEEPSTAKES!

WIN! WIN! WIN! WIN! WIN! WIN! WIN!
Oh yes, lucky reader, you could win big! YOU could actually win JAN OR DEAN! Imagine the envy of your friends when they see JAN sitting on your mantel or DEAN as your doorstop!

Now comes the small print. Since we said "could," it means it might not happen. Oh well, Easy Come, Easy Go. But in lieu of JAN or DEAN as handsome additions to your home, we've rounded up some super special, killer items for the winners!

How would you like to own J&D's official 1981 press kit (as published in SM, complete with 8"x10" glossie)? Or an official Kittyhawk Graphics envelope with logo (8½" x 11")? How about a sheet (unused) of JAN'S personalized music manuscript paper from Phase I (18" x 22")? A Kittyhawk-designed full-color poster advertising MIKE AND DEAN, South Padre Island, 1982? Or a tape

MORE! MORE! MORE! MORE! MORE! MORE! MORE!
* Legendary Masked Surfers "Summer Means Fun" insert card, only included in special mailings of the 45 *
A tape of JAN'S phone answering machine, 1981 *
J&D backstage pass from 1981 * Sealed L.P. featuring cover by DEAN * Macy's poster ad for MIKE AND DEAN at May 1982 opening of Oceans Of Fun, water games amusement park * SM letterhead paper, once folded, now ironed flat *
1973 Radio KEWI survey with "Summer Means Fun" listed * "BUST YOUR BUNS" color logo letterhead, recreated specifically for this contest * Free issues of SM *
[note: items preceding are not listed in categories of first place prize, second place prize, etc., as we're still trying to scrape up goodies. Contributions welcome!]

How to enter: 1-complete the puzzle by answering clues and plugging appropriate letters into the numbered box. Or guess at words and work back to the clues. Once you have "deciphered" the message, copy it <u>exactly</u> on a postcard and send it to SM

of SM's own DOG ROCK from KLWN radio featuring J&D as the "Rock And Roll Lesson For The Day?" Would you like to own an authentic JAN BERRY thumbnail from the hand that worked the board on all those hits we know and love (honest, you guys, this is <u>legit</u>)? What have you got to "lose" by entering? There's even more! Read on!

along with your name, address, age and the title of your favorite J&D song. ONLY ONE ENTRY PER SUBSCRIBER! All entries from the U.S. must be received by October 1st; all foreign entries by October 15th. Winners will be chosen by random drawing.

This contest off-limits to JAN AND DEAN and their families; Doc and Mrs. Rock; Lulu; Frank Kisko; Steve McFarland; Sharon Fox; Papa Doo Run Run; Bel Air Bandits or Aloha Band members. Sorry!

Crypto Clues

1. Dean's name for "Filet Of Soul" FILET OF SHIT
2. Bees live in a HIVE
3. Name of actor who portrayed Jan
4. U.S. summer sci-fi film hit
5. Name of J&D's latest single (unreleased, scb!)
6. To break off an engagement without informing one's affianced
7. Dean's middle name
8. A set of musical ___ does make a ___
9. "The World's Most Greatest Drummer," pal of J&D
10. To suddenly lift something heavy
11. J&D's Phase II manager
12. A copywriter does this to slim down stories
13. Actor who played Dean
14. Thing you stick in the ground to hit a golf ball from

15. Jan's legal first name WILLIAM
16. Small item of formal men's attire
17. J&D's first Phase II band PAPA DOO RUN RUN
18. Digit on human foot TOE
19. Deano's birthday MARCH 10th
20. Musical dot you read (or write, if you're Jan)
21. Jan's natal day APRIL 3rd
22. Stupid person
23. Early name of Bel Air Bandits (band-type, not football)
24. Things which your toes are in direct contact with
25. What was June 20, 1980 proclaimed in Los Angeles? JAN AND DEAN DAY
26. To remove or erase DELETE
27. Title of the first J&D bootleg LP which popped up in 1976
28. A robber
29. Jan's first Coe 45 was
30. One of Jucky "Uncle" Donald's nephews

45. Doc Rock's tribute to Jan and Dean (think pink). SUNSHINE MUSIC

46. The Titanic TWOSOME.

47. Dean was only a boy when he did his duty "for God and my country" and this fellow filled his shoes. ANDY GINSBURG

48. Doctor Altfeld's first name is DAR.

49. DJ friend and collaborator of Jan and Splash, Phase-O 1-0. ROGER CHRISTIAN

50. Intersection where the Jag and Stingray began their fateful rendezvous.

51. Jan's latest solo single that has yet to be released.

52. Jan and Dean were the best possible choice to host the greatest acts in rock and roll "From All Over The World" on _____

53. Liners on J&D's "Command Performance" proclaimed the guys were so funny that they were the "_____"

54. Rallying cry to the Little Old Lady. GO GRANNY GO

55. Dean cleverly masked his voice while playing this 1966 soprano lass at the Torch Club.

56. Jan's pre-Phase II back-up band's name; same as his newly-formed 1982 gang. THE BLOHARDS

31. Where did "Surf City" hit numero 3 in 1979? HOLLAND

32. Slang word for a pimple. ZIT

33. J&D's old friend and early manager. LOU ADLER

34. Reducing one's food intake to lose weight is to DIET.

35. "Tijuana" type; old nemesis of D&J (equal time there!).

36. Stand-off; foreign word used in politics.

37. What did the Boy Blunder do to the transistorized chocolate chip cookie the Little Old Lady gave him? HE ATE IT! (way to go, Boy Blunder!)

38. Agitated to agression; harmful.

39. Jan's remake of a Chuck Berry tune. LITTLE QUEENIE

40. Surname of former Hawthorne, California residents with whom J&D collaborated personally and professionally; they played around with surf-drag music. WILSON

41. Type of Buddhism. ZEN

42. Hard to believe, but there really is a city in Southern California with this unlikely name. There's probably even wild little old ladies zipping through red lights! _____ in PASADENA!

43. Ballerina skirt.

44. They surfed down the Swannee River to backup J&D. THE RHYTHMS

SUNSHINE MUSIC 12 - 13

JAN and DEAN

Jan & Dean cut their first records, "Jennie Lee" and "Baby Talk", in 1958 when many experts were predicting the rapid decline of rock 'n' roll. But rock 'n' roll didn't fade and neither did Jan & Dean. They have kept pace and kept their popularity, especially now that the surfing and hot rod craze is strong. The music of Jan Barry and Dean Torrance is full of the rousing beat of waves and engines, and nothing could be better listening or dancing bait. In the first six months of 1963 they sold over a million singles of "Linda" and "Surf City" and recently have added "New Girl In School" and "Dead Man's Curve" to the list, as well as two smash albums, "Jan & Dean Take Linda Surfing", and "Surf City". Critics who once predicted the downfall of these two sun-tanned boys from California are taking a second look and listen to their enthusiastic sound.

OFFICIAL KIMN HIT PARADE

FOR WEEK STARTING: MONDAY, MARCH 1, 1965

Listen 3 p.m. to 6 p.m. daily for your OFFICIAL HIT PARADE.
Brand new Hit Parade starts every Monday, same time, 3 p.m. to 6 p.m.

THIS WEEK	TITLE	ARTIST	LABEL	LAST WEEK
1.	Eight Days a Week	Beatles	Capitol	7
2.	Birds and the Bees	Jewell Akens	Era	1
3.	Twine Time	Alvin Cash	Blue Cat	2
4.	My Girl	Temptations	Gordy	9
5.	Shotgun	Junior Walker	Soul	20
6.	Jolly Green Giant	Kingsmen	Wand	8
7.	King of the Road	Roger Miller	Smash	12
8.	This Diamond Ring	Gary Lewis	Liberty	4
9.	Can't You Hear my Heartbeat?	Hermans Hermits	MGM	22
10.	Ferry Cross the Mersey	Gerry & Pacemakers	Laurie	14
11.	Red Roses for a Blue Lady	Bert Kaempfert	Decca	11
12.	Red Roses for a Blue Lady	Vic Dana	Liberty	11
12.	Goldfinger	Billy Strange	Crescendo	3
13.	Stop, In the Name of Love	Supremes	Motown	19
14.	Boy from New York City	Ad-Libs	Blue Cat	5
15.	Four by the Beatles	Beatles	Capitol	10
16.	Hurt So Bad	Little Anthony	DCP	24
17.	New York's a Lonely Town	Trade Winds	Red Bird	17
18.	Midnight Special/Cupid	Johnny Rivers	RCA Victor	15
19.	Laugh, Laugh	Beau Brummels	Autumn	6
20.	Send Me the Pillow	Dean Martin	Reprise	28
21.	Please Let Me Wonder/ Do You Wanna Dance	Beach Boys	Capitol	36
22.	Don't Mess Up a Good Thing	Bass and McClure	Checker	42
23.	I Go to Pieces	Peter & Gordon	Capitol	13
24.	It I Loved You	Chad & Jeremy	World Artists	16
25.	It's Alright	Adam Faith	Amy	25
26.	Ask the Lonely	Four Tops	Motown	26
27.	Little Things	Bobby Goldsboro	United Artists	43
28.	Nowhere to Run	Martha & Vandellas	Gordy	44
29.	Stranger in Town	Del Shannon	Amy	46
30.	Goodnight	Roy Orbison	Monument	18
31.	Bye Bye Baby	4 Seasons	Phillips	21
32.	The Race Is On	George Jones	United Artists	32
33.	Do the Clam	Elvis Presley	RCA Victor	39
34.	Tiger by the Tail	Buck Owens	Capitol	23
35.	Don't Let Me Be Misunderstood	Animals	MGM	29
36.	Baby, the Rain Must Fall	Glenn Yarbrough	RCA Victor	5*
37.	I Must Be Seeing Things	Gene Pitney	Musicor	49
38.	People Get Ready	Impressions	ABC-Paramount	31
-39.	Yeh, Yeh	Georgie Fame	Imperial	33
41.	Angel	Johnny Tillotson	MGM	48
42.	Anytime At All	Frank Sinatra	Reprise	50
43.	All Over the World/Freeway Flyer	Jan & Dean	Liberty	KC
44.	Come Tomorrow	Manfred Mann	Ascot	47
45.	Tell Her No	Zombies	Parrot	45
47.	Long Lonely Nights	Bobby Vinton	Epic	KC
48.	Land of 1,000 Dances	Cannibal & Headhunters	Rampart	KC
49.	You Better Get It	Joe Tex	Dial	KC
49.	This Sporting Life	Ian Whitcomb	Tower	KC
50.	I Can't Explain	The Who	Decca	KC

KIMN FIVE STAR PICK HIT OF THE WEEK:
I'm Telling You Now...Freddie & Dreamers...Tower

KIMN FIVE STAR ALBUM OF THE WEEK:
The Impressions' Greatest Hits...ABC-Paramount

★ WHEN AMERICAN TOP TEN WAS PLANNING THEIR UPDATE ON JAN AND DEAN, THEY CONTACTED
★ SUNSHINE MUSIC FOR INFORMATION, PHOTOS, AND SO ON. ONE THING THEY NEEDED WAS
★ SOMETHING TO FILL IN THE GAP BETWEEN PHASE ONE AND PHASE TWO. MANY NEW
★ FANS ARE ALSO MISSING INFORMATION DURING THIS TRANSITIONAL PERIOD. SO,
★ HERE IS THE BRIEF SUMMARY OF PHASE 1½ AS WRITTEN FOR AMERICAN TOP TEN.

Yes, Dean recorded without Jan. He released two versions of a song called "Yellow Balloon," on different labels. One version was "by Jan and Dean," the other by a phony group called "The Yellow Balloon." The latter was the bigger hit!

He recorded a follow-up LP to both songles. Jan, however, refused to allow the "Jan and Dean" version to be released. Only a few copies are known to exist, mostly outside the US, and go for upwards of $300 when they can be found at all.

Dean used his graduate degree in commercial design to open his own company, Kittyhawk Graphics. He won several Grammies for his LP covers (Jan and Dean never won one, probably because rock and roll was ignored by the Grammy folks until the '70s). He did LP covers for Diana Ross, Steve Martin, Nilsson, the Temptations, Bobby Vee, Ventures, Beach Boys, Canned Heat, and many more.

From time to time, he would cut a record with some friends, because music was his life. One project was to re-release their old hit "Sidewalk Surfin'," with updated lyrics to fit the new craze. They were mostly responsible for the first time skateboards were popular, even selling their own "Jan and Dean Little Old Lady Skateboards!" HIs new version was #1 on the charts in San Diego. But the record co., (UA) failed to distribute the 45 nationally, and that was that.

Meanwhile, Jan was recovering from his accident. Among other things, he had to learn to walk, talk, eat, sing, and be nice again. To this day he is paralyzed on his right side. He cut records on various labels from 1967 on. Naturally, he had to give up his hopes of being a surgeon. Like Dean, he had stayed in college. His IQ of 185 had allowed him to write songs and term papers literally simultaneously before the wreck.

Both Jan and Dean cut records independently of one another, with each using the name Jan and Dean or other names, such as Jan, Laughing Gravy, Legendary Masked Surfers, 1 Jan 1, Jan Berry Yellow Balloon, and others. In a variety of styles, none hit the national charts.

Meanwhile, their hits were endlessly repackaged by many labels. Finally, some four years ago, they were talked into a reunion concert in NYC. They had not worked together to speak of for over 10 years!

Inspite of headliners like the Drifters and the Ronnetts, sales were very poor for this show until Jan and Dean were added at the last minute. Suddenly, they were sold out. They added another show. It sold out, too!

Local TV stations taped rehearsals, and featured them on the local news shows. At the concert, Jan and Dean got standing ovations. They could not do an encore, because they had no more material prepared. (The arrangements were found at Jan's father's house. In the old days, Jan had written full arrangements for all thier songs, and recorded an LP, JAN AND DEAN's POP SYMPHONY, convering all their hits with a ful orchestral)

After Jan and Dean left the stage, the other acts had trouble being heard over the chant, "we want Jan and Dean." At this point it was clear that the audience was still interested in Jan and Dean, and more importantly, that Jan was ready for the audiences!

A parallel development was a band called Goodie Two Shoes. In Southern California, there were doing Creedence Clearwater Revival type music at high schools and clubs. One night, just for fun, they did a Jan and Dean song. The response was like nothing they had ever had before. Soon they did Jan and Dean music almost exclusively, and changed their name to Papa Do Run Run (taken from a nonsense line in the Jan and Dean hit record "The New Girl In School").

They contacted Dean, trying to get him to come hear them. Finally, Dean went to a high school dance to hear Papa, and could not believe his eyes! Kids not even born when they had their hits were dancing and singing along with the band! In time, Dean and Papa became good friends, with Dean joining them on stage from time to time.

Then there was the telefilm. "Dead Man's Curve" had been one of their best hits. Deadman's Curve (sic) was a runaway hit on TV. It ran 2 hours, but enough was shot for another 2 hours. In fact, a sequel is talked about. Jan was present on the set everyday, as was Dean, the technical advisor. From the music (the original hits) to the clothes, this was the most (only?) accurate film in terms of reproducing the '50s and early '60s teen life and rock and roll. And the stars of the film, Richard Hatch and Bruce Davison (sic did fantastic jobs of impersonating Jan and Dean. They studied old films. Hatch followed Jan around, learning his aphasic speech patterns and shuffeling walk (passersby thought the actor was making fun of the singer). The end result was tremendous.

In more ways than one. Millions of kids saw the film on TV, and all of a sudden Jan and Dean were in demand. Jan was ready to tour, since he had been touring on his own with a band he organized called Aloha. Now, Jan, Dean, backed by Papa, hit the road. They have been touring eversince, going for a month in Australia this October, 1980. (This was canceled.)

Jan & Dean

Jan & Dean caught the 60s surfin' vogue, and put it on land...with skateboards...

SUNSHINE MUSIC 12 - 13

Jan

Late reports from Southern California inform that Jan Berry has made a few quiet appearances with his new Aloha Band. The shows have been in small clubs with little advertisement, as they are, essentially, rehearsals to get the final kinks out of the stage show prior to touring.

Jan's first two shows were at the rustic Topanga Canyon Corral on June 15th and 16th. Fans lucky enough to have (been living in California and) caught these shows indicate that there were plusses and minuses to the performances. The minuses were mostly technical and to be expected during these "dress rehearsals." There were mixing and feedback problems with sound at the Corral; another report states show number three at the Rumbleseat Garage in Long Beach suffered with feedback squeals as well. Band members displayed some awkwardness at playing in front of a crowd afters weeks of private rehearsal. There were also complaints at the Rumbleseat from disgruntled teenage fans outside who were denied admittance because of minimum-age-21 requirements.

Reportedly, the plusses far outweighed the minuses. "It's a rare treat to see a show like this in the embryonic stages," wrote one observer. "The act has great promise. The band is excellent, a new unit that grows stronger and more solid with each rehearsal. Jan's vocals are tight and clear. Also, after having been a dot in a crowd of thousands seeing J&D last year, it was a wonderful experience seeing Jan close up, in a small, intimate setting. He was mingling with friends, family, and fans at Topanga before and after performing, which made it extra special.

"Members of Jan's family were there, in quiet attendance and support. The music was good and the dance floor was crowded with enthusiastic fans/dancers. It will be interesting to note changes from these samll cabaret shows to righteous concert appearances later on."

The set contains J&D's hits as well as those funtime Beach Boys' standards. Highlights of the shows seems to have been Jan's tribute to John Lennon, "You've Got To Hide Your Love Away," delivered in a moving, soulful manner.

Long Live the King of California Rock 'N' Roll, JAN BERRY!!!

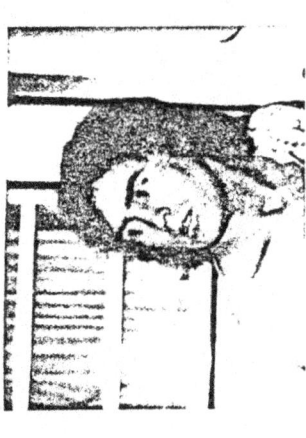

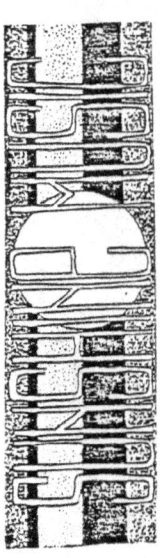

SUNSHINE MUSIC Back Issue Contents Guide--Italics indicate printed lyrics. * indicates interview.

#1 Fall '79
Sunshine Music; introduction to SM; the story* of the J&D 1966 TV series.

#2 Winter '80
Frosty (The Snowman); concert review; J&D live* on tour in the late '50s; survey of fans' favorite songs by J&D; current Holland hit record; survey of J&D LP's of the '60s.

#3 Spring '80
Fiddle Around; letter form J&D's manager; the story* of the FILET OF SOUL LP and the LEGENDARY MASTERS side four; record list with trivia.

#4 Summer '80
I Found A Girl; Skeletons (J&D fan band); concert review; detailed review of bootleg LP OLD WAX AND NEW WAVES; complicated J&D WORD SEARCH game; reprint of '60s teen mag interview; record list with trivia; '60s record chart with Drag City at #10.

#5 Fall '80
Here They Come (From All Over The World); satire of the Paul-McCartney-is-dead-and-there-are-clues-on-the-records craze, "proving" that Dean was replaced with a phony 20 years ago; J&D LP's as released after Jan's wreck; answers to Word Search; J&D radio interview*; newspaper article reprint.

#6 Winter '81
Popsicle Truck; "Rock singer offers words of hope to paralyzed miner" newspaper article on Jan; review of show at Harrah's; 3 newspaper article reprints; The Jan and Dean Criss Cross game; new publicity photo; Jan and Dean: A Reassessment; August '63 Liberty biography; '80 photos.

#7 Spring '81
Yellow Balloon; New Official Biography by Dean Torrence, part one; new official photo; the hidden lyrics of LP cut Sting Ray; the story* of Dean and the song and the group Yellow Balloon; more on phony Dean, including letter from "Arnie Ginsburg"(really Dean).

#8 Summer '81
Poor Little Puppet; new SM logo; part two of New Biography; reprint of 1961 Teen Screen story on J&D split up; typical fan letter (by Dean).

#9 Fall '81
Drag City; 13 pages backstage* with Jan and Dean in 1981; answers to Criss Cross; Dean* tells about Kittyhawk and new record deal requirements.

#10 Winter '82
Ocean Park Angel; new DORE LP release detailed; autographed 8x10 repro.; Retrospect; with Richard Hatch*.

#11 Spring '82
You Really Know How To Hurt A Guy; history of Bomp songs from Jennie Lee on; two stories about Mike and Dean (Love and Torrence) with 8x10; Sept. 9, 1963 Top 40 list; 1966 fan club letter from Kathy Torrence.

ORDERING INFORMATION
Issues 1, 3, 5, and 7 are $2 each. All other issues are $1. Prices subject to change. Cash, or checks payable to Michael B. Kelly.

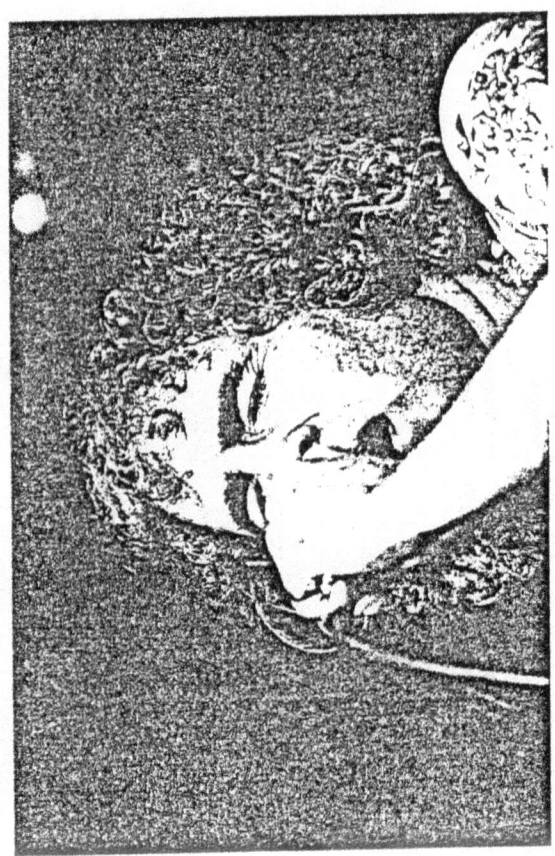

Estelle Bueno/Bonnie Hoyt

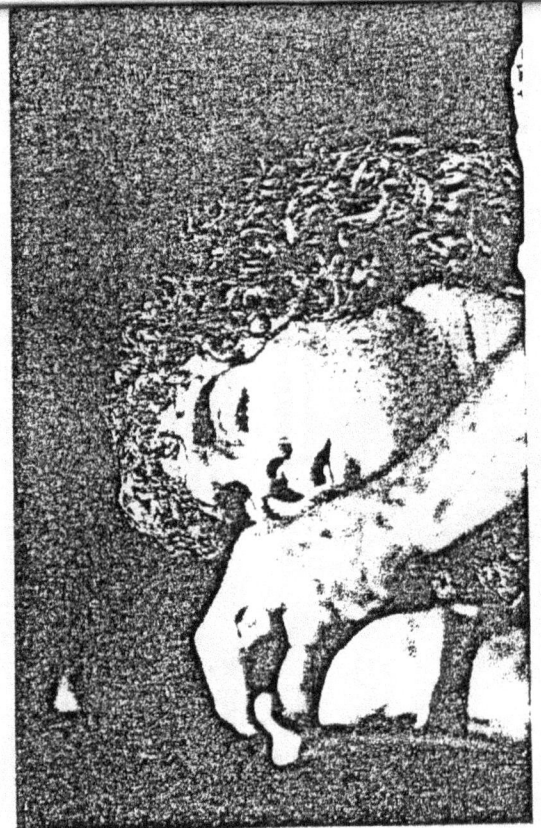

LETTERS

Dear Mike,

The other day, I got another mono copy of the LINDA LP. Have you gotten one yet? *(No, I'm still waiting for a M- at a reasonable price!)*

At the same place, I saw a Murry the K album of live performances, including J&D doing SURF CITY. It appeared to be of recent vintage, sealed, on KFM Records (no #). I was out of cash, and had to pass it up! Just my luck!

Then, on TV I saw a short filler, fifteen minutes long, after a baseball game on TV! Called HOT RODS AND COOL CUSTOMS, it was sponsored by Valvoline and a local auto dealer.

Dean was featured in a short (less than 2-minute) segment on the teenage philosophy behind owning a car in the late '50s, and also about J&D material. J&D songs are in the soundtrack behind the narrator's voice, but the arrangements were unfamiliar. Definitely not Liberty but not quite K-Tel, either.

Are you aware of this program?

Keep up the good work!

George M.

Dear George,

I THINK you should have gotten the KFM LP. I have one, KFM 1001, which matches your description, except it has LINDA, not SURF CITY, listed on the back cover. Incidentally, LINDA is NOT live! The rest of the LP (Angels, Chiffons, Dovels, etc.) is live. However, on another label, FAIRWAY, I have the same basic live show except that J&D do perform SURF CITY, and it IS live.

The TV short is a new one on me. Has anyone else out there seen (or taped) this?

Mike

Dear Michael,

Hi there! Thanks so much for the 10 back issues, all at once! It was so fantastic reading them all straight through cover to cover! I mean, who can ever get enough of Jan and Dean. Reading SM, I felt so close to them. I really admire Dean Torrence, he's an incredible person. Last fall Dean was kind enough to write (or should I say Print?) me a postcard. I was thrilled to death! I can't wait to meet him!

Kathy a Canadian Curfer Girl

Dear Kathy,

Well, by the time you read this, I assume you will have made a stad at meeting Dean with Mike Love at their Canadian show May 25th! Let us know!

Michael

P.S. To George--YOUR SUBSCRIPTION RUNS OUT WITH THIS ISSUE, AS INDICATED BY THE #12 ON YOUR ADDRESS LABEL! HOPE TO GET YOUR RENEWAL SOON!!

For Sale or Auction -- One-of-a-kind rare item. Double LP "Golden Summer" with quality hand painted cover! Picture of tropic sunset on back and original printed front cover. Jan and Dean songs include "Ride the Wild Surf," "Honolulu Lulu," and "Surf City." Plus the Safaris, the Ventures, Fantastic Baggys, Beach Boys and many more. On UA LA627-H2. High Quality LP. Will sell to highest offer, any bids accepted, send SASE to: Paula Moore, &Jan and Dean Lovers Reunite, 33 Short RD, West Falls, NY 14170.

Dear Michael,

Your SUNSHINE MUSIC articles in the past "proving" that "Dean is Dead" have been interesting conjecture. However, I believe you and other SMers have deceived yourselves! Note the enclosed photo, snapped somewhere In The US during J&D's Summer '81 Tour. Dean is very much alive, but note the item in his hand.

Their 1960's career was not as happy-go-lucky as it may have seemed. The item in Dean's hand is a white cane! Mr. Torrence is very much alive--but he is blind!

It's hard to believe we astute scholars of J&D could have missed it but we stalwartly ignored the proof fed to us on J&D LP covers. Let's now take a closer look at those photos. The loss of vision was gradual. It was getting serious by the time they were photographed for their Golden Hits cover. Dean is checking his necktie with investigative fingers to see if it is straight. Neither Jan nor Dean was ready for the picture, which was chosen because of Dean's relatively natural appearance.

He'd lost a great deal of vision when the Linda cover was photographed. He's standing next to a curvy girl--and pays her no attention! Did he even know she was there?

As time went by, the photos documented Dean's squinting mightily to attempt to draw something--anything into clear focus. His squint (due to sensitivity to sunlight) is very pronounced on the back cover of the DMC/NGIS cover, where Jan has copped Dean's protective sunshades!

Jan remained supportive all during this time. Note the copy-cat squint he adopted on the Little Old Lady cover, trying to mask Dean's vain attempt to locate the photographer! On the Ride the Wild Surf cover, Dean is stumbling off a skateboard--his equilibrium was being affected by the loss of his vision. Listen to Dean's sorrowful lament on the LP. The Restless Surfer is obviously an indication of his frustration at not being able to see a surfboard well enough to indulge in his favorite water sport. The lyrics are heart-rendering, as well: "There are no more waves, no more girls to see." The song mentions other towns, obviously Dean metaphorically acknowledging changes in his lifestyle as the fog rolled in.

A number of photos feature Dean in 3/4 view or profile. From this we conclude that Dean retained his peripheral vision for a while. When did The Big Curtain fall? We must surmise that is was shortly after the release of Batman. The LP cover features no photos ans is predominantly black!

After Jan's accident, Dean gratefully dropped out of sight. He appeared again on the Save For A Rainy Day cover. But the mottling on the photo rendered his sunglasses invisible (other photos of Dean taken at this time are actually his sister, Kathy, in a Dean wig).

And Kittyhawk? Dean is responsible for design concepts which cannot render. Note the Beach Boys Fifteen Big Ones LP. Concept by Dean but artwork by Jim Evans!

...to p. 44...

SUNSHINE MUSIC 12 - 13

Estelle Bueno/Bonnie Hoyt

MUSIC

ROCK 'N' ROLL
The Sound of the Sixties
(See Cover)

> *You take some music, hot beats, drumbeats,*
> *Finger poppin' and stompin' feet . . .*
> *It's got this whole wide land.*
> *Rock 'n' roll forever will stand,*
> *Singin' deep in the heart of man.*
> —It Will Stand by the Showmen

The Trashmen. The Kinks. Goldie and the Gingerbreads. The Ripchords. Bent Fabric. Reparata and the Delrons. Barry and the Remains. The Pretty Things. The Emotions. The Detergents. Sam the Sham and the Pharaohs. The Guess Who's. Cannibal and the Headhunters. Them. The Orlons. The Liverbirds. Wump and the Werbles. Like something out of *Malice in Wonderland*, the hordes of shaggy rock 'n' roll singers thump across the land, whanging their electric guitars. Bizarre as they may be, they are the anointed purveyors of the big beat and, as never before, people are listening—all kinds of people.

For the past ten years, social commentators, with more hope than insight, have been predicting that rock would roll over and die the day after tomorrow. Yet it is still very much here, front, center, and belting out from extra speakers on the unguarded flank. Many cannot take rock 'n' roll, but no one can leave it. The big beat is everywhere. It resounds over TV and radio, in saloons and soda shops, fraternity houses and dance halls. It has become, in fact, the international anthem of a new and restless generation, the pulse beat for new modes of dress, dance, language, art and morality. The sledgehammer refrains of Wayne Fontana and the Mind Benders' *Um, Um, Um, Um, Um, Um* can be heard parting the walls of a Yokohama teahouse, a recreation room in Topeka, or a Communist youth club in Warsaw. For better or worse, like it or loathe it, rock 'n' roll is the sound of the Sixties.

Nothing Sacred. The big boost for big-beat music has come, amazingly enough, from the adult world. Where knock-the-rock was once the conditioned reflex of the older generation ("Would you want *your* daughter to marry a Rolling Stone?"), a surprisingly large segment of 20-to-40-year-olds are now facing up to the music and, what is more, liking it. Mostly, the appeal is its relentless beat. It is perhaps the most kinetic sound since the tom-tom or the jungle drum. It may seem monotonous to the musicologist, too loud to the sensitive, but it is utterly compelling to the feet.

The result is that rock 'n' roll has set the whole world dancing. Its shrine is the discothèque, a place of sustained noise, smoky ambiance, and the generally disheveled informality that rock 'n' roll inspires. In a discothèque, it's all records and loudspeakers—since the beat is the thing, who cares about the subtleties of a trumpet solo, even by Miles Davis?

In the past year, some 5,000 discothèques have cropped up in the U.S., and their patrons are not all Coke drinkers in chinos and stretch pants. Starting from Paris' famed Whisky à Go-Go, discothèques by more or less the same name have opened in Milwaukee, Chicago, Washington, San Francisco, Atlanta and Los Angeles. In addition, there is the A-Go-Go in Aspen, Colo., the Bucket A-Go-Go in Park City, Utah, the Frisky A-Go-Go in San Antonio, the Champagne A-Go-Go in Madison, Wis., and the Blu-Note A-Go-Go in Whitesboro, N.Y. And everywhere the couples go-going on the dance floor are like, well, old. Moans one teen-ager: "Nothing is sacred any more. I mean, we no sooner develop a new dance or something and our parents are doing it."

Manhattan now boasts 21 discothèques, where such luminaries as Rudolf Nureyev, Dame Margot Fonteyn, Truman Capote, Baby Jane Holzer, Sammy Davis Jr., ex-King Peter of Yugoslavia, Carol Channing, Peter Lawford, Tennessee Williams and Oleg Cassini mix it up with the hip twitchers. Both New York Senators—Jacob Javits and his wife Marion ("My husband and I just love to frug"), and Bobby Kennedy and Ethel ("I can't believe all that action on such a small floor")—make the discothèque scene. Jackie Kennedy, on her occasional visits to Il Mio, does a sedate version of the frug. Adlai Stevenson, the Maharani of Baroda, and the Duke and Duchess of Windsor have not progressed much beyond the twist, but Walter Cronkite's variations on the frug are a wonder to behold.

Wiggiest Kick. No debutante cotillion or country-club dance is complete these days without a heavy dose of rock 'n' roll. At a charity ball on the roof of the St. Regis Hotel, some of Manhattan's highest society wiggled around the dance floor doing the mule, flapping their hands like mules' ears to the thudding beat of Lester Lanin's orchestra. "It's good for your health," says Lanin, who beefs up his society band with a rock 'n' roll trio called the Rocking Chairs.

On campus, where it once was squaresville to flip for the rock scene, it now is the wiggiest of kicks. Brenda Lee, 20, a tot-sized (4 ft. 11 in., plus five inches of hair) rockette who developed her belting delivery as a high-school cheerleader, outranks Folk Singer Joan Baez and jazz's Ella Fitzgerald on the college popularity polls. "Rock really turns everybody on," says one Princeton senior.

Swinging World. Scholarly articles probe the relationship between the Beatles and the *nouvelle vague* films of

THE FRUG IN CHICAGO

THE JERK IN LOS ANGELES

THE MONKEY IN ATLANTA
Who can sit still?

Jean-Luc Godard, discuss "the *brio* and elegance" of Dionne Warwick's singing style as a "pleasurable but complex" event to be "experienced without condescension." In chic circles, anyone damning rock 'n' roll is labeled not only square but uncultured. For inspirational purposes, such hip artists as Robert Rauschenberg, Larry Rivers and Andy Warhol occasionally paint while listening to rock 'n' roll music. Explains Warhol: "It makes me mindless, and I paint better." After gallery openings in Manhattan, the black-tie gatherings often adjourn to a discothèque.

Even evangelists have adapted to the new beat. A group of Episcopal students from the University of Maryland, armed with electric guitars and bongo drums, have been celebrating with great success a big-beat "rejoice" Mass at several churches in the Washington-Maryland area, including a service that President Johnson and Lady Bird attended. In London, the Salvation Army has formed a rock 'n' roll street-corner group called the Joy Strings, whose repertory includes such numbers as *We're Going to Set the World A-Swinging*. "Our square approach," explains Drummer Captain Joy Webb, "wasn't getting us anywhere."

Rocked Curtain. The rock 'n' roll beat has proved to be more than the Iron Curtain can resist. All over Bulgaria, Beatle-like mushroom haircuts are sprouting faster than the crops—so much so that the government has plastered the countryside with posters ridiculing the hairy youth for their capitalistic degeneracy. They know better in Poland. When a correspondent for the daily Zycie Warszawy wrote contemptuously of Beatlemania two years ago, so many indignant letters poured in that the paper finally had to publicly disassociate itself from the reporter's views. Now Poland is overrun with rock 'n' roll bands, and hundreds more are playing in Hungary and Czechoslovakia, among them, Bratislava's Beatmen and Prague's Hell Devils. Though the "disgusting dynamism" of big-beat music is officially deprecated in the U.S.S.R., a rock 'n' roll group from Jaroslaw is accompanied by an army of finger-snapping fans whenever it goes on tour.

The sudden public acceptance of rock 'n' roll by so many people who supposedly should know better came as no surprise to the record and radio industries. Their surveys have long shown the existence of a vast underground of adult rock 'n' roll fans, including those who were raised on Elvis Presley and, though too embarrassed to admit it, never outgrew their hound-dog tastes. Today more than 40% of the "teen beat" records sold in the U.S. are bought by persons over 20. When a Manhattan rock 'n' roll disk jockey solicited votes for a "rate the record" feature one recent school-day morning, the station was deluged with 18,000 phone calls, all but a few from housewives. The same feature, aired during prime teen-age listening times, never drew more than 12,000 calls. With a seismographic eye on their markets, many of the sponsors for rock 'n' roll radio and TV shows are such Mom-oriented products as detergents, baby lotions and dishwashers.

Out of Misery. The origins of rock 'n' roll go deep—Deep South, U.S.A. There, in the 1930s, in the fields and shanties of the delta country, evolved an earthy, hard-driving style of music called "rhythm and blues"—played by Negroes for Negroes. Cured in misery, it was a lonesome, soul-sad music, full of cries and gospel wails, punctuated by a heavy, regular beat. With the migration to the industrial North after World War II, the beat was intensified with electric guitars, bass and drums, and the great blues merchants, like Muddy Waters, Bo Diddley, John Lee Hooker and Chuck Berry, made their first recordings.

One of the first white disk jockeys to play these "race records," as they were known in the industry, was Cleveland's Alan Freed, a flamboyant, rapid-fire pitchman who sang along with the records, slamming his hand down on a telephone book to accentuate each beat. Borrowing a phrase used in several rhythm-and-blues songs, Freed christened the music "rock 'n' roll." Gradually, the big beat began to take hold.

Then, in the fall of 1956, came Elvis Presley with his flapping hair, three-inch sideburns, and gyrating hips. "Ah wa-ha-hunt yew-hoo. Ah nee-hee-heed yew-hoo," he sang, and millions of teen-agers flipped.

"C'mon, Baby." There was obviously something visceral about Elvis and his music. Because soon there were riots in Hartford, Atlanta, and San Jose, Calif. Theaters were demolished in London and São Paulo, Brazil. Sociologists began to view the phenomenon with alarm. Studies showing that Elvis fans had a below-C average were circulated. A Senate subcommittee started to investigate the link between rock 'n' roll and juvenile delinquency. Pablo Casals condemned rock 'n' roll as "poison put to sound," Frank Sinatra called it a "rancid-smelling aphrodisiac," and Samuel Cardinal Stritch labeled it "tribal rhythms."

Then, in 1959, the payola scandal struck. Freed was indicted for accepting $30,000 in bribes from six record companies for pushing their releases. Rock 'n' roll faltered; record sales fell off 30%. Crooned Bing Crosby: "My kind of music is coming back."

But it didn't. Instead, rock 'n' roll did. Rejuvenation came in 1960 on the wings of a king-sized twister named Chubby Checker. A onetime Philadelphia chicken plucker, Chubby threw his tubby hips into high gear, and issued an invitation: "C'mon, baby, let's do the twist!"

From Noise to Style. The twist did not seem like much of an invention at the time. The participant merely planted

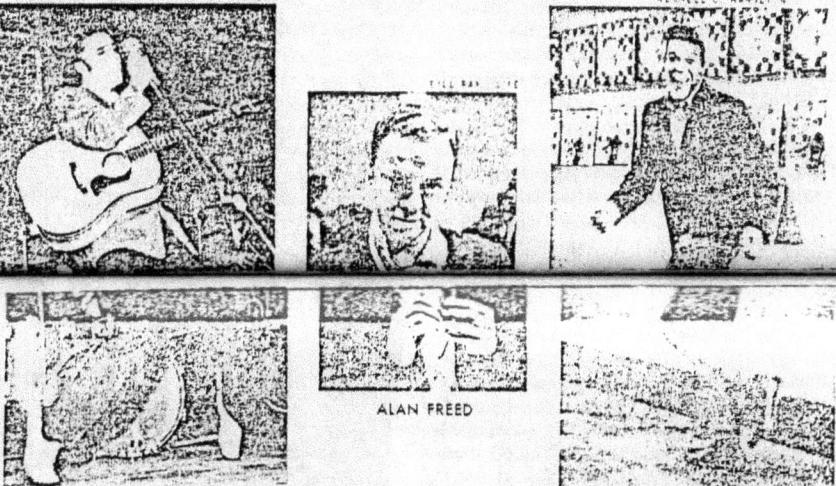

ELVIS PRESLEY (1956)   ALAN FREED   CHUBBY CHECKER
From a forgotten twist, a persistent beat.

his feet opposite his partner, started churning his arms as if shadowboxing, while rotating his hips like a girl trying to wriggle out of a tight girdle. But it transformed rock 'n' roll from a noise on the transistor radio into a teen-age style. For the first time since the decline of the jitterbug, teen-agers had a new dance, and soon, at Manhattan's Peppermint Lounge, the famous and near famous discovered its uninhibited joys. Fashion reacted dexterously. To provide freedom of motion, dress designers shortened skirts and loosened waists to turn out what soon came to be known as the discothèque dress. Nobody, but nobody, went to a mere nightclub any more.

Even then, rock 'n' roll was still dismissable among the sophisticates as a curiously persistent fad. But then came the British. U.S. parents had weathered Pat Boone's white-bucks period, the histrionics of Johnnie Ray, and the off-key mewings of Fabian, but this was something else again—four outrageous Beatles in high-heeled boots, undersized suits and enough hair between them to stuff a sofa. When they appeared on the *Ed Sullivan Show* in February 1964, 68 million people, one of the largest TV audiences in history, tuned in to see what all the ruckus was about.

What they saw was four young chaps having a jolly good bash. In the avalanche of publicity that followed, the Beatles emerged as refreshingly relaxed, if not downright lovable, personalities. Their disarming humor (Reporter: "Why do you wear so many rings on your fingers?" Ringo: "Because I can't get them all through my nose") melted adult resistance.

Back to Fun. There are dozens of rock 'n' roll groups in the U.S., most of them Negro, who can sing better and play better than the Beatles. But somewhere between the "ya da da da da da da" of *Sh-Boom* and the whine of *Hound Dog*, U.S. rock 'n' roll groups became mired in lamenting lost love and other ailments of the heart. By refusing to take themselves seriously, the Beatles made rock 'n' roll fun again.

The Beatles also made it all right to be white. As French Critic Frank Tenot notes: "Since the downfall of the Viennese waltz, nothing in larly dance, has known any success unless associated with one or another of the rhythmic discoveries of the Negro." Beatle music (known as "the Mersey sound") and even Beatle accents are actually Anglicized imitations of Negro rhythm and blues once removed. Says Beatle John Lennon: "We can sing more colored than the Africans."

The Brown Sound. Among the many white rock 'n' roll singers attempting a pure "brown sound" today, the most successful are the Righteous Brothers and the Rolling Stones. The Righteous Brothers, a Mutt-and-Jeff pair of 24-year-old Californians, are referred to by Negro disk jockeys as "our blue-eyed soul brothers" for the spiraling gospel wail and hoarse growl they inject into songs like their bestselling *Just Once in My Life*. Their name, in fact, is derived from the Sunday-go-to-meetin' phrase: "Man, that was really righteous, brothers."

To distinguish themselves from the Beatles, Britain's Rolling Stones have attempted to assume the image of Angry Young Men. "The Stones," their manager proudly explains, "are the group that parents love to hate." They sing Mersey-Mississippi rhythm and blues, backed by a quavering guitar and a chugging harmonica that smacks of cotton-pickin' time down South. With a kind of goggle-eyed conviction, Lead Singer Mick Jagger intones such earthy lyrics as:

Well, I'm a king bee buzzing 'round your hive...
Yeah, I can make honey, baby, let me come inside.
Yeah, I can buzz better, baby, when your man is gone.

At concerts, the Stones' fans greet their heroes by suggestively wiggling two fingers in the air. Their appeal, one 16-year-old girl frankly admits, "is sex—but don't print that; my mother would hit me."

Now Motown. The best brown sound is, of course, that sung by Negroes. Last year 42 of the bestselling rock 'n' roll songs were produced by one man:

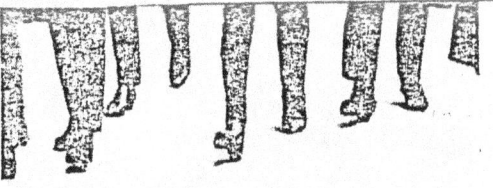

THE BEATLES IN LONDON
Suddenly, it was all happy.

Berry Gordy Jr., 35, who as head of Detroit's Motown Records, employs some 175 Negro artists. A former auto assembly-line worker, Gordy operates out of three adjoining shingle houses which bear the proud banner HITSVILLE, U.S.A. Beginning with a $700 loan six years ago, Gordy has built Motown into the nation's largest independent producer of 45-rpm records (1964 sales: 12 million records). Next to the Mersey sound, the "Motown sound" currently dominates the rock 'n' roll market. It is a swingy city blues sound, propelled by a driving beat, tambourines, violins (from the Detroit Symphony), hand clapping and an ever-present "Oh yeah; oh yeah" refrain from the chorus.

The prize fillies in Gordy's stable are the Supremes, three girls who grew up together in Detroit's squalid Brewster Housing Project. With four consecutive No. 1 records, they are the reigning female rock 'n' roll group, followed by Motown's Martha and the Vandellas. Diana Ross, 21, the Supremes' lead singer, is greatly envied for the torchy, come-hither purr in her voice. Her secret: "I sing through my nose."

Splash in Surf. Distinct from the brown-sound school are the Beach Boys from California: "We're not colored; we're white. And we sing white." They made their big splash with the "surf sound"—clean, breezy orchestration, a jerky, staccato beat and a high, falsetto quaver reminiscent of the Four Freshmen. The Beach Boys' tenor harmony goes so high that it sounds almost feminine, a fact that has all but locked out girl singers from the scores of surf groups performing on the West Coast. Beach Boys' songs, says Jack Good, producer of the rock 'n' roll TV show *Shindig*, "almost sound as if they were sung by eunuchs in the Sistine Chapel."

With hits like *Surfin'* and *Hang Ten* (toes over the edge of the surf board), the Beach Boys—three brothers, a cousin and a neighbor—have sold more than 12 million records, grossed as much as $25,000 for one concert in Sacramento. They write their own songs, following one rule of thumb: "We picture the U.S. as one great big California."

Part of the subculture of the surf sound is the hot-rodders' hit parade. Poaching off their own sandy preserve, the Beach Boys started with *Shut Down*, a classic of pit-stop poetry:

To get the traction, I'm a-ridin' the clutch...
Pedal's to the floor, hear his dual-quads drink...
understood.
I got a fuel-injected engine sitting under my hood.

Extrapolating the style, Jan and Dean (the "Father of Falsetto"), deliberately mix the sounds of surf and drag races into their records until the ear strains to grasp the lyrics. Explains Jan: "If the kids can hear the words, they'll turn their radio down. We want them to turn it up. It sort of relieves a kid's anxieties if he can drown out his parents."

Jan and Dean have endured, at least until next week, which is unique in a market where one-hit-and-forever-miss performances are the rule rather than the exception. Eva Boyd is typical. A few years ago, Eva was a 17-year-old maid working for a husband-and-wife songwriting team. On a dare, she recorded one of their songs, *The Loco-Motion*. It sold more than 1,000,000 copies, and Little Eva, as she was billed, picked up $30,000 and has not been heard from since.

Also Dropouts. Last week the man of the moment was Herman, 16, of Herman's Hermits. An engaging high school dropout who looks like a toy sheep dog, Herman (real name: Peter Noone) smiles a lot, claps his hands over his head, and sticks his finger in his mouth when he sings. His *Mrs. Brown, You've Got a Lovely Daughter*, rendered in a heavy English Midlands accent, was the No. 1 bestseller last week. Right behind it was *Count Me In* by Gary Lewis and the Playboys. Gary is Comedian Jerry Lewis' son. Unfortunately, he favors an overdose of echo-chamber effect, which makes him sound as if he had his head inside a fishbowl.

Rock 'n' roll lyrics have lately taken on urban socioeconomic themes. In the Crystals' *Uptown*, downtown is a place where a man "don't get no breaks" and "everyone's his boss, and he's lost in an angry land." But to hear Petula Clark on the subject, *Downtown* is an island of promise:

> Just listen to the music of the traffic in the city . . .
> How can you lose? The lights are much brighter there.
> You can forget all your troubles, forget all your cares.
> So go Downtown.

For his part, Chuck Berry is going the big apple. If it bumps and wiggles, that's the frug (pronounced froog). The rest are all charades. The dog, for example, is a slow-motion jerk (known in less erudite circles as the bump and grind), which is a slow-motion frug. Add a backstroke arm motion to the frug and you have the swim; add a tree-climbing motion and you have the monkey. Stick your thumbs in your ears and it's the mouse or the mule; up in the air, and it's the hitchhiker—and so on for the woodpecker, Cleopatra, Popeye, Harry James, Frankenstein, etc.

But the names, the gestures, are meaningless pressagentry. All you really have to do is shake your hips a little and then, as Sybil Burton puts it, "dance to suit yourself." Dancing to rock 'n' roll has become such a private reverie, in fact, that a partner, except in deference big-beat dancing have some psychiatrists worried. Says one: "It's sick sex turned into a spectator sport." The *voyeur* aspects are considerable. *Hollywood A-Go-Go*, one of the six nationally aired rock 'n' roll TV shows (including ABC's *Shindig* and NBC's *Hullabaloo*) that have debuted in the past year, features a line of young nubile blondes whose dancing would bring a blush to the cheeks of a burlesque stripper.

Healthy Outlet. Most sociologists, who take this sort of thing seriously, agree that the sensuality of rock 'n' roll is "safe sex." One cynical college observer has concluded that girls "who don't" dance more vigorously than girls "who do." "These dances," says Harvard Psychiatrist Philip Solomon, "are outlets for restlessness, for unexpressed and sublimated sex desires. This is quite healthy."

Many teen-agers consider all the orgiastic screaming as "uncool." The idols themselves have noted that the frantic fans who storm the stages are predominantly homely girls. Says Jeanne Katzenberg, a pretty 16-year-old: "Nobody in my group has crushes on the singers or anything. We all have real boy friends."

Reluctant Seal. Rock 'n' roll still does not exactly have the *Good Housekeeping* seal of approval. But even the most recalcitrant of parents now say: "Well, some of it's okay . . ." Some of it, in fact, is very good, far better than the adenoidal lamentations of a

NBC's HULLABALOO
All this, and adults too.

neither uptown nor downtown, just slightly commercial, and doing well at it. One of the great lowdown blues singers, Berry, 38, now is talking "teen feel," as in his *No Particular Place to Go*:

> The night was young and the moon gold . . .
> Can you imagine the way I felt?
> I couldn't unfasten her safety belt.

After serving time for armed robbery and escorting a 14-year-old Apache girl across a state line for "immoral purposes," Berry was recently granted a reprieve by his parole board in St. Louis and is now one of the most popular singers on the rock 'n' roll circuit. Chubby Checker is back pushing a new dance called the Freddie, a kind of side-straddle-hop routine.

Glazed Reverie. The Freddie is the latest of scores of new dances that have spun off the twist. The pelvis is crucial. If it swings from side to side, that's the twist, and the twist is now as dead as to custom, is not necessary. And that is its great attraction. Since couples neither touch nor even look at each other, all the shyness some men and women have about dancing—clammy hands, missing a beat, stepping on feet, etc.—is removed and, as one club owner says, "Everybody goes off into their own narcissistic bag."

The result is some of the most wildly creative dancing ever seen by modern or primitive man. In a discotheque, where the sound is so loud that conversation is impossible, the hypnotic beat works a strange magic. Many dancers become literally transported. They drift away from their partners; inhibitions flake away, eyes glaze over, until suddenly they are seemingly swimming alone in a sea of sound. Says Sheila Wilson, 18, a student at Vassar: "I give everything that is in me. And when I get going, I'm gone. It's the only time I feel whole."

The highly sensual implications of few years ago. Some of it is still awful, as might be expected in an industry that grinds out more than 300 new records each week. But for the first time rock 'n' roll can boast a host of singers who can actually sing. The music, once limited to four chords, is now more sophisticated, replete with counter-rhythms, advanced harmonics, and multivoiced choirs. Rock recordings, says Jazz Critic Ralph Gleason, "are a lot more interesting than the average jazz release." Conductor Leonard Bernstein likes the Beatles and does not hesitate to admit it: "They are very intelligent, and they have made songs which are really worthwhile. *Love Me Do* is really stirring and very reminiscent in some ways of Hindu music."

Above all, rock 'n' roll today is lively, youthful, aggressive, often funny, seldom heartsick. The lyrics, showing the influence of folk music, are fresher and more intelligible. Coming the other way, the folk types are beginning to feel the beat. Drums and electric guitars, long scorned by folkniks as decadent commercialism, are now featured on the latest album by Bob Dylan, folkdom's crown prince.

Meanwhile, as expressed in the folk-rock song *Walk Right In*, the invitation to join in the big beat is there for the accepting—with a slight qualifier:

> Walk right in, sit right down.
> Baby, let your hair hang down.
> Everybody's talkin' 'bout a new way of walkin'.
> Do you want to lose your mind?

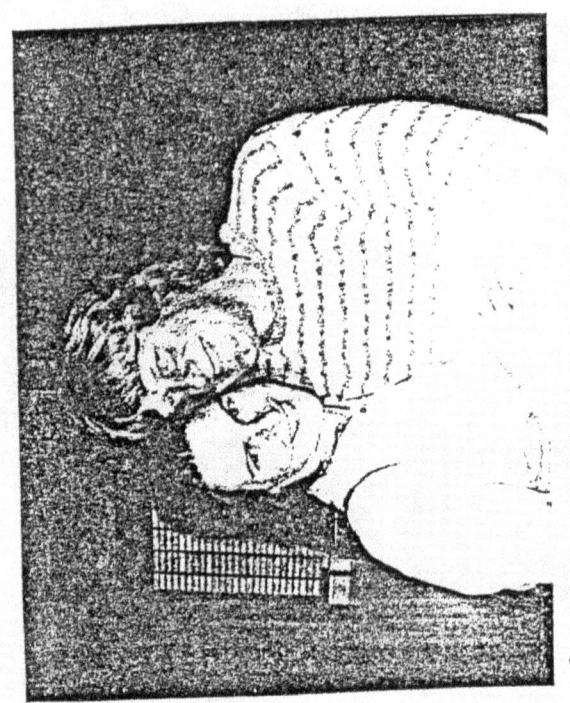

Dean and Susan in Ontario. Photo by Kathy Baxter.

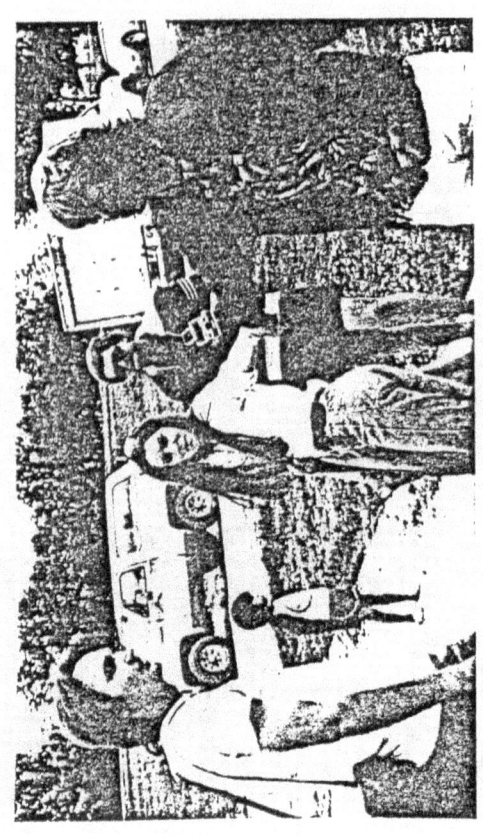

Susan and Dean at Oceans of Fun.

...continuation of...

LETTERS

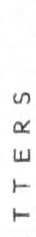

His 1977 cover for The Beach Boys Love You was, as is seen on the record, originally created in a grid framework of raised Braille-type beads so Dean could "see" his work. He wears camoflaging dark glasses in his photos in the liners of that LP.

Definitive and final proof. The color of the Roxy theater, the Palace of Rock on Hollywood's famed "Strip" that Dean designed--and the color of Dean's Porsche--BLACK! I rest my case.

Dr. Venita Bear
Helen Keller Institute

P.S. Is SM available in Braille? It would be nice so Dean could know what is going on!

SHORT CUTS
...CONTINUED FROM P. 4...

OFFICIAL NEWS FOR BEACH BOYS FANS:

Mike Love has shaved!

OFFICIAL NEWS FROM PAT AND KATHY TORRENCE:

The fan club described on page 23 of "Sunshine Music" issue #11, dated June, 1966 (6-66), has not been active for 15 years, nor will it be. Even if it does look like the bargain of the year at $2 per annum, PLEASE DO NOT SEND ANYMORE CHECKS FOR $2. The only current official JAN AND DEAN organization is "Sunshine Music." Thank you!

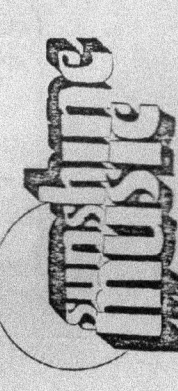

* DEAN TORRENCE MUSIC PHASE II JAPANESE IMPORT - $20.00
* COLLECTOR'S DELIGHT, VARIOUS ARTISTS - THE ORIGINAL DORE CUTS, JAN + DEAN, ETC - $10.00
* LEGENDARY MASKED SURFERS, JAN & DEAN RARITIES - $15.00
* BEACH BOYS / JAN + DEAN, CAPITOL S.M. SL8149 - $6.00
* MIKE LOVE, LOOKING BACK WITH LOVE - $5.00
* ROCK SHOPPE EP, JAN + DEAN, ETC - $11.00
* JAN + DEAN, BATMAN EP - $10.00
* JAN + DEAN, ETC, COKE JINGLE DEMO EP - $14.00

MINT / FACTORY FRESH / POSTPAID USA

DIANE VOSTEEN
5007 DETROIT
CLEVELAND, OHIO 44102
216-631-8444

all the following records are for sale for the prices shown below.
prices are in us dollars.(1 $ = circa £0.7o). all items are originals
unless stated otherwise. = R1

45s 45s 45s 45s

```
jan & dean    we go together/rosie lane(dore 555)usa                      ex/-    $ 1o
jan & dean    heart & soul/midsummer night's dream(london 9395)uk         ex/-    $ 1o
jan & dean    linda/when i learn how to cry(liberty 55531)uk demo         ex/-    $ 8
jan & dean    surf city/she's my summer girl(liberty 5558o)uk             ex/-    $ 6
jan & dean    honolulu lulu/someday(liberty 55613)usa                     ex/-    $ 6
jan & dean    little old lady/my mighty gto(liberty 55704)usa             ex/-    $ 5
jan & dean    fun city/totally wild(ode 66111)usa                         m-/-    $ 14
jan berry     sing sang a song(ode 6612o)usa mono/stereo demo             ex/-    $ 7
jan berry     skateboard surfin'usa(a&m 2o2o)usa mono/stereo demo         ex/-    $ 7
danté/evergreens time machine/dream land(madison 135)usa                  ex/-    $ 12
danté/evergreens yeah baby/what are you ...(madison 143)usa               ex/-    $ 12
yellow balloon yellow balloon/noollab wolley(canterbury 5o8)usa           ex/-    $ 6
yellow balloon stained glass window/can't..(stateside 2124)uk demo        ex/-    $ 6
barracudas   i want my woody back/subway surfin'(cell-out 1)uk            m-/m    $ 6
cantina band summer '81/out in...(millennium 1181o)usa(bb-medley)         ex/-    $ 2
rodney/brunettes little gto/holocaust...(line 1o21)germany                m-/-    $ 5
  (this last one features american spring and, according to a letter from the
   record company, brian wilson on backing vocals)
```

albums albums

```
beach boys    live in london(mfp 5o345)uk R1                              ex/ex   $ 7
various       spectrum usa/dialogue '74(ready marine corps)usa            vg+/ex  $ 9
  (incl "good vibrations" plus cuts by cat stevens, carole king, etc.)
beach boys    rarities(capitol 1c o64 7122931)germany                     m-/m-   $ 9
jan & dean    golden hits(liberty k22p-232)japan (incl lyrics) R1         m-/m-   $ 15
various       memories of the cow palace(rhino 1o5)usa R1                 m /m    $ 11
  (incl j&d's "when the saints" + cuts by ronettes, freddy cannon, etc.)
jan & dean    command performance(liberty 34o3)usa                        ex/ex   $ 18
jan & dean    folk 'n roll(liberty 3431)usa (bit bad pressing)            ex/ex   $ 14
jan & dean    meet batman(liberty 3444)usa                                ex/ex   $ 3o
fantastic baggys surfin' craze(edsel 118)uk (14 songs) R1                 m-/m-   $ 13
marketts      surfin' scene(liberty co62-97043)belgium  re-issue          ex/ex   $ 7
marketts      sunpower(world pacific 2187o)usa                            ex/ex   $ 5
raybeats      guitar beat(dfotm 7)uk                                      ex/ex   $ 7
ronny/daytonas sandy(mala 4oo2)usa                                        ex/vg   $ 19
shut downs    the deuce coupes(crown 393)usa                              ex/ex   $ 25
tradewinds    excursions(kama sutra 8o57)usa (incl "ny's a lonely
                                                         town")           ex/ex   $ 17
```

cassette

```
mike & dean + guests rock 'n' roll city(realistic 51-3oo9)usa             m-/-    $ 1o
  (above one without insert)
```

misc. items

```
beach boys    15 big ones press kit folders(kittyhawk)                    m       $ 1.5o
                (designed by one dean o torrence)
```

trade list with more rarities available on request !

SUNSHINE MUSIC 14

SUNSHINE MUSIC
c/o Doc Rock
2817 Crawford
Parsons, KS 67357

To:

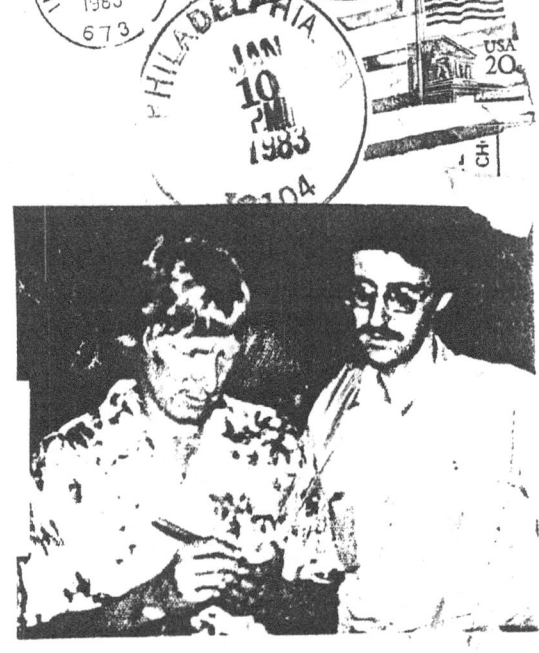

Dean O. Torrence
Frank M. Kisko

Send your photo w/ J or D for display here!!

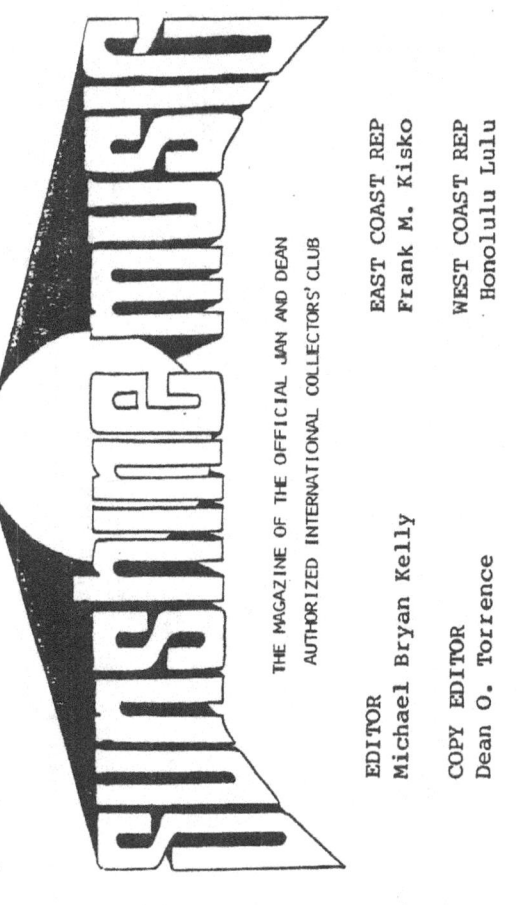

THE MAGAZINE OF THE OFFICIAL JAN AND DEAN
AUTHORIZED INTERNATIONAL COLLECTORS' CLUB

EDITOR
Michael Bryan Kelly

COPY EDITOR
Dean O. Torrence

EAST COAST REP
Frank M. Kisko

WEST COAST REP
Honolulu Lulu

Issue 14   Winter '83

*Contents not already copyrighted are
© 1982 by Michael Bryan Kelly*

SUBSCRIPTIONS

OK Jan and Dean fans world-wide, here is a simplified guide to getting SUNSHINE MUSIC into your mailbox safe and sound:

SAMPLE COPIES of SM are $1 in the US and surface overseas. Airmail, $2. SUBSCRIPTIONS are good for six (6) issues, at the rates indicated below:

USA, mailed in envelope	non-US Surface	Non-US Air	Surface Envelopes Charge is	Air Envelopes
USA $5	$7	$12	$10	$15 for Postage

Please enclose S.A.S.E. (self-addressed stamped envelope) with all letters.

★ *CHECK THE NUMBER ON YOUR ADDRESS LABEL. THE NUMBER THERE IS THE NUMBER OF* ★
★ *THE LAST ISSUE OF YOUR SUBSCRIPTION. IF THERE IS NO NUMBER, LUCKY YOU!!!!* ★

MAKE ALL CHECKS PAYABLE TO MICHAEL B. KELLY---------
-----NEW SUBSCRIBERS, PLEASE INDICATE THE NUMBER ON YOUR
SAMPLE ISSUE OR THE NUMBER YOU WANT YOUR SUBSCRIPTION TO
START WITH, OR ELSE!!---------------------------------

D E A D   M A N ' S   C U R V E

I was cruisin' in my Stingray late one night
When an XKE pulled up on the right.
He rolled down the window of his shiny new Jag
And challenged me then and there to a drag.
I said, "You're on, buddy, my mill's runnin' fine,
Let's come off the line now at Sunset and Vine,
But I'll go ya' one better if 'ya' got the nerve,
Let's race all the way to DEAD MAN'S CURVE!"

It's no place to play, ya' best keep away,
I can hear 'em say, "Won't come back from
DEAD MAN'S CURVE!"

The street was deserted late Friday night
We were buggin' each other while we sat out the light.
We both popped the clutch when the light turned green,
Ya' should'a heard the whine from my screamin' machine.
I flew past La Brea, Schwab's, and Crescent Heights,
and all the Jag could see were my six tail lights.
He past me at Doheny then I started to swerve,
But I pulled her out and there we were, at
DEAD MAN'S CURVE!

"Well, the last thing I remember, Doc, I started to
swerve. And then I saw the Jag slide into the curve.
I know I'll never forget that horrible sight.
I guess I found out for myself that everyone was right...
Won't come back from DEAD MAN'S CURVE!"

THE ROCK SUNSHINE MUSIC 14

Let Me Explain

Well, there was good news, but what happened? What happened to the tours, the record releases, the shows?

Well, look at it this way. Dean and Jan are both grown men. Dean is married. They do not fit neatly into any of the mainstream entertainment categories.

Management difficulties and personal circumstances defeated well-laid plans this year. But there is another perspective. Sure, this year was less exciting in terms of tours and records than we expected.

But, take the pre-CBS movie period, from the wreck onward. Then look at the last year. Reissues, a new live double LP, Mike and Dean on tour, K-Tels records, Sunshine Music... Not bad, really.

As for those people who long to have another Jan and Dean song on the top 40. Well, is that really what we should want? I for one care little for AC/DC, Kiss, Leon Redbone, the Go Gos, and the rest. I see no charm in Slam Dancing, the Pogo, or the Worm. I don't hear the kind of melodies, harmonies, and humor in today's music that I associate with Jan and Dean.

A hit record merely means that the teenagers of middle-class America have decided to buy a record. I don't really care what the teenagers of today listen to or buy. If I did, I would be putting out a Blondie 'zine instead of a Jan and Dean 'zine.

In the '60s, 15 years after his heyday, Frank Sinatra settled in to a stature of established artist who had very few hits but was still a draw. Why can't Jan and Dean assume this kind of image? If Liberty/EMI can reissue a Fantastic Baggies LP, why can't some label release new J&D material for the fans of the music of the '60s without caring if the kids of the '80s get into it or not?

If you are a teenager and groove on J&D, fine. But that may not be a desirable goal in the Phase III days.

What do you think? Let me hear from you. And, Bust Your Buns!!

SHORT C...

LATE ITEMS--TOO LATE TO SHRINK--

"Finally! The First New JAN AND DEAN recording in over fifteen years. Contains live versions of all their big hits. RNDA 1498 $14.98 List."

And so reads the dayglo sticker on the cover of the first new PROFESSIONAL Album by J&D in, well, 15 years!

It is a two-LP album. The cover is a work of art-- a la Torrence/Kittyhawk. And the front cover photo is one of THE best to come out of PHASE II! The back cover lists the 24 cuts: 11 J&D hits, 9 BB5 hits, 2 Beatles songs, and 2 rock 'n' roll standards. Also on the back are 6 graphs of liner notes which are great until the last few sentences.

Inside are some 50 (count 'em, 50) color photos! Holy Kodak! Also a full set of credits. The band is the Bel-Air Bandits, recorded 10-3-81.

New Girl In School--Good bomps from Jan, Dean even does some lead in falsetto! Gonna Hustle You sneaks in at the fade!

Jenny Lee--Once again, Jan carries off the bomps in great style. Dean Ginsburg does a fine whine on the lead, complete with cracking of the voice! The false ending harks back to the '60s fun!

Baby Talk--A highlight of the LP, both Dean and Jan seem to really enjoy this one. The introduction is clever, Jan then leads the Bandits in support of another youthful lead by Dean. The fade gives me goosebumps, as Dean hits all the right falsetto notes, even a steal from She's Still Talkin' Baby Talk!

Linda--AT LAST! A live version of the first J&D song I ever bought! Both Jan and Dean get their alternating leads perfectly, with Dean wisely dueling the lead to match the sound of the hit 45! One of the best live jobs extant!

Drag City--One of the finer touches of the hit 45, and a highlight of the stereo LP, was Jan's "Goin' to Drag City!" Well, it's there. First two verses by Dino, then he switches to background for a most effective rendition.

Honolulu Lulu--It was their 6th biggest chart success for whatever that means, yet it is often neglected as a sort of phantom record lost between Surf and Drag Cities. Appropriately, it is not rushed here. This song is supposed to be done moderato. Jan

...to p. 15....

THE TRUE STORY OF...

In terms of original popularity with the public at large, "Surf City" was once Jan and Dean's biggest song. Then, as they became more known for comedy, "The Little Old Lady (From Pasedena)" became their best-known tune. But, ever since the excellent TV movie DEADMAN'S CURVE (sic), the Jan and Dean "theme song," if you will, has been "Dead Man's Curve."

I was interested in J&D from the beginning in the '50s. When "Linda" became a hit, I bought my first 45. My friend and I almost wrecked his dad's old Ford the day we first heard "Dead Man's Curve" on the car radio. At that point, I began buying every Jan and Dean LP and 45, and I have never quit.

However, there are a lot of funny things about "Dead Man's Curve." Mainly, it turned up on an amazingly large number of records in a variety of forms (see table at end of article). I asked Dean about this.

MK- When I first heard "Dead Man's Curve" on the radio, I quickly went out and bought the Drag City LP because I saw that it had "DMC" on it. Much to my surprise, the "DMC" on the Drag Sitting LP was not the one I had heard on the radio--not at all!

DT- The first "Dead Man's Curve" was the only "Dead Man's Curve" we had, which was the first version that came out on Drag City.

MK- And the mono version of that had a much longer fade than the hit or the stereo Drag City LP version.

DT- Really? That's interesting. The mono version on Drag City?

MK- Yes!

DT- Hum-m-m! I wonder why?

MK- I discovered then that I had to get both the stereo and mono issues of each LP because they would be different.

DT- You know, I'm really glad to hear you say that. Fadeouts are very important to me.

MK- Like the long one on your UA version of "Sidewalk Surfin'" and that marvelously long fade on your Legendary Masked Surfers' "Gonna Hustle You"?!

DT- Well, I just got a Drifters' LP, and it is so disappointing because they faded all of the songs early! Ben E. King did some of the most...neatest vocal things he ever did, they were on the ends. AND THEY CUT OFF ALL OF THEM! Like you're saying, I knew every note and where it went, and when it faded on the singles...

MK- Right!

DT- All of a sudden you get an album, and none of it's there!

MK- If the LP has a longer fade, that's OK...

DT- Oh, yes!

MK- If it's shorter than the single, then it's no good.

DT- Right, exactly!

MK- Now, "She's My Summer Girl"...you never knew what that would be like. The single and different LP versions were all...some end like others begin, some are missing vocal or piano parts. Once, on a radio station, right between two commercials, the DJ played just that one bit you did: "11 bees, 4 wasps, and a turtle; 11 bees, and a bumble bee!" And I'll bet most people had no idea what that was, off the Ride the Wild Surf LP.

DT- Was that on an album?!

MK- "She's My Summer Girl," the flip side of "Surf City"?

DT- Yes!

MK- Figures.. (Then in Dean's send-up voice): They put EVERYthing out on the albums! Boy, get those albums out there!

DT- Well...

MK- I don't remember stuff like that particularly. I do remember the "Dead Man's Curves" though, and that used to bother me after we cut the good one, the hit one.

DT- Really?

MK- The first one, we planned it that way, we knew that that version was going on the Drag City LP. We knew just how we were gonna revise it and redo it, but we didn't have

DT- "OK, new title! Now we can put out an album called New Girl in School and people who have Drag City with "Dead Man's Curve" on it will be attracted to buy the new LP 'cause it has a new hit in the title." Our answer was that "DMC" is a hit, too. "Well," they countered, "We'll put that on the cover, too!" But, mostly, that was to be a "NGIS" LP according to management. They figured it was a residual thing, since many people may not even know that "DMC" was on the other side of "NGIS."

MK- But wasn't "DMC" a bigger hit most places around the country?

DT- Yes, it was, but still "NGIS" (voice) "was a top-twenty record, and top twenty records gotta sell 150,000 albums," which is a lotta albums.

DT- Did you point out that if they'd let you use the original "Gonna Hustle You" words to "NGIS" that it might have been even bigger?

DT- No, we pointed that out and they said, "You're wrong! The original words would sell less because no DJ would play it!" We said, "Whataya mean, 'no one will play it'?" Anyway, you read the liner notes...

MK- Right. For a Jan and Dean fan, those liner notes on ANTHOLOGY were quite a reward for maintaining devotion and searching for records.

DT- Yeah, I was very happy with that, it finalized my involvement with an era, "Phase I," it was nice to compile it, put it all together with my favorite stuff, and then to be able to put on there the most important things, editorially... That was the idea really, to make it an editorial package. More than anything else, that was how we set it up. I put songs on there that had a story to them. Normally, it is the other way around, putting songs on there that have value as songs, and if they happen to have anything to say about anything, you say it. It was set up this different way, and of course it does end up having a lot of hits on it, because there is more to say about hits than there is about stiffs. Still, I tried to say something about the stiffs, like "You Really Know How To Hurt A Guy"...
(note: which song Dean left off the album, but which song I still like very, very much!!)
...without putting them on the album, 'cause I didn't really have room for them anyway!

MK- I was disappointed that "Yellow Balloon" wasn't there. I was hoping I would finally hear it in a stereo mix, to see if it was good that way or not, to see what it was like.

DT- I think I did cut it in stereo.

MK- I'm buying a Save For A Rainy Day from Greg Shaw for $8.

DT- Really? Too Much! Tell him to give it to you or else I won't do his logo for him! Anyway, that is why there were originally two versions of "Dead Man's Curve." After that, anytime it was not the hit version, it was an engineers' mistake.

DEAD MAN'S CURVE DISCOGRAPHY

USA Releases of Liberty Masters

Date	SM/ID#	Disc	Details
11-63	1	LP, Drag City	mono / lyrics include "french tail lights," "and there I was," "ya' won't come back."
	1-s		stereo / same, with shortened fade.
2-64	2	45 #55672 "B" side of New Girl in School	mono only / lyrics include "six tail lights," "and there we were," "won't come back"; added more instruments such as oboe, harp; modified melody line; added vocal parts; added background parts on second verse; added horn part at end of each chorus; shortened fade; added crash, tire, and engine effects. (2-sided picture sleeve)
5-64	2	LP New Girl in School	mono / same as 45 hit release.
	2-s		stereo / same as mono, slightly shorter fade.

45RPM REISSUES:

Date	SM/ID#	Disc	Details
	2	All Time Hit Series	mono, same as hit 45, silver label, "A" side-Drag City.
	2	United Artist Silver Spotlight Series	mono, same as hit 45, Dean designed label, "A" side-Drag City.
11-73	2	United Artists Promotional	mono/stereo, same as hit 45/NGIS LP.
1-65	3	LP Command Performance	mono / no effects; live band; studio vocals; lyrics like 45 except "there I was," and joke recitation.
	3-s		stereo / same as mono.

SUNSHINE MUSIC 14

Certified k·TOP 40
Silver Dollar Survey

Top Big Picks of the Week

Monday

RECORDS INTRODUCED AND HEARD FIRST ON K-TOP
Week of March 16, 1964

Charlie Christian
6--8
You're A Wonderful One
Marvin Gaye

Bob Barber
8--12
We Love You Beatles
Carefrees

Tom Grimes
12--4
Go Tell It On the Mountain --
Peter, Paul & Mary

Bob Harris
4--7
Ain't Nothin' You Can Do
Bobby Bland

Rick Douglass
7--10
Can't Buy Me Love
Beatles

Dave Axton
10--12
Congratulations
Rick Nelson

Prof. J. Jazmo Bop
Midnight--6
Hippy Hippy Shakes
Swingin' Blue Jeans

1. Java — Al Hurt
2. Kissin' Cousins — Elvis Presley
3. High Heel Sneakers — Tommy Tucker
4. I Want To Hold Your Hand/ I Saw Her Standing There — The Beatles
5. I Love You More and More — Al Martino
6. Glad All Over — Dave Clark Five
7. What Kind Of Fool — Tams
8. She Loves You — Beatles
9. Money — Kingsmen
10. Please Please Me/From Me To You — Beatles
11. The Shoop-Shoop Song — Betty Everett
12. I'll Make You Mine — Bobby Vee
13. Blue Winter — Connie Francis
14. Navy Blue — Diane Renay
15. Twist and Shout — Beatles
16. Nadine — Chuck Berry
17. My Heart Cries For You — Ray Charles
18. Hello Dolly — Louis Armstrong
19. Needles and Pins — Searchers
20. Ain't Gonna Tell Anybody — Jimmy Gilmer
21. Fun, Fun, Fun — Beach Boys
22. Tonight I Met An Angel — Chiffons
23. The Way You Do The Things You Do — Temptations
24. Vaya Con Dios — Drifters
25. California Sun — Riverias
26. Good News — Sam Cooke
27. I Wish You Love — Gloria Lynne
28. Crooked Little Man — Serendipity Singers
29. Live Wire — Martha & Vandellas
30. Jailer, Bring Me Water — Trini Lopez
31. My Bonnie — Beatles
32. New Girl In School/ Dead Man Curve — Jan and Dean
33. Bird Dance Beat — Trashmen
34. Stay — Four Seasons
35. Think — Brenda Lee
36. My True Carrie Love — Nat King Cole
37. Hey Bobba Needles — Chubby Checker
38. Worried Guy — Johnny Tillotson
39. Suspicion — Terry Stafford
40. Ebb Tide — Lenny Welch

Pick Album
Columbia---Hey Little Cobra----Rip Chords

SUNSHINE MUSIC 14

...CONTINUED FROM P. 5

carries the lead, a fine job all around.

Ride the Wild Surf--Again the men take turns on lead and on background, just like on the hit! The band does a laudable job of imitating the J&D orchestra, and the pacing is perfect!

Sidewalk Surfin'--Jan uses the Skateboard Surfin' USA lyrics (following some Dixie), Dean sticks to falsetto. Dean is amazing; even Frankie Valli uses his normal voice on the majority of the falsetto parts when he does shows, but Dean of the Falsetto keeps it going all the way!

LOLFP--Just like the hit!

Deadman's Curve--Here we go again! (See story, this issue.) Very authentic. You know, ammy artists feel compelled to "jazz up" or otherwise update their hits when in concert, notably the Beach Bums, Dion, & Elvis. But on this album, even the band sticks to the beat and brings in a solid-gold winner!

Surf City--What can I say? This is IT!

Sure, we all missed the team this last year. But now, you can have your own Phase II concert anytime-- just take the phone off the hook, close your eyes, and drift back with Jan and Dean to ONE SUMMER NIGHT-- L I V E ! ! !

Results of the SWEEPSTAKES.
Due to a mix-up between the lazy bum who devised the sweepstakes and your crud-face editor, the answer to the Sweepstakes puzzle will be published next issue. However, the winners, chosen in random drawings, are: 1st place, Beth Krueger; 2nd, Cindy Porter; 3rd, Rebecca Shugart; 4th, Daniel Bossard. Prize distribution will be announced later, as well. Thanks to all who participated.

9-65	1	LP	Golden Hits Volume II	mono same as original (Drag City LP) version (not hit version), shortened fade.
	1-s			stereo same as original (Drag City LP, stereo) version (not hit version).
1-66	4	LP	Pop Symphony	mono orchestral, non-vocal version, arranged, conducted, produced by Jan Berry and George Tipton, assisted by Dean Torrence.
	4-s			stereo same as mono.
4-66	2-a	LP	Filet of Soul	mono alternate mix of hit 45; no harp; no tire, engine, crash effects; strong lead and drum.
	1-s-a			stereo alternate mix of original non-hit Drag City LP stereo version.
2-72	2-s	LP	ANTHOLOGY	some mono/some stereo side 2 same as NGIS LP, stereo
	5			side 4 live version #2, edited, new joke recitation.
(As of 2-72, "Dead Man's Curve" becomes "Deadman's Curve" for all time.
11-74	2	LP	Gotta Take That One Last Ride	quazi-moto mono (but compatible with quadrophonic or tetrahedral) mono, same as hit 45.
1966	2-s	LP	The Very Best of Vol. I	stereo same as NGIS stereo LP version.
1979	2-s	LP	999 Deadman's Curve	stereo same as NGIS stereo LP version.
1981	1-s-a	LP	Radio Shack The Beach Boys/ Jan and Dean	stereo same as Filet of Soul LP version.

Non-Liberty/Non USA/Non-Releases

Most non-US LP versions are same as US versions of same LPs. Compilations of all the hits (Liberty Masters) tend to have 1 (1-s). 5

Dean and Papa re-cut for K-Tel, widely issued on many labels. 2-a

Bootleg studio Out-takes LP, private version for friends, 45 hit bizarre ending, mono. 2-b

Unreleased 1964 version, mono, no effects on fade, but the effect from "A Beginning From An End" is used here first, during recitation and fade! 6

Dean re-cut alone for TV movie, never used or released. 7

Dean and Mike Love re-cut in 1978-9 for soundtrack LP of movie, with "telephone" recitation, unreleased.

SUNSHINE MUSIC 14

Something Old

DEAN TORRENCE MUSIC PHASE II 1977-1981......$18.00
COLLECTOR'S DELIGHT...ORIGINAL DORE CUTS....$8.00
LEGENDARY MASKED SURFERS...J.&D. RARITIES....$12.00
JAN AND DEAN ODDITIES...17 great cuts......$12.00
JAN AND DEAN DORE 101...GERMAN REPRO......$14.00
JAN AND DEAN BATMAN E.P...w/BOY BLUNDER.....$8.00

Something New

JAN AND DEAN & THE BEL-AIR BANDITS
ONE SUMMER NIGHT/LIVE...THE FIRST NEW JAN AND DEAN
RECORDING IN OVER 15 YEARS. CONTAINS LIVE VERSIONS
OF ALL THEIR BIG HITS...2 RECORD SET......$13.00

Something Else

CELEBRATION...WITH MIKE LOVE,ETC............$4.00
HISTORY OF SURF VOL. 3...BEL-AIR BANDITS,ETC-$7.50
****
ALL ALBUMS ARE FACTORY FRESH...MINT...YOUR
SATISFACTION IS GUARANTEED. FREE INSURED DELIVERY
ANYWHERE IN THE U.S.A.
****************DOLLAR CASSETTE OFFER*************
FOR EACH ALBUM YOU ORDER YOU MAY SELECT ONE OR MORE
OF THE FOLLOWING FACTORY FRESH CASSETTES FOR ONLY A
BUCK EACH;1 ALBUM;1 CASSETTE...2 ALBUMS;2 CASSETTES
ETC, ETC. *CELEBRATION...WITH MIKE LOVE *ELEPHANT
MAN SOUNDTRACK *AIRPLANE SOUNDTRACK *DAYS OF HEAVEN
SOUNDTRACK *MIKE NESMITH LIVE *BEST OF MARK ALMOND.
DIANE VOSTEEN, 5007 DETROIT AVE., CLEVELAND, OHIO,
44102, (216) 631-8444 PHONE ONLY AFTER 6 PM EST...

A FAMILY AFFAIR

Frequently requested by fans is the kind of family information that is often taken for granted, and is seldom if ever published, about Jan and Dean. Marny Koch has vouched for the following as accurate, coming as it does straight to Marny from Kathy Torrence and Mr. and Mrs. Berry. The date and year of birth is provided where available.

★ Mr. Maurice Dean Torrence   December 12
  Mrs. Natalie Ormsby Torrence   April 10
  Dean Ormsby Torrence   March 10, 1940
  Kathleen Jane Torrence   March 23, 1945
  Susan Vogelberger Torrence (Mrs.) ?
  Mr. William Laden Berry   ?
  Mrs. Clara Lorentz Berry   October 12, 1937
  Luana D. Berry   April 3, 1941
  William Jan Berry   November 1, 1942
  Kenneth W. E. Berry
  Bruce Berry (deceased)
  Brian L. Berry   June 22, 1948
  Aleta K. Berry   July 17, 1852
  Steven G. Berry   February 24, 1959
  William B. Berry   September 9, 1961
  Melissa L. Berry   February 11, 1963

As you can see, Jan is from a bunch of Berries, while Dean came in Torrents...

PIX PICKS

Frequently requested by fans are photos of Jan and Dean. Here are the names and addresses of people who have photos for sale. Please send an SASE with all inquires, and good luck!

Connie Celentano   Arlene Coletti
4639 Los Feliz Blvd.   Box 396
Hollywood, CA 90029   NY NY 10002

Smile Photos (Dean ordered Arlene Richie
Box 15293   these!)   5527 S Braeswood
Chesapeake, VI 23320   Houston, TX 77096

Sharon Pirosko   Marty Ross
3205 Lucerne AV   1423 Palxyra RD
Parma, Ohio   Warren, OH 44485

STARS ADDRESSES

Frequently requested are the home addresses of Jan and Dean. Tough noogies!

LETTERS

Dear Doc,
  Enclosed is check for $15 for the first 10 back issues and a subscription. Are J&D going to tour the East Coast soon? Any word on releases by them?
                                          Surf's Up!
                                            J. K.

Dear J. K.,
  Thanks for the support! No tour dates set, but there is a new release!
                                            Doc Rock

Dear Myke,
  Please renew me for 6 more great issues! I really look forward to each one. How do you like "One Summer Night" live? I like it! All of the new packages really surprised me! Did you see that Liberty/EMI reissued an abridged version of Tell 'Em I'm Surfin'? Anyway, keep up the great work!
                                          Yours In Surf,
                                            Doug K.

Dear Doug,
  Wow! A reissue of the Fantastic Baggies LP? I had to special order it in '65, and then the clark ribbed me for being into surf, still! Thanks!
                                            Myke

Dear Michael,
  Enclosed is a check for $20 for all of the back issues and a subscription. I loved the sample double issue! I've got some J&D LP's and 45's for sale, some mint. How and/or where can I sell them? Thanks for everything.
                                          Sincerely,
                                          Karen Shraeder/72 E. St Honeoye Falls NY 14472

Dear Karen,
  Thanks to you! And I think we just solved your problem of the records!
                                          Sincerely,
                                            Michael

Dear Sunshine Music,
  I am a collector of J&D video. Could you ask other subscribers if they want to trade or something?
                                          Best,
                                          Tim Smith/42 Village Trail Honeoye Falls NY 14472

Dear Tim,
  Sorry, I can't do that! (TWO LETTERS IN A ROW FROM HONEOYE FALLS!! WOW!!)
                                          Sunshine Music

Dear Mike,
  Here is my $7 renewal! Keep up the good work! By the way, here's one: On page 38 of Alan Clark's booklet, red cover, there is a trade ad for for a film, JAN AND DEAN MEET MYRON THE MUSICAL APE, (Dunhill Films, Inc., A Paramount Release). A film short? A Long Lost Musical? Who is this ape, anyway? The ad also mentions the COMMAND PERFORMANCE LP, datain the ad. Any ideas? Readers guesses?
                                          Take it easy,
                                            George

Dear George,
  You have a sharp eye! Maybe it was a misprint, and meant to say, JAN AND DEAN MEET BRIAN THE MUSICAL APE?
                                            Mike

Dear Doc Rock,
  You wouldn't believe what happened! I forgot to renew! Am I mad at myself! Here is my check! Sned #11, fast! I saw on MTV today that J&D are supposed to have a new LP, double, out soon. I can't wait!
                                          Thanks,
                                            Ken H.
P.S. Recently bought MALIBOOZ RULES with Dean and Walter Egan. Great!
                                            Doc Rock

Dear Ken,
  New LP? What new LP?
P.S. Keep those renewals coming in!

Hi Mike!
  How is Doc Rock doing these days? I've neglected all of my subscriptions lately--even National Geographic! Today I got the Wailers on Nrtional Etiquette ET-6, distributed by Liberty. "We're Goin' Surfin'" b/w "Shakedown." The curious part is the composer credits for the former: (Dangel-Ormsby-Morrill). Address on the label, Box 682, Tacoma, WA. Valet Pub. Co. Just thought that Dean (a.k.a. Nat Ormsby) might have had a hand in this one??
                                          Take care,
                                          Steve, Alberta Canada

WELL, DEAN, IS THIS YOU??????

Dear Sunshine Music,
  I'm a big J&D fan, have most of the LP's, and want to subscribe. Here's my $12. Do you know where I can get J&D's GOLDEN HITS, OLD WAX AND NEW WAVES, SPARD, JAN'S WD LP, and the Beach Boys ANAHEIM '78?
                                          All the Best,
                                          Daniel Bossard
                                          Gotthelfweg 9
                                          5036 Oberentfelden
                                          Switzerland

Dear Daniel,
  Thanks. Let's hope you get some LP offers!
                                            SM

Doc Rock,
  Here is my Sweepstakes Entry. There's a new Japanese release, JAN AND DEAN SING THE ORIGINAL RECORDINGS FROM DEADMAN'S CURVE." Brck cover has hatch and Davison. Included are some extra songs from the DMC/NGIS LP. Alos, got a promo of "Miss America" by Drnte and his Friends. Any J&D involvement?
                                            Doug

Doug, Thanks for the news. J&D never sang on any Dante record.
                                            Doc Rock

Dear Michael,
  Here's $7 for issues 2,4,6,8,10,and 11. I really liked my first one (12-13)! I just got the SURF CITY LP and it plays really well. It was 25¢. Did I get a good deal? They were really crazy together! When Dean got out fo his car, I asked for a picture. Hn said, "Sure." I also got his autograph! He was really nice! Keep up the good work.
                                            Dalia I.

Dear Dailia,
  Isn't Dean the greatest! (Except for Jan, of course!).
                                            Michael

SUNSHINE MUSIC 14

Dear Mike,
Was really surprised to read of Dean's wedding. More, I was amazed that there was no network coverage. I assume it went off with a hitch. I hope someone told Dean that there are two questions that a bachelor was never asked:
1. Where are you going?
2. Who was that on the phone?
After I got married, I found out that "None of your business" was not the suitable response! Where will the newlyweds be parking their skateboards?
I was wondering, has the collectors' club considered delving into video tapes? I need DMC on Beta. A tape called "60's R&R Revival" has the Titanic Twosome on it, but there must be more?
Later,
Bob

Dear Bob,
Glad to hear you are happily married! Skateboards are always parkkd in an old violin case. As for video tapes, let's hear from the readers!
Mike

Dear Mike,
Congratulations on issue 12-13--very enjoyable! Here is my renewal! How send me all the back issues!
Paul L.

Dear Paul,
Thanks!
Mike

Dear Michael,
Unre is a phot for the back cover. Can anyone read the back cover of the PHASE II LP? Also, can SM print photo copies?
Bust your buns,
Linda and Pam M.

Dear Linda and Pam,
I am sure Ryuichi can read it. SM loves to print photo copies, but the quality is much better if I can use the original!
Michael

Dear Michael,
There is a bootleg of DORE 101. An exact copy from Germany. The sound is superb! It can be identified by the absence of the words "Album by Container-Kraft" and the sidewise writing on the back. On the disc, the boot has the name DORE in the run-out groove area. Also, the photo is washed out on the front. It is a good LP, but I'd hate to see someone pay $100.00 for a phoney. Lew of DORE says it is news to him.
Diane Vosteen

Dear Diane,
Thanks for the word. However, I have a DORE 101 that I bought about 10 years ago that fits your description. It is thick wax like the regular DORE with the Container-Kraft bit. So, if it is a boot, they made it long before the late-70's J&D boom! Perhaps my LP, if not yours, is just a second pressing or a pressing from a different plant? The fades are a little different from the Container-Kraft version.
Michael

Dear Myke,
Your issue 12-13 arrived the day I had Susan's parents here for dinner. The Vogelbergers were in L.A. on business, and it was great to have SUNSHINE MUSIC to show them pictures of Susan and Dean (page 45). We all enjoyed the magazine, its articles and pictures. Decided it was time to pay for our subscription! Also, thanks for the correction on the final page. (Still got money and two letters for Kathy's newsletter last week!).
On page 44 last issue, there is a letter from Dr. Venita Bear of the Helen Keller Institute suggesting that Dean is blind. Please direct her attention to the picture on the opposite page, of Dean and his bride. One look at Susan is proof that Dean is not blind!

And, Myke, this goes for you, too. The snap of Mrs. Rock with Mike and Dean is proof that your eyesight is excellent, too!
Anyone who calls information for the number of Dean Torrence Senior--and I just direct them to get a sample of SUNSHINE MUSIC! This saves me a lot of time, since SM answers all of their questions!
Thanks again for all of your clever writing and your labor.
Sincerely,
"Pat" Torrence

P.S. Please send a gift subscription to the name and address below. These are 2nd cousins we will be visiting. Thanks, Pat.

Dear Pat,
THANKS! Your letter made it ALL worthwhile!!!
Sincerely,
Myke

SUBSCRIBER ADS---$1---SUBSCRIBER ADS---$1---SUBSCRIBER ADS---$1---SUBSCRIBER ADS

Many misc. photos of J&D, $1.50 each. Sharon Fox 5742 W. Giddings Cht. 60630

For sale, $60 each: Videocassette DEADMAN'S CURVE; J&D'S CALIFORNIA SPECIAL; J&D COMPILATION (Dinah, TODAY, Midnite Special, Sha Na Na, etc.); TAMI SHOW; Add $2 for P&H. Louise Texler, 2825 W. 12th ST B'klyn, NY 11224

J&D Photos available from HOLLYWOOD BOOK CITY COLLECTABLES 6625 H'wood Blvd. 90028
Also from Connie Celentano, 439 W. Valencia, Burbank, CA 91506

WHEN ANSWERING ANY AD, PLEASE MENTION SUNSHINE MUSIC. THAT IS ANY AD IN SM, OK?

JAN & DEAN

Since their first hit in 1958, Jan & Dean went on to become "surf" legends with their special sound. A car accident in 1966 interrupted Jan's career, and he still walks with a limp. But Dean, 40, and Jan, 39, continue to play concerts all over the U.S. They play some oldies and delight audiences with new songs!

RECORDS FOR SALE Please mention Michael Kelly and SM when ordering records from any ad in SM!
Special just arrived Bel-Air Bandits w/ Torrence $6 pp.
Diane Vosteen, see large ad for address.
Caution: The guy who had the auction inserted inside the last issue never paid for his ad--cost SM bundle, too! I personally wouldn't buy records from him... Rip Ace Dealer Rip Lay has mint 45s for sale. $4. Rip is a great dealer. SUNDAY KIND OF LOVE, $4. TENNESSEE, $4. Johnny Crawford's JUDY LOVES ME, written/produced by Jan, $3. Postage, $1.75, inc. insurance. Box 342, Concord, CA 94522.

5. DEAD MAN'S CURVE

I was cruisin' in my stingray, late one night
When an XK-E pulled up on the right
He rolled down the window of his shiny new Jag
And challenged me then and there to a drag.

I said, "You're on, buddy, my wheel's runnin' fine
Let's come off the line, now, sun settin' fine
But I'll go you one better if you got the nerve
Let's race all the way to Deadman's curve."

Chorus: Deadman's curve is no place to play
Deadman's curve, you must keep away
Deadman's curve, I can hear 'em say
Won't come back down Deadman's curve.

The street was deserted late Friday night
We were buggin' each other while we sat out the light
We both popped a clutch when the light turned green.
And you should've heard the whine from my screamin' machine.

I soon passed the fresh mobs of girls in bright
And all the Jag could see were my six tail lights
He passed me at Dohini, then I started to swerve
But I pulled out and there we were, at Deadman's curve

Deadman's curve is no place to play, Deadman's curve

Well, the last thing I remember, Doc, I started to swerve
And then I saw the Jag slide into the curve
I know I'll never forget that horrible sight
I guess I found out for myself that everyone was right.

Won't go back down Deadman's curve
Repeat Chorus twice

● DEAD MAN'S CURVE

*) Jan Berry, Roger Christian, Artie Kornfeld and Brian Wilson

I was crusin' in my Sting-Ray late one night
When an XK-E pulled up on the right
He rolled down the window of his shiny new Jag and challenged me then and there to a drag.

I said you're on buddy my mill's runnin' fine
Let's come off the line now at Sunset & Vine
But I'll go ya one better if ya got the nerve
Race all the way to Dead Man's Curve Dead Man's Curve, Dead Man's Curve
Won't come back from Dead Man's Curve

The strip was deserted late Friday nite
We were buggin' each other while we sat out the light
We both popped the clutch when the light turned green
You should have heard the wind from my screamin' machine
I flew past Labrea, Schwabs and Crescent Heights
And all the gang could see were my frenched tail lights
He passed me at Domeny and started to swerve
But I pulled her out and there I was at Dead Man's Curve, Dead Man's Curve.

Well the last thing I remember Doc I started to swerve
And then I saw the Jag slide into the curb
I know I'll never forget that horrible sight
And this I found out for myself
That everyone was right
Ya won't come back from Dead Man's Curve, Dead Man's Curve, Dead Man's Curve, Dead Man's Curve, Dead Man's Curve.

© Copyright 1968 by Screen Gems-Columbia Music, L.a.

Total number of release version of Liberty Masters........12
Total number of other versions........................5
                                                      ――
                                                      17 Grand Total

SUNSHINE MUSIC 15

SUNSHINE MUSIC

JAN BERRY AND THE ALOHA BAND

Issue 15

SUNSHINE MUSIC
c/o Doc Rock
2817 Crawford
Parsons, KS 67357

To:

FIRST CLASS MAIL

If this ends with "X", it's time to renew!!!

Dean O. Torrence
Peter M. Ciccone
Send your photo
with Jan or Dean

SUNSHINE MUSIC 15

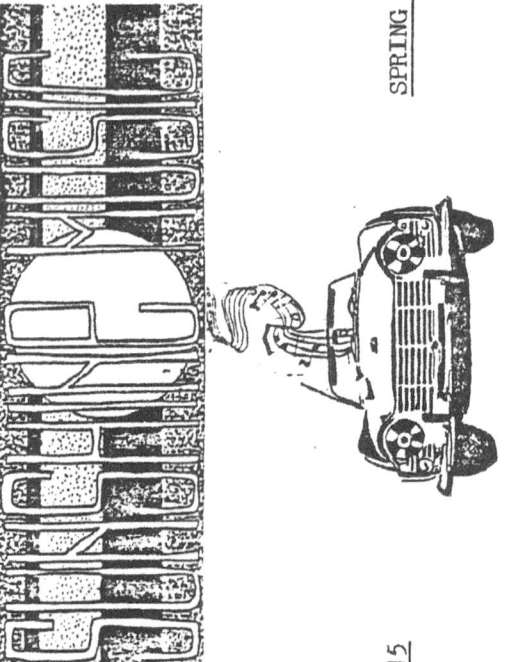

ISSUE 15 SPRING 83

THE MAGAZINE OF THE OFFICIAL JAN AND DEAN
AUTHORIZED INTERNATIONAL COLLECTORS' CLUB

EDITOR   ASSOC. EDITOR
Michael Kelly, M.A., Ph.D.   Frank M. Kisko

COPY EDITORS   GRAPHICS
Jan Berry   Buzzie Gentry
Dean Torrence   Honolulu Lulu

Contents Not Already Copyrighted are
© 1983 by Michael Bryan Kelly

SAMPLE COPIES of SM are $1 in the US and surface overseas. Air-mail, $2. SUBSCRIPTIONS are good for six (6) issues, at the rates indicated below:

USA, mailed   non-US   Non-US   Surface Air   Envelope
in envelope   Surface Air   Envelopes Envelopes Charge is
$5 $7 $7 $12 $10 $15   for Postage

Please enclose S.A.S.E. (self-addressed stamped envelope) with all letters.

★ *CHECK THE NUMBER ON YOUR ADDRESS LABEL. THE NUMBER THERE IS THE NUMBER OF*
★ *THE LAST ISSUE OF YOUR SUBSCRIPTION. IF THERE IS NO NUMBER, LUCKY YOU!!!!*

MAKE ALL CHECKS PAYABLE TO MICHAEL B. KELLY
----NEW SUBSCRIBERS, PLEASE INDICATE THE NUMBER ON YOUR
SAMPLE ISSUE OR THE NUMBER YOU WANT YOUR SUBSCRIPTION TO
START WITH, OR ELSE!!

"BE TRUE TO YOUR BUD"

MIKE LOVE
DEAN TORRENCE
GARY GRIFFIN
●IRVING/ALMO MUSIC

WHEN SOME LOUD BRAGGART
TRIES TO PUT ME DOWN
AND SAYS HIS BEER IS GREAT
I TELL HIM RIGHT AWAY
NOW WHAT'S THE MATTER BUDDY
AIN'T YOU TASTED MY BEER
IT'S NUMBER ONE IN THE STATE

('N PROBABLY THE WORLD)

SO BE TRUE TO YOUR BUD
JUST LIKE YOU WOULD
TO YOUR GIRL OR GUY
BE TRUE TO YOUR BUD, NOW
LET YOUR COLORS FLY
BE TRUE TO OUR BUD

THE KING OF BEERS
IS WHAT THE GANG ALL CHEERS FOR
WHEN WE'RE OUT HAVIN' FUN
LET'S HAVE ANOTHER ONE
THE OTHERS TAKE THE BACK SEAT
TO THE NATIONAL CHAMP
BUDWEISERS NUMBER ONE

SO BE TRUE TO YOUR BUD
JUST LIKE YOU WOULD
TO YOUR GIRL OR GUY
BE TRUE TO YOUR BUD, NOW
LET YOUR COLORS FLY
BE TRUE TO OUR BUD

WE'LL ALL BE WORKIN ON A
SIX PAC TONIGHT
BECAUSE OUR TEAMS GONNA WIN
WE'RE GONNA ROUT 'EM
AND THE ONLY WAY TO PARTY
IS TO DRINK THE RIGHT BREW
THAT'S WHY BUDWEISERS IN
THAT'S WHY WE'RE SHOUTIN'

SO BE TRUE TO YOUR BUD
JUST LIKE YOU WOULD
TO YOUR GIRL OR GUY
BE TRUE TO YOUR BUD, NOW
LET YOUR COLORS FLY
BE TRUE TO OUR BUD

RAH, RAH, RAH BE TRUE TO YOUR BUD
RAH, RAH, RAH BE TRUE TO YOUR BUD
RAH, RAH, RAH BE TRUE TO YOUR BUD
RAH, RAH, RAH BE TRUE TO YOUR BUD
(RE-PEAT)

SHORT CUTS

Back in the early '70s, I was on the edge of trying to start a Jan and Dean club of some sort. But, just at that time, I learned of Mark Plummer's brand new RIPPED BUGGIES CLUB, so I dropped my plans and instead wrote some things for his newsletter.

A few years later, he told me he was sick of Jan and Dean, never wanted to hear their names again (?), and was sending me his membership list and mercy he had taken in so that I could carry on with RIPPED BUGGIES.

Well, I never got the names or the money, but after a discussion with Dean, I did launch SUNSHINE MUSIC. I had no idea at that time that, someday not too far off, there would be a movie, tours, Aloha, Mike and Dean, albums, tapes, and who knows what else. There has been a Jan and Dean explosion since PHASE I. Mostly, rock 'n' roll is much more accepted these days than it was in the '60s. I mean, to get your own movie in three days, you literally had to be Elvis, the Beatles, or Bill Haley! Today, Jan and Dean have finally been getting the recognition that was robbed them by Jan's accidents in the mid-60s.

So, now in 1983, there is room for many different kinds of Jan and Dean clubs. SUNSHINE MUSIC is geared toward record collecting, divides its coverage about equally between PHASE I and PHASE II interests, and is the only source officially authorized to use PHASE I photos and material. CALIFORNIA MUSIC covers International Surf Music by all kinds of artists, written from the Australian perspective. Although it no longer comes out monthly, it remains an unparalleled source of obscure information. Write to Stephen McParland, 2 Kentwell Ave., Concord, 2137 NSW Australia.

In addition, there are two new clubs, one established by Dean, the other being started under the auspices of Jan and his father.

SURF SCOUTS is the name Dean has given his organization. A typical Deano satire on the Boy Scouts, this is a club aimed at the fans of Jan and Dean, the Bel-Air Bandits, Mike and Dean, the Mailbozz, Papa Doo Run Run, and the Beach Boys. Their address is SURFSCOUTS, Box 240, Roslyn, NY 11576.

Bonita Hoyt tells us about her Jan Berry publication: "At Last, we may have a network of people formed to provide information for the fans of Jan Berry and the Aloha Band. I have been truly surprised at the swelling group of devoted fans who followed Jan from his early days with Arnie and later with Dean to the present. Since Dean got married and began pursuing other courses, Jan has decided to continue entertaining on his own with a new band.

"Jan, being the perfectionist that he is, auditioned many musicians before personally selecting the present members for his group. They not only had to be talented instrumentally, but also for their vocal and harmony parts. Each is personable, warm and entertaining, as is Jan himself. They not only enjoy playing the Jan and Dean type music, but are versatile and play other rock, pop, and country styles.

"I recently made a 36-hour round trip to see and hear them and I certainly was not disappointed. I found them to be gentlemen through and through, fun to be with, and a credit to the music fraternity.

"They have been playing all around the country now for several months, and to sell-out crowds, even in these strained economic times. People surely want to attend their performances. The standing ovations and repeated requests for encores are a tribute to their entertainment abilities.

"I am greatly surprised at the wide range of ages of people who are enjoying the Jan and Dean music. At first it seemed to be a nostalgic experience, but the younger people are showing an appreciation for the happy lively unique sound that Jan was so instrumental in creating.

"We are planning to get a newsletter out every month and also to send postcards to Fan Club members to notify them of an appearance of the group if it is to take place within a 100 mile radius of the club member.

"Also we expect to have offers from time to time which will be available to Club members only. The Fan Club will be a non-profit organization strictly, the income from dues to be used for such expenses as printing, photographs, post cards, and postage. Our purpose and hope is to provide fans with information and a source of communication that Jan would like to do but is not in a position to do personally. Should you have questions or interesting tidbits that you feel should be passed on to other members, send us a note and we will try to accomodate. Also if there are clubs in your area where you would like to see them perform, send us the name and number and we will try to get them booked here for you. Dues are $1.00 per month.

"Jan Berry and Aloha Fan Club
% Bonnie Hoyt
185 Lakeview AV Apt. 1-2
New Canaan, CT 06840"

Even newer than Bonnie's club is a terrific Jan and Dean/Beach Boys/Surf 'zine from, of all places, Sweden! The first issue came out in April, 1983, and features a novel photo of Jan and Dean with Kathryn Miner, the Little Old Lady from Pasadena. (Speaking of Kathryn, I saw her on an old I SPY rerun the other night. I first saw it in 1967. She wins a jackpot on a Las Vegas slot machine, but the silver dollar belonged to Robert Culp and Bill Cosby!) Outside of Europe and Scandinavia, the rate is $1.50 per issue. Write to:

Orran Tunefelt
"Surfer's Rule"
Lilla Nygatan 16
111 28 Stockholm
Sweden

So, Jan and Dean fans, there is no reason why you can't get into Jan and Dean just about as much as you want to. But, please, since SUNSHINE MUSIC has always led a policy of giving free publicity to other clubs, even though in a way they are competition, keep your SUNSHINE MUSIC subscription up to date. When a new issue is coming out, and I have to delete from the subscription mailing list the names of people I have been in touch with for months and years, it is very sad. True! And remember, the more members we have, the better the 'zine can be. Without making any promises, I can tell you that I do have a goal of upgrading the printing and illustration reproduction process used for SM, although it will cost considerably more than the subscription price (why not--after all, the present method already costs more!).

So, RENEW, (or get sales!! THEN write to SURFSCOUTS, CALIFORNIA MUSIC, JAN BERRY AND ALOHA FAN CLUB, and SURFER'S RULE, OK?

Jan Berry Appearing at the 35th Annual Grand National Roadster Show--Oakland Coliseum,
January 15, 1983   by Carol Robbins

Jan's band, the Alohas, opened the show with "Surfin' USA." Then Jan came out wearing slacks, a pink dress shirt, and a new sports jacket. He performed all of the J&D favorites, plus a few Beach Boy tunes. The crowd at the 3 pm show was full of hard-core J&D fans, many wearing Jan and Dean shirts from previous years' shows!

Jan's performance brought rousing applause and cheers following each song. One fan tossed a gold chain up to the stage, for which Jan thanked the entire crowd. The encore was "Little Old Lady (From Pasadena)." But when Jan returned to the stage to sing it, a girl who had been standing next to me took a rose bouquet to the stage and gave it to Jan. He expressed his thanks, saying it was the most beautiful rose he'd ever gotten. Throughout that final song, he held the rose up to the crowd and sniffed it.

Before he left the stage for good, he told everyone how much he appreciated and loved them. He was obviously touched by the devoted crowd.

There was a second show at 8 pm, but I had to miss it if I was going to catch the last subway and return to San Francisco that night. But it is an afternoon I shall remember!

QUAZI-MOTO MONO

A Story About Stereo Rock 'n' Roll

During the '50s and '60s Golden Age of Rock 'n' roll, records were, by and large, monaural, or as sometimes said, monophonic. There were some stereo 45's in the '50s, by such artists as Conway Twitty and Frankie Avalon, but as late as the mid-sixties some labels (notably EPIC) still released all albums in mono (as non-stereo is also sometimes called) or in re-channeled stereo.

But, we are getting ahead of ourselves. What is stereo? In simple terms, stereo means a music program (although talking can also be in stereo) with different but integral signals coming out of two separate speakers. Stereo was first created many years ago, immediately after the phonograph was invented. Early versions had two different needles and tone arms playing different tracks on a record. Lawrence Welk once broadcast a stereo TV special, with one-half of the sound coming out of the TV and the other coming out of an AM radio.

The first stereo hi-fi sets got one side of the stereo from an FM radio station and the other half from an AM radio station. In 1960, an AM radio station in Kansas City broadcast stereo for a while. To get the stereo effect, one had to tune one AM radio a bit to the left of the usual dial setting for that station, and another AM radio a bit to the right.

The best success in stereo radio has been in FM, however. This is not because FM is better for stereo. Rather, it is because stereo signals take up more room on a radio dial or frequency. When the FCC gave out the FM permits, they gave wide frequencies to permit stereo. But when the AM frequencies were assigned, stereo had not caught on, so only narrow frequencies were allocated. (You ever notice how close together AM stations are on the dial compared to FM stations?)

What about Jan and Dean? What was the first Jan and Dean record recorded in stereo? Probably "Linda."

In 1964, Jan and Dean had released several stereo LP's. However, I never bought them, because they cost $1 more than the presumably identical mono versions. Even the cover was the same, except that the front was pasted a little lower for stereo, revealing an extra row of stars!

Then, one day a well-meaning friend got me my first copy of the LINDA LP for my birthday. Unable to find a mono copy, she got me the stereo version, paying the extra $1 I was never willing to pay. Well, was I surprised when I played that sucker—for the first time I knew what that extra speaker on my record player was for!

I immediately went out to get stereo versions of the other Jan and Dean LP's. It was not easy. Take GOLDEN HITS. It was not recorded in stereo, so I was out of luck. (Later, Liberty Records released GOLDEN HITS in a stereo version of sorts. This released version and the simultaneous mono release can be easily detected by the pink stripe across the cover.)

A large cross between a department store and a discount store, the French Market, had no stereo LP's at all. I asked the manger, and he told me that they never stocked stereo rock and roll, because no kids had stereo players or wanted to pay the extra $1! This was in 1964!

Eventually, I got a full set of stereo Jan and Dean. The value of this was that the stereo LP's sounded different. However, I soon learned that different often did not mean better.

On GOLDEN HITS, Liberty had the master tapes. Since the music had been recorded first and the vocals later, they could create a phony stereo by splitting a song in two. The effect was much like the King who would settle a dispute about which woman should get to keep a baby. A rock and roll song, like a baby, can be killed by being split in two.

However, another problem grew from having an engineer mix the stereo version of an LP that Jan and Dean had carefully mastered in Quazi-Moto-Monural:

to p. 11

CALIFORNIA COLLECTORS SERIES

Ever since the PHASE II interest in Surf music in general and Jan and Dean music in particular began 10 years ago, there have been rumors of many rare but unreleased tracks in the genre. As the decade passed, many of these were in fact released on such records as ODDITIES, STUDIO OUTTAKES, and OLD WAX AND NEW WAVES.

Now, a new series of EP's has come out, featuring many of these heretofore unreleased songs, and what is rarer than unreleased material, after all!

These EP's have an extra bonus feature, liner notes—or, should I say, sleeve notes—documenting just what the heck these songs are! And, what they are, is GREAT!!

Volume One of the Collectors' Series features 1/2 of Jan's unreleased Warner Brothers LP. Since the other half was previously released on 45s by WB in the '60s, we now, at last, have access to all 12 of the cuts from the project which Jan tackled soon after his early recovery. "Carnival of Sound" has top harmony, "Mulholland" was originally called "Ian and Dean on a Trip," and "Stay" is possibly the best version of Maurice Williams' composition that has ever been recorded. "Blowin' My Mind" is the closest Jan ever got to hippie music, "Louisiana Man" is a version totally unlike the version on J&D records, and "Laurel and Hardy" is sung this time by—DAVY JONES! There are two previously unreleased photos of Jan, as well.

Volume Two, FIVE RARE TUNES, boasts three cuts by Jan and Dean's trusty background singers, the Fantastic Baggies. These songs are from the groups' second LP, which was released in 1966 in, of all places, South Africa, only! "Hot Rod USA" is the song made famous by the Rip Chords (aka Bruce and Terry), "How Wrong You Can Be" is a new song, and "Get A Chance With You," and a 1977 Beach Boy song by Brian Wilson.

(Originally, Volume Two was to have featured the original, uncut, 7-minute version of "Surfer Joe" by the Surfaris. Let's hope a later disc does give us this unreleased, longer track.)

Volume Three has Jan doing his favorite Beatles' song, "Hide Your Love Away," Brian (Mickey Mouse With A Sore Throat) Wilson doing "Don't You Just Know It," and Brian's demo of "Gonna Hustle You" (aka "Gotta Chance With You" and "New Girl In School"). Side 2 is a Jan and Dean session witch would have gone onto the IMTWAV LP had Jan completed it and/or not had his accident. Unfinished, it is a cross between "A Teenager In Love" and "Poor Little Fool," Jan at his production best!

DEAN TORRENCE PHASE I 1964-1967 is Volume Four. An alternate version of Jan and Dean's LP cut "The Restless Surfer" features Gary (Yellow Balloon) Zekley, as does the flipside, "When I Go To Sleep." "Theme From Leon's Garage" was the flip of a rare release by Dean of "Summertime Summertime" in 1966. "Like A Summer Rain" is a version never heard before, and the only one besides the Columbia version in stereo! "Vegetables" is Dean's original version as released on White Whale records under the name Laughing Gravy.

Finally, Volume Five consists of 4 novel Beach Boy cuts. Lauri contributed these comments on Volume Five. "Bootlegs seem to serve two purposes. One is to annoy the artists whose material is being pressed and made available to the public without the artist's receiving any monetary compensation. The other is to allow devout fans the luxury and pleasure of hearing 'new' material.

"'Loop De Loop' was first recorded in 1970. Written and produced by Al Jardine, this song is one of the finest examples available of the Beach Boys use of harmony and production to further the lyrical content of a song.

MK- Besides "Sidewalk Surfin'" and "Old Lady," "Anaheim, Azusa and Cucamonga Sewing Circle, Book Review, and Timing Association" sound better in mono.

DT- I think I picked all of three out in mono on the ANTHOLOGY album, I used mono whenever I could. And the management always fights me, because they feel that everyone is... "Into stereo." I think stereo is fine for records with exciting, like strings and extra horns and stuff like that...

MK- UP SMIRK!

DT- Sure. That's nice, because there are enough components that you can get the feel of an orchestra around you, and that can be very interesting. But as far as a straight rock and roll record, you just don't give a damn about "Where the orchestra is." It's just all together, all mish-mashed, coming at you, that is the exciting part, not having it taken apart and killed. Yeah, you're right. These stereo mistakes were from the engineer, but sometimes any stereo is a mistake...

MK- I always play my mono LP's. To me, the stereo is just sort of a novelty on most songs.

So, that is why Mr. Dean put out GOTTA TAKE THAT ONE LAST RIDE in "Quasi-Foto-Monaural." Many people felt there was some kind of mistake. But if you play the mono versions of those songs against the stereo versions, even when it is the exact same recording, the mono has an impact that cannot be matched by the stereo, or pseudo-stereo versions!

"The words refer to a barnstorming exhibition in the sky. The song is joyful and exuberant, guaranteed to make the listener laugh and smile. This piece was reputed to have been prepared for the SUNFLOWER LP, but was never included. Then, it was one of the proposed tracks for TEN YEARS KNOWN, released last year. It was scrapped at the last minute, Jardine saying it would be released "when it's done." It seems inconceivable that the song is 'incomplete.' The quality of the track on this EP is excellent, well worth the price of the disc for this selection alone.

"Carl Wilson, Dennis Wilson, and Al appeared on THE DAVID FROST SHOW in 1971 and performed live. Two cuts from that show are included on this LP. "Vegetables," an amusing cut from the Beach Boys SMILEY SMILE lp, appears here in an acoustic version, much as if the Beach Boys were sitting in your living room performing for fun! It's like the Beach Boys PARTY lp, revisited! The song is done for fun, and the quality is very good for a television track. Also performed on the show was "Falling In Love," a beautiful love song by Dennis. He released this on a single as "Lady," it quickly vanished and is a collector's item today. Al and Carl provide backup support.

"The final cut is "Brian is Back," Mike Love's tribute to his cousin, Brian Wilson. Originally recorded in 1976 when Brian's comeback was toasted in the media, the Beach Boys deliver this in achingly pure harmonies with a guitar line reminiscent of "Don't Worry, Baby." It was originally released on a special Dick Clark radio broadcast. This version is the shortened, "sweetened" track, with Mike overdubbing his vocal, a shortened break, and an augmented guitar line.

"The sound quality of the EP is excellent, considering some of the songs were taken from a TV show. It is not to be missed by any appreciator of the Beach Boys!"

Well, it sounds like Lauri is a fan of the Beach Boys, all right. But, no doubt about it, the material is not to be missed on these CALIFORNIA COLLECTORS' SERIES EPs!

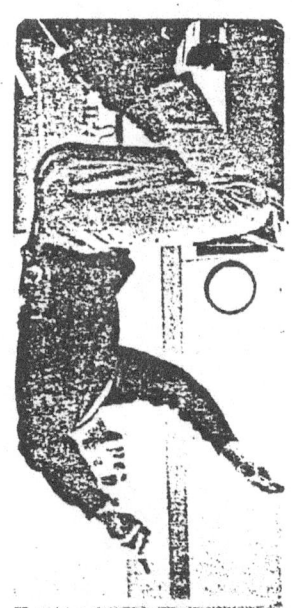

JAN BERRY'S POP SYMPHONY
IN
TRUE STEREO

Harp   Tympani   Oboes Flutes Clarinets   Bass Guitar
Piano   Strings   Bassoon   Drums Horns   Trumpets
                              Glockenspiel   Rhythm Guitar

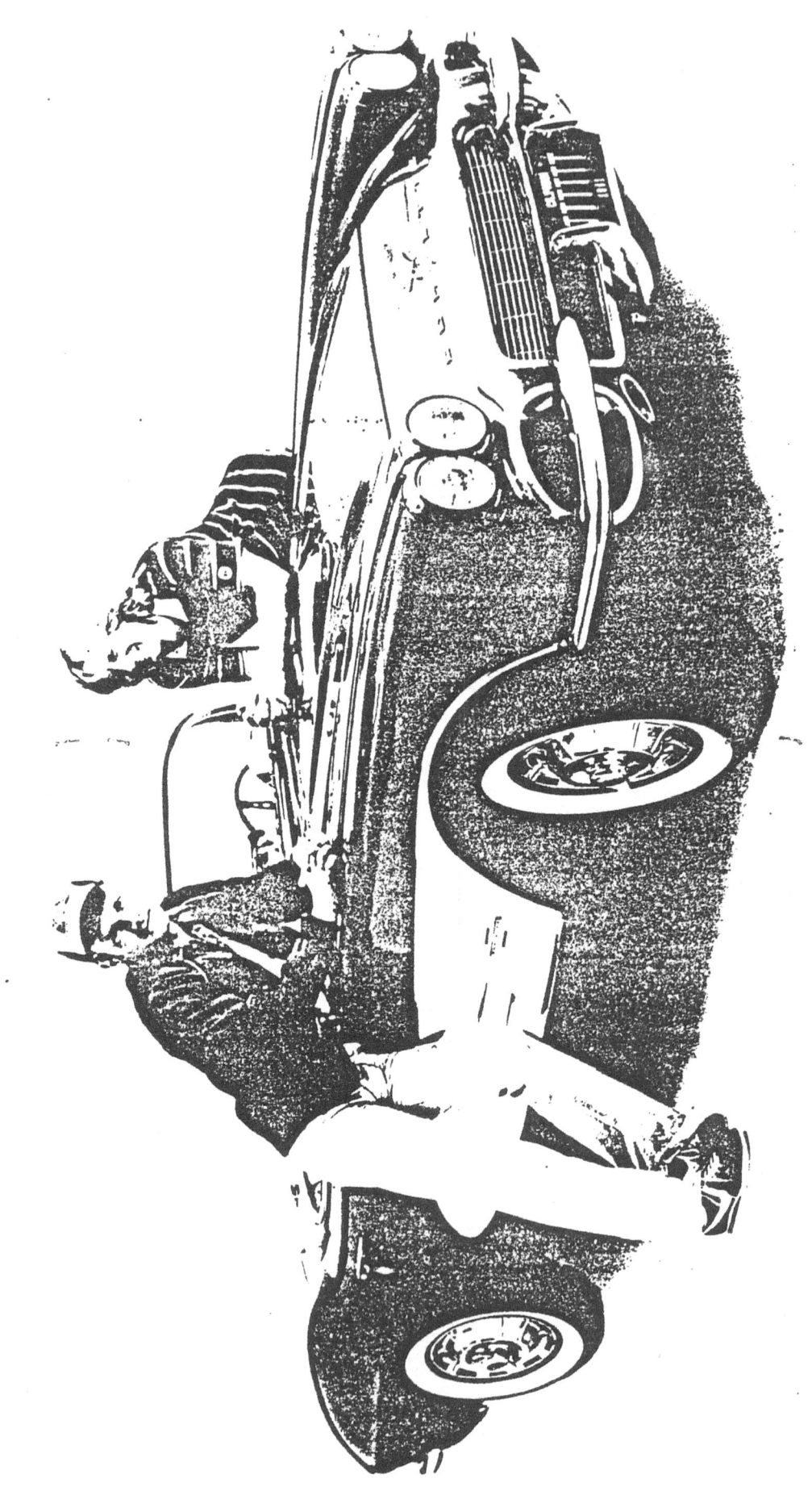

SUNSHINE MUSIC 15

DIANE VOSTEEN, 5007 DETROIT AVE, CLEVELAND, OHIO, 44102
(216) 631-8444 (PHONE ONLY AFTER 6PM EASTERN TIME)
***THE BEL-AIR BANDITS WITH DEAN TORRENCE...FACTORY
FRESH 12 INCH EP...POSTPAID/INSURED...$6.00...LP
***JAN AND DEAN WITH THE BEL-AIR BANDITS...ONE SUMMER
NIGHT LIVE...THEIR FIRST NEW RECORDING IN 15 YEARS...
CONTAINING LIVE VERSIONS OF ALL THEIR BIG HITS...TWO
RECORD SET. SEALED...POSTPAID TO YOU...ONLY $13.00...LP
***JAN AND DEAN DORE 101...GERMAN REPRO...$14.00...LP
***JAN AND DEAN BATMAN EP...w/BOY BLUNDER...$8.00...EP
***LEGENDARY MASKED SURFERS...RARITIES...$12.00...LP
***COLLECTOR'S DELIGHT...w/J.&D. DORE CUTS...$8.00...LP
***BEACH BOYS/JAN AND DEAN...REALISTIC...$6.00...LP
***CELEBRATION...WITH MIKE LOVE,ETC...JAN AND DEAN ON
THE COVER...SEALED LP POSTPAID/INSURED...$4.00...LP
***MIKE LOVE...LOOKING BACK WITH LOVE...$4.00...LP
***ROCK SHOPPE BEACH YEARS EP w/JAN AND DEAN...$8.00EP
***HISTORY OF SURF VOLUME THREE 1980-1982...WITH THE
BEL-AIR BANDITS,ETC...POSTPAID TO YOU...$7.50...LP
***PAPERBACK BOOK..."HOT SHOTS"...90 PAGES OF ROCK
STARS DOING FUNNY THINGS FOR THE CAMERA LIKE ON PAGE
54 IS THAT DAVY JONES LETTING IT ALL HANG OUT? YOU
BET IT IS *YOU DON'T NEED A NOTE FROM YOUR MOTHER..
JUST SEND $3.95...POSTPAID/INSURED...$3.95...BOOK
***THE BEACH BOYS...160 PAGES...238 PICTURES...THIS
OVERSIZED 8 1/2 X 11 INCH PAPERBACK WAS PUBLISHED IN
1979 FOR $8.95. BYRON PREISS DID A SLICK JOB...IT'S
FUN,FUN,FUN AND GOOD VIBRATIONS ALL THE WAY...$5.00 BK
****
ALL ALBUMS AND BOOKS ARE FACTORY FRESH...MINT...YOU
MUST BE SATISFIED...AND AS ALWAYS FREE POSTAGE AND
INSURANCE ANYWHERE IN THE USA...OUTSIDE OF THE USA..
PLEASE WRITE FOR AN EXACT QUOTE ON YOUR POSTAGE COST.
****
DIANE'S DIVINE DIZZY DOLLAR DIVIDEND...FOR EACH ALBUM
OR BOOK YOU ORDER YOU MAY SELECT ONE OR MORE OF THE
FOLLOWING FACTORY FRESH PRODUCT; CELEBRATION WITH
MIKE LOVE CASETTE TAPE; MIKE NESMITH LIVE CASSETTE
TAPE; MIKE NESMITH INFINITE RIDER LP; MIKE NESMITH
RADIO ENGINE LP; CHARLES LLOYD WEAVINGS LP..$1.00 EACH
WONDERFUL JOYCE YARROW JUMPING MOUSE LP....
****
SEND FOR NEW FREE LIST
DIANE VOSTEEN, 5007 DETROIT AVE., CLEVELAND, OHIO, 44102
(216) 631-8444. PHONE ONLY AFTER SIX PM
*DAVY JONES' BUNS??

Let Me Explain

Who would have believed that so much could be happening in the world of Jan and Dean in 1981! It's wonderful!

First, there are Jan's tour dates with Aloha. It is always great to see Jan performing his songs with his great group. And there are Dean's shows with Mike Love. Theirs is the kind of music that the words "good-time rock and roll" were invented for. Now, I told you last issue that the only thing the separate tours of Jan and Dean would mean was twice as many chances to see them in concert. In fact, within a couple of weeks of each other, both Jan and Aloha as well as Mike and Dean played Austin, Texas!

But, did any of us expect any new Jan or Dean record releases by only the second month of 1983? I don't think so! Well, read on!

The first big surprise was a new cassette tape/LP to be sold only in Radio Shack stores or from the Radio Shack catalog. So far, all I have seen is a prototype of the cassette. The music has something for everybody..."60s tunes, "80s production, Jan and Dean material, Beach Boys, and for those who are so inclined, stereo.

A highlight of the 12 cuts is Dean's wild version of "Wild Thing," originally a hit record by the Troggs (rhymes with froggs). And they said Deano has no soul! Or, is it more satire? I'll leave that judgement up to you! I will say that I can't wait to hear what Harry Young, who publishes the Lou Christie 'Zine LIGHTNIN' STRIKES, says about Mike and Dean's version of that song. Dean's solo effort, "Baby Talk," a candidate for the TV movie soundtrack, is a rare treat. And to top off the dozen is Mike and Dean doing "HER Boyfriend's Back!" Complete with motorcycle sound effects!

I've said it now and I'll say it then, when selecting songs that were hits by other artists to do for LPs, Jan and Dean have always picked all of my Top 40 favorites. It is uncanny. After J&D, the Angels, who had the hit "My Boyfriend's Back" in the summer of Surf City, are perhaps my favorite artists!

Then, as if that weren't enough, Mike and Dean have a new single. It will probably be a limited pressing with distribution only for promotional purposes. This version resembles the one Dean did in the late '70s with Papa more than anything else, with the incomparable falsetto of Dean's shining through. It is in stereo, and the flip side is the same song, minus the lead vocals.

Since I first began SUNSHINE MUSIC, it has been my goal to publish tour schedules. So far, I have not been able to do so. The main reason is that it takes approximately six weeks to get an issue in the mail AFTER ALL OF THE MATERIAL HAS BEEN WRITTEN AND PREPARED. Since tour dates are usually set only one month in advance, any dates I print would be out of date by the time you read them. For instance, I am writing this on March 7th. I have here in front of me a letter from Dean giving me these dates for Mike and Dean shows:

    march 15   Padre Island
    march 17   Daytona Beach
    march 23   Ft. Lauderdale
    March 24   Back to Daytona Beach
    March 31   Destin, Florida

Don't get me wrong. I very deeply appreciate Dean's letting me know about these. And I will try to contact any 5hers who live in those areas. But, the only way I can print dates in time for you to read them and act on them is if I get show dates right after everything is proofread, corrected, sent to Jan and Dean for approval, returned from Jan and Dean with approval, photo-reduced (this reduction alone takes a week in the U.S. mail), pasted up with photos, page numbers, and headlines, but right before I actually go to press. That way, I can stick them in, unreduced, at the very last minute. Allow a week for printing and transportation, and a few days for the mails, and you would be reading them just 10 days or so after I got them.

LETTERS

Dear Myke,

I wish to express my viewpoint on the current situation of Jan and Dean. In LET ME EXPLAIN of issue #14, you expressed the opinion that Jan and Dean should adopt a kind of Frank Sinatra-type act. I feel that, if the boys released a tune that was close to the style of their pre-crash music, it would indeed reach the magical top ten (if properly promoted).

Look at the Beach Boys. At their concerts, the kids are yellin' for the oldies ("I Get Around," "Deuce Coupe," "Surf City," etc.), yet the BBS do not have the common sense to release a song in the same vein as their hits from their golden period. They apparently feel that they should not rely on their past success to keep in business, that it would not be proper for artists of their stature to fall back on their hit style to support them. So what happens? They keep playing their oldies to screaming audiences while their current work fails to reflect any notice of that interest.

Perhaps J&D should team back up with Usher, Christian, Altfeld, and the others who were teamed with them in Phase I. It could result in a guaranteed hit!

The time is ripe, the public is enthused with the new muscle cars (I'll reserve my own comments on this subject), sports such as jet skiing are immensely popular, it is almost like the early '60s again.

Another area J&D might look at is video. Their songs are perfect for this medium. Just imagine "Dead Man's Curve" on video!!

Sorry to be so welcome on the subject, but I have a bad case of generation lapse—I am 19, but my taste is 20 years behind the times. I drive a muscle car, I go surfing, and I love any form of Surf and Drag music.

Sincerely yours,
John L., Piscataway, NJ

Dear John,

I agree with you. I think Dean does too, as evidenced in the new Mike and Dean LP/cassette available from Radio Shack. Of course, these songs are not exactly in the old style, and not all of the same people are involved as were in the old days. But as far as I am concerned, so far, so good!

Your idea of J&D video is a good one. I have often reflected on the elaborate video productions lavished upon many two-bit artists of the '80s, unlike the many hits of J&D that were never realized in video just because they were a bit previous! Thanks for writing!

Myke

Dear Myke,

Thanks for the recent issue of SM. Very enjoyable again, though there isn't a lot of Jan and Dean news at the moment.

Jan and Dean's ONE SUMMER NIGHT LIVE is excellent. My album of 1982.

I also enjoyed the "Dead Man's Curve" interview with Dean and all of the facts on "Deadman's Curve." Have you heard Flash the Slash's version (Dindisc 28, England)?

The Dore bootleg has been available since 1979 in shops and mail order from Germany, Holland, and sometimes Switzerland.

Finally, I would like to see a box LP set of classic Jan and Dean, say 7 records of 12 songs each, covering their hits as well as other significant cuts. Do you think there is any chance of this?

Sincerely,
Daniel Bossard
Switzerland

Dear Daniel,

Thank you for your letter and suggestions for a box set. As for news about Jan and Dean, I think this issue will be making up in that department.

I agree with you about ONE SUMMER NIGHT. On the topic of the Dore LP, I bought 2 copies in 1973. One was an original issue, the other was a second pressing by Dore. The only difference was that the fades were somewhat different on a few songs, and the back cover had that containercraft variation.

Thanks,
Myke

Dear Myke,

Let ME explain! I am a 16-year-old girl who thrives on J&D and the BBs (Let's not forget Bruce!). I, too, am glad that they're not classified with the new rock groups of today. I may not know what the number one album is on the charts, but, my Lordy, I do know what J&D's new LP is!

I'm proud of my record collection, consisting of J&D, the BB, Rick Nelson, Dion.... It's great having oldies radio stations coming up. Although I missed this music when it originally came out (not my fault!), I'm not missing it this time. Which leads me to TV. If they can show old FATHER KNOWS BEST, why can't they show the T.A.M.I. (whatever that stands for) Show?

When I've gone to BB concerts—I would include J&D but I haven't seen them yet (that's a hint, guys)—I get "high" on the music and singers, and it lasts for weeks. I really don't categorize this with the "rock concerts" where the audience and group are stoned.

One more thing: why do you say it may not be desirable for a teenager to "groove" on J&D in Phase III? I may be the only one at school who doesn't know (or care) who sings "Dirty Laundry," but I'll bet ya I'm the only one who knows where the bongos in "Jennie Lee" came from!

Bustin' my Buns in Dayton, Nevada,
Paula Thrisimovic

P.S. You seem to have a typographical error in abundance when spelling Beach Boys. "Boys" is spelled B-o-y-s, not B-u-n-s, alright?

Dear Paula,

Well, actually I'd say it is the BB15, judging from the aggregation I saw on stage last time. Or, if the rumors of Beach Buns breaking up are true, the BB1 (Mike Love).

Your collection sounds pretty good. T. Teenage A. America M. Music I. International has been on TV. Most of it was on ABC, hosted by Dick Clark, and with live guests J&D, same 10 years ago!! However, due to a clause in their contract, the BB137 portion was deleted after the original release.

I agree with all your comments. But, you are not the kind of teenager I was referring to. What I meant was, if Jan or Dean put out the kind of music which could be a hit seller these days, I fear it would be in a style I would detest. Now, it is true Sinatra had some teen-hits in more or less his old style—"That's Life" and "Strangers in the Night"—but that was back in the days when the Top-40 had diversity.

Actually, I'd love for kids to dig J&D music, as long as J&D don't have to compromise their good-time sound in the process.

Myke

Michael,

I'm 23, and would love to have some J&D sheet music. Can SM readers help me?

Best your Buns,
Tod Lewis
Box 42
Goldsboro, PA 18424

SUNSHINE MUSIC 15

Hi, Mike—

I just got your latest issue—it's great! I love the "D.M.C." theme and feature. I hear that song all the time on the radio. Your mag has a lot of spirit—makes my Lou Christie LS [Lightnin' Strikes] look dry by comparison!

New LP, Impact (Canada) BC 319 ROCKIN' KAHN'S SOLID GOLD RADIO SHOW side 1 cut 2 is "Sidewalk Surfin'" (rerecorded, courtesy of S.J. Productions). And, Lou has a new LP of Motown songs coming out soon, and a gig in Vegas at the Tropicana. See ya'.

Harry Young
LS, APT. 10-H
1645 E. 50th ST
Chicago, IL 60615

Dear Harry,

You are too kind and too modest. I recommend LS to all S&rs!

Mike

Dear Mike,

Here is my renewal. I'm still reading #14. And, I agree with your editorial (Let Me Explain). Although I always hoped there would be a new J&D record on the charts, after I read your column, I feel the same as you do. I don't particularly care what the '80s teenagers buy, either. I always felt lucky that I grew up with J&D, the Beatles, Beach Boys, Elvis, etc.!

I'm also pleasantly surprised there is still an SM! I was afraid that when J&D split, that would be the end of SM! Keep up the good work!

Alice S.

Dear Alice,

Thank you very much for your support!!

Mike

Hi, Michael,

A lot of J&D songs are hard to understand. Could you print the words to "Jennie Lee," "The Piece...," "Little Queenie," "Sing Sang A Song," "Mother Earth," "Tennessee," "Clementine," "I Gotta Drive," "Back In the USSR," and "New Girl In School."

Debbie

Dear Debbie,

In time, in time....

Michael

Dear Michael,

Thanks for a superb issue #14. It was always my hope that there might be a version of "Dead Man's Curve" with a really long fade—as long as "Hot Stacker." Maybe in the vaults somewhere? Here in England, the B.B.C. seldom played entire rock 'n' roll records, since it only played that kind of music a few minutes a day at all! Of all things, they always cut DC at the crash!! Even so, it stood out as a classic!

Yours,
Mike Smit

Dear Mike,

Funny thing. My brother, the Beatles' fan, used to chide me for liking songs with trivial lyrics and topics such as sidewalk surfing, cars, and old ladies. He was, of course, into songs with relevant lyrics, like war, drugs or sex. Especially, he thought that repetition, such as that in longer fades, was bad.

At least, until "Hey, Jude" came out with its 5-minute fade. Then, his criticism was that J&D's fades were not long enough!

I'm like you. About 3 years ago, I edited my own version of DMC. Lasts for about 10 minutes, includes a long fade, extra drag race and crash effects, as well as crowd and ambulance sounds. Real neat!

Michael

P.S. Boy, I can't wait to read the letter my brother will write when he sees this issue!

Dear Myke,

How's the "Sidewalk Surfin'" in Kansas during winter? Enclosed is an article on J&D from the time of my birth, October, 1960! OK, don't think you are going to get that item without a couple of questions. First, what ever happened to the movie Easy Come, Easy Go? Was it cancelled because of the accident? Question no. 2, are there any J&D picture discs other than Oldities? Last question, are they giving any awards for spending 25% or more of your weekly paycheck on J&D records and related items? Well, gotta go scrub my white tennis sneakers that are black!

Sincerely,
Karen

Dear Karen,

Here in Parsons, they don't spread sand or salt on the pavement—they spread gravel! The movie ended due to Jan's previous accident. They were filming the last scene of Easy Come, Easy Go aka Jan and Dean Go Wild aka Jan and Dean a-Go-Go Wild when the trains being used crashed and Jan broke his leg. I had a story I was going to run, but it was reprinted in the excellent booklet advertised a few issues ago. I suppose I could still run it...what do you think? (If only the director had not decided to film the final scene first!)

I don't know about picture discs. However, the award you ask about does exist! It is a subscription to SM—assuming you have paid your dues!

Myke

Dear Michael,

I found an LP—Hanna Barbara promo HLP 8505, JEAN KING SINGS FOR THE IN CROWD—which has inside liner notes. I quote: "Though the album was recorded in a studio, it was not in a studio atmosphere, but in a party one—that's exactly what it was, an in-crowd party. Among Jean's personal friends, admirers and well-wishers were Jan and Dean, Billy Page, composer of 'The In Crowd,' Shorty Rogers, who is 'in' all by himself, and many, many others of the in crowd." Engineer: Bones Howe. Drums: Hal Blaine! Jean King is black, for what that is worth. I don't hear Jan or Dean. Anyone have any ideas?

Diane Voorteen

EPs

CALIFORNIA COLLECTORS SERIES vol. 1 - 5   (EP's)   (Autralia)

CARNIVAL OF SOUND   - JAN BERRY   Bitchen Records 001
Carnival Of Sound / Mulholland / Sty / Blowin My Mind /
Louisiana Man / Laurel & Hardy

FIVE RARE TUNES   - FANTASTIC BAGGYS,   Bitchen Records 002
Hot Rod U.S.A. / Goes To Show / Debbie Be True (Fantastic Baggys) / Surfer Joe (Surfaris) / Endless Summer-
vokal (Sandals)

BEACH BOYS & JAN & DEAN - BEACH BOYS, JAN & DEAN   Bitchen Records 003
Gonna Hustle You / Don't You Just Know It (Brian Wilson)
Hide Your Love Away / A Teenage Bat (Jan Berry)

DEAN TORRENCE MUSIC PHASE ONE   Bitchen Records 004
Vagabond / When I Go To Sleep (Gary Zekely) / Theme From
Leon's Garage / Like A Summer Rain / Vegetables

LIVE & UNRELEASED   - BEACH BOYS   Bitchen Records 005
Vegetables / Fallin In Love / Loop De Loop / Brian's
Back

Now, you can get all of these great Collectors' Records by direct mail order! Single copies are $10. Or, you can get a discount of 20% by ordering five or more EPs! For example, the full set of all five EPs is just $40. Or, you can get five of the same EP for $40!

West Coast Services
Dept. SM
Box 699
Blacktown, 2148
Australia

THE MAN WHO CAME BACK FROM DEADMAN'S CURVE

After having eight years of tremendous success; first as JAN & ARNIE, and then as JAN & DEAN, collecting such classic hits as *Jenny Lee, Linda, Surf City, Honolulu Lulu, Drag City, Deadman's Curve, Little Old Lady, Ride The Wild Surf*, and *Sidewalk Surfing*, tragedy struck Jan Berry.

Jan had just completed three years of pre-med at UCLA and was attending the California College of Medicine to complete his doctorate in surgery, when in April of 1966 the Corvette he was driving crashed into an illegally parked truck only a few blocks south of "Deadman's Curve", on Sunset Blvd. The song, *Deadman's Curve*, was written by Jan and Brian Wilson of the Beach Boys, and had sold almost a million records just two years previously. It appeared that it would be unlikely that Jan would survive the accident. The firemen at the scene of the accident struggled for almost an hour to free Jan from the twisted wreckage. Jan was in a coma for over a month and in intensive care for over three months. His prognosis was that he would probably never walk, talk, move his limbs, or lead a normal life ever again.

With four years of agonizing therapy and sheer determination, Jan learned to talk, write, and walk again. He overcame what doctors described as impossible obstacles through his will to recover.

His tragedy and his long road to recovery had been such an inspiration to so many people that a television movie entitled "Deadman's Curve" was filmed about his experience.

Today, Jan is still an inspiration to millions and an example of a true life come-back story. Jan didn't quit then and won't quit now. Despite the physical limitations forced upon him by his accident, Jan enthusiastically continues to give the world his music and is the living legend of the Man Who Came Back From Deadman's Curve!!

12 New Rock 'n' Roll Recordings

- California Dreamin'
- The Letter
- Wild Thing
- Lightning Strikes
- Sealed With A Kiss
- Walk Away Reneé
- The Locomotion
- Baby Talk
- 96 Tears
- Da Doo Ron Ron
- Sugar Shack
- Her Boyfriend's Back

REALISTIC Cat. No. 51-3009

Rock 'n' Roll City
—MIKE LOVE of The Beach Boys
—DEAN TORRENCE of Jan and Dean

® & © 1983 Hitbound Records

ALL RIGHTS RESERVED. UNAUTHORIZED DUPLICATION IS A VIOLATION OF APPLICABLE LAWS.

Side 1 Lightning Strikes—Mike & Dean • Walk Away Reneé—The Association • The Letter—Mike Love • The Locomotion—Mike Love • Sealed With A Kiss—The Ripchords • Sugar Shack—Mike Love

Side 2 96 Tears—Paul Revere & The Raiders • California Dreaming—The Beach Boys • Baby Talk—Dean Torrence • Wild Thing—Dean Torrence • Da Doo Ron Ron—Mike Love • Her Boyfriend's Back—Mike & Dean

CUSTOM MANUFACTURED IN U.S.A. FOR RADIO SHACK, A DIVISION OF TANDY CORPORATION, FORT WORTH, TEXAS 76102

ROGERS & COWAN, INC.
PUBLIC RELATIONS

9465 WILSHIRE BOULEVARD
BEVERLY HILLS, CALIFORNIA 90212-1692
(213) 271-8181   TELEX 687-442

CABLE ADDRESS ROCOPUB
BEVERLY HILLS, CALIFORNIA

ROCK 'N ROLL CITY

"Rock 'N Roll City" is an enjoyable new release of 60's classics by some of the most popular artists of the past two decades. Mike Love of The Beach Boys; Dean Torrence of Jan and Dean; The Association; Paul Revere; Terry Melcher of The Ripchords and Bruce Johnston of The Ripchords and currently of The Beach Boys, have combined their talents to present refreshing renditions of many memorable hits from the past.

In an effort to bring music to the consumer at a reasonable price, the Tandy Corporation and Hitbound Records developed the "Rock 'N Roll City" project. Radio Shack stores, a subsidiary of the Tandy Corporation, will exclusively distribute and sell the "Rock 'N Roll City" cassette, which will be available in all 8,300 outlets nationwide.

"Rock 'N Roll City" includes newly recorded versions of "Da Doo Run Run" by Mike Love, "Baby Talk" by Dean Torrence, "Walk Away Renee" by The Association, "Sealed With A Kiss" by Bruce Johnston and Terry Melcher, "96 Tears" by Paul Revere, and a special recording of "California Dreamin'" by The Beach Boys.

Providing a fun look back at the sound of the 60's, combined with the added touch of contemporary arrangements, "Rock 'N Roll City" is sure to be welcomed by all fans who appreciate the early roots of popular music.

* New York Office: 122 East 42nd Street, New York, New York 10168 (212) 490-8200 Cable: ROCOPUB New York, New York
London Office: 27 Albemarle Street, London W1X 3FA, England • 499-0691 • TELEX 211-21171

Instead, I often get dates right after an issue comes out, or else weeks before hand. Either way, I am grateful, even though I know I cannot print them!

Or, can I!! Today, March 24, 1983, Jan sent me the following valuable information. Important to <u>all</u> Jan and Dean fans, no matter where you live in the world!

May 3   The National Orange Show, San Bernardino, CA
         Reunion of JAN AND DEAN with the BelAir Bandits!

May 4 thru 30   Marina Hotel, Las Vegas
                Jan Berry and the Aloha's

July 1, 2, 3, 4   San Diego Wild Animal Farm
                  Escondido, CA
                  Special Concert Featuring
                  JAN AND DEAN!

July   Concert Tour by Jan Berry And the Aloha's

17 Klamath Falls, Oregon
19 Richland, Washington
20 Hillsboro, Oregon
21 To Be Determined
22 Bremerton, Washington
23 Thorne, Washington
24 Everett (Seattle), Washington
25 Tentative

(Other dates are being scheduled.)

So, if that isn't good news, I don't know what is!

SUNSHINE MUSIC 15

LETTERS

Hello!

You surprised me when you said that the DORE LP was priced too high. A Goldmine set sale had it at $80, with no poster insert included. I have seen minimums of $20-30, but the high bids are in excess of $150, with photo. My local dealer has sold his third copy for over $100. On picture sleeves, I always thought that $20 was high for "From All Over The World," but Goldmine listed it for $50! "The Universal Coward" and "Gee" go for up to $100!!

There is a new video, "That Was Rock," which included J&D from the intro to the TAMI SHOW, as well as "Sidewalk Surfin'."

Barbara, Phoenix

Dear Barbara,

Nice to hear from you. I got most of my Jan and Dean stuff when it first came out, or else later in cut out bins in the '60s. To me, the high collector prices are ridiculous. The Dore poster used to be rumored to have been included in only the promotional copies. This makes sense, since even today, radio sations get many LP posters sent to them by record companies. Further, since many stations tend to keep LPs, and keep them in good condition, this could explain why there are as many around in nice condition as there are. However, some non-promo copies have also been found with posters, so....

When I got into the fanzine/collecting world 11 years ago, Jan and Dean stuff was no more valuable than any other important artist, such as Lesley Gore, Freddie Cannon, or Bobby Vee. Then, three things happened during the 1970's. 1, the fanzine THE ROCK MARKET PLACE did the best J&D article ever written. 2, Frank Kisko, Myke Kelly, Mark Plummer, and Thomas DeTomaso began bidding against one another for J&D material, 3, raising the prices higher and higher by trying to outbid one another. 3, the movie DEADMAN'S CURVE came out.

Before these factors began to effect prices, I astounded an established dealer by bidding #27.27 for a mint 78 of "Jennie Lee." He told me that this was the highest bid he'd ever had for any record. Before these three factors took effect, I got the J&D SAVE FOR A RAINY DAY LP for $8 and DORE for $25, and Dean told me that I had been swindled! Before these factors, I GAVE Dean a DORE LP because he had not even seen one since 1964. Before these factors had their effect, Rip Lay sent me free and unsolicited a mint DORE poster (the only one I have ever seen and which I didn't even know what it was) just 'cause he knew I was a J&D fan and would appreciate it! I was the only J&D fan ordering from him 10 years ago!

Now that these factors have taken effect, the new, current prices are ridiculous. So, while I am happy that J&D records are so popular/valuable, I regret the price gouging. Rip Lay still sells DORE picture sleeves very reasonably. Write to him (Rip Lay, Box 342, Concord, CA 94522) and tell him Michael Kelly from Kansas sent you.

Remember, GOLDMINE has such a large readership that dealers can ask high prices--their ads will reach the few rich extremists. Plus, GOLDMINE dealers have to pay for the ad, raising their costs. A dealer down the street in a small shop cannot reach the extremist collectors and does not have the cost of the ads. "Frosty, the Snowman" goes for $75 in California auction lists, but goes for 75 cents in a used record shop in downtown Joplin, Missouri.

A bidding tip: I once ran a COLDMINE list of several hundred 45s and LPs. I made several hundred dollars, even though I sold only 10% of the records listed! Of the records sold, only a couple had more than one bid! That means that any low bid was usually also the only and therefor the high bid! That is why dealers list minimums--you are bidding against the dealer's minimum, since there will usually be no other bidder! In essence, a minimum bid is often a set sale price!

Another collector was heard to say that he never won a record by bidding. Rather, when he got a record in an auction, he knew he had been overcharged for it!

Here is what Dean had to say about record prices when I asked him a few years ago (1973).

MK: This afternoon, I'm going over to United Artists to see a guy who is going to sell me, after years of searching, a copy of the DORE LP and a copy of the RAINY DAY LP.

DT: I have the RAINY DAY LP but I don't have a DORE LP.

MK: He's charging $8 for the RAINY DAY and $20 for the DORE.

DT: <u>Really!</u> I'd almost buy the DORE for $20. I'd like to have that. Just saw one recently for the first time in years.

MK: I've never seen one.

DT: How many does he have? Just one?

MK: Just one. He said he was thinking about giving it to you guys, but he didn't think you cared.

DT: Who was this?

MK: Greg Shaw.

DT: What da ya' mean, he didn't think... You tell him-- $20!! --You tell him to give you the DORE LP or I won't do his logo for him. (Note: I tried Dean's suggestion, but it didn't work--MK.) Well, unless he paid about that much for it. Tell him I said to give you a deal. Tell him $20 is too much to pay for ANY album! I don't care WHO it is. If he get's $20 from you I'll... Tell Greg I'd sure like to have a DORE LP too. Maybe Lou will give me one...

Later, I got another copy of DORE, so I sent Dean the one I got from Shaw. It was only later I realized the one I sent was the original pressing, and the one I had left was a later, authentic DORE pressing!!

Doc

Dear Doc,

What can I say--sorry! Here is my double renewal, 10 bucks, please send the two double issues and do your best to restore me to good standing with "SM!"

Bob, NJ

Dear Myke,

I have really incredibly sad news to tell you. Louise Texler, who was suffering from horrible cancer, has passed away earlier this week. She was a wonderful person, a dear friend, and a true Jan and Dean fan. She really loved Jan and Dean with all her heart and soul. I know they liked her, too, and will feel so bad when they hear this most awful news.

Ilene Diamond

Dear Michael;
Here's my $5 to renew. You can't go wrong when you're getting the best magazine you can find anywhere!
I thought the article on Jan and Dean vs The Beatles was a great one! I guess there's a couple of people who didn't seem to think so, because they thought you were giving *your* opinion alone. But I thought the article was very interesting, whether it be for or *against* The Beatles. I really liked the way you compared them, though. Even in your reply to the letter in #18-19, it all makes sense! Good Stuff!
Hey, that's a clever idea about having a fav. LP in every issue! Every J&D LP is my favorite, too! I can't wait to find out which album you pick for the next SM!
Here is the picture of the Blue Fox I made for my fiance, Gary Ost. I am not telling him I sent it to you, so when he gets his next issue, will he be surprised!!

Bye Bye, Paula, NY

Dear Michael,
Great new issue, especially the JAN AND DEAN vs. THE BEATLES. I think I may do a similar article about LOU CHRISTIE vs. ELVIS for my 'Zine, LIGHTNIN' STRIKES!

Harry, Chicago

Dear Myke,
Great double issue once again! Especially Jan and Dean vs. Beatles #2. Thought I'd tell you about some new J&D LPs I have added to my collection:
1. Ride the Wild Surf-Greenlight Records, 1981. UK Import #2011. All the '63-'64 hits, plus 2 Fantastic Baggys, 20 in all! Cover is from LINDA LP!
2. Greatest Hits-K-Tel, Holland. #N8333006. Includes biggest hits, 3 BB tunes, and Dore cuts. Great Phase II action photo of Dynamic Duo on cover. By the way, I've been seeing some familiar faces on General Hospital-Gary Griffin and Chris Farmer!

Bust your buns, Melanie, Mass.

Dear Michael,
Here's my reply to the reply of a letter I sent you some time ago containing my renewal and condemning your article on Jan and Dean vs. The Beatles. My reply is in the same form as yours was: paragraph by paragraph.

(MICHEL: HERE IS YOUR LETTER IN TOTAL. MY NEW REPLY TO YOUR REPLY TO MY REPLY TO YOUR LETTER APPEARS BELOW IN CAPS LIKE THESE.)

1. Why compete? Just admit that there are good and inferior quality things about both groups?

I AGREE COMPLETELY. HOWEVER, I HAVE SEVERAL REASONS FOR RAISING THE COMPETITION. ONE, I FEEL THAT A JAN AND DEAN FAN CLUB SHOULD BE UNRESTRAINED IN ITS SUPPORT OF JAN AND DEAN. TWO, I PERSONALLY FEEL THAT JAN AND DEAN ARE GREATER. THREE, I DID NOT CREATE THE COMPETITION. SINCE 1964 PEOPLE HAVE BEEN COMPARING MY JAN AND DEAN MUSIC TO THEIR BEATLE MUSIC, ALWAYS TO THE DETRIMENT OF JAN AND DEAN. FOURTH, I EXPECTED TO GET SOME DISAGREEMENT, AND I HOPED THAT SM READER INTEREST WOULD BE PIQUED. IT IS IMPORTANT TO HAVE FIRE AND CONTROVERSY IN A PUBLICATION IF YOU ARE GOING TO MAINTAIN INTEREST!

2. I would say that I agree with Tim but I don't know Elvis that well.

ME, TOO, BUT I HAVE NO ELVIS LPS EXCEPT SOME SECOND-HAND COMPILATIONS.

3. Who can tell? AGREE.

4. Agree. AGREE.

5. When did Jan and Dean have a number-one hit in England?

I NEVER SAID THEY DID. I STATED THAT SALES/POPULARITY ARE NOT SIGNS OF "GREATNESS" AS THE TERM WAS USED IN THE ORIGINAL ARTICLE. THEREFORE, THE QUESTION OF JAN AND DEAN'S HAVING A NUMBER-ONE HIT IN ENGLAND IS IRRELEVANT. IF YOU DISAGREE WITH MY DEFINITION OF "GREATNESS," WHICH EXCLUDES RELATIVE CHART SUCCESS, THEN YOU WILL REJECT MY WHOLE ARGUMENT. IF THE DEFINITION OF "GREATNESS" DID INCLUDE RELATIVE CHART SUCCESS AS THE MEASURE OF "GREATNES, AS IT DOES TO MOST PEOPLE, THAN MY ARTICLE WOULD BE POINTLESS, AND I WOULD HAVE TO AGREE WITH YOU AND WITH TIM, THAT THE BEATLES ARE GREATER (SOLD MORE RECORDS THAN) JAN AND DEAN.

6. Agree.

AH, SO YOU DO ACCEPT MY DEFINITION OF "GREATNESS!" NOW THE DISCUSSION CAN MOVE RIGHT ALONG!

7. Agree. AGREE.

8. Agree. But why weren't Jan and Dean chosen for this hype?

GOOD QUESTION. ACCORDING TO INTERVIEWS IN THE HBO SPECIAL THE COMPLETE BEATLES, THE FORCE BEHIND THE BEATLES WAS BRIAN EPSTEIN. APPARENTLY BRIAN WAS RESPONSIBLE FOR ALL THE HYPE. AND, WHEN HE DIED, SO DID THE FAB FOUR. I WOULD SAY THAT JAN AND DEAN WERE NOT CHOSEN BECAUSE THEY WERE NOT BRITISH, AND BRIAN LIVED IN ENGLAND AND KNEW ONLY BRITISH TEENS.

9. Agree. AGREE.

10. AND 11. Agree. See 8. AGREE.

12. Agree. AGREE.

13. and 14. When Liberty re-released a Jan and Dean's greatest hits album nothing happened. Why?

I WOULD NOT SAY THAT NOTHING HAPPENED. THE LEGENDARY MASTERS ALBUM HAS GONE THROUGH SEVERAL PRESSINGS. PLUS, THERE HAVE BEEN SALES ENOUGH TO JUSTIFY THE GOTTA TAKE THAT ONE LAST RIDE ALBUM, THE TWO SUNSET LPS, LP 999 DEADMAN'S CURVE (A HITS COMPILATION), PLUS ENDLESS K-TEL COMPILATIONS, AND MORE. THE BEACH BOY'S LP TOOK OFF ONLY AFTER THE TV ADS BEGAN. BUT, I SHOULD NOT EVEN BE ANSWERING THIS ONE... RELATIVE SALES/POPULARITY ARE NOT PART OF THIS DISCUSSION, REMEMBER?

15. 16. 17. Agree. AGREE.

HAD A RECIPROCAL RELEASE ARRANGEMENT WITH THE BEATLES BRITISH LABEL, PARLOPHONE, GOING BACK TO THE PRE-ROCK 'N' ROLL DAYS. CAPITOL AUTOMATICALLY GOT THE RIGHT TO RELEASE ANY PARLOPHONE MATERIAL IN THE USA, INCLUDING, AS IT HAPPENED, THE BEATLES' MATERIAL. HOWEVER, FAR FROM SIGNING THE BEATLES IMMEDIATELY, CAPITOL TURNED DOWN EVERY SINGLE BRIAN SENT THEM, SO BRIAN SENT THEM TO SMALLER LABELS, SUCH AS VJ, TOLLIE, AND SWAN, AS WELL AS LARGER LABELS SUCH AS ATCO AND MGM. THESE LABELS RELEASED SOME SINGLES, BUT WITHOUT THE $50,000 PUSH AND HYPE FROM CAPITOL, THE SONGS FLOPPED. NOTICE I DID NOT SAY THE SONGS WERE FAILURES OR WERE NOT GOOD. THEY JUST DID NOT SELL.

LATER, WHEN THE BEATLES WERE BIG, CAPITOL SUED ALL THOSE OTHER LABELS, AND WON. THE SMALL LABELS EACH HAD TO TURN OVER THEIR BEATLES' RECORD PROFITS TO CAPITOL, BECAUSE OF THE OLD PARLOPHONE AGREEMENT. BUT THE BEATLES WERE NEVER SIGNED TO CAPITOL, JUST TO PARLOPHONE OF THE UK.

CAPITOL OF CANADA WAS PART OF THE SAME AGREEMENT, AND DECIDED TO RELEASE A LITTLE OF THE BEATLES' MATERIAL THAT US CAPITOL PASSED UP.

WHY DID JAN AND DEAN GET STUCK ON LIBERTY? LET ME QUOTE THE OLD ARABIC SAYING: "SHOW THEM THE DEATH, AND THEY WILL ACCEPT THE FEVER." PUT ANOTHER WAY, "FEED A MAN GRAVEL, AND HE WILL THEN APPRECIATE HARDTACK." OR, AFTER THREE RECORDS ON ARWIN, DORE LOOKED GOOD, AND AFTER A FEW YEARS ON DORE, LIBERTY LOOKED GREAT!! TO QUOTE DEAN: "IN 1961, WE WERE DETERMINED TO SIGN WITH A MAJOR COMPANY AND NEVER TO DEAL ANYMORE WITH COMPANIES THAT CARRIED ON BUSINESS OUT OF A TENT IN AN EMPTY LOT. SO WE CUT A SONG THAT...WAS RELEASED ON CHALLENGE RECORDS. WELL, AT LEAST THEY DIDN'T CARRY ON BUSINESS OUT OF A TENT. THEY HAD AN ALMOST NEW CAMPER WITH DECALS OF TROUT ON THE SIDE AND CHALLENGE RECORDS PAINTED ON THE DOOR, ALL IN LOWER CASE." LATER, "IT WAS TIME TO LOOK FOR A NEW COMPANY ONCE AGAIN. THIS TIME WE WOULD NOT COMPROMISE. ONLY THE BEST. AND AFTER BEING TURNED DOWN BY ALL THE BEST, WE SIGNED WITH LIBERTY RECORDS."

SO, JUST LIKE THE BEATLES WHO WERE TURNED DOWN BY ALL THE BEST (AND ALL THE WORST) IN 1962-63 IN THE US, JAN AND DEAN MOVED UP, ALBEIT TO LESS THAN THE BEST. STILL, IN 1961 ROCK 'N' ROLL WAS LESS THAN BIG BUSINESS, AND MOST ACTS FROM 1958-59 WERE LONG GONE. BUT, TALKING OF BIG LABELS, IN 1966 WHEN JAN AND DEAN'S CONTRACT EXPIRED, (JAN AND) DEAN SIGNED WITH A VERY BIG AND OLD LABEL, COLUMBIA! ACCORDING TO DEAN, THEY COULD HAVE RENEWED THEIR EXPIRED 5-YEAR WITH LIBERTY, BUT LIBERTY WAS OFFERING THEM THE SAME MONEY THEY HAD ORIGINALLY SIGNED FOR AFTER THE CAMPER COMPANY. BUT NOW, JAN AND DEAN HAD DOME TAMI, THEY HAD A TV SHOW, A MOVIE, AND A STRING OF BIG HITS. SO THEY PLANNED J&D RECORDS, AND AFTER JAN'S ACCIDENT, DEAN WENT TO COLUMBIA. A BIG LABEL.

26. Yes, the Beatles were imitated, but who imitated the surf sound, the car sound, the "protest" sound?

I'LL SKIP THE PROTEST SOUND, SINCE JAN AND DEAN'S PROTEST SONGS WERE REALLY "TEST" (ANTI-PROTEST) SONGS, SATIRES, LIKE "FOLK CITY," WHICH SATIRIZES THE DYLAN TYPE. BUT WHO IMITATED SURF AND DRAG? WELL, ALMOST EVERYONE. EVER HEARD OF "BACK IN THE USSR?" (A SATIRE, TOO.) EVERY RADIO STATION IN THE WORLD USED THE SURF SOUND FOR THEIR JINGLES, STATION IDS, AND "GOLDEN" AND "DOUBLE GOLDEN" DROP-INS. TO ME, THE ESSENCE OF ROCK 'N' ROLL IS, AS YOU SAID, SOUND, NOT LYRICS. HARMONY, FALSETTO, BOMPS AND PAHS. LISTEN TO THE BEATLES (PAPERBACK WRITER, DAY TRIPPER), THE TURTLES (SHE'D RATHER BE WITH ME, HAPPY TOGETHER, SURFER DAN), THE MAMAS AND PAPAS (MONDAY, MONDAY, CALIFORNIA DREAMIN'), THE SUNSHINE

18. Why didn't they get this type of promo? Was the Jan and Dean sound too "Californian?"

IN MY MIND, THE QUESTION ISN'T WHY DID JAN AND DEAN NOT GET THE BIG PROMOTION. JAN AND DEAN GOT THE STANDARD TREATMENT THAT THOUSANDS OF OTHER ARTISTS GOT. THIS IS A REPEAT OF #8.

19. I disagree but I respect your opinion.

THANK YOU. NOTE THAT I USED THE WORD "ENORMOUS" SUCCESS. YOU MUST ADMIT, HAD ONLY CAPITOL BEEN RELEASING BEATLE RECORDS IN 1964, ONE AT A TIME ACCORDING TO THEIR OWN RELEASE SCHEDULE, THEN THE BEATLES COULD NOT HAVE, FOR EXAMPLE, HAVE HAD THE TOP FIVE SINGLE ON BILLBOARD AT THE SAME TIME, SINCE THEY WOULD HAVE HAD ONLY ONE SINGLE OUT! THAT IS FOR CERTAIN. WHAT WE DON'T KNOW IS, WHAT WOULD HAVE HAPPENED IF A LARGE NUMBER OF LABELS HAD RELEASED AND PROMOTED HEAVILY ($50,000 WORTH) MANY OF JAN AND DEAN "A" SIDES AT THE SAME TIME.

20. See 19.

DID YOU KNOW THAT SOME BEATLE WRITERS ATTRIBUTE A LARGE PART OF THE BEATLES' SUCCESS (SALES) TO THE ASSASSINATION OF PRESIDENT KENNEDY? THEY SAY THAT AMERICAN YOUTH HAD LOST ITS BIG HERO AND WAS REAL DOWN AT THE END OF 1963, AND THAT THE BEATLES' PHENOMENON CAME ALONG AND FILLED A VACUUM.

21. Agree. AGREE.

22. What was Liberty doing at the time?

ACCORDING TO DEAN, THE LIBERTY EXECUTIVES WERE LIKELY TO BE VACATIONING IN HAWAII OR WHATEVER WHEN NEW JAN AND DEAN MATERIAL CAME OUT. KEEP IN MIND THAT RCA WAS A HUGE CORPORATION, PART OF NBC RADIO AND TV, AND HAD BEEN AROUND FOR DECADES WITH ARTISTS SUCH AS GLEN MILLER. LIBERTY, ON THE OTHER HAND, WAS A FAMILY-RUN RECORD LABEL, ESTABLISHED IN 1956. THIS ENTIRE LABEL WAS BEGUN WITH A LOAN OF ONLY $2,000 (4% OF THE AMOUNT SPENT ON THE BEATLES PROMOTION IN JANUARY, 1964) BY SY WARONKER.

23. You cite only five of the 20 or more singles that were released and still, "Get Back" was released in 1969!

GOOD POINT. I WAS TRYING TO BE BRIEF. LET ME JUST SAY THAT SINCE THE 1970'S, DJ RECORDS HAVE ONLY ONE SONG, THE "A" SIDE ON BOTH SIDES. NO DOUBT THIS INHIBITS TWO-SIDED HITS THESE DAYS! AND, HAD BOTH SIDES OF EACH BEATLE 45 BEEN ROCKERS (THEY WERE CALLED THE BEAT-LES, NOT THE SOFT-LES), THE ADULT/MOR STATIONS WOULD NEVER HAVE PLAYED BEATLES' RECORDS AND CONTRIBUTED TO THE LEGEND.

24. Same as 23, change the names.

SAME ALSO. CAPITOL WAS A VERY OLD LABEL AND A GIANT CORPORATION.

25. Note how quicky they were signed to Capitol. (In Canada, they were on Capitol as early as February, 1963 with the release of "Love Me Do"/"P.S. I Love You," Capitol 72076.) Why did Jan and Dean get stuck on Liberty?

THE BEATLES WERE NOT SIGNED TO CAPITOL, QUICKLY OR OTHERWISE. CAPITOL

COMPANY (HAPPY, BACK ON THE STREET AGAIN), SPANKY AND OUR GANG (MAKIN' EVERY MINUTE COUNT, LAZY DAY), THE BYRDS (ALL I REALLY WANT TO DO, TURN TURN TURN), HARPERS BIZARRE (59TH STREET BRIDGE SONG, ANYTHING GOES), PLUS DOZENS OF OTHERS. AND 50% OF THE TV COMMERCIALS OF THE 1970S, FROM SUNKIST TO WRIGLEY'S GUM. SURE, THEY DID NOT MENTION STICK SHIFTS OR KNOTS ON THEIR KNEES, BUT THEY ALL COPIED THE SURF SOUND, AND STILL DO. ALONG WITH THE BRITISH INVASION AND THE SAN FRANCISCO SOUND, SURF WAS ONE OF THE MAJOR MUSICAL INFLUENCES ON THE ROCK ERA (1964-ON). AND EVEN THE SAN FRANCISCO SOUND WAS LARGELY A SURF DERIVITIVE, UNTIL THE LSD TOOK OVER.

(I WON'T EVEN MENTION RONNY AND THE DAYTONAS, THE RIP CHORDS, THE DETERGENTS, AND TRASHMEN. THE TIMERS, THE QUADS, THE SHANGRI-LAS, THE SURFARIS, BRUCE AND TERRY, THE HONDELLS, JIM MESSINA AND HIS DRAGSTERS, THE FIRST CLASS, THE WOMBLES, THE SUNRAYS, AND DOZENS OF OTHERS WHO DID SING ABOUT STICK SHIFTS AND KNOTS ON THEIR KNEES)

27. And 28. Agree. AGREE.

29. But as opposed to Pet Rocks, and Vega-matics, people still buy them.

TRUE. BUT I EXCLUDED COMPARATIVE SALES FROM THIS DISCOURSE IN THE ARTICLE LAST YEAR. THE BIGGER THE ORIGINAL SALES OF A SONG OR ARTIST, THE MORE COPIES ARE SOLD AS OLDIES.

30. Quite right. AGREE.

31. and 32. Agree. Again, why didn't they change.? Any other competitor, any other label would surely have signed them if they saw in them such talent and musical genius there just ready to explode.

BELIEVE YOU ME, THEY WANTED TO CHANGE, BUT LIBERTY HAD THEM IN AN IRON-CLAD 5-YEAR CONTRACT. AS SOON AS IT ENDED, THEY WERE LAUNCHING J&D, WHERE THEY WOULD RELEASE NOT ONLY JAN AND DEAN SONGS, BUT SONGS OF OTHER ARTISTS THEY WOULD PROMOTE AND/OR CREATE WITH THEIR GENIUS. JAN WOULD PRODUCE, DEAN WOULD DESIGN. THEN JAN HAD HIS CRASH.

BUT, LOOK! WITH JAN (WHO WAS THE DRIVING FORCE OF THE MUSIC IN TERMS OF PRODUCTION WRITING, AND ARRANGING) IN A COMA, MAJOR COMPANY COLUMBIA STILL SAW ENOUGH GENIUS IN LITTLE 'OL DEAN TO SIGN HIM FOR A 45 AND AN LP AND PROBABLY MORE.

I BELIEVE THAT ONCE OUT OF THEIR LIBERTY CONTRACT, ON THEIR OWN LABEL OR ON COLUMBIA, WITH THEIR MOVIE AND TV SERIES, JAN AND DEAN WOULD HAVE BECOME TRULY MAJOR ARTISTS, EASILY OUTSELLING THE BEATLES. BUT WE WILL NEVER KNOW....

34. The Singing Nun also had a hit with her first record.

AND NO FOLLOW-UPS, ALTHOUGH SHE TRIED, EVEN LEAVING HER ORDER TO PURSUE A CAREER IN SHOW BUSINESS. ACTUALLY, I DON'T KNOW THAT THAT WAS HER FIRST RECORD. BUT, YES, MANY ARTISTS GREAT AND NOT-SO-GREAT HAVE HAD HITS WITH THEIR FIRST RECORDS.

35. What about being there at the right time?

SURE, THAT HELPS. JENNIE LEE MAY HAVE BEEN A RESULT OF BEING AT THE RIGHT PLACE AT THE RIGHT TIME. AFTER THAT, JAN AND DEAN MADE THEIR OWN RIGHT PLACES AND RIGHT TIMES.

36. Agree. AGREE.

37. Agree. But I note your note. THANKS.

38. Disagree. Beatles would have had a greater degree of success.

PERHAPS. BUT MY EDITORIAL CAN ONLY GIVE MY OPINION. IF I DIDN'T BELIEVE THE WAY I DO, I COULD NOT DO "SUNSHINE MUSIC." INSTEAD, I WOULD BE DOING A 'ZINE CALLED "MERSEY MUSIC." AND I AM WILLING TO BET THAT NO BEATLE WOULD BE GIVING ME THE EDITORIAL SUPPORT AND JAN AND DEAN DO!

39. 40. Probably. THANKS.

41. Am I glad they didn't! Still, some promoter would have noticed them.

RIGHT. SURE. THAT IS YOUR OPINION.

42. I wonder what would have happened to them trying to break into the European and British markets. Still, you can't change the past. Beatles sound was more suitable to the US than surf sound and car sound in a continent where the sea was cold and dirty and the price of gas made car cruising prohibitive, and that's when you could afford a car.

VERY GOOD POINTS. ONE SMer WROTE THAT HE HEARD "DEAD MAN'S CURVE" ON THE BBC RADIO IN 1964 SEVERAL TIMES, BUT THE DJ ALWAYS CUT THE RECORD BEFORE THE CRASH!! COMPARE THAT TO THE THE WAY AMERICAN STATION PUSHED BEATLE RECORDS LIKE VEGI-MATICS!!

43. That's your opinion.

YEP!

* I suppose you like better Jan and Dean's cover versions of Beatles' songs than the originals?

I (letter writer) personally prefer Jan and Dean's best songs to some of the Beatles' weakest but all in all, the Beatles are Number 1 to me.

YES, I DO, ALTHOUGH THEY ARE NOT COVER VERSIONS (THEY WERE NOT RELEASED TO COMPETE WITH THE BEATLES' VERSIONS OR TO CAPTURE A SINGLES MARKET NOT TAPPED BY THE BEATLES). WHEN MY BROTHER PLAYED HIS BEATLE LP (I DON'T KNOW WHICH ONE IT WAS) THAT HAD NORWEGIAN WOOD, MY REACTION WAS THAT THE SONG SOUNDED PRETTY BAD. BUT AS A NONSENSE SONG/NOVELTY TUNE, TAKEN AS RAW MATERIAL, I THOUGHT THE SONG WOULD PROBABLY BE QUITE NICE IF DONE BY JAN AND DEAN. IMAGINE MY PLEASED REACTION WHEN IT SHOWED UP IN SEVERAL VERSIONS BY THE DYNAMIC DUO!

YOU KNOW, DOZENS OF SONGS IN THE OLD DAYS WERE POPULAR BY DIFFERENT ARTISTS AT THE SAME TIME IN DIFFERENT PARTS OF THE COUNTRY. EXAMPLES INCLUDE WONDERLAND BY NIGHT (LOUIE PRIMA, BERT KAEMPFERT), ALLEY OOP (THE HOLLYWOOD ARGYLES, THE DYNA-SORES, DANTE AND THE EVERGREENS), AND "PARTY DOLL (BUDDY KNOX, STEVE LAWRENCE). MY EXPERIENCE IS THAT WHICHEVER ONE WAS HEARD FIRST IS CONSIDERED BEST. MANY IS THE ARGUMENT I HAVE HAD OVER THE YEARS ABOUT WHICH VERSION IS THE "TRUE" VERSION WITH FRIENDS WHO GREW UP LISTENING TO STATIONS THAT PLAYED THE VERSIONS I DID NOT HEAR ON MY

STATIONS.

SINCE I PLAY JAN AND DEAN ALL THE TIME, MY DAUGHTERS HEAR IT. ONE DAY, THEY HEARD PAUL'S MICHELE ON THE RADIO, AND ALMOST GAGGED, THEY SO GREATLY PREFERRED DEANS!

SPEAKING OF ORIGINAL'S BEING BETTER THAN COVERS, WHICH VERSION OF "BLUEBERRY HILL" DID YOU PREFER, FATS DOMINO'S ORIGINAL OR PAT BOONE'S COVER. MOST PEOPLE FEEL THAT PAT SHOULD NOT HAVE TRIED TO DO ANY RHYTHM AND BLUES SONGS THAT LITTLE RICHARD OR FATS DOMINO HAD DONE. OF COURSE, THESE PEOPLE PROBABLY DON'T REALIZE THAT BLUEBERRY HILL IS NOT A RHYTHM AND BLUES SONG, BUT A 1940 HIT BY GLEN MILLER!!

* Strangely, the Beatles never played "Surf City" in any of their US tours. No surf sound, no car sound, nothing that was so popular in the US and the West Coast at the time.

DISAGREE. FIRST, SONGS LIKE TAXMAN AND HELLO GOODBYE SHOW A STRONG INFLUENCE OF THE SURF SOUND (NOT SURF LYRICS).

SECOND, THE ABSENCE OF SURF CITY IS NOT STRANGE AT ALL. THE ONLY THING THE BEATLES KNEW ABOUT THE US WAS WHAT THEY SAW OUT OF THE HOTEL WINDOW. THEIR MUSICAL INFLUENCES WERE THE RECORDS BROUGHT TO THE PORT CITY OF LIVERPOOL BY US SAILORS. NOW, THIS MAY COME AS A SHOCK TO YOU, BUT MOST OF THE US MERCHANT SAILORS WHO SAILED THE ATLANTIC WERE FROM THE EAST COAST, NOT THE WEST COAST. SO, THE RECORDS THEY BROUGHT TO ENGLAND WERE BLACK, URBAN, AND SOUTHERN, SUCH AS CHUCK BERRY AND THE COASTERS. IMAGINE IF ENGLAND WERE ACROSS THE PACIFIC, NOT THE ATLANTIC! THEN THE BRITISH INVASION WOULD HAVE SOUNDED TOTALLY DIFFERENT, PROBABLY REFLECTING THE SOUND OF DICK DALE, JAN AND DEAN, AND LIBERTY RECORDS!

THIRD, AS YOU SAY, THE BRITISH COULD NOT RELATE TO CARS AND SURFING. BUT, THEY COULD RELATE TO CROWDED URBAN POVERTY, AND THAT IS WHAT SAILORS FROM NY BROUGHT ON 45S TO LIVERPOOL. SO, AGAIN, IT IS NOT STRANGE AT ALL THAT THE BEATLES DID NOT DO SURF CITY. BUT, THEY DID DO THE SURF SOUND AS THEY DEVELOPED AND BECAME EXPOSED TO IT WHEN THEY HAD THE MONEY TO GET OUT OF THE STRIP JOINTS IN HAMBURG.

* How can you compare "Horace The Swingin' School Bus Driver" to "Elenore Rigby?"

ARE YOU SERIOUS? I HAVE NEVER PLAYED "ELENORE RIGBY" IN MY LIFE EXCEPT WHEN IT MIGHT HAVE BEEN REQUESTED ON MY RADIO PROGRAM, BUT I HAVE PLAYED "HORACE" HUNDREDS OF TIMES! "ELENORE RIGBY" HAS NO RELEVANCE TO ME, I THINK THE SOUND IS TOO SELF-CONSCIOUS AND PREACHY, AND IT SOUNDS VERY LITTLE LIKE ROCK 'N' ROLL TO ME. TO ME, ROCK 'N' ROLL IS FOR FUN, NOT DRUG-INDUCED MYSTICISM AND SYMBOLISM.

ON THE OTHER HAND, MY PARENTS HAVE COLOR HOME MOVIES OF MY FIRST DAY OF KINDERGARTEN, CLIMBING ON A SCHOOL BUS. I RODE A BUS IN JUNIOR HIGH SCHOOL AND LISTENED TO "IT'S MY PARTY" AND "SURF CITY" ON MY TRANSISTER WHILE RIDING THE BUS IN 1963. AFTER COLLEGE BEFORE I GOT MY FIRST PROFESSIONAL JOB, I DROVE SCHOOL BUSES IN 1978 AND 1979. TO ME, "HORACE" NOT ONLY HAS BETTER HARMONIES AND BETTER USE OF WOODWINDS THAN THE BEACH OR THE BEATLES EVER MANAGED, BUT THE LYRICS OF HORACE, ALBIET SECONDARY, ARE DAMN NEAR AUTOBIOGRAPHICAL. I HEARD "ELENORE RIGBY" HUNDREDS OF TIMES ON THE RADIO, AND I HAVE NO IDEA WHAT IT IS ABOUT, NOR DO I CARE!

DID YOU KNOW THAT SONGS LIKE HELTER SKELTER, RECORDED UNDER THE INFLUENCE OF DRUGS, RAN OVER 40 MINUTES, BUT WERE EDITED DOWN FOR RELEASE PURPOSES BY THE BEATLES PRODUCER? SUCH GENIUS!

* How many songs did Jan and Dean write entirely by themselves?

I HAVE NO IDEA. PROBABLY STUDYING FOR MEDICAL SCHOOL AND COMMERCIAL DESIGN SCHOOL CUT INTO JAN AND DEAN'S SONGWRITING. I GUESS THEY SHOULD HAVE STAYED WITH JENNIE LEE AT THE STRIP JOINT AND HUNG AROUND BACKSTAGE WRITING SONGS TO PROVE THEIR GREATNESS.

SARCASM ASIDE, UNLESS THE LYRICS HOLD SPECIAL IMPORTANCE FOR SOMEONE, ONE SONG IS ABOUT THE SAME AS ANOTHER. IT IS THE PRODUCTION THAT MAKES A ROCK 'N' ROLL SONG GREAT. HOW GOOD WOULD "PIECE OF MY HEART" HAVE BEEN BY GARY LEWIS AND THE PLAYBOYS? HOW GREAT WOULD "ALLEY OOP" HAVE BEEN BY FRANK SINATRA? HOW WOULD ELVIS HAVE SOUNDED DOING "HERE THEY COME (FROM ALL OVER THE WORLD)?" WOULD YOU HAVE LIKED "DA DOO RON RON" BY CHUBBY CHECKER? LOOK HOW DIFFERENT THE SONG "DO YOU WANNA DANCE" SOUNDED WHEN DONE SUCCESSIVELY BY BOBBY FREEMAN, THE BEACH BOYS, THE MAMA'S AND PAPAS, AND JOHNNY RIVERS. IN OPERA, THE SONG IS EVERYTHING, AND EACH SINGER IS SUPPOSED TO MAKE IT SOUND THE SAME, BUT BETTER. IN ROCK 'N' ROLL, THE SONG IS SORT OF A NECESSARY EVIL. IT IS THE PRODUCTION THAT MAKES THE RECORD, NOT THE SONG.

ANOTHER POINT. WHEN LENNON AND MCCARTNEY "WROTE" A SONG, THEY DID A LYRIC AND A MELODY, MAYBE SOME CHORDS. BUT, THAT WAS IT. ALL THE REST WAS DONE BY A PRODUCER SUCH AS GEORGE MARTIN, PHIL SPECTOR, OR SOME OTHER PRODUCER.

COMPARE THIS WITH JAN'S ACCOMPLISHMENTS. JAN TOOK A MELODY AND A LYRIC, WHICH HE MAY OR MAY NOT HAVE NOT HELPED WRITE (BUT HE ALWAYS REVISED THE LYRICS AND TUNE WHILE RECORDING IT), AND MADE IT INTO A RECORD. HE SCORED THE SONGS FOR AS MANY INSTRUMENTS AS NECESSARY, INCLUDING AT VARIOUS TIMES A HARP, VIOLINS, OBOES, CLARINETS, VIOLAS, TYMPANI, FRENCH HORN, FLUTES, AND OTHERS. THE BEATLES COUL NEVER HAVE DONE THIS THAT IS WHY IT WAS GEORGE MARTIN, NOT LENNON OR MCCARTNEY WHO CREATED THE THE ORCHESTRAL LP TITLED OFF THE BEATLE TRACK, BUT IT WAS JAN (WITH GEORGE TIPTON-AFTER ALL, JAN WAS IN MEDICAL SCHOOL AT THE TIME) WHO CREATED POP SYMPHONY. AND THERE IS THE LEGENDARY INCIDENT WHEN JAN AND DEAN WERE IN A FAR-FLING CITY FOR A CONCERT, AND DISCOVERED THAT THEIR MUSIC HAD BEEN LOST. JAN SAT DOWN AND WROTE SHEET MUSIC OFF THE TOP OF HIS HEAD FOR A

Cover Photo Courtesy
SHer Kathy Baxter, Canada

MAMAS AND PAPAS, AND MANY OTHERS WOULD NEVER HAVE HAD THEIR HITS.

TREND SETTERS? HOW MANY ARTISTS SANG ABOUT HOLDING HANDS AND FIELDS OF STRAWBERRIES JUST 'CAUSE THE BEATLES DID? NOT TOO MANY!

AS I SAID BEFORE IN THE ORIGINAL ARTICLE, IMITATING SOMETHING DOES NOT MAKE IT GOOD. IF A HUNDRED TV SHOWS COPY DALLAS, I STILL WON'T THINK DALLAS IS GREAT. IF 2,000 ADS FOR BAMBOO STEAMERS AND FISH POPPERS COPY THE ORIGINAL VEGI-MATIC AD, I WILL NEVER COLLECT VIDEO TAPES OF VEGI-MATIC ADS. AND IF 10 MILLION ARTISTS FOLLOW TRENDS SET BY THE BEATLES, I WILL NOT THINK THEY ARE GREATER THAN JAN AND DEAN. THEREFORE, THE ARGUMENT OF SETTING TRENDS IS NOT VALID.

HOWEVER, SINCE YOU BROUGHT IT UP, I WILL MENTION THAT JAN AND DEAN WORE "BEATLE BOOTS" BEFORE THE BEATLES DID (SEE THE GOLDEN HITS LP COVER). MOREOVER, ALL ROCK 'N' ROLLERS WORE SUITS UP THROUGH THE MID-60S. BUT JAN AND DEAN SET A TREND EARLY, BY WEARING CALIFORNIA CLOTHES, SWEATERS AND BERMUDA SHORTS, IN THE '50S, AND WHITE LEVIS AND BOATNECKS AND T-SHIRTS IN THE '60S. YOU COULD SAY THAT JAN AND DEAN SET THE STYLES FOR THE FUTURE!

* Would you put your head in fire that neither Jan nor Dean never took drugs?

OF COURSE NOT. MY AUNT TAKES (ABUSES) DRUGS WHEN SHE TAKES TOOTH PAIN KILLERS PRESCRIBED BY HER DENTIST, WHEN SHE HAS A HEADACHE WEEKS LATER. BUT I HAVE FOUND THAT ARTISTS WHO DO MUSIC I LOVE TEND TO HAVE SOMETHING IN COMMON: I WOULD WELCOME THEM AS HOUSE GUESTS. THESE ARTISTS SMILE DURING PERFORMANCES, DRESS NICELY, HAVE A NEAT APPEARANCE AND RESPECT FOR THE CONVENTIONS OF POLITE SOCIETY. BASED ON THIS AND THE TOPICS OF THEIR SONGS, I WOULD GLADLY OPEN MY HOUSE TO JAN AND DEAN, EVEN IF THEY HAVE EXPERIMENTED WITH DRUGS. ON THE OTHER HAND, BETWEEN JOHN'S NUDITY AND ALL OF THE BEATLES SMOKING CIGARETS (SLOW DEATH—NO ASHTRAYS IN MY HOUSE), OPEN USE OF DRUGS, AND SLOBBY APPEARANCE AROUND 1970, I WOULD NOT WANT THEM IN MY LIVING ROOM.

USING A LITTLE DOPE IS SORT OF LIKE FUDGING ON YOUR INCOME TAX. BUT, OPENLY FLAUNTING YOUR ABUSE OF DRUGS IS LIKE BEING A PROFESSIONAL CROOK.

Yes, I am one of the millions that disagree with you. Still, I didn't watch "Lou Grant" or "The Dukes of Hazard." The best TV shows that I liked were cancelled: "Get Smart" and "Police Squad." The first years of Saturday Night Live were great as well as SCTV.

DID THOSE SHOWS SET TRENDS, WERE THEY IMITATED, WERE THEY THE MOST POPULAR SHOWS ON?

Finally, I may be one of the few to subscribe to "Sunshine Music," "Add Some Music," "The Beatles Book," and "Beatles Now" at the same time.

Please tell me if Jan and Dean ever toured Canada and will they ever again?

I DON'T KNOW.

That's all for now,

Michel Bisson, Canada

SIXTEEN-PIECE ORCHESTRA IN TIME FOR THE REHEARSAL AND SHOW THE SAME NIGHT! NO BEATLE COULD HAV DONE THAT!

IT WAS GEORGE MARTIN'S IDEA TO PUT STRINGS ON "YESTERDAY," BUT THE BEATLES WERE GIVEN CREDIT FOR PUTTING STRINGS ON ROCK 'N' ROLL RECORDS. NEVER MIND THE STRINGS THAT JAN AND DEAN HAD ON THEIR RECORDS ON THEIR EARLIEST LIBERTY RECORDINGS!

IN OTHER WORDS, THE LEGEND OF THE BEATLES HAS GROWN OUT OF PROPORTIONS. THEY ARE GIVEN CREDIT FOR THINGS THEY NEVER DID, OR DID NOT DO FIRST. STRIP AWAY THE LEGEND, AND YOU HAVE A NICE LITTLE COMBO WHO DI NICE ROCK 'N' ROLL UNTIL THEY GOT INTO HEAVY DRUGS.

* What innovations did they bring to the recording industry? Oh, I forgot: they were the first to record a skateboard "live" on a sidewalk.

INNOVATIONS? I SUPPOSE YOU THINK THAT STARTING A RECORD WITH FEEDBACK IS AN INNOVATION? IF JAN AND DEAN HAD TRIED TO RELEASE A RECORD THAT HAD FEEDBACK AT THE BEGINNING, I WOULD HAVE STOPPED THEM IF LIBERTY HADN'T. IN FACT, WHEN THEY TRIED THE INNOVATION OF THE FILLET OF SOUL LP, LIBERTY REFUSED TO RELEASE IT! I HAVE A SNEAKY SUSPICION THAT MANY PEOPLE HAVE HAD FEEDBACK ON RECORDING SESSIONS. THE BEATLES JUST WENT A STEP FURTHER AND LEFT IT ON THE FINAL VERSION. THE FEEDBACK ON "I FEEL FINE" WAS ONE OF THE MAJOR SETBACKS OF ROCK 'N' ROLL. IN MY OPINION, SPAWNING A SLEW OF IMITATORS WITH JARRING, EAR-INJURING NOISE, NOT MUSIC. GIVE ME A SKATEBOARD ANY DAY!

I SUPPOSE THAT PLAYING A TAPE BACKWARDS (AS ON STRAWBERRY FIELDS) IS SUPPOSED TO BE INNOVATIVE. I USED TO PLAY MY YELLOW WAX KIDDIE GOLDEN RECORDS BACKWARDS WHEN I WAS A TODDLER IN 1953. BIG DEAL.

I KNOW OF NO TRUE INNOVATIONS THAT THE BEATLES BROUGHT TO THE RECORDING INDUSTRY, OTHER THAN HOLDING RECORDING SESSIONS UNDER THE BLATANT INFLUENCE OF DRUGS, WHICH THEY MADE FASHIONABLE.

* They followed the trends. Surf, car, and protest sound. Even satire with me. "Batman" and "Folk City." The Beatles created trends.

YES, THE BEATLES CREATED TRENDS. TRENDS LIKE DOING LSD IN THE STUDIO, PLAYING TAPES BACKWARDS, LETTING FEEDBACK GET ON THE RECORD, WEARING RIDICULOUS CLOTHING INSPIRED BY A GURU WHOM THEY LATER RENOUNCED AS BEING A FAKE AND A RIP-OFF ARTIST. I'M GLAD THAT WAS A TREND THAT THE BEACH BOYS AND NOT JAN AND DEAN FELL FOR.

BUT, YOU ARE MISTAKEN. JAN AND DEAN DID CREATE TRENDS. THE BEACH BOYS COPIED JAN AND DEAN (LISTEN TO BABY TALK AND THEN TO SURFIN'. LISTEN TO TENNESSEE AND THEN TO PAUL SIMON'S SONGS LONE TEEN RANGER AND MOTORCYCLE. LISTEN TO I FOUND A GIRL AND POPSICLE, THEN LISTEN TO SHE'D RATHER BE WITH ME. LISTEN TO GAS MONEY AND THEN TO 409. THE RIP CHORDS DID SURF CITY, DRAG CITY, AND GAS MONEY ON THEIR LPS. RONNY AND THE DAYTONAS DID BUCKET T. THE WHO DID BATMAN, BUCKET T, AND BARBARA ANN. BARBARA ANN WAS A TAKE OFF ON JENNIE LEE. JAN AND DEAN CREATED THE TREND OF "BOMP" RECORDS, AS CHRONICLED IN SM #11. AFTER JAN AND ARNIE AND JAN AND DEAN BECAME BIG, MANY ARTISTS COPIED THEIR NAME, INCLUDING DON AND JUAN, DEAN AND JEAN, DANNY AND GWEN, DICK AND DEE DEE, AND MANY OTHERS. I COULD GO ON, BUT THIS IS GETTING RATHER LONG.

WITHOUT THE PRODUCTION TECHNIQUES JAN PIONEERED, THE BEACH BOYS, THE

SUNSHINE MUSIC 16 - 17

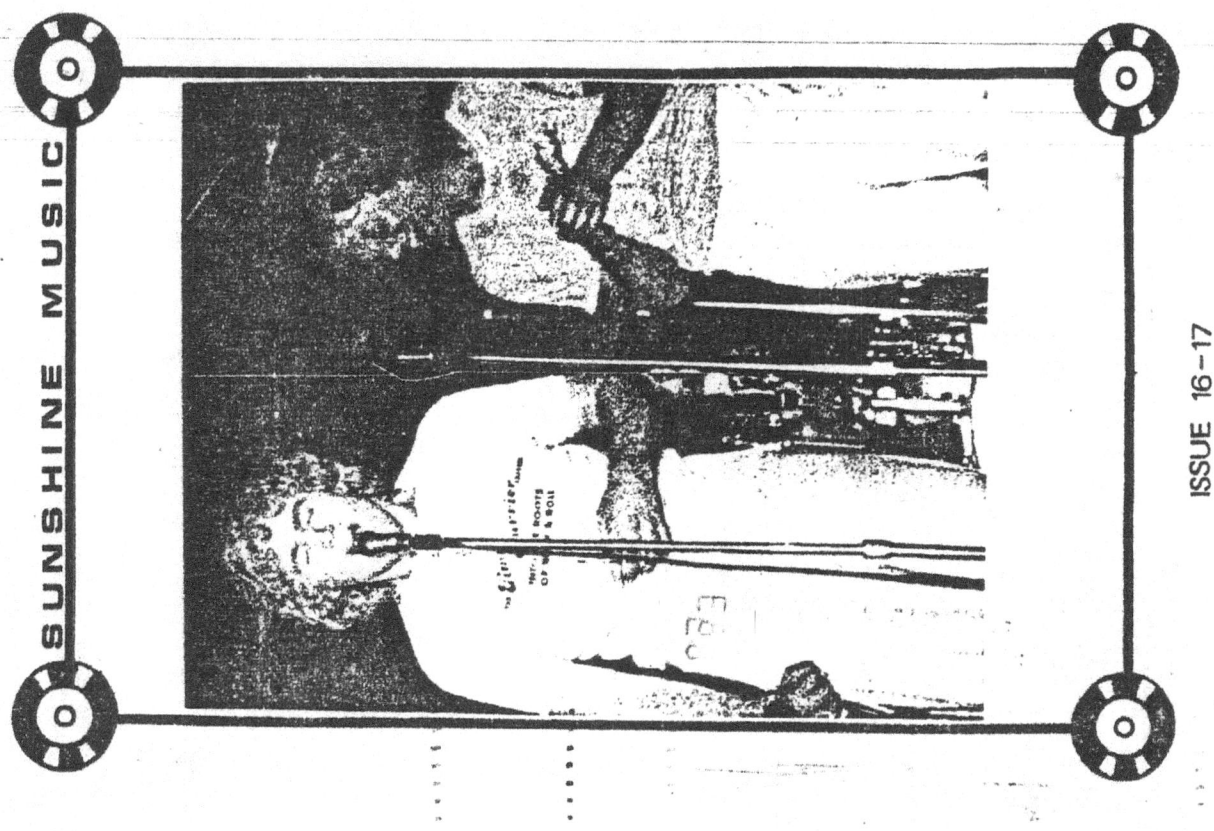

ISSUE 16-17

SUNSHINE MUSIC
c/o Doc Rock
2817 Crawford
Parsons, KS 67357

To:

FIRST CLASS MAIL

If this ends with "R", it's time to renew!!!

SUNSHINE MUSIC 16 - 17

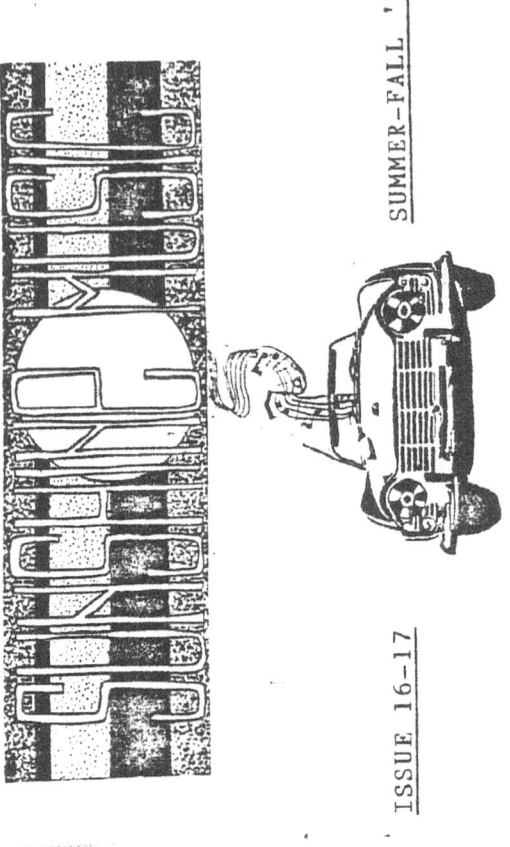

ISSUE 16-17

SUMMER-FALL '83

THE MAGAZINE OF THE OFFICIAL JAN AND DEAN
AUTHORIZED INTERNATIONAL COLLECTORS' CLUB

EDITOR
Michael Kelly, M.A., Ph.D.

ASSOC. EDITOR
Frank. M. Kisko

COPY EDITORS
Jan Berry
Dean Torrence

GRAPHICS
Buzzie Gentry
Honolulu Lulu

Contents Not Already Copyrighted are
© 1983 by Michael Bryan Kelly

SAMPLE COPIES of SM are $1 in the US and surface overseas. Airmail, $2. SUBSCRIPTIONS are good for six (6) issues, at the rates indicated below:

	USA, mailed in envelope	non-US Surface $7	Non-US Air $12	Surface Envelopes $10	Air Envelopes $15	Charge is for Postage
USA $5						

Please enclose S.A.S.E. (self-addressed stamped envelope) with all letters.

★ CHECK THE NUMBER ON YOUR ADDRESS LABEL. THE NUMBER THERE IS THE NUMBER OF
★ THE LAST ISSUE OF YOUR SUBSCRIPTION. IF THERE IS NO NUMBER, LUCKY YOU!!!!

MAKE ALL CHECKS PAYABLE TO MICHAEL B. KELLY---
---NEW SUBSCRIBERS, PLEASE INDICATE THE NUMBER ON YOUR SAMPLE ISSUE OR THE NUMBER YOU WANT YOUR SUBSCRIPTION TO START WITH, OR ELSE!!----------------------------------

BEGINNING FROM AN END

(As recorded by Jan & Dean/Liberty)
CLEVE HERMAN
JAN BERRY
GEORGE TIPTON
ROGER CHRISTIAN

She looks like you in every way
And I love her more with each passing day
But that doesn't mean I don't miss you
The way she cries (miss you)
Those baby eyes (miss you)
Her tender sighs
But that doesn't mean I don't miss you.

She reminds me of the morning
When you left me without warning
But that doesn't mean I don't miss you
Whenever I'm holding her near
I seem to sense you presence dear
I even get the feeling
That I could reach out and touch your hand
She wakes each morning smiling bright
She takes my hand and she'll squeeze it tight
The way she cries (miss you)
Those baby eyes.

I can still remember that stifling antiseptic smell of the hospital corridor
As you clutched my hand and we hurried down the hall
I think you knew as you looked up at me
That we'd never see each other again
And I felt so all alone
As they wheeled you through the door
And told me to wait
And there was a cry
And the doctor came out
And showed me our baby girl
You never saw her sweetheart
But she must have known you somewhere
Because she looks and acts and talks the way I remember you
But that doesn't mean I don't miss you
The way she cries (miss you)
Those baby eyes (miss you)
Her tender sighs
(Repeat chorus).

* Copyright 1965 by Screen Gems-Columbia Music Co., Inc.

Cover: Estelle Bueno, the Bottom Line, 5-7-79

JAN & DEAN vs. the Beatles

In our house there was a constant battle—my Jan and Dean music versus Tim, my brother's, Beatle music. Every time he got bigger speakers, I'd get a new amplifier. It is true, he did buy "Surf City" before I did, but I bought MEET THE BEATLES before he did, not to mention the classic 45, "Linda."

In the debate continues to this hour—who was greater, Jan and Dean or the Beatles? Of course, Tim thinks the answer is obvious. After all, except for the King, no one sold more records or made more money or had a bigger influence on music than John, Paul, plus George and Ringo. But other than Tim, I am sure, feels that the Beatles even outclassed Elvis in the end.

Well, I submit that Jan Berry, along with partner Dean, was in fact a greater genius, musically and otherwise, than John and Paul, along with partners George and Ringo.

First, let me stipulate that the Beatles are more famous than Jan and Dean; that they did sell more records; that they did have bigger and more hits; that they are richer; and so on.

Big deal.

To me, selling more records does not make the Beatles greater than Jan and Dean. Books by the author of CONAN outsell the works of Shakespeare—but does that make Conan's author a greater writer than Shakespeare? Of course not! I mean, you can sell Americans pet rocks, cigarettes, whole-life insurance, unsafe automobiles, or anything else, by the millions, regardless of quality.

Now, how do you sell things to Americans? Promotion. The Beatles did not do well in America without promotion. Decca, Tollie, Swan, Atco, and even Capitol turned down the Beatles contract and music pre-1964. Vee-Jay records got them for free, no extra charge when they paid for the American rights to distribute Britisher Frank Ifield's hits "I Remember You" and "Lovesick Blues." When they released the Beatles' "From Me To You" in August of 1963, it failed to make the U.S. top 100! It would take another half a year, several more releases, and a lot of promotion before the Beatles could have an American hit with "I Want To Hold Your Hand" in January, 1964.

What happened in that half a year? Well, there was a lot of pre-British Invasion publicity. Jack Paar filmed the Beatles in Great Britain doing "She Loves You" and showed it on American TV in the fall of '63. Capitol shipped "I Want To Hold Your Hand" to record stores without waiting for it to get on the radio or the charts. There was publicity in Time, Billboard, and a special "newspaper" distributed to record stores nationwide, free, by Capitol records, telling the recording-buying teens all about the Beatles. Not only had the Beatles yet to have a hit, Capitol even goofed and put the wrong tune in the cutlines under the Fab Four's photos!

So, with that much publicity, and the merchandising that followed, how could the Beatles miss? I feel strongly that with similar publicity and financing, Jan and Dean could have been as big as the Beatles. Say, if their TV show had not been stopped by Jan's accident. I mean, look at the Monkees. With members who had from little to no musical ability or experience, who were complete strangers to one another, they immediately sold millions and had #1 hits due to promotion and exposure on TV and, coupled with widespread merchandising in retail stores of dolls, toys, and so forth, such like the Beatles before them. By contrast, I never have known anyone who was able to find a "Little Old Lady Skateboard!"

The Monkees are not the only example. In the Fall of 1954, actress Joan Weber sang a song on a live TV drama. The next day, millions of American TV viewers ran to their record stores to buy the record, but were disappointed to find that this song was an

---

SHORT CUTS

Elaine Williams of 712 Ashe ST, Key West, FL 33040, would like to correspond with people who are into Jan and Dean record collecting, video tapes, other related music, fishing (?), growing orchids (?), and tropical plants.

Meanwhile, Kathy Baxter, 1338 Seagull DR, Mississauga, Ontario, Canada L5J 3E7, has one copy of Jan and Dean's 1980 Forum concert on VHS. Excellent quality, for sale ($60 US) or trade for Jan and Dean's California Special.

OK, I CUT THE DEAL. EVEN IF J&D ARE NOT GOING TO BE ON MTV SOON (AND WASN'T A VIDEO VERSION OF THE ORIGINAL "DEAD MAN'S CURVE" MADE?), IT SEEMS LIKE J&D VIDEO SHOULD BE INCLUDED UNDER THE HEADING OF JAN AND DEAN COLLECTABLES. SO, STARTING NEXT ISSUE, SUNSHINE MUSIC WILL FEATURE A VIDEO TAPE CLEARING CENTER. ANYONE WHO HAS VHS OR BETA MACHINES, AND ANYONE WHO HAS ANY JAN AND/OR DEAN VIDEO, PLEASE WRITE AND LET ME KNOW. FIRST, WE NEED TO GET A COMPREHENSIVE LIST OF ALL OF THE J&D VIDEO AVAILABLE. THEN, WE NEED TO FIGURE OUT HOW TO MAKE IT AVAILABLE TO THE MAXIMUM NUMBER OF FANS. PARTICIPATION IS, OF COURSE, VOLUNTARY. BUT PLEASE LET ME KNOW WHAT YOU HAVE OR ARE LOOKING FOR, AND WHAT, IF ANYTHING, YOU MAY HAVE FOR TRADE OR SALE.

Back to Stax of Wax, don't forget West Coast Services' Jan and Dean collectors' EP's. Full details are in the last issue, or you may write them at Box 699, Blacktown, 2148 NSW AUSTRALIA.

From Deborah K. Hush: Wanted—all Jan Berry lovers to write me also want anyone who has the compilation tape can pay a little but not much. And, especially want cassette tapes of Jan's live shows in the California night clubs acts please contact me soon, thanks. Write Deb at RR #3, box 250, Bloomfield, IN 47424.

LOVE AND TORRENCE are performing in CAFE OLD over Labor Day weekend, September 3, on The Hyannis Village Green at noon! And, it's free, as usual!

BERRY AND TORRENCE dates are in the works.

JAN BERRY AND ALOHAS are having a very successful and busy summer! July had a string of dates. August 10 and 11, Jan will be recording material in Hawaii! The rest of the schedule:

August
1 Marine Air Station, Oahu
2 Pearl Harbor, Hawaii
3 Pearl harbor, Hawaii
4 Coconut Grove, Honolulu
5 Coconut Grove, Hawaluhu
6 Kauai Resort, Honolulu
7 Lahaina Civic Amphitheater, Maui
8 Blue Max, Lahaina, Maui
9 Blue Max, Lahaina, Maui
10 Recording
11 Recording
12 Kona Lagoon Longhouse, Kona
13 Kona Lagoon Longhouse, Kona
14 Maniloka Surf Crown Room, Hilo
20 Louisville Fair, Kentucky
21 Andy's Picnic, Salerno Fair, Vallejo, CA

October
3 Marina Hotel, Las Vegas

November
1-30 Melbourne, Perth, Sidney, Australia

THE FAB FOUR

So, sales and fame do not greatness make. How about chart success? The Beatles had five—count 'em, 5—songs at once on Billboard, all at once, in positions 1,2,3,4, and 5. Even when "Ride the Wild Surf," "The Anaheim Azusa and Cucamonga Sewing Circle, Book Review, and Timing Association," "Sidewalk Surfin'," and "When It's Over" were all being played on the radio at the same time, Jan and Dean did not monopolize the nation's top 5!

So how did the Beatles do it? Well, those five hits were on different labels, and had already been hits in England over a period of two years. I mean, it would have been interesting to have seen "Surf City," "Drag City," "Dead Man's Curve," "Little Old Lady (from Pasadena)," and "Baby Talk" each as a different record label, released all at once, with coverage in all national magazines, news shows, and all of the rest! I dare say, that would have sold more 45s than Liberty did in 1964.

So, when the Beatles hit the US, they had a backlog of hit productions, simultaneous release and push of their records by numerous record companies, and tons of free publicity. All of this I feel led to a band-wagon effect. This is a common advertising and sociological concept which describes a situation in which people join a movement not out of personal taste, but to be like the crowd, because it is the in-thing to do.

Might there be a similar explanation for the numerous two-sided hits the Beatles had, compared to only three for Jan and Dean. People assume that the Beatles had more two-sided hits just because their music was such high quality. But there is at least one alternative explanation.

First, due to the backlog of material and the simultaneous release by many companies, people were accustomed to there being more than one Beatles song at a time. In fact, it is likely that most radio listeners had no idea which songs were flip sides, since the DeeJays never announced it on the air. More importantly, though, only a minority of radio stations in the mid-sixties played rock and roll.

An old-line record label, RCA, had been using this technique since the fifties, and gotten Elvis two-sided hits by simply putting a ballad on his rock and roll record flip sides. Then, while the teen stations played the rocking side, the more adult and country stations could be in and play the ballad side without offending their conservative listeners too badly. Voila, two-sided hits!

Well, the Beatles did the same thing, allowing the non-teen stations to get on the Beatle bandwagon:

Rocking	Ballad Flip
She Loves You	I'll Get You
Thank You Girl	Do You Want To Know A Secret
Twist and Shout	There's A Place
Ticket To Ride	Yes It Is
Get Back	Don't Let Me Down

THE DYNAMIC DUO

original composition for the TV production and had never been recorded. By popular demand as it were, Weber went into the studio immediately, and by November, "Let Me Go Lover" was the number one hit in the USA!

In the later '50s and early '60s, Dick Clark's AMERICAN BANDSTAND made Philadelphia a world center of rock and roll by having local kids sing (lip sync) local records on that network TV show. The publicity made these kids instant stars, regardless of ability (the Fabulous Fabian, for one). Besides the singing stars who came on the show, the national exposure given the local high schoolers who danced on the show made them so popular that they had their own fan clubs!

Later, the Partridge Family and Bobby Sherman had a lot of hits—until their TV shows were cancelled.

In the early '70s, the Beach Boys couldn't give away their concert tickets. When they played the University of Kansas in those days, they drew less than 1,000 students and townies in a town of 50,000, a University of 20,000, and a field house which could hold 18,000. (And they played mostly Stores and GQB-type material). Then Capitol passed a two-record set of their hits and LP cuts endlessly on TV and made them better-known stars than they had been in the '60s.

Suddenly, the Beach Boys were superstars who could draw huge crowds anywhere they played! They came back to KU and overflowed the 18,000-capacity field house to the point of standing room only. People even had to settle for standing outside and listening through the walls! (And, the band did only Beach Boy material!)

Similarly, Chubby Checker did a little thing called The Twist...." "Hi, I'm Chubby Checker—I did a little thing called The Twist...." "Hi, I'm Joey Dee and the Starlighters "Peppermint Twist"!" In spite of the fact that none of Chubby's hits was even on the LP or the commercial, this publicity made him a star in constant demand at a time when he could get no bookings at all!

As a final example of how fast being on TV can make a career, there is a new cable TV service called MTV, Music Television. The idea was to show videotapes of hit artists doing their new songs. But the record companies balked, and it was left to independent producers to make their own tapes of unknown artists if MTV were going to have enough material to stay on the cable.

Soon, in spite of the fact that probably less than 5% of all homes have MTV, the record stores of America were full of kids asking for non-existent records by these kids who were being shown on MTV. These unknown artists, with no hits on the radio at all, soon were outselling the known, "hit" artists of the day! Now, because they serve as host "Veejays" (video "Deejays") on MTV, today, even the totally unknown young people who introduce these videotapes are superstars with the kids of America, such as Dick Clark of Bandstand fame.

Reminds me of what Capitol did with the Beach Boys. . . .

Little Deuce Coupe | Surfer Girl
Be True To Your School | In My Room
I Get Around | Don't Worry Baby

Imagine, if Jan and Dean had gotten picked up by a major label like RCA or Capitol, or imagine if the Beatles had been stuck on Liberty!!!

One claim Tim (my Beatle-loving brother, remember?) makes for the Beatles' greatness is the fact that so many groups and producers have imitated the Beatles style in music, clothes, and hair. Well, it doesn't take genius or greatness to set a style or to be imitated!

I remember when the girls who danced on American Bandstand set a new clothing trend out of wishing, totally by accident. It seems they came to the show immediately after school, Catholic school, and still wearing their school uniforms. Well, the mars objected to the girls' wearing their uniforms on TV, but if the girls went home to change, they'd lose their places in line to other kids. The only solution was to wear sweaters over the blouses of their school uniforms.

The result: teen girls nationwide searched the stores for non-existent dickies to wear under those resto sweaters, like the kids in Philly wear to school. The point is that people will imitate anything. And while imitation may be the sincerest form of flattery, it does not define greatness or genius!

It is therefore possible to attribute much of the super-star status attributed to the Beatles to factors other than genius. It is time to look at Jan and Dean to see what qualities they had that could be seen as making them inherently better than the Beatles.

First, of course, there is the fact that, in spite of very bad personal misfortune, and the lack of the push and other advantages outlined above in connection with the Beatles, Jan and Dean had a major rock and roll career on what you might call their own artists.

And on a shoe string! When the Beatles cut an LP, they had unlimited resources. Compare that to the LINDA LP, completed probably in one day, with no chance to do songs over to get rid of mistakes, let alone experiment with playing tapes backwards and the like. Besides the budget and time restrictions imposed by the label, Jan and Dean were restricted artistically. Liberty wouldn't let them say "Come Bastie You," and if they had tried to play tapes backwards (as on "Strawberry Fields Forever") or to have a five-minute fadeout (as on "Hey, Jude") Liberty would not have released it, the stations would not have played it, and the public would not have bought it.

Nothing succeeds like success. Because of the promotion and bandwagon effects, the Beatles could release material that, even if it sounded identical, would have been rejected if released by another artist. It is sort of like the glamorous way Liz and Dick mess around, behavior which would never be tolerated if committed by other actors or by our neighbors.

Here's a sure measure of success, perhaps indicative of success, that makes Jan and Dean clearly superior to the Beatles. John and Paul were together making music for five years in the UK before they could manage to squeeze out a hit. And in the USA, they went through numerous record companies and many flops before they finally caught on.

But Jan, with no dues-paying, borrows a microphone from his father's collection (which included such recently developed models as the latest RCA Ribbon mic and a German Telefunkin mic), makes up a song for a party, and bingo, with no promotion, on a teeny-tiny record label, had a national #1 hit first rattle out of the can!

If that isn't genius, I'd like to know what is!

Moreover, after losing his partner, Arnie Ginsberg, Jan proves it wasn't a fluke by starting anew with Dean, going to another itsy-bitsy label, offering another homemade tape, and having another hit with no promotion to speak of! Two national #1's in a row!

Later, at Liberty, another small label, company executives almost killed the act with their input, never realizing the genius that Jan and Dean had. Finally, the company gave up on the duo and left them to sink or swim on their own. Naturally, they swam, all the way to "Surf City" and #1 again!

Perhaps the most important factor in support of the contention that Jan and Dean were greater than the Beatles is the fact that, in addition to the commercial effort put out by the US industrial complex on behalf of the Beatles, the Mustops themselves bent their every effort to the making of hits. They were into rock 'n' roll full-time.

Contrast this situation to the extreme part-time nature of Jan and Dean's rock 'n' roll music making. Unlike the Beach Boys, the Beatles, Elvis, and over 99.99% of all rock and roll-acts before or since, Jan and Dean were FULL TIME STUDENTS throughout their musical careers. Be it junior high, high school, college, or graduate school, Jan and Dean were students first and artists second.

Between classes, homework, and dating, music was relegated to weekends, both in the studio and on the road. Fly to the East Coast on Friday night, come back Sunday night for school! Why, at the time of Jan's accident, they were about to cut the vocals on a new LP. What Dean heard that Jan had had an accident, but had no idea Jan was really hurt, his first reaction was relief that the evening's recording session was cancelled and he could go out on a date!

So, scenario one: Take the Beatles, strip them of their publicity, promotion, financing, multiple labels, and all of the rest. Instead, make a rule that they have to stay in school, do music part time, and if they don't get a hit immediately (with no five-years of practice first), put 'em on a podunk label. Where would they be? NOWHERE! It took them five years, full-time, and several releases to get a hit in England, and two more years and many more releases before they got a hit in the USA.

Scenario two: Take Jan and Dean, let them practice for five to seven years, let them have several chances to get a good record, have them do music full time, then put them on Capitol, Tollie, Veeday, Atco, Swan, and MGM, and then promote the heck out of them. You'd have the biggest hit since, well, since Elvis Presley!!

In summary, you cannot argue with facts such as sales, hits, and celebrity. However, you can question whether these things are a measure of genius, or due largely to circumstances. In point of fact, comparing Jan and Dean with the Beatles is like comparing apples and oranges. In light of the casual approach Jan and Dean took to music, and considering all of the obstacles they had to overcome, it is either proof of genius, or it is a plain miracle, that they had any hits at all.

As for the Beatles, there is no doubt in my mind that any four men, pushed like the Beatles were in America, would have been the biggest thing since Elvis.

To quote Spleen, "These recordings are for fun and dancing only and not for the purpose of competing musically or artistically with any other artist's recordings."

But, when someone says the Beatles are greater or greatest, a comparison is implied. So, while I agree with Green, the question forced on us is, if you handicap the Jan and Dean/Beatles race like Uley do horse racing, golf, bowling, and dog racing, who would come out the greater? Scenarios one and two are self-explanatory—

JAN AND DEAN ARE GREATER THAN JOHN AND PAUL AND GEORGE AND RINGO!

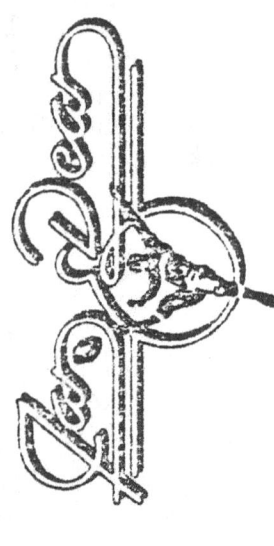

SUNSHINE MUSIC 16 - 17

SURF'S UP!!!

FOR THE BEST SELECTION IN **the Beach Boys** JAN & DEAN AND ALL SURF-RELATED RECORDS

ROCKAWAY RECORDS
P.O. BOX 24197 DEPT.SM
LOS ANGELES, CA 90024
U.S.A.
Phone (213) 479-1674
Or (213) 479-1364

WRITE FOR OUR NEWEST SET SALE/AUCTION CATALOG OF SURF, 60's/70's/80's ROCK PSYCHEDELIC, PICTURE DISCS & RARE ITEMS

• FANTASTIC BAGGYS • DYLAN • SUNRAYS • SPRINGSTEEN • SURF RAIDERS
• BRUCE & TERRY • THE BEATLES • SAGITTARIUS • PRESLEY • THE HONEYS
• JOY DIVISION • HONDELLS • BOWIE • SURFARIS • THE JAM • RIP CHORDS • COSTELLO

Let Me Explain

For new readers, SUNSHINE MUSIC comes out four times a year, Summer, Fall, Winter, and Spring. A subscription is for six issues, or one and one-half years. Sample issues and back issues are $1 in the US, except for certain back issues which have been reprinted and therefore cost $2. Issue 12-13 was a double issue, costs $2 in the US, and includes a detailed guide to all back issues prior to 12-13. When asking for a sample issue or a subscription, always tell me what issues you already have, or what issue you want the subscription to start with. Otherwise, you are likely to get a duplicate. Correspondence gets answered much more quickly if you enclose an SASE. Thanks!

MUSICAL COLUMNS:

The July COLUMNS magazine featured Mike and Dean. Our resource they used in preparing their feature was back issues of SUNSHINE MUSIC. A nice mention of SM in the "Fanfare" column has netted us a number of new subscribers.

An upcoming COLUMNS will feature a Celebrity Baby Photo Contest, including a photo of Dean. It was taken by Dean's doting uncle "Red" Ormsby. "Red" is a writer, who started as editor of THE PELICAN, a University of California humor magazine. He now edits SALES TALK, which goes to advertising agencies.

NEWLYWED NEWS:

Dean's antique home was originally owned by Humphrey Bogart. Now, Dean's sweetheart (get it?) has transformed this house into a comfy, attractive, flower-laden home. Jeano has made this garden into a potential prize-winner! Under the drawbridge (!) to his house, he has created a fish pond, with natural rock outlining the terraces.

Water cascades down the terraces and over the rocks from a quiet pump, so the garden has that delightful "plop-plop" sound that one hears either by a brook, or in this case sitting by one of Dean and Susan's livingroom windows!

Colorful water lilies are growing in the pond. Red, pink, and lavender impatiens thrive in the rock garden. Add the blue of the lilies of the Nile, hanging baskets of fuchias, and it is indeed pretty!

Susan and Dean like to bar-b-que (imagine getting an invitation!) on their open-air porch. Their guests are treated to great food, piped-in, long-playing music, and the sound of waterfalls! All of this in the shadow of the huge HOLLYWOOD sign on the hill behind them!

For Dean and Susan, the honeymoon certainly is not over.

SINGLE PICKS

RECORD WORLD

JAN & DEAN—United Artists 50859
VEGETABLES (Sea of Tunes, BMI)
Perhaps this previously unreleased master should have been credited to Jan & Dean & Brian. Beach Boy Brian Wilson is not only its co-writer and co-producer, but can also be heard singing back-up. With spins, sure to catch on. Brilliant.

JAN BERRY'S 1958 CORVETTE

On November 6, 1961, Jan Berry was riding the crest of popularity of "Heart and Soul." Jan and partner Dean Torrence were appearing in New York that fateful day. Back in Bel-Air, California, fire completely destroyed 485 houses, including Berry the residence.

Jan's white Corvette was parked in the driveway at the time. The fire glazed the windows, peeled the paint, gutted the interior--in short, burned the sportscar to a crispl

Fortunatly, neither the tires nor the fuel tank were ingited by the massive conflagration. Jan's brother was able to guide the car down the hill, where he left it, pending Jan's return, in the care of a friend. On his return, Jan decided to have his car repaired, and the exterior repainted black.

Two years later, Jan was riding the even higher crest of "Surf City." He decided it was time to get a new 'vette, so he sold his fire car, a through classified ad, to classic-car buff Jim Blanchard.

Jim kept the car for twenty years. As time passed, he restored the car, going to extremes to obtain original-equipment parts from seat covers to screws. He traced the serial number to the date of manufacture, stripped the back and white pait and repainted fire-engine (Signet) red, and buffed it to a high polish. He rechromed the trim, and began entering the results in Classic Car Shows, winning a Trophy, which attests to the excellence of his work. He is still improving the job he has done on the car.

April 14, 1983, Jim took the car back to the scene of the fire, and parked it in front of the same (rebuilt) house, in the same driveway. He thought Jan would enjoy seeing his old car again after 20 years. He was right!

ORIGINAL JAN + DEAN
... ALL RECORDS AND COVERS
GRADING AT LEAST VERY GOOD+

✱ GOTTA TAKE THAT ONE LAST
RIDE — $15.00
✱ GOLDEN HITS VOLUME 2 $12.00
✱ GOLDEN HITS VOLUME 3 $12.00
✱ COMMAND PERFORMANCE $10.00
✱ DRAG CITY $10.00

ALL POSTPAID AND INSURED
IN USA

: MINT / FACTORY SEALED
✱ J+D LIVE . . . $13.00
✱ ODDITIES . . . 12.00
✱ AMERICAN DREAM . .

VARIOUS ARTISTS ... JAN +
DEAN TRACK "FUN FUN FUN" — $5.00
ALL POSTPAID
✱ BEL-AIR BANDITS EP (12")
WITH DEAN $6.00
✱ J+D BATMAN EP $8.00

A GREAT BOOK ... "ROCK
RECORD" 526 PAGES LISTING
25,000 ROCKERS/ETC ON 30,000
ALBUMS ... SALE—$7.00 POSTPAID
DIANE VOSTEEN 5007 DETROIT 15
CLEVELAND, OHIO 44102 (216) 631-8444

As anyone who knows Dean (or who has read the liner notes from GOTTA TAKE THAT ONE LAST RIDE) knows, Dean is opposed to musical reviews on principle. But, he did make an exception, once...

SUNSTROKED...
by Dean Torrence

GOLDEN SUMMER
Various Artists
United Artists (UA-LA627-H2)

To review this album properly, I'll have to become schizophrenic once again. You see, when I was recording with my partner, people would continually ask me if I was Jan and Dean. And I would reply, "Yes, I was one of the main guys in the group."

Since I stand to make some bucks on this turkey, I am somewhat more interested in the commercial potential of this album then I am in how it fits into my record collection. Personally, I am really knocked out to finally have an album with both the Beach Boys and Jan & Dean almost side-by-side. Having some of the most important surfin' bands ever recorded on the very same lp is pretty bitchin' in itself.

The Marketts sound great, just like a studio band, and then there are The Ventures, those fun-lovin' surfers from Yakima; The Frogmen, those holldoggers from Fargo; Dale Dick and the Dick-tones, and the Trashmen, who prove they were appropriately named. Plus, Jack Whatshizname, that tube-shooting New York arranger, and those wiped-out kids from Pitts-berg—The Surfaris!

But that's not all! How can we forget the two that had the biggest effect on surfin' music and surfin' consciousness. They degraded the whole California scene to a level so low that it was almost irreversible. Thank you Frankie (Avalon) for all that hot knee-boarding you did on the silver screen and all those bitchin' beach parties on the back lots of American International and last but least, all those great Italian surfin' songs! Likewise, thank you, *Annette*, for showin' Middle America that the typical California surfer girl is not blonde, thin and golden-skinned, but rather Italian, chunky and has a make-up man providing the bronzing. And *can she surf!*

Wow! She and Frankie would ride side-by-side on a nine-foot slider while discussing how *Frank-ee* had gotten red lipstick on his fly when *her* lips were baby-pink.

Personally, I really don't mind them being on the album, cuz they were a part of it all, even if it was all negative. They were just doing what they were told to do (e.g., Martin Bormann) and just trying to make a buck.

But commercially, it seems to me the producers of this album were to concerned with trying to assemble an historic lp instead of a playable one. There are only a small bunch of us fools left that don't give a shit what the music is, as long as we got it! But the average record-buyer is younger now, and into music that turns him or her on.

Pop music is just not all that damn important. It's just, after all, rock 'n roll.

P.S. In conclusion., after re-reading this review, my mind hasn't been changed. I still say all reviewers suck.

Dean Torrence is not Jan Berry. He is merely one-half of the duo that rode the wild surf (and the record charts) with the help of a diminutive, elderly woman from Pasadena.

Crawdaddy

ROGERS & COWAN, INC.
PUBLIC RELATIONS

9661 WILSHIRE BOULEVARD
BEVERLY HILLS, CALIFORNIA 90212-2192
(213) 271-4181   TELEX 687-442

CABLE ADDRESS ROCOPUB
BEVERLY HILLS, CALIFORNIA

DEAN TORRENCE   a biography

A surprising group burst upon the 1958 music scene, tragically disappeared in 1966 and then reappeared miraculously in 1978.

Surprising -- because this group recorded their first hit about a friend's stripper girlfriend on a home tape recorder in their family garage. The song, "Jenny Lee," hit number one in most markets and the group, Jan and Dean (Jan Berry and Dean Torrence) were on their way to rock 'n roll stardom while they still attended college.

Between 1958 and 1966, Jan and Dean obtained top chart status for 25 songs, with seven of them in the Top 10. But their skyrocketing careers were abruptly halted when Jan was involved in a near-fatal accident. Jan's unfortunate twist of fate left him in a state of aphasia where he had to learn to read, write, talk and walk again at the age of 26.

During Jan's long recovery, Dean turned his attention to design, which he had studied at U.S.C., and began a very successful graphics company, Kittyhawk Graphics, which specialized in music industry packaging, advertising and merchandising. He has designed album covers for The Beach Boys, Steve Martin, Nitty Gritty Dirt Band, Nilsson, Anne Murray, Linda Ronstadt and Walter Egan. Four of his albums have been nominated for Grammys, with one winning the best

New York Office: 122 East 42nd Street, New York, New York 10168 (212) 490-8200 Cable: ROCOPUB New York, New York
London Office: 27 Albemarle Street, London W1X 3FA, England · 499-8601 · TELEX 291-23371

DEAN TORRENCE/page 2

album of the year honor.

Jan and Dean reappeared as a group in 1978, after a 12-year absence, just about as surprising as they started: in a feature television film, "Deadman's Curve," which told the story of Jan and Dean to millions.

This reappearance is what Dean terms, "The Second Phase," and the band still spreads the same musical magic that they produced so well for so long. Dean says the music cannot be "oldies" or go through a "revival," because the tunes have stood on their own throughout the 12-year absence of Jan and Dean.

"People want to hear sunshine music in summer and winter," Dean explains. "It is not always seasonal."

The current Jan and Dean following of young people in their late teens and early twenties bears him out. "They don't attend the concerts out of nostalgia," he says. "They come because the music is good rock 'n roll."

Since the television special, "Deadman's Curve," Jan and Dean have toured with The Beach Boys and on their own, with the Papa Doo Run Run Band.

"In the Sixties, we spent a lot of time in Florida," Dean says. In fact, Jan and Dean fans are most numerous in the South.

Dean will be joining Beach Boy Mike Love for a series of "Spring Break" concert dates. This mini-tour, sponsored by Anheiser-Busch/Budweiser, will kick off March 15 at Padre Island, Texas.

# # # #

Contacts:
West Coast: Sandy Friedman
              Nancy Sullivan
              Ann Toler
              (213) 275-4581

East Coast: Joe Dera
              Linn Tanzman
              Penny Staples
              (212) 490-8200

ROGERS & COWAN, INC.
PUBLIC RELATIONS

9665 WILSHIRE BOULEVARD
BEVERLY HILLS, CALIFORNIA 90212-2393
(213) 271-4181 TELEX 687-442

CABLE ADDRESS ROCOPUB
BEVERLY HILLS CALIFORNIA

MIKE LOVE -------- a biography

Mike Love has been featured as the leader of The Beach Boys band since its inception in the early 1960's. Not only has he served as the band's lead singer and spokesman, but he has also contributed to the group's success and popularity by writing and co-writing such hits as "Good Vibrations," "California Girl," "Fun, Fun, Fun" and "Do It Again."

With such wide ranging talents, it's no surprise that Mike Love has ventured out on his own to develop his versatility.

Mike has completed his first solo album project, "Looking Back With Love," and is performing on tour with his "Endless Summer Beach Band," although he still plays an important role in the present Beach Boys band.

In addition, perhaps because he was a trend-setter in the sixties, Mike is now becoming increasingly involved in the video spectrum of rock 'n roll entertainment. As creator and executive producer of "The Spirit of America Spectacular" television and FM stereo simulcast in July of 1981, he attracted the largest nation-wide audience for a live simulcast in history.

Along with Dean Torrence, Mike will be performing at a series of "Spring Break" concert dates. This mini-tour, sponsored by Anheiser-Busch/Budweiser, will kick off March 15 at Padre Island, Texas, and will include appearances in Daytona Beach and Ft. Lauderdale.

New York Office: 122 East 42nd Street, New York, New York 10168 (212) 490-8200 Cable: ROCOPUB New York, New York
London Office: 27 Albemarle Street, London W1X 3FA, England • 499-6091 • TELEX 851-27371

MIKE LOVE/page 2

Mike credits his ability to withstand the pressures of touring and changing music scenes with daily Transcendental Meditation, TM-Sidhi sessions, a regular routine of aerobic exercise and Nautilus workouts.

Although he has seen a kaleidoscope of changes in the entertainment world over the last twenty years, Mike is challenged by what he has experienced.

"I think the future will be even more exciting," he says.
"I'm looking forward to making movies and soundtracks as well as enjoying the promotional and performing aspects of the entertainment business, while trying to do the best job I can so I can look back with pride on what I've accomplished."

###

Contacts:

West Coast: Sandy Friedman
Nancy Sullivan
Ann Toler
(213) 275-4581

East Coast: Joe Dera
Linn Tanzman
Penny Staples
(212) 490-8200

NOTE: Mike and Dean have recorded two more Hitbound/Radio Shack LPs. One is oldies like the first, the other is a CHRISTMAS ALBUM!

Mike & Dean SOLD OUT

Sunshine Flockers Meet West Coast Rockers in a Beach-Music Blow-out!

After all, what good is the beach without the sounds of surf? And keeping surf music alive and kicking, are two legends of the sound—Mike Love of the Beach Boys, and Dean Torrence of Jan and Dean. Together with the Endless Summer Beach Band, Mike and Dean have been leaving Spring Break student audiences breathless and shouting for more. SRO in Daytona Beach. Twenty thousand fans in South Padre Island. Swaying and stomping to *"Surfin' U.S.A."*, *"Ba-Ba-Barbara Ann"*, and *"Little Old Lady From Pasadena."*

"I can't wait to be back," exclaims Mike Love, "I'm really just a life-long student." Love has been the leader of the Beach Boys since the groups inception in the early 60's. Not only the band's leading singer and spokesman, he has also contributed to the group's popularity—by writing or co-writing such hits as *"Good Vibrations"*, *"Fun, Fun, Fun"*, *"California Girls"*, *"Do it Again"*.

Additionally, Mike has recorded his own solo album, "Looking Back With Love," performs on tour with the Endless Summer Beach Band, and still plays an important role in the present Beach Boys.

Dean Torrence burst upon the music scene in 1958 teamed with Jan Berry. Better known as *Jan and Dean*, they were early collaborators with the *Beach Boys*. Their careers were halted abruptly when Jan was involved in a near-fatal accident. The television movie, "Deadman's Curve" recounted the story of the duo's fame and misfortune.

Subsequently, Dean turned his attention to design and spawned Kittyhawk Graphics, specializing in music-industry merchandising. He has designed album covers for the Beach Boys, Steve Martin, Nitty Gritty Dirt Band, Nilsson, Anne Murray, Linda Ronstadt and Walter Egan.

"But I can't stop performing for the college crowd," glows Dean. So he joined forces with Mike in 1982, and Budweiser sponsored a Spring Break tour. The results were spectacular: "Everyone was in a party spirit...and the band delivered," reported the Daytona Morning Journal. The Dallas Morning News gave front-page coverage to the cheering crowd: "The perfect culmination..."

To keep warm through the winter, Mike and Dean and the band are engaging in a "Be True to Your Bud" college concert tour, again sponsored by Budweiser Beer.

Needless to say, Spring Break 1983 will find Mike & Dean, searching out those special places where the priorities are sand, sun, and fun. Delivering two hours of nonstop entertainment to aficionados (and who isn't) of the sounds of surf rock.

If you're planning a Spring Break vacation, you'll find Mike & Dean rocking through South Padre Island, Texas, on March 15 (raindate—March 16); double-teaming in Daytona Beach March 17 and the 24th; riding in with the tide in Fort Lauderdale on March 23; and taking the plunge in Destin Beach on March 31. All brought to you, FREE, by Budweiser, the King of Spring.

If you do see Mike & Dean, say, "Thanks guys," for keeping the *"Good Vibrations"* happening.

the ALOHAS

LETTERS

Dear Michael,

I was really glad to get my first issue of SM so soon! I've been into J&D since '61, but news has been hard to find! I've become a serious collector in the last several years. I'm impressed with your newsletter. It looks like you really work hard to find info your readers couldn't get elsewhere, as well as take a lot of care to insure your info is accurate. Here is $2 for the double issue that has the back-issue guide!

Thank you very much,
Karen B., North Carolina

P.S. I trusted your newsletter enough to subscribe sight-unseen, because 1) I've heard of it before, 2) I've never met a serious J&D fan who was a rip-off artist. Maybe I've been lucky, or maybe it is because people who like the fun J&D music are honest.

THANK YOU VERY MUCH, KAREN. READ ON!!

Dear Dec,

Enclosed is a buck for a sample issue. I would like to see an issue or two before I subscribe. I am rather cautious because of a bad experience I had with another J&D club, the Ripped Buggies. I sent them $5, and never heard another word.

Still, I am looking forward to an issue—it sounds very good!

Sincerely,
Dennis D., Texas

DENNIS, FOR A FULL STORY ON THE RIPPED-BUGGIES RIP-OFF, SEE SM #1

Dear Myke,

Do you ever receive negative letters?

Frank M. Kisko

YES, AND I HAVE PRINTED THEM ALL IN PAST ISSUES!!

Dear SM:

Urk! Summer's here and I forgot to renew! Here-take my money, please! I'll try to see that it never, ever happens again!

Kathy D., Los Angeles

Michael,

What does the "Little Old Lady (from Pasadena)" do when her Dodge breaks down?
She does some "Sidewalk Surfin'" to the nearest telephone booth, of course!

Frances L.

Dear Sunshine Music Readers:

I am planning an official SUNSHINE MUSIC/Jan and Dean T-Shirt! Just think, at concerts, you can wear the shirt, and the guys on the stage will know you are a trufan. Plus, you will be able to spot other SM-ers in the audience!

Groovy Records

by
Frank M. Kisko
and
Michael B. Kelly

THE MEANING OF
THE CRYPTIC RUN-OUT INSCRIPTIONS
SEEN ON JAN AND DEAN 45'S AND LP'S

1. Jennie Lee   Arwin PM-108-45   April, 1958   First pressing.

   Side 1: "Jennie Lee"   Self-explanatory.
   Side 2: "Gotta Get a Date"   Self-explanatory.

2. There's A Girl   Dore 45 531   October, 1959

   Side 1: "Baby Talk" "A is P" The hurras were University High School's car club in which Jan and Dean and Arnie were members. This was, by the way, in West (W) Los (L) Angeles(A)! "A is P" stands for "Lou Adler is a Pimp."
   Side 2: "TDHS" This stands for the fraternity Jan was a member of. This was also much later the name of Jan's music publishing company on Ode and A&M.

3. You Really Know How To Hurt A Guy   Liberty 45 55792   April, 1965

   Side 1: "JAND & JILLY" Some copies do not have this and inscription or any other. However, it refers to the fact that Dean did not sing on You Really Know How To Hurt A Guy, and Jill Gibson (once a member of the Mamas and Papas) sang the high harmony on the flip side. Some may have "DEAN & JACKIE" on the "A" side, a sort of equal-time for Dean and his girlfriend, Jackie Miller.

4. Like A Summer Rain/Louisiana Man   J&D Record Co. 402   October, 1966
   At least three versions of this 45 are known to exist.

   a) LASR, timed at 2:35/L Man, no time listed on label, sang starts with quacks. Has no special etching.
   b) LASR timed at 2:35/L Man, timed at 2:31 w/quacks. Its etching. LASR has "ARM" and a heart shape, plus 7450 RE1, Dean no longer recalls what "ARM" stood for. "RE 1" stands for "remix" or version #1.
   c) LASR, timed at 2:35, mix very clean/L.. Man, timed at 2:31, without quacks. Its etching. LASR has "Thanks IZ," which is a thank you to Lou Zacaglini, the promotional head of J&D records. L Man has "Thanks IZ, LUT + SRP and another heart shape. LUT is Dean Ormsby Torrence, while SRP must be Sanne, after all

5. Mother Earth/Blue Moon Shuffle, Jan Barry Ode 66023 November, 1972

   Side 1: Three different mixes were released, indicated by runout-groove notations "M1," (Mix One) "M2," and "M3."
   Side 2: Many mixes of this exist, but there are no groove notations here.

Interested? Write me and let me know. Vote what colors you'd like, what style of shirt, fabric content, what you think should be included in the design. Perhaps the SM car, or bottle cap, as illustrated in past issues?

Let's hear from you!

Best Your Bans,

Michael "The Rick" Kelly

Dear Mike,

Please forgive my lack of mental stability. Enclosed is a check for $10. Please renew my subscription to SUNSHINE MUSIC! with a double subscription!

Thanks,

Frank B., Missouri

Dear Michael,

My wife Denise has blessed me with our first child—a Boy!
Kiley Michael Lynch
6-1-83 6:10 PM
Keep up the good work of SUNSHINE MUSIC! Regards to your family!

Cordially,

Paul V. Lynch, Rhode Island

Hi Michael!

I've been noticing some things that are on same of my albums. There are little sayings on the records around the labels. Who puts these messages on the records?

Frances Lind

Dear Frances,

Well, I thought you deserved a good answer, and that the other SMers would enjoy reading it. So, here goes.

The space between the end of the music grooves and the label is called the "run-out grooves." In the run-out groove area, record companies put some information. Usually this information is 1) the record release number, 2) the side of the record, such as 1 and 2 or A and B, 3) the matrix (master tape ID) number of the record(s), and 4) the delta number which indicates the pressing plant that manufactured the disc, and from which the release date may be determined.

Sometimes this information is typeset, other times it is hand written. Either way, it must be done in backwards, or mirror writing on the master plates that will be used to mold the records if it is to be readable on the final record.

Many years ago in the '50s, Jan and Dean, and especially Dean, began putting extra, personal information in the run-out grooves of 45s, and later LPs. As evidenced by the handwriting and the style of humor, Dean is responsible for the majority of the messages in Jan and Dean record run-out grooves. One interesting point: because of the nature of the record-pressing process, the etching had to be done in "mirror writing," backwards, in order to come out correctly on the final pressings!

Frank Kisko, your Associate Editor, is a real J&D trivia expert. I consulted with him, and then with Jan and Dean, and here is what we all 4 came up with:

6. Don't You Just Know It/Blue Moonlight, Au Oki 66036, June, 1973

    Side 1: "B1" or "B2" indicate different mixes.
    Side 2: "N4" or "N5" indicate different mixes.

7. Skateboard Surfin' U.S.A. (Sidewalk Surfin' With Flo)/How Do I Love Her, Am Perry A&M 2000-S, April, 1978

    Side 1: There is a mono mix, clearer than the stereo mix, which is marked "Stereo" on the paper label, but marked "A&M 1200E(mono)-R2" in the runout grooves.

8. Vegetables/Snow Flakes On Laughing Gravy's Whiskers, The Laughing Gravy November, 1967

    a) DJ copy, dark blue label, no concentric circles on label, etching: "LG + BW" for "Laughing Gravy plus Brian Wilson." Artist: The Laughing Gravy. Laughing Gravy was a dog in a Laurel and Hardy movie.
    b) Light blue label, no concentric circles on label, no etching. Artist: Laughing Gravy.
    c) Light blue label, with concentric circles on label, no etching. Artist: The Laughing Gravy. Flip side has "Whiskers" misspelled "Whiskors" on this pressing.

9. Summertime, Summertime/The Theme From Leon's Garage, Our Gang Br'er Bird 001 August, 1966

    Side 1: None.
    Side 2: "STOP COPYING ITS HEADLEYS" "JB DRESSES FUNNY" "BK*ER BIRD LIKES MAMS" "TO THE OLD LIQUOR R"

10. Gonna Hustle You/Summer Means Fun, Legendary Masked Surfers, UA XW270-W July, 1973

    a) One pressing, both DJ and regular, has no special etching, and side one is the .88D LP cut, unmodified.
    b) Another pressing, DJ only, is a newly modified version of the .88D LP cut, and has etching:
    Side 1: "TR/TLY/JLB" and a heart shape. "A Mystery Lady", I love you, Dean Ormsby Torrence.
    Side 2: "BJ/JM/BH" are the initials of the persons who modified the recording, Bruce Johnston, Terry Melcher, and Dean Ormsby Torrence.

11. Surf City/She's My Summer Girl Liberty 55580 May, 1963

    Side 1: On many copies, there is a "q" followed by from one to six or more hatch marks, indicating subsequent pressings of this record which outsold all other 45's.
    Side 2: Nothing.

12. OUTTA TAKE THAT ONE LAST RIDE 2-LP Set UA LA 341-H2 November, 1974

    Side 1: "THANKS BRIAN" and a heart shape; "CHERRES RULE."
    Side 2: "DJT + CJM" and a heart shape.
    Side 3: "THERE'S MIA" (see listing #2)
    Side 4: "I AM 1"

13. One Summer Night Live: 2-LP Set Rhino Records 1498 November, 1982

    Side 1: "SEE SHIE TWJ"
    Side 2: "KAHANA NANA LEI U" (self explanatory)
    Side 3: "PARTICIPATE WITH PARTY HATS"
    Side 4: "WHERE ARE SHE FIVE AND SIX."

14. The Bel-Air Bandits with Dean Torrence Permanent Records No. 2 1982

    Side 1: "We love you Brian"
    Side 2: "Take the money and limp, babys"

15. You Really Know How To Hurt A Guy Liberty "All-Time Hit" Series 56569 1966

    Side 1: "Juno & Jilly" Same as #1.
    Side 2: Nothing.

SO, FRANCES, THAT SHOULD ANSWER YOUR QUESTION. NEXT QUESTION?

Sincerely,

Frank and Michael

SUNSHINE MUSIC 16 - 17

FROM THE FILES

JAN & DEAN FOREVER!

I just read your January issue, and I was so thrilled when I read a letter from someone saying how much she loved Jan and Dean. I feel the exact same way about them. They not only sing about surfing, but other kind of music as well. This only proves how much talent they really have. I, too, have all of their albums, and I cut out every picture and article I can find on them. Jan and Dean will certainly be popular long after the British groups are forgotten. Jan and Dean forever!

S. M.
Long Island, N. Y.

Handsome Jan Barry likes boots so much that he decided to have some made for him. He outlined his size 12-D's carefully and sent this with his foot measurements to a very exclusive shop in London. "I got back the greatest pair of suede boots with stacked wooden heels I've ever had," he enthuses. "Everybody went wild over them, so I ordered lots more pairs in all colors. But this time I made the mistake of putting Mr. Jan Barry on the order. When I got the new boots, they were a lot different from my first pair—because the first time they thought I was a girl, with size 12 feet, and they sent me girls' boots. I didn't like the men's boots at all," he sighs. "Boy those other ones really were a gas!"

WHERE'S DEAN?

We are writing to inform you (in case you didn't know) that there are TWO people in the singing group Jan and Dean. Not just one named Jan! Sure, Jan got his leg all raunched up and it was a terrible accident, but that's not any reason to go off and forget good old Dean! He may not be as good-looking as Jan, but looks aren't everything! Jan probably wouldn't be where he is today without Dean, so we think he deserves some mention too! What does the poor guy have to do, go out and break his leg too? If so, we'll do the job for free!

Geri & Shell
Boston, Mass.

HERE IS THE ANSWER KEY:

ANSWERS

```
Y . . . . . . . . . . . . . . . . . . . . .
. A . . . . . . . . . . . . . . . . . . . .
. . R . . . . . . . . . . . . . . . . . . .
. . . G D . P A S A D E N A . . . . . . . .
. . . . N R . E . . . . . . . . . . . . . .
. . . J . . A V . . . . . . . . . . . . . .
. . . . A . T G O L E . . . . . . . . . . .
. . . . . N . . S U R F . . . . . . . . . .
. . . . . . . . . K I . . . . . . . . . . .
. . . . . . . T . . L P . . . . . . . . . .
. . . . . . . . O . . E D . . . . . . . . .
. . . . . . . . . R R A . . . . . . . . . .
B . . . . . . . . . E N L . . . . . . . . .
. E . . . . . . . . N I . E . . . . . . . .
. . A . . . . . . O . C . . . . . . . . . .
. . . R . . . . . A . E . . . . . . . . . .
. . . . T . . . . D . . . . . . . . . . . .
. . . . . C . . N . . . . . . . . . . . . .
. . . . Y . H . I . . . . . . . . . . . . .
. . . . . . . I . . . . . . . . . . . . . .
. . . . . . B . L . T O P F O R T Y . . . .
. . . . . E . . S U . . . . . . . . . . . .
. . . . R . . . . . N . . . . . . . . . . .
. . . H . B . . . . . S . . . . . . . . . .
. . I . . E . C . . . . H . . . . . . . . .
. T . . . . S . U . . . . I . . . . . . . .
. . . . . . . H . . . . . . N . . . . . . .
. . . . . . M . . . . . . . . E . . . . . .
. . . . O . . . . . . . . . . . . . . . . .
. . P . . . . . . . . . . . . . . . . . . .
P A L . . . . . . . . . . . . . . . . . . .
```

Friday, May 20, 1983/Las Vegas Review-Journal/7D

Jan & Dean alive

Jan Berry keeps music of

By Gary Ebbels
Review-Journal

There is something about the sound and the lyrics of surfin' music that sets it apart.

It's Southern California.

It's beaches.

It's drag racing.

It's Hawaii.

It's Jan and Dean.

The Jan end of that combination — Jan Berry — is appearing at the Marina Hotel with his band, the Alohas. They do many of the old Jan and Dean numbers, duplicating the original sound, as well as some Beach Boys tunes and a Beatle number.

Many of those in the audience were parents of teen-agers in the 1960s when Jan and Dean were pumping out hit record after hit record. Maybe those people frowned on their music then, but no more.

"It's happy, clean music," said Dave Loe, who sings the harmony with Berry. "We seem to attract all ages with it."

"One of the reasons we might draw an older crowd in Las Vegas is because it is a vacation city," said Berry. "It's one of the best cities on our tour."

"When we're in Los Angeles and San Diego and so forth we get younger crowds."

"It's surprising the number of teen-agers we draw, too," added Jeff Todd, who plays bass. "It's just happy music and everyone seems to love it."

Berry and his band are not just trying to sell surfing music from the 1960s. His plans are to record some new surfin' music next month when the tour slows down.

"I have two, maybe three songs that I want to record," said Berry.

One of the songs will be "Rock City," a number that will fit in with the Jan and Dean hits "Surf City" and "Drag City."

The other two are "Almost in Love" and "Surfin' Again."

Berry and the Alohas got together in April of 1982. They put the show and the songs together in the same garage in Belaire that Berry and Dean Torrence used when they put together their act in 1962.

Then came the first tour.

"We started the tour in Eugene, Ore.," said Berry. "Then we went to North Carolina and then Texas. I think—we did 12 dates in 12,000 miles, traveling in a motor home."

Future tours include Hawaii, Australia and Japan. In September the group will return to Las Vegas.

Although Torrence is no longer a part of the act, Aloha drummer Jim Ebert looks a lot like him. When Berry is out by the hotel pool with members of the band, fans often come by insisting that he is, indeed, Torrence, catching some sun with his buddy Jan Berry.

And Jan and Dean remain friends even though they have split up professionally.

"Dean got married and settled down," said Berry. "He still does some shows with Mike Love (of the Beach Boys) and sometimes he comes in and does a show with me. In fact, there's a chance he'll be here to sit in with us before we leave at the end of the month."

The song "Dead Man's Curve" is included in the show. The song was a big hit for Jan and Dean in 1964.

"I've thought many times it was an omen," said Berry. In 1966 Berry nearly lost his life in an auto accident just a half mile from the Dead Man's Curve about which the song was written.

"That's past," he said. "We're just moving on."

JAN BERRY: at the Marina

SUNSHINE MUSIC 16-17

SECOND ANNUAL
JAN AND DEAN
WORD SEARCH
WORDS

Well, here we go again! This time there are twenty words for you to search for in the puzzle preceeding. A clue--only two words are printed normally--that is, straight across, horizontally, left to right!

To save your eyes and tempers, this is being printed in nice, large type. Nice, huh?

Oh, yes, the solution may be found in this issue, but don't cheat!

Alhoas
Dore
Jan
Dean
LP
Pasadena
Stingray
Surf
Torrence
Arnie
Berry
Drag
Liberty
Popsicle
Mikelove
Sunshine
Linda
Hit
BeachBums
TopForty

CALIFORNIA MUSIC: 2 Kentwell Avenue, Concord 2137 Australia. CM63 is NOW AVAILABLE. 60 pages detailing the Surf Music Revival including Jan & Dean, the Beach Boys and all the others who have kept the musical genre alive. $6.00 a copy AIRMAIL. (If paying by cheque not in AUSTRALIAN $ add $3.)

THE SECOND ANNUAL JAN AND DEAN WORD SEARCH

```
OYHQUWIOEBSZCWLRYMR
BAZNDDDVKFQBZYMQXH[E
CKKRHDOPASADENAFJFWU
SKMVGDOWHDI[WPLNJDVZ
NEOYVNRPWGWEH[ZOVDMM
BRUJOSIAZHSWVXFSXM[H
VIBLVAYNTGXFNFONPMUBF
VKDLYNKTS[TG[NLNSEGPI
RBNYIKYCUHOTMIKEDL
UVOJLJ[BSNSSXXIEOTIZR
QVXWYPTKKVDUJRMYHNM[J
LVXRRXYYHPWIJRMYHNM[J
LVKRPLKWFGZIKMGFNDGJX
FEICNFHDXGUVMWWRRKLJ
BWECZHTHOITMXCDSD
LLCZHTHOITMXCDSD
JEWRWBFISDKEHRKFFAHO
DBNOAHPRMSDINGETNLHX
WSUNDRLSRNMNIFDBBNIC
BVJUGTNEMMFRRKTNCPOQ
HLSDRBMISEIRLDJIEOV
QNUZVQZZBMISTELPBXFSWGBKK
ZQSGIZNFYBELPBXFSWGBKK
FFSOBTT[W]BDTWEXLMFF
ONZCPHQIFSXLM[VQKPFWSHMO
VEIGTTFGLUDRVPUHZMUMU
WWBRKENZEPBIVSTOPFORTYNUE
CKELZEPDKUSKTOBHWCSYFEI
QNYNYTCYGRKESTNGL[YHMNZ
NSKYHIHIYLKNHVSLZQL[H
UQCKKJBCURTSNGHHJGBV
ZGVYXUIGGAPBCJHRUGT
LVDHVSQWMHPTNBPHNK[R
QMSTPORNOSBDTFBZPEDI
VOZOJ[FLSUSCNOXWFJYQ
IUPXFSAVMQUUKLUKWDUF
```

199

JAN & DEAN

WHAT STARTS OUT AS SIMPLY COMIC HAS a way (especially in California) of turning out sort of cosmic, as Jan and Dean, those clown princes of rock & roll found out. From their first vinyl gag "Jenny Lee" to that mysterioso business of "Deadman's Curve" they were, "the funnybone of rock & roll, the ganglia of schlock and humor," as David Marsh diagnosed them in his liner notes. As Marsh suggests, what "endeared Jan and Dean to their hard core fans was their absolute refusal to acquire the garb of pretension. . . ." They were in it for the party, that one last ride on the green curling surf.
Their career came to an abrupt end in April 1966, when Jan Berry slammed his Stingray into a parked truck and suffered severe brain damage.

Here, in Dean Torrence's own liner notes for the Jan and Dean Anthology Album, is how it all began:

We both made the varsity football team in our last year at University High and by chance happened to get team lockers next to one another . . . it wasn't long before a bunch of us on the team discovered that the sound in the shower room was the best echo around. Group songs were popular that year, and a bunch of other guys started singing the songs of the day in the University High shower room: "Get A Job" by the Silhouettes, "At The Hop" by Danny and the Juniors, "Tell My Why" by Norm Fox and the Rob Roys.

The football season ended which meant that the showers were now being used by the baseball team, so the group, now called the Barons, had to start practicing in the boys' restrooms.

Jan Berry was a joker, a ~~master thief (he borrowed~~ ~~the auditorium mike for their rehearsals~~), an electronic whiz (simulating that ineffable shower room echo by creating a tape delay on two tape recorders) and a certified wise guy (he had an IQ of 185). But if Jan was the Charlie Brown of West Los Angeles University High School, Jan's jokes were, well, almost serious. "He rarely did anything for fun," explains Dean. "He had four or five rationales for everything he did. There would even be a rationale for the accident." Jan has recovered sufficiently to be back recording a solo album again, but he is in a semi-aphasic condition, and we may never know what put-on was behind the put-on that got them their first hit record.

"Jenny Lee," in the spring of 1958. They'd made it in Jan's garage for a friend's party as a joke and ended up with a recording contract.

Everybody at the party said it sounded like a real record, and Arwin records when they heard it thought so too. They put it out and holy moly if it didn't make it to number three nationwide.

Through Sam Cooke, Jan had met Lou Adler, who became their future producer. It was to be an historic relationship, their joint ingenuities developing what later became the California sound: soft layered vocal harmonies, multi-tracked voices and sound effects, all backed by a group of advanced session musicians — Hal Blaine on drums, Leon Russel (who played keyboard for Jan and Dean until 1963) and Glen Campbell among others.

It wasn't until they were working on "Linda," 10 singles and 3 labels later in the Fall of 1962, that they hit upon the sound which became the surfing sound, trademark of the Beach Boys and Jan and Dean. Liberty hadn't given them much of a budget for the album. Jan and Dean had to do all the background vocals themselves with lots of multi-tracking on two four track recorders. On one take Dean sang lead in a falsetto voice just like a girl. If it weren't for that androgynous vocal effect we wouldn't have the Beach Boys, the Byrds, Love, Buffalo Springfield and Crosby, Stills, Nash & Young (which is almost all of California right there). Dean put it this way on the liners for *Greatest Hits Volume Two*: "I said, do you really think you can get me to sing like a girl . . . But Spleen he said in his easy going voice (not the one he sings with) I'll give you some milk duds and some gum if you just warble some high notes for me."

The reaction was truly torrential: "Linda" sold nearly a half million copies. So it wasn't so bad sounding like a girl after all. And as fate would have it, enter the Beach Boys. "The Beach Boys opened up the surfing field, they got the sound from us, we got the beaches and wheels from them," Dean says matter-of-factly about this historic exchange. While hanging around Western Recorders, Brian Wilson (the apotheosis of Beach Boy mystique) was tooling around the piano and the song just happened to be that sybaritic vision of the surfer's dream dreamed aloud, the two girls for every boy of Surf City. This was the male teen dream even for landlocked mods, Boston boppers and midwestern teenagers; the ultimate California equation "Summer Means Fun": cars cruising, chickadees, pendeltons, woodies, St. Christopher medals, "shootin' the breeze," the "asphalt aisle," baggies, and madras.

"Linda" was followed in early 1963 by their biggest hit, "Surf City," written for them by Brian Wilson, and a string of surf drag smashes: "Honolulu Lulu," "Drag City," "The New Girl in School" and "Dead Man's Curve."

"Schluck Rod,"
"Drag City," a typical Jan and Dean novelty nugget which was a goof on "Alley Oop" broadened the topics that could be treated. Subject matter now consisted of such items as a drag-racing old lady ("The Little Old Lady From Pasadena"), "Sidewalk Surfin'," a senior citizen car club, a taco wagon, "Batman," and "Popsicle."

Today Dean, who is a graphic artist with his own company, Kittyhawk, is almost scrupulously casual about it all:

1963-1983

Yesteryear's Hits

Change-of-pace programming from your librarian's shelves, featuring the disks that were the hottest in the land 5 years ago and 10 years ago this week. Here's how they ranked in Billboard's charts at that time.

POP SINGLES—5 Years Ago
July 20, 1963

1. Surf City—Jan & Dean (Liberty)
2. Easier Said Than Done—Essex (Roulette)
3. So Much in Love—Tymes (Parkway)
4. Tie Me Kangaroo Down, Sport—Rolf Harris (Epic)
5. Memphis—Lonnie Mack (Fraternity)
6. Fingertips (Part II)—Little Stevie Wonder (Tamla)
7. Wipe Out—Surfaris (Dot)
8. Sukiyaki—Kyo Sakimoto (Capitol)
9. (You're the) Devil in Disguise—Elvis Presley (RCA Victor)
10. Pride and Joy—Marvin Gaye (Tamla)

POP SINGLES—10 Years Ago
July 21, 1958

1. Hard Headed Woman/Don't Ask Me Why—Elvis Presley (RCA Victor)
2. Yakety Yak—Coasters (Atco)
3. Purple People Eater—Sheb Wooley (MGM)
4. Splish Splash—Bobby Darin (Atco)
5. Poor Little Fool—Ricky Nelson (Imperial)
6. Patricia—Perez Prado (RCA Victor)
7. Rebel-Rouser—Duane Eddy (Jamie)
8. When—Kalin Twins (Decca)
9. Endless Sleep—Jody Reynolds (Demon)
10. Secretly/Make Me a Miracle—Jimmie Rodgers (Roulette)

R&B SINGLES—5 Years Ago
July 20, 1963

1. Easier Said Than Done—Essex (Roulette)
2. Hello Stranger—Barbara Lewis (Atlantic)
3. Surf City—Jan & Dean (Liberty)
4. Pride and Joy—Marvin Gaye (Tamla)
5. Just One Look—Doris Troy (Atlantic)
6. Fingertips (Part II)—Little Stevie Wonder (Tamla)
7. So Much in Love—Tymes (Parkway)
8. Not Me—Orlons (Cameo)
9. One Fine Day—Chiffons (Laurie)
10. No One—Ray Charles (ABC-Paramount)

POP LP's—5 Years Ago
July 20, 1963

1. Days of Wine and Roses—Andy Williams (Columbia)
2. Moving—Peter, Paul & Mary (Warner Bros.)
3. The James Brown Show—(King)
4. Surfin' U.S.A.—Beach Boys (Capitol)
5. West Side Story—Soundtrack (Columbia)
6. Lawrence of Arabia—Soundtrack (Colpix)
7. Peter, Paul & Mary—(Warner Bros.)
8. I Love You Because—Al Martino (Capitol)
9. I Left My Heart in San Francisco—Tony Bennett (Columbia)
10. The Barbra Streisand Album—(Columbia)

JULY 20, 1968, BILLBOARD

Back Cover: Dee LeClair
Dixon, Ca., May Fair, 5-8-80

"The lifestyle of the beach was the key to our music, the California sound was almost more of a lyric. We never started off with what are we going to write about, but mostly just from the images like the "Little Old Lady From Pasadena" came about when I was watching this Dodge Commercial on TV.... That was what was so beautiful about Endless Summer, just sounds and images."

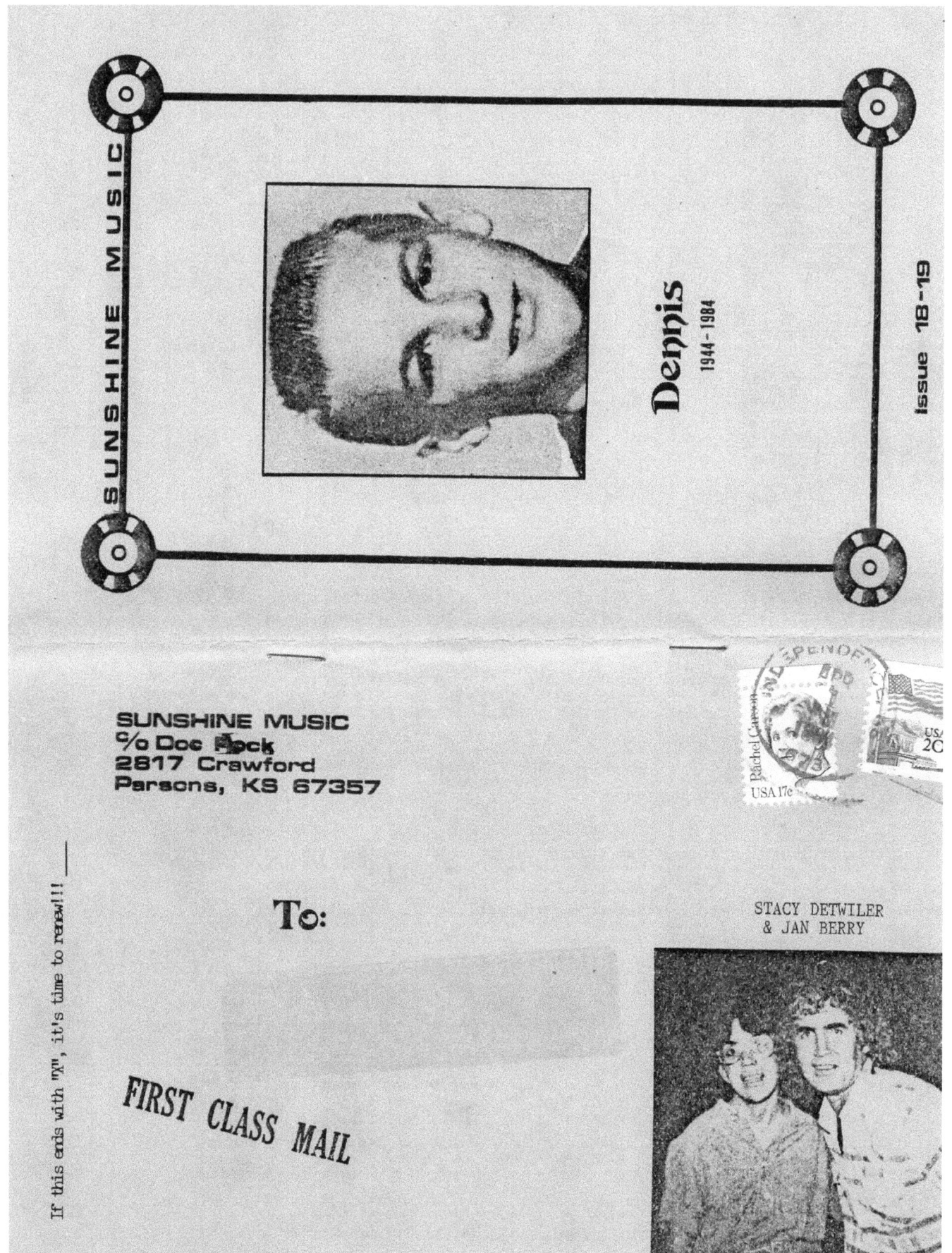

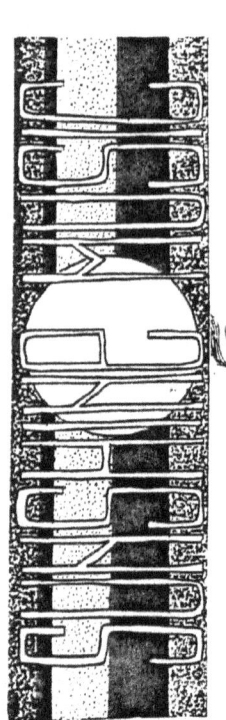

ISSUE 18-19   WINTER-SPRING 1984

THE MAGAZINE OF THE OFFICIAL JAN AND DEAN
AUTHORIZED INTERNATIONAL COLLECTORS' CLUB

EDITOR
Michael Kelly, M.A., Ph.D.

ASSOC. EDITOR
Frank M. Kisko

COPY EDITORS
Jan Berry
Dean Torrence

GRAPHICS
Buzzie Gentry
Honolulu Lulu

Contents Not Already Copyrighted are
© 1984 by Michael Bryan Kelly

SAMPLE COPIES of SM are $1 in the US and surface overseas. Air-mail, $2. SUBSCRIPTIONS are good for six (6) issues, at the rates indicated below:

USA, mailed   Non-US   Surface   Air Envelope
in envelope   Envelopes   Envelopes Charge is
$5   USA, mailed $10 $15   for Postage
     in envelope
     $7

Please enclose S.A.S.E. (self-addressed stamped envelope) with all letters.

★★ CHECK THE NUMBER ON YOUR ADDRESS LABEL. THE NUMBER THERE IS THE NUMBER OF THE LAST ISSUE OF YOUR SUBSCRIPTION. IF THERE IS NO NUMBER, LUCKY YOU!!!! ★★

MAKE ALL CHECKS PAYABLE TO MICHAEL B. KELLY----------
-----NEW SUBSCRIBERS, PLEASE INDICATE THE NUMBER ON YOUR SAMPLE ISSUE OR THE NUMBER YOU WANT YOUR SUBSCRIPTION TO START WITH, OR ELSE!!-------------------------------

BUT ONLY DENNIS GOT HIS FEET WET!

by John Martin

Dennis Wilson, the second of the Wilson brothers, provided the initial impetus for the Beach Boys "Surf Sound."

The only member of the group to ever actually catch that illusive wave, it was Dennis who came in from a day on the surf in 1961 with the suggestion that Brian write a song about the surfing craze. Brian obliged him with *Surfin*, which became the first Beach Boys record and the beginning of their fifteen-year career. That song's title, in turn, inspired the Pendletones to become the Beach Boys.

Dennis became the group's drummer, occasionally stepping down to sing (his slightly flat, but nonetheless exuberant rendition of Dion's *The Wanderer* will be found on the 1964 BEACH BOYS CONCERT album). In 1971 a hand injury forced him away from the drums, and he took on the less-taxing keyboards. His wound now healed, he is currently pounding the skins again with full vigor.

Dennis' musical background has led to numerous original compositions, among them *Steamboat*, *Only With You*, and *Got To Know The Woman*. He is always quick to acknowledge his secondary role to big brother Brian Wilson, however. "We all like to get involved in what we put down, but Brian is the leader," Dennis affirms.

Like everyone who grew up in the 60's, Dennis' life has seen many phases, including the customary flirtation with the psychedelic sub-culture. He has only recently managed to live down his brief association with composer Charles Manson and his clan, who were later convicted of mass murder. *Never Learn Not To Love*, a Manson composition, was sung by Dennis on the Beach Boys' 20/20 album.

Nowadays, Dennis continues to surf whenever possible, but is more often seen riding the waves in his sailboat, aptly dubbed the *Harmony*. On shore, he makes his home in a rented beach house with his third wife, actress Karen Lamm. He is currently at work on a film score and studying acting.

"There's a parallel between what we do as musicians and acting," he notes. "What we're there to do in both cases is entertain the audience." ●

And that, as Dennis himself will tell you, is what he and the Beach Boys do best.

Let Me Explain

There is a change in the SM subscription/membership rates. The post office will no longer let me mail outside the US without an envelope. At least, that is what my post office here tells me. So, the non-envelope rate will be discontinued. For those who have a current subscription, don't worry. This will not affect you until you renew.

Sometimes people ask why I charge extra for envelopes. Well, the envelopes cost over 6 cents each. Plus, they weigh so much, that even in the USA, as they add 17 cents to the postage fee. Overseas, they add much more, especially air mail.

Say, how come SM has not been out as often lately? Well, as I have mentioned in the past, I never promised a certain number of issues per year. The main thing that determines how often SM comes out is how long it takes, for the appropriate amount and kind of material to accumulate. Lately, there has not been as much J&B activity and so on. So, SM has not been out as often as before. I have kept to the 4 seasons, 4 issues per year schedule, though, when you take into account the double issues. So, have faith and patience!

I had planned to use a new printer for this issue. The new printer is closer. The round trip drive would be only about 250 miles, instead of 400, and he was almost as cheap as the old one. But, something went wrong. Now, I may have to do another double issue to keep up the informal publication schedule followed so far. We shall see!

SURFERS' RULE

Do you get restless between issues of Sunshine Music? Well, try this! The surfmusic magazine from Scandinavia. All in English. Only $6 for 4 issues (air), no checks, please. Write to: Goran Tannfelt, Lilla Nygatan 16, 11128 Stockholm, SWEDEN!!!

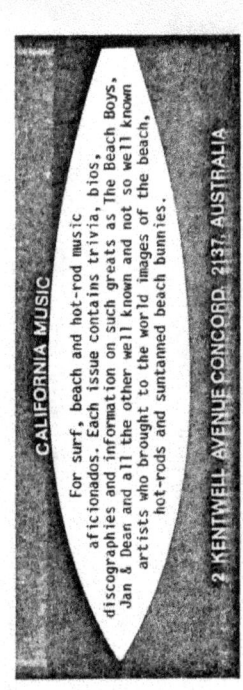

CALIFORNIA MUSIC

For surf, beach and hot-rod music aficionados. Each issue contains trivia, bios, discographies and information on such greats as The Beach Boys, Jan & Dean and all the other well known and not so well known artists who brought to the world images of the beach, hot-rods and suntanned beach bunnies.

2 KENTWELL AVENUE CONCORD 2137, AUSTRALIA

BE THE FIRST ON YOUR CONTINENT TO GET ISSUE #1 OF THE VERY CLEVER NEW JAN AND DEAN 'ZINE, SURFIN' AGAIN!! WRITE: D. BOSSARD, GOTTHELFWEG 9, 5036 OBERERTFELDEN, SWITZERLAND (IT'S IN ENGLISH!)

MY FAVORITE JAN AND DEAN LP

PART I

BY DOC ROCK

The year was '64, and a good year it was for Ban and Spleen. Their hits and other assorted tunes had been zipping up the charts with a regularity that must have given pause to the likes of Beachlamb Brian and Rippedchord Terry. Well, all of a sudden like, I went to my local record store (actually the Zip Drug Store), and lo and behold, there on the rack was Jan and Dean. I mean, on the record rack was a new Jan and Dean song that I had not even heard yet on the radio. And what a song! And what a picture sleeve!

Yes, ladies and folks, there was Bean standing next to his clothes, and Ban standing next to his! And all of the lyrics (even sum that were not on the record!) were printed right there on the sleeve!

Soon, the whole dingidy-danged country was warbling, "Go, Granny, Go!" along with Jan, Dean, Hal Blaine, and the Fantastic Baggys.

Soon again, there was a slick LP out, with a cover that topped the 45 sleeve! The 45 was called "The Little Old Lady (From Pasadena)." The LP was called "THE LITTLE OLD LADY FROM PASADENA." And I would have to say that this is my favorite Jan and Dean LP ever released 6 months (12-64) after the single became a hit in 1964.

First, the covers. I mean, compared to the covers of the British groups or American artists like the Newbeats or the Four Seasons, Jan and Dean's cover alone on this LP was worth the price of the LP ($5, stereo, $4 mono, list). The front shows a Jan and Dean somewhat older and more worldly wise than a similar pose on their earlier LP, NEW GIRL IN SCHOOL/DEAD MAN'S CURVE...but not as old or worldly wise as the chick standing between them! Except for Jill Gibson on the cover of LINDA, this babe, Kathryn Milner, is the only woman to share a Jan and Dean cover--ever!

She is, of course, THE Little Old Lady From Pasadena, and famous from local Dodge car commercials. In fact, she and her commercials inspired the song. It was only after the record was out that Jan and Dean learned that the commercials were not seen nationally. Oh, well.

Two highlights of the front cover. One, Dean's famous The Blue Fox sweatshirt. Two, the supposed difficulty the graphics artists had fitting one title on the label, The Anaheim, Azusa and Cucamonga Sewing Circle, Book Review, and Timing Association! Whew!!

Finally, it is worth noting that an early alternate version of the cover to this LP is evidenced on the back of the simultaneously-released Ride the Wild Surf LP cover. Here, a song is listed that is not on the Little Old Lady From Pasadena LP as released. It is, "Put A Dodge in Your Garage, Honey." It is tempting to speculate that this song was an early title for the instrumental, "Old Ladies Seldom Power Shift," but for the fact that this song is also shown on the cover of the alternate cover art. So, that leaves two possibilities likely. One, "Skateboarding--Part II" before skateboard sound effects were added could have been called "Put A Badge In Your Garage, Honey." (i.e., there could have been another instrumental—or vocal)—which has never been released! At any rate, I suspect Bean had input on this cover art, since only the released version, and not the alternate version, has The Andaluz, Azusa and Cucamonga Sewing Circle, Back Review, and Timing Association stopping (or shopping) over onto the photo portion of the cover!

So much for the cardboard. Now down to the real LP, the vinyl! Side one, band one, is the classic, "Little Old Lady From Pasadena!" This song was one of the many novelty tunes penned and submitted to Jan and Bean by Don Altfeld and LA DJ Roger Christian. The difference is, this one, Jan and Bean accepted!

The probable reason Jan and Bean accepted this particular tune, not only to record but to release as the "A" side of a 45, was the series of Little Old Lady From Pasadena Dodge commercials which were running on TV in those days. Little did Jan and Bean know that those ads were not seen outside of LA! As suggested in "Jan and Bean versus the Beatles," had the ads been nationally shown, as Jan and Bean thought they were when they did the tune, the additional exposure would undoubtedly have made this song, even a bigger hit than it was. Up until the movie "Deadman's Curve," "Little Old Lady from Pasadena" was easily Jan and Bean's best known song.

The pattern of lead alternating with background, set in "Surf City," is maintained. But here, the sound is much more sophisticated. The Hootenanny movement of 1963-64 is represented by Jan's use of harmonica. Bean's falsetto is the best ever. In short, this is a classic!

Next, Chuck Berry's "Memphis." Or, is it Johnny River's "Memphis." You see, this song was the only hit by another artist that Jan and Bean recorded (but not a hit) by its composer, Chuck Berry, back in the 1950s. Then, in May of 1962, guitarist Lonnie Mack had a big hit instrumental version of "Memphis." Since this was the same month that "Surf City" was released upon the world, it was natural that Jan and Bean would include "Memphis" on their "City" LP later that summer.

Now, a year later in the spring of 1964, Johnny Rivers, former demo artist, had a hit with the same song. Since Jan and Bean had always liked both the song and the composer, they did a new version, which mimicked the "Live at the Whiskey A-Go-Go" hit recording by Rivers, and improved on it by easing out the excess soul which Rivers put into the song but which the song itself did not warrant.

A rarity on Jan and Bean LPs is a ballad. But here we have one, written by Jill Gibson and Bean and Horace Altfeld, and sung solo by Jan. "When It's Over" is a mournful ode, about a young man fearful of how his life may become empty without his love, when they, as most all teens, must break up, "When It's Over."

My older sister was not overly fond of Jan and Bean, but "When It's Over" was her favorite song on this LP, so I guess you could say that Jan and Bean ballads are not only rare, but uncharacteristic of Jan and Bean. My Beatle-loving brother Tom (remember him from "Jan and Bean vs. The Beatles"?) felt in later years that this song was inspired of influenced by "Yesterday" by the Beatles, because of its string arrangement. Indeed, the Beatles were hailed as innovative in the extreme for using strings on a rock and roll song. The problem is, "Yesterday" (originally an instrumental called "Scrambled Eggs") was released 6 months after Jan and Bean put out "When It's Over!" We see again how the Beatles' extra publicity made them seem to be even greater than they were.

The sound and lyrics of "When It's Over" are hauntingly evocative. This is a side of Jan and Bean seldom heard. Perhaps it is worth noting that Jan's long-time girlfriend and sometime Piano and Papa wrote on this song. If you listen from her point of view, the song takes on a new, personal meaning.

On band three, we return to more conventional Jan and Bean fare, the immortal "Horace, the Swingin School Bus Driver." Never in the annals of the big Yellow Follow has there been such a ride to and from school as Horace provided. Many was the time I sang this song over and over to myself on high school field trips, or in later years when I was a part-time school bus driver myself! This sounds like the kind of song you expect to be written by the Altfelds and Roger Christian, but, no, this is the music of the Fantastic Baggies, Phil Sloan and Steve Barri. (For an excellent article on Sloan and Barri, see the new issue of CALIFORNIA MUSIC.)

At this point, the Baggys became honorary members of Jan and Bean, backing them up, in much the same way that Mike and Brian in the Beach Boys were backed up by the Rums. And when this extended "Jan and Bean Group" wanted to, they could put out harmonies that neither the Beach Boys nor the Lettermen could top! Put on your headphones and listen to this track. The richness of the background harmonies on this tune show how well the voices of Jan and Bean and the Baggies blended. Add to that the use of woodwinds, sound effects of a honking horn, and the clever lyrics, and you have a highlight of this excellent LP!

What would a Liberty Jan and Bean LP be without at least one auto and drag instrumental hit? We'll never know, because they all have one here, band five is called "Old Ladies Seldom Power Shift." Power shifting is shifting gears, as in a race, without letting up on the gas pedal between gears. Jan and Bean have composer credits, and the sound effects, so a part of the Jan and Bean sound are present on the mono version of this LP. It is an encore appearance of the crash used on "Dead Man's Curve," as well as every other crash song Jan and Bean did. The sound effects record they used was widely distributed. This same crash was used on the Red Skelton TV show years after, as well as in innumerable radio commercials and movies.

The crash is great as used here. However, the stereo version has its own attraction for the collector. In the stereo mix, the engineer made a mistake, and left out the crash. Instead, we hear some music which sounds very much like that heard some time later on the famous Jan and Bean "Pop Symphony" LP version of "Surf City!"

Rounding out side one, we have the first LP appearance of "Sidewalk Surfin'." This song, is Jan and Bean at their musical, lyrical, and satirical best. "Sidewalk Surfin'" began life as a Beach Boy LP cut called "Catch A Wave," obviously a surfing song. However, it was Jan and Bean's new words and arrangement that made the song a hit. Today, many people think that "Catch A Wave" was a bit. It has been included on Beach Boy hit compilations, such as "Surfin'" and "Surfin' Safari" have been included on Jan and Dean compilations. To the non-expert, these different versions sound alike. But, to the collector, the words to "Sidewalk Surfin'" are superior to the awkward lyrics ("eat them with a fork and spoon"?) of the "Catch A Wave," and musically, "Sidewalk Surfin'" totally eclipses the earlier "Catch A Wave." Boots Randolph's yakety sax, followed by a great French horn break, gives the feeling of skateboarding down first a sidewalk, then a smooth blacktop. The sound effects are great. To get them, Jan ran a microphone cable out the front door of the recording studio building, and skated past the mike!

Here we come across another little engineer's mistake. The mono LP has the hit 45 version of "Sidewalk Surfin'." However, on the stereo LP a different mix of the same recording is used and, besides being a little fuzzy sounding, it is missing the sound effects.

After such a good side one, how can it be topped? Well, by none other than the classic follow up to "Little Old Lady From Pasadena," "The Anaheim, Azusa and Cucamonga Sewing Circle, Book Review and Timing Association!" Bean described it as being influenced by "a certain Bach chorale linked quite smoothly with 'I Get Around.'" It always seemed to me that the harpsichord in "The Anaheim, Azusa and Cucamonga Sewing Circle, Book Review, and Timing Association" was a British influence. (Interestingly, the original British theme to the TV series Secret Agent Man aka Danger Man was a harpsichord instrumental!) However, it is probable that this is more of Jan's bringing his college musical training into his rock 'n' roll. This is supported by the use of oboe and bassoon. "This was Jan's 'Good Vibrations,' two years to the month before Brian Wilson got around to doing his own. Perhaps Jan was ahead of his time. By the time rock and roll got as complex as this song, Jan had returned to the simplicity of 'I Found A Girl.'"

One of the neatest parodies in musical history is found in "the Anaheim, Azusa and Cucamonga Sewing Circle, Book Review, and Timing Association," in which the TV commercial for Dodge is satirized. "Go, Granny, Go" becomes "Go, Grannies, Go!"

"Summer Means Fun," the next cut on side two, was written by Sloan and Barri for Bruce and Terry. Terry's did married Boris Day and ran Jan and Arnie's label, Arwin. Bruce and Terry later became the Rip Chords, and Bruce still later became a Beach Boy. It was recorded in time by Bruce and Terry, Jan and Dean, the Fantastic Baggys, Flash Cadillac and the Continental Kids, and The Legendary Masked Surfers! The "Surfers" group was mostly Dean and Bruce overdubbing voices and music onto this LP track. It was a great early '70s 45, but, due to another engineer's mistake, most copies of the 45 were of the original recording, not the doctored one. (See back issue article on Groovy Records.)

One minute and forty-four seconds later, we have experienced a drag race between a Mustang and a T-bird, the Thunderbird driven by a surf bunny of some description. The Mustang was supposed to be driven by Jan and Dean, but due to still another engineer's mistake, the demo recording by composers Sloan and Barri was put on the LP instead.

The ultimate sidewalk surfing instrumental, "Skateboarding—Part II," rolls in next, and is a neat reworking of "Frere Jacques," or if you know Spanish, "Fry Felipe." Probably every skateboard sound effect Jan recorded is included here, and some sound familiar from "Sidewalk Surfin'." With headphones on, or sitting between stereo speakers, the back and forth sound effects are a sure-fire gimmick which raises this instrumental to the level of Jan and Dean classic.

And, speaking of classics, the Little Old Lady From Pasadena cycle is brought full swing, and the LP to an end, by "One-Piece Topless Bathing Suit." For those too young to know, this suit was a designer creation which was the novelty headline of 1964. Not as revealing as it sounds, this had long, over-the-shoulder straps, and did not sell all that well. Written by the Baggys with Don Altfeld, it was recut by the Rip Chords/Bruce and Terry, and made the radio airplay lists. But, not being Jan and Dean, they changed the 94-year-old Little Old Lady From Pasadena into a four-year-old toddler!

Final notes: The Fantastic Baggys, besides writing songs for this landmark LP, also sang background on it. Jan, in turn, sang with Bruce and Terry on the LP "Three Window Coupe, which contined such songs as "Surf City" and "Gas Money." And, the new incarnation of Liberty Records has recently rereleased this LP. The only changes were the removal of ads for "Other exciting Liberty albums by Jan and Dean for your collection" and the deletion of two songs, "Memphis" and "Summer Means Fun." Check out your local dealer, and maybe this will become your favorite Jan and Dean LP, too!

Discography

All on Liberty unless noted.

45	55704	The Little Old Lady (From Pasadena) 5-64 (a pirate version seems to have been pressed, as well)
LP	3377/7377	The Little Old Lady From Pasadena 5-64
LP	3361/7361	The New Girl In School/Dead Man's Curve 5-64
LP	3368/7368	Ride The Wild Surf 8-64
LP	LN-10151	The Little Old Lady From Pasadena 1981
45	Imperial	Move Out Little Mustang 66036 The Rally Packs 1964
45	Imperial	It's As Easy As 1,2,3 66068 Jill Gibson 1964
45	Imperial	Memphis 66032 Johnny Rivers 5-64
45	Columbia	One-Piece Topless Bathing Suit Rip Chords 43093 8-64

CALIFORNIA COLLECTORS SERIES
VOLUME 6
VERY LIMITED EDITION

Just released! SIX more FANTASTIC BAGGYS' songs on one EP, complete with liner notes and coloured sleeve. ONLY 150 copies.

"Summer In New York City"
"Do What You Did"
"Move Out Little Mustang"
"I Love You When You're Mad"
"Skateboard Craze"
"Swintine U.S.A."

SEND $11 (includes AIRMAIL) to:
Stephen J McParland
P.O. Box 106
NORTH STRATHFIELD, 2137
AUSTRALIA

SUNSHINE MUSIC 18-19

Radio Shack — A Division of Tandy Corporation

"Rock'n'Roll City"
Dolby Cassette Starring
Mike & Dean
Only $4.99

A Radio Shack exclusive! 12 new Rock'n'Roll recordings by Mike & Dean with special guests: The Beach Boys, Paul Revere & The Raiders, and The Association. New recordings of 60's hits will make you feel 18 again. Produced by Daryl Dragon.

The FTC power rating for the STA-112 is 35 watts per channel, minimum rms into 8 ohms from 20-20,000 Hz, with no more than 0.05% total harmonic distortion. Come into your nearby Radio Shack and experience the sonic superiority of the STA-112 receiver. Only $339.95.

Take it from Mike Love of The Beach Boys and Dean Torrence of Jan and Dean:
"It's slim and trim like I am, and simple enough for Dean to use."

GET YOUR FREE 1984 CATALOG
184 Full-Color Pages Show You What's Really New in Electronics!
Mail to Radio Shack, 300 One Tandy Center, Fort Worth, TX 76102

Name _____
Address _____ Apt.# _____
City _____ State _____ Zip _____
84A-091

*Reprinted with permission from August, 1983 issue, STEREO REVIEW magazine. Copyright © 1983 by Ziff-Davis Publishing Company All rights reserved. Prices apply at participating Radio Shack stores and dealers.

...from p. 41

be doing reggae." So intrigued by the Carribean-style tunes, Jan & Dean made two nightly appearances at an island hotel where reggae was the feature of the band on stage. Dean also had nothing but praise for Michael Jackson and Company saying they were, "precise, craft, and a sharp team." He also raves on Hall & Oates and 10CC.

Planned for this afternoon, the Confederate Air Force will start off the concert with a performance at 1 p.m. followed by Austin's The Fabulous Thunderbird at 2 p.m. and Jan & Dean will make their appearance at about 4 p.m. at the picnic area in Isla Blanca Park.

LIGHTNING STRIKES THE LOU CHRISTIE NEWSLETTER
THE UNIVERSAL MIND/PRESS/FOUNDED 1977/EDITED, DESIGNED AND WRITTEN BY
TRACEY YOUNG / P.O.B. 643 LEGIN ST. CHICAGO IL 60605/(312) 555-1212

...from p. 43

Red Skelton — Color 1963 clip of
TV Show — unique version of
  Surf City (edited).
Super night of — 2-20-84
Rock 'n' Roll
NBC TV Special

Dean Martin — Surf City
Premier Episode — 9-16-65
TV Series

*   B   *

Jan Berry survives 'Dead Man's Curve'

By BOB BLASKEY

They were at the top of their world, riding the crest of a wave that seemed like it would never end.

"They" were Jan Berry and Dean Torrence — better known to countless of admiring fans as "Jan and Dean."

The pair met each other in junior high school and went on to meet fame singing about the beach, the ocean and California freeways. Whether it was "Little Old Lady From Pasadena" or "Surf City," the team's harmonizing caught the nation's fancy.

Jan Berry was the driving force of the duo, writing most of their songs. One of the most popular songs came in 1964 — "Dead Man's Curve," telling the story of how a man's love for his car could have a tragic end.

Two years later, Jan Berry's song uncannily came to life for him. Since that near-fatal accident, his windmill has been a 17-year attempt to recover and lead a normal life.

While still at the top of the musical world, Jan realized he would someday outgrow music. He prepared for the future by entering medical school.

On that fateful day in 1966, he was on his way to answer a draft induction letter. On Whittier, near Sunset Boulevard, Jan was passing a car when his Stingray's wheel came off and he was hit broadside by an oncoming truck — just a few blocks from the location he sang about in "Dead Man's Curve."

"I was unconscious and couldn't get out of the car," Jan says. His rescuers ultimately needed a torch to cut through and pull him away.

The ambulance rushed him to Beverly Hills Hospital where the attending physician took one look at Jan and said he could do nothing to save him.

He was then taken to the UCLA Medical Center where surgery was performed to remove parts of his brain. Doctors found that Jan's nerves were so badly damaged that most of his right side was paralyzed. A tracheotomy was needed to allow him to breathe.

Jan lay in a hospital bed for three months in a coma. When he finally regained consciousness, he found himself in an oxygen tent, unable to talk.

Doctors — and Jan — discovered that the coordination between his body and his mind had been affected. The brain damage left Jan with the ability to think and create, but no easy means of expression.

TILTING AT WINDMILLS:

The most famous of all idealists, Don Quixote, is best remembered for his battle against windmills. Idealists like him keep pursuing their quests, seeing their impossible dreams come true.

Tilting at Windmills is about these idealists, some of whom may even be your neighbors.

"I had the mind of a 25-year-old," Jan recalls slowly, "but the body of a baby. I could think, but not communicate."

Then began the long and slow process of learning how to read, write and talk all over again.

"I had to learn words in groups of 30 at a time," Jan says.

This was a frustrating time, but Jan believes his basic makeup helped him persevere. "As an Aries, I'm a stubborn, bullheaded so-and-so," he says with a smile. "That helped me continue fighting to get better."

There was another key ingredient to his recovery — music.

Lou Adler, Jan's longtime friend and record producer, brought him into a recording studio as therapy. Since Jan's memory wasn't affected and he already knew all the words to the songs, singing alleviated the frustrating problem of having to search for the right word in sometimes encounters in conversations.

Pursuing medicine was ruled out after the accident — but the chances of reviving a career in music started looking better and better.

With music as therapy and a driving force, Jan continued to improve. Relying on his stubborn fighting spirit, he refused to give up and set his sights on a new windmill — continuing his musical career.

In 1975, he returned to the stage, performing his old songs. In 1980, he was joined by Dean Torrence, then he teamed up with The Alohas earlier this year.

"My therapist is encouraged by my progress and the future," Jan says.

The future certainly does look bright for this man who was once written off for dead.

A new Jan and Dean album is in the works, featuring five old songs and five new ones on which Jan is working. Jan admits that the creative process is slower now, and he has to find the right means of expression. But he's learned to slow down, and expect this.

After being on top of the world professionally, then have to fight back just to function properly, it only would be natural if Jan were bitter or if he lived in his past glories.

But that's not the case. "Today is today and the future is the future. There's nothing in the past — it's gone," he says.

Hearing him talk, you know that Jan Berry is sincere — and that he will succeed in what he sets out to do.

At a recent benefit softball game, one of the many fans who flocked to see him commented that except for his curly hair, he's just like he was in the '60s. Actually, there are signs of the accident — the tracheotomy indentation hidden behind a gold chain, the slow and thoughtful speech pattern and the limp and non-use of his right side.

But none of this is as memorable as Jan Berry's inspiring determination and his talent. When he sings, the old quality is immediately evident. In rehearsals, he knows exactly what he wants from himself and others, hearing the music in his head as all good arrangers and producers do.

What does the future hold for this courageous man who refused to give up his dream of leading a fulfilling and creative life?

"I want to develop the act more," he says, "and make more records. I think it's my turn to do it and I think we're going to make it. It's a slow process but I'll keep on chugging away."

It may be a slow process, but Jan Berry's windmills already are showing signs of defeat. And it's a sure bet they'll quit before Jan will.

· · ·

```
AVAILABLE FROM
CRYSTAL BALL RECORDS
       ED ENGEL
  45-10 KISSENA BLVD.
  FLUSHING, N. Y. 11355
```

Collectors Series Volume 1-4
(Previously Unreleased from 1976-77)
$13 each USA, postage included.
Overseas, add additonal for postage.

```
         Volume 1  New Album
         Volume 2  Adult Child
Volume 3  Merry Christmas from the Beach Boys
         Volume 4  California Feeling
```

JAN AND DEAN--RAREITIES $13
   Unreleased songs,
roots back to Jan and Arnie and the Barons.

JAN AND DEAN--ODDITIES $9
   Late rare material.

DEADMAN'S CURVE $8
PAPA DOO RUN RUN--FEATURING DEAN TORRENCE
         1977 TV Soundtrack.

```
AVAILABLE FROM
CRYSTAL BALL RECORDS
       ED ENGEL
  45-10 KISSENA BLVD.
  FLUSHING, N. Y. 11355
```

Papa Doo Run Run

P.O. BOX TWO-FIFTY-FIVE, CUPERTINO, CA 95014

PAPA DOO RUN RUN

IS

ALIVE AND WELL

by

BARBARA BURBES

A large part of Jan and Dean Phase II is attributable to a band called Goodie Two Shoes, AKA Papa Doo Run Run. They began playing music around 1970 in the Creedence Clearwater Revival style. When they once threw in a few Jan and Dean songs as a joke, they found the music brought the house down and they switched to surf music for good! Later, they interested Dean Torrence in their music, and Dean and Papa even recorded a song together—"SUNSHINE MUSIC!!"

Current Papa members are Don Zirilli, keyboards; Jimmie Jo Rush, bass; Krazy Jim Shippey, drums (all of whom toured with Jan and Dean); Steve Barone, lead guitar; and Steve "Surf" Bronueck, rhythm guitar.

The only brand new member is Steve Barone. Steve "Surf" was a member back before the Jan and Dean tours, and Steve co-wrote the song—"SUNSHINE MUSIC!!"

January 17, 1986, we attended the "1986 Annual World of the LP" in Phoenix to see the 8:00 and 9:30 Papa shows. Each show featured a new 45-minute set, and was repeated at Sunday's two shows.

It's being Friday the 17th, things had to go weirdly. After announcing that "Keeping the Summer Alive" was on their new LP, the power on stage went off!

It seemed a good time to ask Don if we could look at this new record. It is a 5-song EP titled "PAPA DOO RUN RUN" on Twin Towers records (TT-C414) and is distributed though wharehouse record chain. Other cuts include "Do It Again," and two bou Z. originals, "On Fire," and "Sail Away." Special guest on the EP is John Stamos ("Blackie" on General Hospital) on drums. John is a good friend who appears with Papa at Disneyland.

As the power was still off, the band mingled with the crowd. Steve Surf came over to ask about our Bel-Air Bandits shirt. Just as the conversation was getting interesting, the power came on. The music was better than ever.

After the show was an autograph session and sale of Papa items. We asked why they did not sell the Papa jackets. Steve Surf said that it was 2 years before he got one!

After the second show, Steve came over to tell us good-by, but we said we'd be back on Sunday.

We were, and Steve recalled us by name. In the sets, besides surf music, the band shows their roots with a Creedence medley, and Check Berry and Beatles tunes. "Country" Steve Barowe does a country medley with plenty of clowning by the other Steve. Of course, they let Krazy Jim do his legendary "Wipe Out." And Steve Surf took the spotlight, spinning around playing "Pipeline," as the other band members hid behind the amps.

When Jan and Dean and Papa Doo toured together, one could wonder whose contribution to the live music was greatest. Now, I know that Jan and Dean are great, and that Papa is equally great in its own right. Their joint show still rank as an ultimate surf show!

VERY LIMITED EDITION

Just published, a 90-page book full of JAN AND DEAN related material, including 66 pages of handwritten lyrics (with notes). Many are of songs never recorded or released. Also in tht book are numerous clippings and original Fan Club flyers. This quality book is available in a limited edition for only $14.98 plus $3.70 for AIRMAIL postge and handling. The size is approximately 8" x 10".

This is, of couse, a once-in-a-lifetime opportunity to aquire something of historical and musical value and there are only 100 numbered copies being offered for sale. So, be quick and order your copy now while the supply lasts.

SEAGULL PRODUCTIONS
P.O. BOX 106, NORTH STRATHFIELD 2137, AUSTRALIA

BEACH BOYS BOOKLET
16 pages of clippings, photos and cartoons detailing the James Watt-Beach Boys July 4th Fiasco. Limited number now available.
Send $3 plus $1 for AIRMAIL - CASH ONLY to:

SEAGULL PRODUCTIONS
P.O.BOX 106 NORTH STRATHFIELD
2137, AUSTRALIA

Coming Soon
FROM SEAGULL PRODUCTIONS

A 116 PAGE BOOK DOCUMENTING THE ALBUMS OF THE SURF, HOT-ROD, CALIFORNIA MUSIC GENRE COMPLETE WITH FULL TRACK LISTINGS AND SINGLES RELEASED BY THE "ALBUM" GROUPS FEATURED. INCLUDED ALSO ARE TWO ADDITIONAL SECTIONS - SURFING CELLULOID, AND AUSTRALIAN SURF MUSIC

FURTHER DETAILS TO FOLLOW:

SEAGULL PRODUCTIONS
P.O.BOX 106 NORTH STRATHFIELD
2137, AUSTRALIA

SUNSHINE MUSIC 18-19

'The sad part is that a lot of Jan and Dean stuff is hard to get because people wore it out.'

Jan/Dean fan rides crest of surfer song craze

Les Kasten, 28, has been collecting surfer music, particularly that of Jan & Dean, since he was about 22. With a $3,000-$4,000 investment he has formed what many consider to be one of the largest and most comprehensive collections of Jan & Dean records in the United States. He holds a rare album; in background is part of his collection.

10L/Nevadan/Sunday, June 27, 1982

SUNSHINE MUSIC 18-19

SOUND OF MUSIC

THE KIOA TOP 9 PLUS 40 SOUNDS OF MUSIC
(For Week Ending October 3, 1964)

GOOD GUY SANDY SHORE 6 AM - 9 AM
GOOD GUY PETER McLANE 9 AM - 12 NOON
GOOD GUY PHIL THOMAS 12 NOON - 3 PM
GOOD GUY HAL MOORE 3 PM - 6 PM
GOOD GUY STU ADAMS 6 PM - 9 PM
GOOD GUY JIM MICHAELS 9 PM - 1 AM

9 + 40

1. LAST KISS — J. FRANK WILSON
2. *DO WAH DIDDY DIDDY — MANFRED MANN
3. *THE ANAHEIM, AZUSA AND CUCAMONGA SEWING CIRCLE, BOOK REVIEW AND TIMING ASSOCIATION/RIDE THE WILD SURF — JAN AND DEAN
4. FUNNY — JOE HINTON
5. BABY I NEED YOUR LOVIN' — THE FOUR TOPS
6. SLOW DOWN/MATCHBOX — THE BEATLES
7. A SUMMER SONG — CHAD STUART AND JEREMY CLYDE
8. LITTLE HONDA — HONDELLS
   LITTLE HONDA/WENDY — BEACH BOYS
9. *WHEN I GROW UP (TO BE A MAN) — BEACH BOYS

10. Dancing In The Street — Martha And The Vandellas
11. It Hurts To Be In Love — Gene Pitney
12. From A Window — Billy J. Kramer
13. We'll Sing In The Sunshine — Gale Garnett
14. *Have I The Right? — The Honeycombs
15. *Chug-A-Lug — Roger Miller
16. Let It Be Me — Betty Everett And Jerry Butler
17. *Pretty Woman — Roy Orbison
18. *House Of The Rising Sun — The Animals
19. Devoted To You — Brian Hyland
20. *Remember (Walking In The Sand) — The Shangri-Las
21. Tobacco Road — The Nashville Teens
22. Maybe I Know — Lesley Gore
23. *Over You — Paul Revere And The Raiders
24. *Save It For Me — The Four Seasons
25. On The Street Where You Live — Andy Williams
26. Do You Wanna Dance? — Del Shannon
27. *Beach Girl — Pat Boone
28. Michael — Trini Lopez
29. *Good Night Baby — The Butterflys
30. You Must Believe Me — The Impressions
31. G. T. O. — Ronnie And The Daytonas
32. *All Cried Out — Dusty Springfield
33. *I'm Crying — The Animals
34. *Baby Be Mine — The Jelly Beans
35. *Move It Baby — Simon Scott
36. Softly As I Leave You — Frank Sinatra
37. I Like It — Gerry And The Pacemakers
38. *Baby Love — The Supremes
39. She's Not There — The Zombies
40. *I Don't Want To See You Again — Peter And Gordon
41. *I See You — Cathy And Joe
42. Cousin Of Mine/That's Where It's At — Sam Cooke
43. Why You Wanna Make Me Blue? — The Temptations
44. That's What Love Is Made Of — The Miracles
45. Mercy, Mercy — Don Covay
46. Come A Little Bit Closer — Jay And The Americans
47. Funny Girl — Barbra Streisand
48. The Door Is Still Open To My Heart — Dean Martin
49. Shaggy Dog — Mickey Lee Lane

*-Denotes Previous KIOA Pick-Hits

LISTEN FOR THE KIOA PICK-HITS...
The KIOA Good-Guys pick the best of the new record releases as soon as they are received by KIOA/940, where you hear hits first!

THE KIOA PICK-ALBUM OF THE WEEK...
People — Barbra Streisand

THIS KIOA SURVEY IS TABULATED WEEKLY BY THE KIOA GOOD GUYS FROM ACTUAL RECORD SALES, AND REQUESTS RECEIVED BY KIOA.

TOP SOUND OF MUSIC SONG LYRICS ON BACK

Les Kasten happily admits he's living in the past.

He has been stuck in the '60s for about six years now, ever since he was afflicted with an overwhelming desire to collect surfer music and memorabilia.

At 28, Kasten has what is believed to be one of the largest and most impressive collections of Jan and Dean music in the country.

"I'm originally from Minnesota and there's no ocean up there." But "Beach and surfer music is 100 percent American," and he can "really identify" with the people who played and sang it. "They were kind of rowdy and that's the way I was when I grew up.

For the most part, surfer music centered around a Southern California lifestyle that involved surfing, fast cars and/or girls.

With hits like "Jennie Lee," "Linda," and "Deadman's Curve," Jan Berry and Dean Torrance epitomized the surfing-music craze that swept out of Southern California during the late-'50s and early-'60s.

But they struggled several times throughout their careers for the type of popularity enjoyed by groups like the Beach Boys.

From late 1963 to the beginning of 1965, the group released an album once every three months or so. Most didn't do that well.

The two were supposed to be in the movie, "Ride the Wild Surf," but "Dean inadvertently got involved in the kidnapping of Frank Sinatra Jr. as a college prank and Columbia Pictures asked them to drop out of filming."

To top it off, on April 23, 1966, Jan was driving his '66 447 Corvette in Beverly Hills when he lost control of it, and slammed into a parked truck. He was going about 90 mph.

He suffered head and internal injuries that left him in a coma for three months. At the time, he was studying at UCLA to be a doctor. The accident ended those plans and, almost, his career in music.

As he slowly recovered, he found he could barely sing and the popularity and personal closeness of the duo gradually deteriorated.

"Jan cut three singles with Warner Brothers from '66 through '67. Again, they went nowhere."

So "Jan basically withdrew through the '60s and early part of the '70s."

Dean gravitated toward the graphic-arts end of the record industry. He helped design album covers for groups through his business, Kitty Hawk Graphics.

"Over the years from 1974 to '78, Jan's singing ability improved a lot. Each record got a little bit better."

"Within the last five years, there's been a big rebirth of surfer music in Southern California.

"Jan and Dean got back together in 1978 with the Beach Boys. The response was so great that they more or less decided to stay together and do some touring, even though they hadn't had a record on the charts since 1966."

It was during a January, 1979 Beach Boys convention aboard the Queen Mary in Long Beach, Calif., that Kasten fulfilled a dream: to meet Jan. "I went over to his apartment and he even sang for us. I had probably the best time of my life."

With the current revival of interest in Jan and Dean music, "their records are exceptionally sought after today."

Most of Kasten's records are stored on shelves in a converted bedroom of his four-bedroom house. Rarer discs are kept in storage at a bank vault.

One of his choicest is a 45-r.p.m. copy of the release, "Hawaii," which runs about $75. Then, there's an original copy of the duo's first album, "Jan and Dean Sound," which runs about $150.

Two of his most treasured finds are black and blue vinyl copies of the stereo album "Save for a Rainy Day," which was issued in extremely limited numbers. The blue-vinyl version is worth about $400.

Kasten still has a long list of Jan and Dean records he is looking for, including a Columbia demonstration album of "Save for a Rainy Day" that runs about $400-$600.

"The sad part is that a lot of Jan and Dean stuff is hard to get because people wore it out."

He figures he has $3,000-$4,000 tied up in the collection and that the collection now is worth $12-$15,000.

Kasten sometimes lends part of his collection to KOMP-FM radio for use during it's "Prehistoric Rock" program on Sundays, and to KOMP's sister station, KENO-AM which has an "oldies" format.

He does collect other surfer music, such as the Beach Boys, but not as enthusiastically. "As far as I'm concerned, Jan and Dean is the way to travel as far as surf records."

— Brad Peterson

LETTERS

Dear Michael,

Here's my change of address. Here is my shirt design idea. "Groovy Records" was a great article.

I recorded "She's Still Talkin' Baby Talk" off the radio. Have you heard it? Was it on an album?

Thanks,
Leila

Dear Leila,

Got your new address OK.

"She's Still Talkin' Baby Talk" is the flip side of "Frosty (the Snowman)." It was never on an LP. The 45 goes for about $70. I have never seen any but LJ copies. It was bootlegged on the LP RARITIES. I, too, love it. It is rare, and I have heard it on the radio only once. I requested "Baby Talk" on an oldies show, and was I surprised when I heard the follow up! I later got the DJ to give me the stations copy!

Thanks for the SASE, glad you liked "Groovy Records!"

Bye!
Sincerely,
Michael

Dear Karen,

Thank you for your wonderful letter. I suspect it will appear, in part, in the next SM. (oops! After I wrote the answer to your letter, I lost it! Sorry!)

On the Liberty 45s, the "p" indicates that it was pressed on the East Coast.

The Era 45, I have had for years. Keep looking! Also, look for a reissue on Dore, with a black label and a colored leather!

"Carnival of Sound"-- I believe it was never released.

Thanks a million! Your letter was the best one I have ever gotten!

Sincerely,
Michael

Dear SM,

Here is my $7. I love #1's, so please start me with #1b. I have a question. In the movie "Deadman's Curve," "Jan" sings a song in the studio that has a weird... What is the name of this song?

Thanks, Eric H.

Dear Eric,

That was no song. It was just a thing made up on the set on the spur of the moment by members of the band, Papa Do Run Run. It was kind of catchy, wasn't it!?

Michael

Dear Sunshine Music,

I need the LP "Command Performance." Can you help me?

Kimberly Sorrell
205 Elmwood AV
Warwick, RI 02888

Dear Kimberly,

I don't have any LPs for sale, but I will print your letter, and a dealer will probably read it and write to you. OK?

Thanks,
Michael Kelly

Dear Bee,

What's this? My subscription ran out? Good Grief! Well, here is my cash! Yes, I am interested in 38 T Shirts. Also, Bee, after getting your book, "The Fitness Factor," I have been wanting, nay, craving September with free weights and Beautibar! Thanks, Bee.

Bark H.

Dear Bark,

Triple Thanks!

Bee

Dear SM,

I really enjoy your magazine, cannot wait for the next issues. Here is my $7 renewal. Could you tell the story of the LP "Save for a Rainy Day," and tell me how to get a copy of "Bear Torrence Music Phase 11?"

#1 Jan and Dean Fan in Georgia,
Ken Mobley, Jr.
PO Box 401
Monroe, GA 30655

Dear Ken,

I'll do a story on the Rainy Day IP. As for BB Phase II, I will print your letter, and I have a feeling a dealer or two may write.

Doc

Dear Myke,

Just had to write and tell you how much I enjoyed the new double issue. Although I always enjoy SM, this one was exceptionally interesting and informative. Keep up the good work!

Nancy A.

Dear Nancy,

Love your buns.

Myke

Dear Michael,

Now, how can I resist printing a letter like that!!

Had a wonderful summer, got married the 18th of June. We are a perfect match, we both love "oldies," and are looking forward to enjoying our first Jan and Dean concert together. My new husband, Jerry Kelly's family is from Kansas. Any relation?

Becky Kelly

Dear Becky,

No relation.

Michael

Dear Myke,

Good article of J&D vs Beatles, well written. Also cryptic run-outs was excellent. How about an indepth article on DJ copies, and a J&D price list. Is the "Gee" sleeve really worth $40, and is in the "Universal Coward" sleeve worth $200?

Any info on the Radio Shack 45? To be honest, your artwork is pretty hokey. How about a heavier cover, like "Lightning Strikes?"

Lees B.

Dear Lees,

I have been trying to get Honolulu Lulu to do a new cover for months (she did not do the original, which is a take-off on the ANTHOLOGY album cover!). Frank Kisko, who has the worlds largest DJ copy collection, says he will collaborate on an article. He also says $200 is too steep!

As for price listing, how does this sound. Anyone who has bought any Jan and Dean record or collectable in 1983, write me with the item, condition, and price you paid. I will summarize it all into a price guide. OK?

The Hitbound 45 (HR-101) is proving elusive. Frank Kisko suggests writing to Hitbound Records, 101 Mesa Lane, Santa Barbara, CA 93109. Be sure to tell them about Sunshine Music!

Myke

Dear Doc,

If you think you have to be old to like Jan and Dean, I am only 17, and they are my favorite!

Phil S.

Dear Myke,

A dream come true! Dean and Mike on Cape Cod! I never thought I'd ever see Jan or Dean. Thanks for the great double issue. Here is my $5 renewal.

Melanie S.

Dear Michael,

Please don't refer to me as a "former subscriber." I'm sorry I forgot to renew. Please, please forgive me. Can you give me an address for Dean. I'll enclose a bribe--best I could do. Thank you, and please keep SM alive!!

Karen

Dear Karen,

I don't give out the address, sorry. But, thanks.

Myke

Dear Myke,

On the SM/J&D shirts, we wanna have the SM logo and J&D's pix, of course. Your article "Jan and Dean vs the Beatles" is very good, but I've never heard of that mysterious second group before!

Surf's still up,

Danile B., Switzerland

Mike,

Just received #16-17. Another gem! Sure it can't come out monthly?

Yes, do a T-shirt. Yellow, red, or blue is perfect, cotton is nice. The design should feature both J&D and SM. The classic J&D pose (Ride the Wild Surf) of the Phase II Hawaiian-Shirt pose would be good. Here are some sketches. I'll try to be helpful in any way.

Mike W.

and many more.

Now, you would not argue that the dynamics or Anita Bryant were "better" than the Beatles, just because the Beatles chose to sing their songs? Someone records a song, for many reasons. Two are paramount. First, because it is commercial. The whole idea is to make money. With the possible exception of "Wanted, One Girl" b/w "Something A Little Bit Different," I would be surprised if Jan and Dean released or performed any songs that they did not feel would progress their career.

Second, people record songs because they like the songs. But, since group like songs that were never popular, this is not a sign that a group is automatically below another group. "Baby Talk" was originally done by the Laurels on the Spring record label. Since Jan and Dean did this song, does that mean that the Laurels were better?

I expected a lot of mail from JAN & DEAN vs. THE BEATLES last issue, but instead, I got just a few pro, and one con. However, as predicted, my brother Tim disagreed strongly, and I don't want you to misunderstand my position. So let me briefly clear up any misunderstandings caused by the article.

The point of the article was not to compare music. As Dean so eloquently stated on the GOTTA TAKE THAT ONE LAST RIDE album, "These recordings are...not for the purpose of competing musically or artistically with any other recording artists recordings." Notice that Dean is so neutral that he does not even refer to "music," sticking with the inarguable term, "recordings." Now, there were some misunderstandings about what I said last issue.

So, paragraph by paragraph, let me briefly review what I said or meant to say last issue.

1. Tim and I die (and do) compete, musically, through Jan and Dean and the Beatles.
2. The Beatles and Elvis are the Princes and King of rock 'n' roll.
3. Maybe Jan and Dean had more musical genius--potential but not realized due to circumstances.
4. The Beatles outdistanced Jan and Dean in fame, sales, chart success, money, and so on.
5. "Is that all there is?"
6. Greater sales of records (or of anything) does not mean better recordings, be they by The Beatles or by Jan and Dean.
7. Many labels turned the Beatles down, and the records that were released before 1964 in the US were not hits.
8. The Beatles were given the biggest promotional hype in the history of show business in the US in 1964.
9. Promotion can sell (jet rocks, vegematics, bamboo steamers, magazines, or Monkees' records) regardless of quality.
10. The Monkees' TV show was produced to sell records by Hollywood businessmen who knew that they could, by imitating the Beatles' promotion and movies, duplicate much of their chart success.
11. Nationwide exposure on TV's Bandstand made even non-recording teenage amateur dancers famous and popular.
12. TV also made Bobby Sherman and The Partridge Family recording stars.
13. & 14. TV promotion renewed the Beach Boys' popularity in the early '70s.
15. TV gave Chubby Checker's career a new lease on life.

Dear Mike,

Thanks for your input on the shirt. As for SM being monthly--do you realize what that would entail? Just collating, stapling, folding, stapling again, putting on address labels, postage, and putting in envelopes, rubber stamping, etc., takes an entire week of evenings. And that does not even cover the "creative" process, writing and paste-up, which takes even longer. Did I mention that I have to drive 240 miles round trip to get it printed each issue? (And the price charged for subscriptions does not cover my costs?) Thanks, but impossible!

Mike

Dear Michael,

It's been a hectic summer. Thank you so much for the reminder that my subscription has run out. Here is my $7.

Linda M.

Michael Kelly,

Here is my renewal. But, don't go on insulting my intelligence (and that of millions of others) by stating that Jan and Dean are (or were) better than the Beatles. I don't remember the Beatles playing Jan and Dean's music at their concerts.

Don't go on comparing apples and oranges!

Michael, Canada

P.S. If I were fluent, in English, I would write you a 10-page reply!

Dear Michael,

Thanks for the renewal.

I don't know what songs the Beatles did at their concerts. The one I attended in Kansas City in 1964 was too noisy to tell what songs they were playing. However, on records, the Beatles recorded songs which had been hits by many other artists:

Misery...Dynamics 11-62 #44
Chains...Cookies 11-62 #17
Boys...Shirelles LP cut
Baby, It's You...12-61 #8
Twist & Shout...Isley Brothers 7-62 #17
Rock & Roll Music...Chuck Berry 11-57 #8
Honey Don't...Carl Perkins LP cut
Long Tall Sally...Little Richard 3-56 #8
Slow Down...Larry Williams LP cut
Dizzy Miss Lizzy...Larry Williams 4-58 #69
Bad Boy...Larry Williams LP cut
Matchbox...Carl Perkins LP cut
Roll Over Beethoven...Chuck Berry 6-56 #29
Til There Was You...Anita Bryant 2-60 #23
Money...Barret Strong 2-60 #23
Act Naturally...Buck Owens Country hit
Take Good Care of my Baby, Bobby Vee, #1

HAD HAD ONLY ONE SHOT AT STARDOM?

ANSWER: NOWHERE.

42. WHAT IF JAN AND DEAN HAD SPENT FIVE YEARS (TIME IT TOOK BEATLES TO GET FIRST BRITISH HIT) OR SEVEN YEARS (TIME IT TOOK BEATLES TO GET FIRST US HIT) DEVELOPING THEIR MUSIC, HAD RECORDED MANY SONGS FOR MANY LABELS, HAD QUIT SCHOOL AND WORKED ON MUSIC FULL TIME, HAD HAD RELEASED ALL OF THEIR PROVEN HITS IN ANOTHER COUNTRY RELEASED IN THE US ON MANY LABELS SIMULTANEOUSLY, AND HAD BEEN PROMOTED AS NO ACT HAS EVER BEEN PROMOTED IN THE HISTORY OF SHOWBUSINESS?

ANSWER: VERY MUCH BIGGER STARS THEN THEY HAVE BEEN.

42. Sure, musical history tells us the Beatles were greatest in popularity. But circumstances must be accounted for. Comparing the careers of the Beatles and Jan and Dean historically is like comparing apples and oranges, due to their varying circumstances.

43. Taking circumstances into account, it would have been a miracle if the Beatles had not been big, and it was either a miracle or pure genius that Jan and Dean were.

To summarize, this has been no comparative review of musical output or quality. Musical taste is subjective and personal, and I personally prefer Jan and Dean's weakest material or LP to any music by the Beatles. Therefore, I leave this out of my discussion.

My only position:

Many mitigating circumstances can and do affect the size or even aquisition of success, and the masses spend money on many poor quality products, so one may not accept evidence such as number or size hits by any artist as proof of greatness or genius.

Had the career circumstances of Jan and Dean and the Beatles been reversed, we would have never heard of the Fab Four, but the Dynamic Duo would have had the success that favorable circumstances can give to many artists.

With the possible exception of side two of Meet the Beatles, there is not a single Beatles' LP that I can listen to clear through without being so irritated by the sounds that I have to turn it off. Now, I realize that I am not representative of the general public. But....

Let me close with this. Yes, I admit the Beatles, in spite of being blatent users and advocates of drugs, and of being failures in school, sold many more records than Jan and Dean did. However, in terms of musical quality and accompanying lifestyle, Jan and Dean were without a doubt greater artists.

Yes, there are millions of people who would disagree with me, just as there are millions that feel the Dukes of Hazard is a better TV show than Lou Grant. Aren't we lucky to be living in a country where quality and quantity are both allowed to exist side by side?

---

16. MTV makes stars and sells records merely on the basis that there was a video made to accompany a recording.

17. The Beatles had the top five songs in Billboard at the same time.

18. These five were several years worth of British hits released all at once in the US. Had Jan and Dean had tons of promotion and all of their previous five-years' hit recordings released at once, they would have sold more records than they did in 1964.

19. While the Beatles' sales record is great, it may have been due to factors not inherent in the Beatles or their music. I feel the Beatles' enormous success in 1964 was due to release of records and promotion by many labels at once.

20. The same push may explain the two-sided hits.

21. Few stations in 1964 played rock 'n' roll.

22. RCA got Elvis MOR station airplay, and two-sided hits, by putting slow songs on flip sides.

23. The Beatles and/or Capitol repeated this technique.

24. As did Capitol/The Beach Boys.

25. Imagine if Jan and Dean had been on a major label, like Capitol, or if the Beatles had been on a small label, like Liberty (note how poorly the Beatles did do in 1965 on the small label, VJ).

26. The Beatles were imitated, but this is not necessarily a sign of greatness, since many ungreat things are imitated.

27. & 28. Bandstand set teen styles with exposure, artistic quality aside.

29. Much of the Beatles' status is attributable to factors other than musical genius.

30. With tragedy and little establishment help, Jan and Dean had a career in rock 'n' roll.

31. & 32. Jan and Dean recorded on a shoestring and had to fight label restrictions and censorship, the Beatles did not.

34. The Beatles made music for 5 years before their first British hit, Jan and Dean' first year out got them a hit. This makes Jan and Dean greater, but NOT because hits are indicative of greatness. Rather, it is because, before the hype was piled on, with Jan and Dean on a sort of an equal footing with the Beatles, Jan and Dean did all at once what it took the (Silver) Beatles many years of performing and recording to do: score a hit.

35. If that isn't genius, what is?

36. Losing half his group and his contract with a (very small) label, Jan found a new partner and another (small) label and had another national top hit.

37. At liberty, Jan and Dean hit the top again. Note that I merely state these facts. I do not say that these facts (hit records) mean that Jan and Dean are great or greater than the Beatles.

38. Perhaps the biggest factor that does say that Jan and Dean were greater than the Beatles is the amount of effort each put into music to get success. This assumes that success is absolute, not relative. In other words, each was successful, but because of the factors enumerated above, I do not accept greater sales as indicative of being greater. Thus, the position I take is that without the unique circumstances above, but with the same musical potential, the Beatles would probably have had a degree of success in the US approximately equal to that enjoyed by Jan and Dean. The Beatles did rock 'n' roll full time.

39. & 40. Jan and Dean were probably the only major rock 'n' rollers in the '60s to go to school full time all the while they were recording artists.

41. WHAT IF THE BEATLES HAD HAD NO SPECIAL PROMOTION, HAD GONE TO SCHOOL FULL TIME, HAD DONE MUSIC PART TIME AND HAD BEEN ON A SMALL LABEL, AND

DIANE VOSTEEN
(216) 631-8444

MINT ALBUMS: - NEW -
DORE 101 .... GERMAN
IMPORT ... ONLY $12.00
DEAN TORRENCE ... 1977 -
1981 ... IMPORT ... $17.00
AMERICAN DREAM ...
JAN & DEAN, OTHERS
SPECIAL ...; $5.00

A GREAT VERY GOOD +
COPY OF COMMAND
PERFORMANCE ... $8.00

RCA FULL COLOR POSTER
... ELVIS, A CANADIAN
TRIBUTE ... $4.00 FOLDED;
$5.00 ROLLED

MIKE & DEAN RADIO
SHACK TIE-IN BUTTONS...
COLOR, 2 1/4 INCH ... $2.50
EACH OR ONLY $1.50 WITH
ANY OF THE ABOVE.

ALL PRICES U.S.A. POSTPAID
5009 DETROIT AVE
CLEVELAND, OHIO, 44102

Dear Mr. Peck,

ROLLING STONE says that Eddie and the Cruisers is about Bruce Springsteen, but I think that it is really about Jan and Dean!

1. Eddie Wilson drives a "57 Chevy—a reference to "Hot Stocker."
2. Eddie's last name, Wilson, probably a mistake by someone who thought J&D really liked the B.B.'s and some guy named Brian.
3. The song "Wild Summer Nights," trying to fit "Ride the Wild Surf" and "She's" by Summer Girl" into one song.
4. Eddie's statement in the recording studio scene are stolen almost verbatim from D.M.C., about inventing a new sound and making it big.
5. Eddie's car wreck. Eddie was upset with his record company, The Establishment. Jan had a witch wife upset with the Draft Board, the Establishment.

These five alone should be enough for Jan and Dean to file suit for royalties and a share of the profits!

(Signature misplaced—Sorry!)
Susan B.

Dear Michael,

I'd like to subscribe. I have found no other that satisfies my curiosity etc... about Jan and Dean!

Dear Blythe,

Who said Jan and Dean never come to Cape Cod. I did, and I guess I was wrong! Mike and Dean, WITH Jan!! Dean was real nice, signed COMMAND PERFORMANCE, Jan signed ONE SUMMER NIGHT LIVE. Mark Ward and Jim Armstrong were great, too!

Cape Cod is as far from LA as one can get. It was a miracle, and a dream come true! Thanks guys!

Belaine B.

P.S. Enclosed is a picture for the back cover!

Dear Mike,

Mike and Dean's ROCK AND ROLL CITY cassette is an Lp in Japan, titled LISTEN TO THE AIR. Includes "Alley Oop" in place of "California Dreaming," and is number VIE 28138. About $12 plus postage. Wanted: video tapes and magazines on the Honeys, Superstocks, Crystals, Barry and Tami Lynne, Secrets, alike Ronettes (video only).

Sincerely,

Ryoichi Tanaka
4-21-10 Tsukushigaoka
Kashiwa, 277
JAPAN

SUNSHINE MUSIC 18-19

HAD HAD ONLY ONE SHOT AT STARDOM?

ANSWER: NOWHERE.

42. WHAT IF JAN AND DEAN HAD SPENT FIVE YEARS (TIME IT TOOK BEATLES TO GET FIRST BRITISH HIT) OR SEVEN YEARS (TIME IT TOOK BEATLES TO GET FIRST US HIT) DEVELOPING THEIR MUSIC, HAD RECORDED MANY SONGS FOR MANY LABELS, HAD QUIT SCHOOL AND WORKED ON MUSIC FULL TIME, HAD HAD RELEASED ALL OF THEIR PROVEN HITS IN ANOTHER COUNTRY RELEASED IN THE US ON MANY LABELS SIMULTANEOUSLY, AND HAD BEEN PROMOTED AS NO ACT HAS EVER BEEN PROMOTED IN THE HISTORY OF SHOWBUSINESS?

ANSWER: VERY MUCH BIGGER STARS THEN THEY HAVE BEEN.

42. Sure, musical history tells us the Beatles were greatest in popularity. But circumstances must be accounted for. Comparing the careers of the Beatles and Jan and Dean historically is like comparing apples and oranges, due to their varying circumstances.

43. Taking circumstances into account, it would have been a miracle if the Beatles had not been big, and it was either a miracle or pure genius that Jan and Dean were.

To summarize, this has been no comparative review of musical output or quality. Musical taste is subjective and personal, and I personally prefer Jan and Dean's weakest material or LP to any music by the Beatles. Therefore, I leave this out of my discussion.

My only position:

Many mitigating circumstances can and do affect the size or even aquisition of success, and the masses spend money on many poor quality products, so one may not accept evidence such as number or size hits by any artist as proof of greatness or genius.

Had the career circumstances of Jan and Dean and the Beatles been reversed, we would have never heard of the Fab Four, but the Dynamic Duo would have had the success that favorable circumstances can give to many artists.

With the possible exception of side two of Meet the Beatles, there is not a single Beatles' LP that I can listen to clear through without being so irritated by the sounds that I have to turn it off. Now, I realize that I am not representative of the general public. But....

Let me close with this. Yes, I admit the Beatles, in spite of being blatent users and advocates of drugs, and of being failures in school, sold many more records than Jan and Dean did. However, in terms of musical quality and accompanying lifestyle, Jan and Dean were without a doubt greater artists.

Yes, there are millions of people who would disagree with me, just as there are millions that feel the Dukes of Hazard is a better TV show than Lou Grant. Aren't we lucky to be living in a country where quality and quantity are both allowed to exist side by side?

16. MTV makes stars and sells records merely on the basis that there was a video made to accompany a recording.
17. The Beatles had the top five songs in Billboard at the same time.
18. These five were several years worth of British hits released all at once in the US. Had Jan and Dean had tons of promotion and all of their previous five-years' hit recordings released at once, they would have sold more records than they did in 1964.
19. While the Beatles' sales record is great, it may have been due to factors not inherent in the Beatles or their music. I feel the Beatles' enormous success in 1964 was due to release of records and promotion by many labels at once.
20. The same push may explain the two-sided hits.
21. Few stations in 1964 played rock 'n' roll.
22. RCA got Elvis MOR station airplay, and two-sided hits, by putting slow songs on flip sides.
23. The Beatles and/or Capitol repeated this technique.
24. As did Capitol/the Beach Boys.
25. Imagine if Jan and Dean had been on a major label, like Capitol, or if the Beatles had been on a small label, like Liberty (note how poorly the Beatles did do in 1963 on the small label, VJ).
26. The Beatles were imitated, but this is not necessarily a sign of greatness, since many ungreat things are imitated.
27. & 28. Bandstand set teen styles with exposure, artistic quality aside.
29. Much of the Beatles' status is attributable to factors other than musical genius.
30. With tragedy and little establishment help, Jan and Dean had a career in rock 'n' roll.
31. & 32. Jan and Dean recorded on a shoestring and had to fight label restrictions and censorship, the Beatles did not.
34. The Beatles made music for 5 years before their first British hit, Jan and Dean' first year out got them a hit. This makes Jan and Dean greater, but NOT because hits are indicative of greatness. Rather, it is because, before the hype was piled on, with Jan and Dean on a sort of an equal footing with the Beatles, Jan and Dean did all at once what it took the (Silver) Beatles many years of performing and recording to do: score a hit.
35. If that isn't genius, what is?
36. Losing half his group and his contract with a (very small) label, Jan found a new partner and another (small) label and had another national top hit.
37. At Liberty, Jan and Dean hit the top again. Note that I merely state these facts. I do not say that these facts (hit records) mean that Jan and Dean are great or greater than the Beatles.
38. Perhaps the biggest factor that does say that Jan and Dean were greater than the Beatles is the amount of effort each put into music to get success. This assumes that success is absolute, not relative. In other words, each was successful, but because of the factors enumerated above, I do not accept greater sales as indicative of being greater. Thus, the position I take is that without the unique circumstances above, but with the same musical potential, the Beatles would probably have had a degree of success in the US approximately equal to that enjoyed by Jan and Dean. The Beatles did rock 'n' roll full time.
39. & 40. Jan and Dean were probably the only major rock 'n' rollers in the '60s to go to school full time all the while they were recording artists.
41. WHAT IF THE BEATLES HAD HAD NO SPECIAL PROMOTION, HAD GONE TO SCHOOL FULL TIME, HAD DONE MUSIC PART TIME AND HAD BEEN ON A SMALL LABEL, AND

BIOGRAPHY

MIKE LOVE, lead singer of THE BEACH BOYS since the bands inception and DEAN TORRENCE, sometimes lead singer of the duo, JAN AND DEAN, met in the early sixties. Both groups did extensive touring together and participated on each others recordings throughout the sixties. BRIAN WILSON, Chief Writer and Producer of most all THE BEACH BOYS classics also co-wrote many of JAN AND DEAN'S greatest hits, including JAN AND DEAN'S all time biggest seller, "SURF CITY". DEAN TORRENCE sang lead on THE BEACH BOYS monster hit, "BARBARA ANN". MIKE has also contributed to THE BEACH BOYS success and popularity by writing or co-writing such hits as, "GOOD VIBRATIONS," "CALIFORNIA GIRLS," and "FUN, FUN, FUN". DEAN TORRENCE has also contributed his writing talents as to create such classics as "SCHLOCK ROD" parts one and two and "LITTLE OLD LADY'S SELDOM POWER SHIFT".

After JAN BERRY'S untimely automobile accident in the late sixties, DEAN started his own music design and packaging company, Kittyhawk Graphics. One of DEAN'S first jobs was to design a music trade ad for THE BEACH BOYS. Ten years later, DEAN designed five BEACH BOYS albums and also developed and designed THE BEACH BOYS logo. To date, Kittyhawk Graphics has been responsible for over two hundred album cover designs for such artists as THE BEACH BOYS, THE NITTY GRITTY DIRT BAND, LINDA RONSTADT, STEVE MARTIN, DIANA ROSS, ANNE MURRAY, NILSSON, etc. DEAN was nominated for "album cover of the year" four times in a row and won a Grammy in 1972. Kittyhawk presently designs all promotional and advertising materials for MIKE AND DEAN.

Both MIKE AND DEAN are very versatile. Both were aware of the Video spectrum of rock and roll entertainment. In 1976, DEAN and a friend wrote a treatment for a movie made for television titled, "DEADMAN'S CURVE". A year later, the film debuted on CBS Television and was a overwhelming success. DEAN arranged for MIKE to have a speaking part in the film. DEAN also co-wrote the screenplay and Produced all the sound track music. Since that first airing of "DEADMAN'S CURVE," the movie has played on network television one more time and has played numerous times via syndication.

In 1981, MIKE LOVE was the creator and executive producer of "THE SPIRIT OF AMERICA SPECTACULAR," television and FM stereo simulcast on America's Birthday, July 4th. This special attracted the largest nationwide audience for a live-simulcast in the history of television broadcasting. MIKE made sure his old buddies, JAN AND DEAN, were included as special guests in his special.

The mass appeal for their classic hits had lead MIKE AND DEAN to another unique situation, performing in corporate sponsored concerts. DEAN says that, "our corporate sponsorship is a pure one in every sense of the word. The other corporate sponsorship associations of note (i.e., THE ROLLING STONES, THE WHO, etc.), should not be called corporate sponsorships because the consumer still has to buy a non-reduced priced ticket. So who cares if Jovan or Schlitz Beer presents somebody if a ticket still costs fifteen bucks". "A real corporate sponsorship picks up the tab". In MIKE AND DEAN'S association with Budweiser, the consumer has been treated to eight free Spring Break concerts averaging over 15,000 people per concert and two free summer concerts. Last Fall, MIKE AND DEAN toured through Texas and Louisiana colleges in a "BE TRUE TO YOUR SCHOOL" concert series, also sponsored by Budweiser. These concerts were played at smaller Universities that could not possibly afford big name talent. The more than reasonable ticket price of $2.00, was given back to the school and in most cases ended up in the schools scholarship fund.

MIKE AND DEAN'S success in live performances has paved the way for yet another unique venture. They have collaborated on a newly recorded album titled, "ROCK AND ROLL CITY", and the unique part is that it was produced, performed and manufactured by MIKE AND DEAN and it is exclusively distributed not by a record company, but by the Radio Shack chain. By bypassing the traditional middle men, the product retails for a most reasonable price of $4.99. This is indeed a revolutionary move by most recording industry standards. MIKE AND DEAN plan to continue their revolutionary music business strategies. Stay tuned.

JAN AND DEAN--The popular 60's duo of Jan and Dean, shown above, signed autographs locally Wednesday. They were scheduled to perform to Spring Break crowds today on the Island. See article, page 7A. (PRESS Photo)

Jan, Dean reunite for concert

By JEFF KEPLINGER
Staff Writer

How many muscians do you know can endure 25 years of making music?

Releasing their first hit single, *Baby Talk* in July of 1959, Jan Berry and Dean Torrence have survived where other rock and roll groups have fallen to the rigors of the fastlane associated with rock.

Originally singing with Arnie, as Jan & Arnie, Jan's songwriting talent led him to release *Jenny Lee* with Arnie in 1958 before Arnie dropped out and Dean came back from a tour in the Army.

As a team, Jan and Dean have released 44 singles and 21 albums bringing surfers and beach lovers a pop sound that will never fade away.

Summers on the beach would never be the same without hearing classics like *Little Old Lady From Pasadena, Surf City* and *Deadman's Curve.*

Tragedy hit the duo in the summer of 1966 as, ironically, the Corvette Jan was driving hit a parked truck on Whitier Boulevard in California in 1966. Years of rehabilitation was required for him to learn to read, write, talk and walk again.

According to Dean, who handles most of the promotion for the duo, they will be working on a new album together for Radio Shack. Down on record companies, Dean sees their work for the electronic store as heaven-sent. They receive a purchase order, and bingo-they're paid within 30 days, unlike the record companies.

A two-concert tour is all Jan & Dean will perform this summer, the first on South Padre Island and the second at Fort Lauderdale. Dean warns fans for a few surprises for this year's gala Spring Break event. Dean's past two performances on the island were with Mike Love of the Beach Boys who is currently in Acapulco for a concert.

As far as music goes today, Dean said he would "love to

Thanks in most part to one Siler, Linda Hunter, and to your Assistant Editor Frank M. Kisko, we have a list of Jan and Dean video tape things. Now you know what to collect. Maybe soon, we can figure out HOW to collect them! Write Linda at 5606 Kirk Road, Youngstown, Ohio, 44515, as she may be able to help!

("V" indicates known to be on VHS home video format. "B" indicates known to be on Betamax home video format. "*" means known to have been televised or filmed, and may become available on VHS or Beta at some point.)

TITLE	NOTES	V/B
The Dick Clark 25th Anniversary Show	15 seconds of BABY TALK, 1st TV appearance B & W 1959	V
Today Show Interview	7-80, 8 minutes	V
Roots of Rock 'n' Roll	'81, 2.5 min.	V
Beach Boys' Long Beach Queen Mary TV Special "Spirit of America"	7-5-81 J&D Segment	V
Midnight Special "Salute to Jan and Dean"	5 min., 15 sec. 12-31-79	V
California Summer Special wit Papa Doo Run Run	1980, 45 minutes	V
America's Top 10	7-27-80 #1 30 sec. #2 2.5 min., #3 3.5 min. #4 2 minutes "Top Ten Duos of the rock era" ("Little Old Lady" from the TAMI Show)	V
Shu Na Na TV Show	Conversation and Baby Talk, 4.5 min., 2-7-79	V
Bob Braun Local Cincinnati Show	1-80, 16 min.	V
Dinah Shore Show	18 minutes, 6-16-79	V
Dick Clark's Good Old Days	1.5 min., 10-11-77	V
Dick Clark's Good Old Days Part II	11-29-78	V
Ride the Wild Surf	Title Theme J&D music	V
T.A.M.I. Show	This is it! Phase II 1965, 85 minutes	V
Bandman's Curve	CBS TV Movie, 90 minutes	V
Live at the Forum with Papa	1980, 50 minutes	V
Entertainment Tonight TV Show	Mike and Dean 30 sec. from behind at Oceans of Fun Kansas City, Missouri 6-83, Mike and Dean 3 minutes	V
	12-29-83 Jan on Dennis Wilson's death 1.5 minutes	V
	12-30-83 Dean on Dennis Wilson's death 1.5 minutes	V
1981 Concert Video by Fun w/ Kel Air Bandits	1981	V
Ad Los Angeles	Local TV Mike and Dean 3 minutes	V
Little Old Lady Dodge Commercial	Very Brief	B x W
People's Court TV Show	'81 Jennie Lee 10 minutes	V
PM Magazine	Dean in a Hart to Hart baseball game — no talking or music by Dean, 3 minutes	V
Mike Douglas Show	11-7-78 3-20-79	V
Hollywood Palace	2-27-65 "From All Over The World" lip sync, and Dean lip-lamounth.	*
Kasey Kasim Show	7-24-77	*
Lloyd Thaxton Show	Several appearances in the 1960s	*
Rock Concert TV Show	5-5-79 "Surf City" and Little Old Lady from Pasadena	V
"You" TV Show	7-7-79	V
Celebrity Game TV Show	Host: Carl Reiner	*
Youngstown, Ohio	Dean on local TV show	*

to p. 10...

Sunshine Music
c/o DOC ROCK
2817 Crawford
Parsons, KS 67357

TO:

Roland Coover, Jr.   20
1537 E. Strasburg Rd.
West Chester, PA   19380

FIRST CLASS MAIL

An "X" here means it is time to renew!!!

Melanie R. Salone
and
Dean O. Torrence

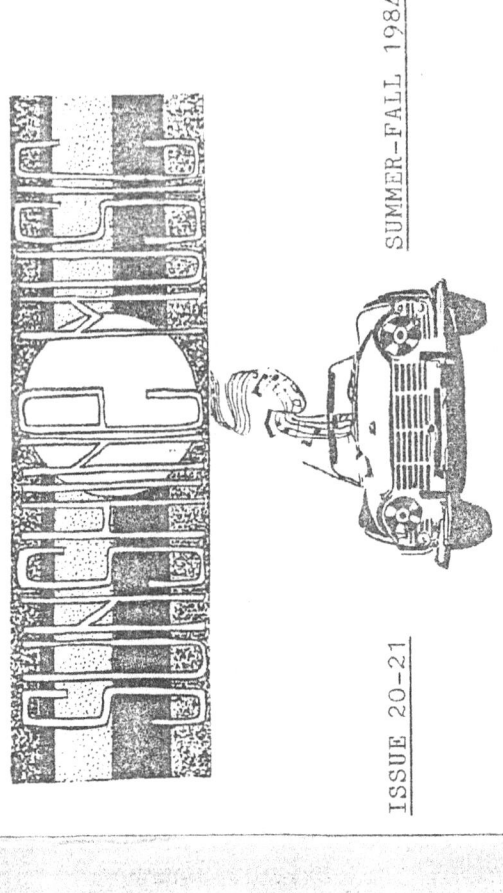

ISSUE 20-21   SUMMER-FALL 1984

THE MAGAZINE OF THE OFFICIAL JAN AND DEAN
AUTHORIZED INTERNATIONAL COLLECTORS' CLUB

EDITOR   ASSOC. EDITOR
Michael Kelly, M.A., Ph.D.   Frank. M. Kisko

COPY EDITORS   GRAPHICS
Jan Berry   Buzzie Gentry
Dean Torrence   Honolulu Lulu

Contents Not Already Copyrighted are
© 1984 by Michael Bryan Kelly

SAMPLE COPIES of SM are $1 in the US and surface overseas. Air mail, $2. SUBSCRIPTIONS are good for six (6) issues, at the rates indicated below:

	USA, mailed in envelope	Non-US Surface	Air Envelope Envelopes Charge is for Postage
USA	$5	$7	$10 $15 with all letters.

Please enclose S.A.S.E. (self-addressed stamped envelope) with all letters.

★ CHECK THE NUMBER ON YOUR ADDRESS LABEL. THE NUMBER TELLS IF THIS IS
★ THE LAST ISSUE OF YOUR SUBSCRIPTION. IF THERE IT IS BETTER, PAY THE TOLL!!

MAKE ALL CHECKS PAYABLE TO MICHAEL B. KELLY.
---- NEW SUBSCRIBERS, PLEASE INDICATE THE NUMBER ON YOUR
SAMPLE ISSUE OR THE NUMBER YOU WANT YOUR SUBSCRIPTION TO
START WITH, OR ELSE!!----

★ SIXTEEN YEARS AGO TONIGHT
HOWARD GREENFIELD   KENNY KAREN
JACK KELLER

Bop a dip dip ching ching
Doo ba bop a dip dip ching ching
Doo-ba-bop a dip dip ching ching
Doo ba bop a dip dip, sixteen years ago tonight
Bet your mommy was nervous
And your daddy was a sight
Way back in forty seven, my baby came from heaven
Sixteen years ago tonight bop-a-dip dip
Sixteen years ago tonight
The stork delivered seven pounds of pure delight
I bet your dad applauded
When he saw the daughter he ordered
Sixteen years ago tonight
While ev'ryone was thinkin' 'bout your future
The angels did some plannin' from above
They knew that someday I would be your future
And be the only boy that you would love
And now there's sixteen candles shining bright
At last we've come of age
And I can hold you tight
I feel so happy hearted
To think our love got started
Sixteen years ago tonight.
Copyright © 1962 by Alison Music, Inc. (A Nevins-Kirshner Affiliate)

THESE ARE LYRICS TO A SONG FROM THE JAN AND DEAN ERA.
I HAVE NEVER HEARD THIS SONG, WHICH LOOKS
LIKE IT COULD HAVE BEEN RECORDED BY
JAN AND DEAN.
DOES ANYONE KNOW WHO DID RECORD THIS?

RARITIES!

Hootchie McCoochie! Last issue (remember that--it was not so long ago--for a change!!) there was this nice ad for Ed Engel, a dealer and Jan and Dean fan of some standing. Well, that ad offered THE JAN AND DEAN RARITIES. Big deal, right? We all have that bootleg, right?

WRONGO!!! This is a new RARITIES,

CONTAINS
RARE
AND NEVER BEFORE
HEARD CUTS
DATING BACK TO THE
ROOTS OF JAN AND DEAN
!

Nice large cover photo, black cover with yellow writing, and the back has each cut!

SIDE A

1. Drag City, live with Papa. Dicey lyrics!
2. Laurel and Hardy in a totally unique version, radically different lyrics.
3. Little Queenie features somewhat different lyrics, a different take.
4. Here is a REAL treasure, a cut that was cut form the SAVE FOR A RAINY DAY LP before it wasn't released! Remember how nice Dean sounded on the LINDA LP doing Rhythm of the Rain? You ain't heard NOTHIN' yet. Full studio stereo, too! This would have been the second or third best cut on the LP, had it stayed on and had the LP come out. This is the kind of thing you don't even dream about!
5. Before Captain Jan and Dean, the Boy Blunder, there were Batman and Robin. A rare EP came out a few years ago (thanks, Frank) with these practice skits. Now, the best one, full of flubs and ad libs, is available again!
6. BEFORE MOTHER EARTH, Jan recorded, not Pretty Lady Love (the CBS movie song), but The Magic of Making Love! Jan's first lead vocal since the accident, and it is a terrific song with infectious rhythm. Jan had it, and always will!
7. Will miracles never cease? Here is the original garage track of Jan and Arnie's hit, Jennie Lee, before Arwin added instrumentation. Hear Jan play the piano! Here Arnie play metal sticks and sing nasal! Wow!!

Side B

1. More miracles. Ever try to understand the lyrics on the J&D records version of Doug Kershaw's Louisiana Man? Well, on this track, the mix is clear, and Dean's vocal parts are amazing!
2. Jan's girlfriend, Jill Gibson, doing her Imperial 45 of Easy As 1, 2, 3. Quite a shock after Jano and Jilly's version on Liberty, but a treat, too!
3. The original version of Mother Earth, without background singers! Jan does great lead and overdub harmony on a classic track!
4. An "oldie" from the Papa tours, Do It In The Dirt.
5. Yipes! The instrumental flip side, Blow Up Music, is one of Jan's most rare and intriguing tracks. Here it is, WITH JAN SINGING LEAD!!
6. From the people who brought you Jan and Judy (Lovejoy, DEAN's girlfriend) on an unreleased duet, Come on, baby.
7. In the early '70s, Jan recut his fav Beatle cut, Hide Your Love Away, then he hid the track away. Here it is, folks!
8. Last, but not least, the most rare of all the tracks, something that no one ever dreamed of hoping that it ever would be recorded, let alone saved! From the people who brought you Jill and Judy, Jano and Jilly, Jan and Dean, and Jan and Arnie, here is (guys, hold on to your girls, and girls, you just hold on), a song called There Is The Night by...the pre-Jan-and-Arnie

B-A-R-O-N-S-!-!

When ordering, please tell Ed that you read it here!

LET ME EXPLAIN

Nothing to explain this time. Oh, yes. Some people have had problems with Concert Clothes, the place in LA that advertised Jan and Dean shirts and jackets in SM a few issues back. They have also failed to answer my last several letters, and they have not returned my calls. I would not advise that anyone order from them, or at least order only a little bit at a time so that you do not lose your shirt (no pun intended).

If you have had trouble, complain to me, and I will give you the Concert Clothes address and phone number so that we can both hassle them. I forwarded all orders to them.

The Japanese Mike and Dean LP LISTEN TO THE AIR is not an LP version of the US cassette ROCK 'N' ROLL CITY. Besides having Alley Oop, it has Dean and a DJ exchanging pleasantries, as well as unique cover art.

In the works--a special issue of SM covering DOT ART--the graphics/design work of Dean O. Torrence/Kittyhawk Graphics. Don't miss it!

Go to your local grocery store or other place that sells paper cups, and look on the SOLO cup packages. There is a record offer there that you may find interesting!

Word also comes of two "new" LPs from Japan. BEACH BOYS VS. JAN AND DEAN: HOT ROD EDITION and BEACH BOYS VS. JAN AND DEAN: SURF EDITION. They are from Capitol, so they should be the good recordings!! (Thanks Barbara!)

ITINERARY FOR JAN & DEAN, AND FOR JAN & ALOHAS

1984

Date	Event	Act	Location	State
JAN. 2	ROSE BOWL, FOOTBALL GAME	JAN & DEAN	PASADENA	CA.
MAR. 15	CONCERT	JAN & DEAN	PADRE ISLAND	TX.
APR. 8	CRAZYHORSE SALOON	JAN & DEAN	SANTA ANA	CA.
APR. 20,21	KNOTT'S BERRY FARM	JAN & DEAN	BUENA PARK	CA.
APR. 26-MAY 17	CONCERT TOUR, 3 WEEKS	JAN & ALOHAS	SOUTHERN U.S.	
MAY 27	CONCERT	JAN & DEAN	VANCOUVER	WA.
JUNE 2	ON STAGE AMERICA (TV)	JAN & DEAN	AIRED WORLDWIDE	
JUNE 2	CARSON PARADE GR. MARSHALLS	JAN & DEAN	CITY OF CARSON	CA.
JUNE 15	SEGMENT (DICK CLARK - TV)	JAN & DEAN		
JUNE 16	PORTLAND ROSE FESTIVAL	JAN & DEAN	PORTLAND	OR.
JUNE 25-JUL. 7	SANDS HOTEL	JAN & DEAN	LAS VEGAS	NV.
JUNE 27	SEGMENT(SOLID GOLD PROGRAM)	JAN & DEAN		
JULY 8	ORANGE COUNTY FAIR	JAN & DEAN	COSTA MESA	CA.
JULY 15		JAN & DEAN	ROCHESTER	NY.
JULY 19		JAN & DEAN	ONTARIO, CANADA	
JULY 20		JAN & DEAN	CHICAGO	IL.
JULY 21		JAN & DEAN	CINCINNATI	OH.
JULY 22	RESORTS INTERNATIONAL	JAN & DEAN	ATLANTIC CITY	NJ.
JULY 23	FENWICK	JAN & DEAN	OCEAN CITY	MD.
JULY 25		JAN & DEAN	WILKES BARRE	PA.
JULY 27	CLUB BENET	JAN & DEAN		NJ.
JULY 28	CRUISE (BUDWEISER)	JAN & DEAN	BOSTON	MA.
JULY 29	HAMPTON	JAN & DEAN	HAMPTON	NH.
AUG. 3,4,5	SAN DIEGO WILD ANIMAL PK.	JAN & DEAN	ESCONDIDO	CA.
AUG. 8	SAN JOAQUIN FAIR	JAN & DEAN	STOCKTON	CA.
AUG. 11-18	RIVERSIDE COUNTY FAIR	JAN & DEAN	HEMET	CA.
AUG. 10	CRUISE SHIP	JAN & DEAN	MIAMI	FL.
AUG. 29	ANTELOPE VALLEY FAIR	JAN & DEAN	LANCASTER	CA.
SEPT. 16-29	CONCERT TOUR	JAN & ALOHAS	NORTHWESTERN U.S.	

1985

JAN.21-FEB.10	CONCERT TOUR	JAN & DEAN	AUSTRALIA & N. ZEALAND	

Revised 06-15-84

SATURDAY, JULY 21, 1984

Surf's up at Malibu North

BY ALAN NIESTER
(From yesterday's late editions)

WE LIVE in strange times. Can you imagine, way back in 1963, that a young music fan would forsake his own musical heroes to spend an evening celebrating music written well before his birth — that of Glenn Miller, say? To a generation busy growing Beatle bangs and memorizing the lyrics to She Loves You, it would have seemed preposterous.

Yet Thursday night at the Ontario Place Forum, at least 50 per cent of the audience of 15,000 on hand for the triumphant return of Jan and Dean were not alive when the duo was recording its long string of hits. There is something unsettling in watching 15-year-old blond girls in Hawaiian shirts singing all the lyrics to Surf City. How do they know these songs? Does K-Tel have that much effect on the nation's consciousness?

Anyway, if there was any doubt that we are deeply entrenched in a nostalgia boom, it was laid to rest Thursday night. This was an audience ready to celebrate. They came in print shirts, carried beach balls and one fan even had a cardboard cutout of a surf board. They sang, danced and generally carried on as if it was Michael Jackson down on the revolving stage. This was the happiest, most responsive audience I've ever seen at the Forum.

Jan and Dean were backed by a five-piece outfit called The Belair Bandits, an energetic and competent cover band that seemed able to imitate anyone who lived on the West Coast from 1958 to 1966. With all five of the Bandits adding to harmonies, there were seven singers up there, meaning that even difficult surf classics such as Good Vibrations and California Girls could be handled with ease.

More than half of the material was not vintage Jan and Dean. There were lots of Beach Boys songs (some of which either Jan Berry or Dean Torrence might have written or actually performed — there was a great deal of interweaving between the two outfits in the early sixties), including Darlin', Help Me Rhonda, Dance, Dance, Dance and Little Deuce Coupe. There was even a so-called "East Coast surf song" — The Cowsills' Indian Lake.

As almost everyone knows, Berry was involved in a serious motor accident in 1966, which left him partially paralyzed and with speech difficulties. The only song on which the audience hushed all evening was Dead Man's Curve, the hideously prophetic number about a car crash, on which Berry sang lead. It garnered one of the biggest ovations of the night.

The other hits? Most were presented in enthusiastic, authentic fashion. The duo went all the way back to 1959 for Baby Talk, and carried through to 1964's Sidewalk Surfin'. In between, the songs included Ride the Wild Surf, Little Old Lady From Pasadena and New Girl In School. With the audience so solidly behind them, Jan and Dean presented what will probably prove to be one of Malibu North's best concerts of the summer.

MY FAVORITE JAN AND DEAN ALBUM: PART 2

The year was '63, and it had been a great year for rock 'n' roll. Girl groups, Jan and Dean, Beach Boys, Randy and the Rainbows, Four Seasons, Neil Sedaka was still around, Great Stuff. Jan and Dean won me over with Linda, Surf City, Honolulu Lulu, and Drag City! They were great on the radio, and irresistible on the juke boxes!

Then, it was 1964, and Dead Man's Curve/New Girl In School went zipping up the charts! My best friend and I were cruising the campus of the University of Kansas the first time we heard Dead Man's Curve on the car radio. When the DJ said "Jan and Dean," we got our hopes up. When we heard the title, "Dead Man's Curve," we sat up and listened! When we heard those opening horns, we looked at each other in astonishment! Up 'til then the sounds of Drag City and Fun Fun Fun had seemed like the ultimate in car songs, but this Dead Man's Curve was something!!!

I won't even try to describe our reaction when we heard the crash, the recitation, and the screeching fade. Up until this time, I had taped Jan and Dean songs off the radio with my reel-to-reel recorder (I still have those "Summer-of-Sixty-Three" tapes). I had also bought two copies of Linda. But now, I really had to have a copy of Dead Man's Curve.

To the record shop. Yep, there is a Dead Man's Curve LP alright, and it even has New Girl In School and Linda! Yipes! On the other hand, there also was the Drag City LP, with Dead Man's Curve and Drag City. That's the one I'll get, then. An LP cost $4 (mono, or $5 stereo) in the record store, but a dollar less at the discount house over in Kansas City. So, next time we drove into Kansas City, I went to the record rack and dug up my two-and-a-half week's allowance for the Drag City LP. Up to this time, I had two LPs in my collection, Bobby Vee's Greatest Hits (still my favorite non-Jan-and-Dean LP), and Teenage Triangle. Somehow, as much as I wanted Drag City, I could not make myself part with the cash. So, I gave my brother Tim the money and the LP and told him to buy it for me after he had made his selection. I also told him that if I changed my mind and asked for the money back, to refuse to comply. He said OK.

Minutes later, I chickened out, but he followed my instructions and bought the LP over my protest. Am I glad he did! When I got home, I discovered the wonderful world of Jan and Dean LPs, and I heard, for the first time, my favorite Jan and Dean LP!

I feel that this is an autobiographical LP of a guy who is Jan/Dean. What do you think?

Drag City. What can be said. The opening sound effects are unmatched for excitement, and set the pace for the song (and LP) that follows. Best of all, the sound is not that of a junker with a bad muffler, but of a finely-tuned machine. Then, just as the car engine begins to recede, but before the excitement can fade, in comes the best harmony since the first barber shop quartet was formed: "Burn up that quarter mile!" At the time, I thought they were saying "Turn on that border line," whatever that meant. But, knowing nothing about cars or racing, least of all that races were often one-quarter mile in length, it was really just the sound, not the lyrics, that I was into. The pounding drum rolls, the four-four piano, the guitar chords, the cymbal keeping the pace, Dean's high voice pulling Brian's and Frankie's by comparison, Jan's lower voice turned up all over the mix, and his "listen to 'em" after each line was a great touch.

The lyrics went by so fast, I never knew what they all were until I bought my copy of the new SONGS AND STARS magazine. Then, I discovered

Kinda gutsy, following a song about a hearse with a song about a death. Hey! Something is wrong! Doesn't sound like the radio version! Well, later I found out the story, and it is told in SM #14. When I played this for my friend (remember him—we were in his car up in the second paragraph), he figured it was a version by the Beach Bums! Well, this song had (or should have had) the sound effects of the first two cuts, the pacing of the third cut, the satire of the last two cuts—sounds like a committee job, and it was, being written by Jan, Roger, Art, and Brian. As time passed, I learned to value this as an alternate version, a peek into the development of a hit. It is excellent in its own right, and takes it rightful place on the LP. However, the later refined version is even better, so at the time I was disappointed.

Schlock Rod. In case anyone missed the satire in Dead Man's Curve, and I did for years, the whole thing became very lappy with the next cut. I had played Schlock Rod (Part 1) on the free juke box at the rec center. (Jan and Dean songs were made to appeal to the kids at surburban rec centers, you know. I mean, how many Eastern inner-city youth can relate to cruising freeways when there is no place to park a car and the streets are as congested as Malibu in July?) Schlock Rod was Jan's answer to Alley Oop, which had three hit versions four years earlier by the Hollywood Argyles, the Dyna-Sores, and Dante and the Evergreens. The third group were aquaintances, so it figured.

Up to this point on the LP, the comedy quotient was on the constant upswing throughout side one. Liberty should have seen this and not been surprised when Filet of Soul came up for release (see SM # 3 for Liberty's reaction to a Jan and Dean comedy LP). Side two maintained the flow, with a second chapter to the saga of Jan/Dean's Stan-and-Ollie car, begun on the rec center juke box, Drag City flip side. So now, time for a straight song, right?

Popsicle Truck. Wrong. With all the bomps, Barry Mann should have been involved with the composing of Popsicle Truck, but instead, Buzz Cason and Bobby Russel gave us a song which was not really a satire of anything. I mean, a funny song about popsicles is logical, compared to a funny song about gapping spark plugs! From the first hearing, this was a favorite, but I must admit it was a surprise when it came out as a single in 1966, under the shortened title, Popsicle. Unless I miss my bet, this is the only Jan and Dean song to ever feature falsetto bomps! The bomps are a fine tribute to the Jan and Dean sound of the early sixties just past, the harmonies are beautiful, and Glen Campbell's guitar is perfect. The background part has a nice touch, the "ding-a-ling" after the prolonger "ooooh." Great Stuff!

Surf Route 101. On their previous two Liberty LP's, Linda and Surf City, Jan and Dean had produced their own versions of other artists hits. Now, Jan, Roger, Art, and Brian composed their own version of "Dion does Dragstrip," although the influence may have been from Dion through Dickey Lee, whose I Saw Linda Yesterday also very Dion-esque and might have inspired Linda), and Schlock Rod (Alley Oop). Now, the Jimmy Gilmer and the Fireballs hit Sugar Shack is reworked. But, whereas Gilmer's dream girl worked in a coffee house along a Southern country road, Jan and Dean's dream girl was a surfer who hungout down the freeway on the beach (Holy Ocean Park Angel!!).

The snapping bass guitar is a big hint that this is a take-off on Sugar Shack. The line, "We Stopped at the Sugar Shack for chow and some jivin'" settles the matter. But, the "we" is Jan/Dean and the Angel. Unlike Jimmy Gilmer, who observed his dream girl from afar so to speak, Jan/Dean made a good friend!

Sting Ray. Ah, at last, the song I was waiting for!

that Jan had changed a lot of the words in the studio, anyway! (See inside front cover of SM #9 for the clipped lyrics from SONGS AND STARS that I corrected in 1963!) Jan, Roger Christian of KFWB who wrote the liner notes, and Brian really did an excellent composing job on this song.

But there is a risk taken when the first song on an LP is so outstanding...can the rest of the LP measure up? Is it possible to do a whole LP of I-Want-To-Hold-Your-Hands, or of Fun-Fun-Funs? In my opinion, it has seldom, if ever, been done. But, Jan and Dean did it! I Gotta Drive. Roger Christian and Barry Mann wrote this ode to drag racing. Barry Mann wrote many of my all-time favorite songs, including Who Put The Bomp, I Love How You Love Me, Footsteps, and Sweet Little You. Now, he's doing stuff for Jan and Dean! Wow!

After Drag City's sound effects, it would have been a let down had I Gotta Drive not featured some non-musical sounds. It did. Right at the start, a car engine revs, but goes nowhere. Quickly, we hear the drumbeat that symbolizes the driver (Jan/Dean) slamming the hood of his machine just before the race. "MY SENTIMENTS "Been waitin' for eight years, I had been growing up with a rock 'n' roll EXACT.Y. For such a long time...." MY SENTIMENTS that was too Eastern-urban, too soulful, too sexy, too uneducated, or too pop for me. Now, I have met my musical match, Jan and Dean. Middle-class school kids enjoying themselves.

The recitation ends, the car takes off, and the promise of Drag City is fulfilled again! The pace is up to par, and the background singing is perfectly complementary, and the band replicates its Drag City success. "Why isn't this a single, too?" I asked myself. I didn't know until many years later that I was not alone in asking this question, and it WAS a single, on the Colpix (Col-Pix, Columbia Pictures, get it?) label. Also know as Screen Gems, who use the same Statue of Liberty log as Liberty and which published the songs on this LP. The single on Colpix was the same recording, with Jill Gibson doing the recitation, and the Matadors, who sang background parts, getting label credit as artist. Drag Strip Girl. The pace had to let up, or else we'd all faint from exhaustion. So, just as a good horror movie follows a tense, scary scene with some comedy relief, Jan and Dean bring us Jan and Art Kornfield's satire on Surfer Girl, titled Drag Strip Girl. While I was and am a huge Beach Boy fan, I never cared for their slower songs, and Surfer Girl was one I never played. So, most welcome was the humor; "My drag strip girl, she's got just what it takes, when she adjusts my brakes, the chassis never shakes!"

Surfin' Hearse. Such chutzpah! Starts off with the theme from Laurel and Hardy, "The Cuckoos." A strong hint tha this is not to be taken too seriously, folks! Then, Jan and Dean do Jan and Roger's song in a very Dion-esque style, with the Matadors and Jan and Dean on background parts sounding like the Belmonts. But this is really a down subject, a hearse, especially on an LP about a dangerous pasttime, car racing! This song give the same treatment to songs like Shut Down and Drag City that Drag Strip Girl gave to Surfer Girl and Honolulu Lulu (not that Lulu was all that serious of a song!).

Again, the lyrics were tough, took me years to get "It's got a lot of fancy engraving on the side" and some other lines. But the sound was 100%, and Jan purposely buried the vocals so that in trying to hear the words we would turn up the record player or radio and hear the songs at the proper volume. But, heavens! My English teacher may have told me about foreshadowing, yet I never expected to find it on a Jan and Dean LP!

Dead Man's Curve. Ah, at last, the song I was waiting for!

SHORT CUTS

SUNSHINE MUSIC--Lots of last-minute news. This is, as you see, another double issue. Jan and Dean are so hot these days, compared to back when SM began, that the material accumulates much more rapidly than it used to.

LITTLE OLD LADY--Jan and Dean and Mike have been at it again. Watch MTV for THE LITTLE OLD LADY FROM PASEDENA!!! It is a new video. Amazing! Haven't we all dreamed of the video possibilities of songs like DEAD MAN'S CURVE or SIDEWALK SURFIN'? The original Lady, the late Kathryn Milner, is replaced by a new Old Lady, Ethel Sway. She is 76. Also in the video--The Beach Boys!

VIDEO--For dreamers, there is also a new video TAPE called BEACH PARTY, which was previewed on Solid Gold's two hour special countdown of the 40 biggest summer hits. It featured Carl Wilson and 2/3rds of The Angels in person. I was disappointed in that PALISADES PARK (Billboard for 13 weeks, peaked at #3) was included but SURF CITY (Billboard for 13 weeks, peak at #1) was not! The tape is from "CENTEL PRODUCTIONS" and released by MEDIA MUSIC.

TAMI--I recently found two sources for the Legendary TAMI show video tape starring Jan and Dean. One was a mail-order source, a collector who offered many rare videos for sale and trade. The quality was poor, because the stuff was bootleg. Why do I use the past tense? Well, the FBI, which frowns on bootlegging, visited this fella in the middle of the night recently, and he is, to say the least, out of business.

The other source is a legal one, a tape called THAT WAS ROCK (Music Media, $29.95). It combines both TAMI and the sequel, TNT. However, they cut the shows severely. Originally totalling 189 minutes, now they run just 90 (!!) minutes, and that includes new footage of Chuck Berry! You won't see much J&D on THAT WAS ROCK.

SOLO--More from the Solo Cup Company. Besides the LP offer on the cup packages, there is a second offer that comes with the records. It includes two 45s, Mike and Dean JINGLE BELLS, and Dean BABY TALK b/w DA DO RON RON!

GOLDMINE--Last year, GOLDMINE MAGAZINE asked SM to supply baby pictures of J&D for a contest. In this issue is a reprint of the contest and of the photos. NOTE: THE CONTEST HAS ENDED. DO NOT SEND ENTRIES!

SHIRT BY: Paula Moore

MODELED BY: Gary Ost

Sting Ray with Jean Sharp. Jean's husband Jim was the producer on the hit version of Sting Ray by the Routers. The horn gimmick makes this fit well into a car LP that emphasizes the lighthearted, and the Matadors contributed some L.A.-Mexican Spanish (see SM #7).

Little Deuce Coupe. Just as Jan's favorite Beatle song is probably Hide Your Love Away, Dean's favorite Beach Boy song seems to be Little Deuce Coupe. And when Dean sings a solo lead, as on this cut, one may assume that he likes the song a lot. Written by Roger and Brian, it fits the LP nicely. And, Jan and Dean prove once again that they are the only artist who can do a Bum's song justice!

Hot Stocker. As the comedy became more dominate over the course of side one, the pace slowed on side two, just as it does after a car race. In a sense, on this LP we spent some time with Jan/Dean, an afternoon at the strip (Drag City), discussing hopes (I Gotta Drive), with his girl (Drag Strip Girl), kidding with the guys (Surfin' Hearse), and past race (Dead Man's Curve), discussing his woodie (Schlock Rod), goofing off in the school yard (Popsicle), cruising and meeting a new beach bunny (Surf Route 101), and singing along with a Beach Boy song on the car radio (Little Deuce Coupe). Probably a pretty typical week in Jan and Dean's lives!

Rather than satire or excitement as the prime motivation for recording the song, it would seem that the main purpose in Hot Stocker was to see how many car terms Jan, Roger, and Artie could fit into one song. While skipping harmony and background vocals, Jan did not sacrifice arrangement, instrumentation, pacing, or excitement. The longer, mono version is especially exciting, and shows that, while harmony was a big part of the Jan and Dean "sound," the basic production worked even without intricate vocal styling. This is a factor in Jan and Dean music which set it apart from groups which were basically combos and played their own instruments (Beach Boys and Beatles come to mind as examples) or were primarily vocalists and could not really do songs that were primarily instrumental in nature (Four Seasons and Jay and the Americans, for instance).

The cover design of Drag City has all of the excitement of the music. Dean in white levis, sweatshirt, and tennies, Jan in stylish jacket, jeans, and "Jan and Dean" boots (as I called them ever since the Golden Hits LP cover, later known as "Beatle" boots), a pair of dragsters whizzing past. Dean and Jan are ignoring the race, probably oggling a drag strip girl, admiring a surfin' hearse woodie, or perhaps looking for the Popsicle truck for a whistle-wetter.

The back cover has a unique slant--literally--that transmits a feeling of movement and excitement. The drawing of racing cars shows an art style which turned up again on the Dead Man's Curve 45 sleeve (where the front cover photo also reappeared). And Roger's liner notes tell the tale as far as what this LP is going to be about.

What made such a fine LP possible? Jan and Dean had several solid hits, Lou Adler let Jan have his head in' roll recordings, Dean's had 7 years of experience in making rock 'n' roll recordings, Dean's voice was never better, and the budget was larger than that for any Jan and Dean LP yet. Plus, Jan and Dean had something to sing about--cars. Up until this time, they had only girls/love to sing about. As seen on the Surf City LP, such topical limitations led, in those days, to an adult career as a pop singer- With surfing, and cars, Jan and Dean had someplace to go musically. The result? My first, and still favorite, Jan and Dean LP!

Jan and Dean catch a wave of applause

By JOHN WEEKS
Sun Staff Writer

SAN BERNARDINO — Surf rockers Jan and Dean, performing together for the first time since an angry spiltup a year ago, electrified a National Orange Show audience of almost 4,000 Tuesday night.

Jan Berry and Dean Torrence, who had met for a single rehearsal the previous day, performed for an hour and a half in the Orange Pavilion, and had the standing-room-only crowd cheering, dancing, singing along and calling for more. After their encore medley, they walked from the stage arm-in-arm.

The concert was a third beginning in Jan and Dean's checkered career, which ended the first time in a 1966 car crash that crippled Berry, and which ended a second time last May in a hailstorm of angry words.

Ironically, both the breakup last year and the reunion this year took place in San Bernardino.

At last year's Orange Show, Torrence performed without Berry and that evening announced the breakup of Jan and Dean in an exclusive interview with The Sun. He called Berry a "tyrant," accused him of ruining their national tour of the previous year because of temperamental outbursts, and said he would never perform with Berry again "except on a really limited basis, for a lot of money."

Berry, interviewed later that week at his home in Los Angeles, called Torrence a "conniver," accused Torrence of undermining him during performances, and said, "I don't ever want to play with Dean again."

Since then, the two have patched up their nearlifelong friendship, which began in high school in Los Angeles, developed into a singing partnership, and culminated between 1960 and 1966 with the sale of 20 million records, including such hits as "Surf City," "Deadman's Curve" and "Little Old Lady from Pasadena."

After their career was brought to a halt by the 1966 car crash in Los Angeles that left Berry crippled and speech-impaired, Jan and Dean reunited in 1979, after a television documentary about them sparked a wave of national interest.

They reunited again Tuesday night in San Bernardino.

Backed by Dean Torrence's band, the Bel Air Bandits, Jan and Dean performed a basic sampler of California surf rock, including all their own old hits and a number of Beach Boys standards.

Performing is something of a heroic challenge for the crippled Berry, but he was game for it Tuesday night, and seemed radiant at the enthusiastic audience response. When he took the spotlight alone and sang his now-ironic classic, "Deadman's Curve," it was a sentimental highpoint of the evening.

The musical highlight was a surprisingly gregarious vocal solo, on "Dancing in the Streets," by Bel Air Bandits' drummer John Cowsill, an alumnus of the Cowsills, a singing family group popular in the '60s.

But it was Torrence who was ringmaster of stage and audience. With an eager guitar and voice, he led the band and repeatedly urged the crowd to join in. Fans responded with abandon, and at one point a couple of women rushed the stage. They were led off by security officers.

Nobody minded when the music hit an occasional rusty snag. The party was too much fun.

Torrence made a convincing public showing of his rapprochement with Berry, conferring often with him before numbers, bantering with him, and exchanging several "gimme-five" handshakes with him.

Berry has indicated he would be agreeable to a permanent reunion of Jan and Dean. Torrence, however, has said he wants to keep it "limited and special." Interviewed earlier in the week, Torrence said, "As long as it can be fun, that's great, that's wonderful, and we'll take it from there. I've told Jan that these are test dates. We'll see what happens in San Bernardino."

What did happen in San Bernardino Tuesday night couldn't help but encourage him.

THURSDAY, MAY 5, 1983

(BOYS WILL BE BOYS....)

SUNSHINE MUSIC 20-21

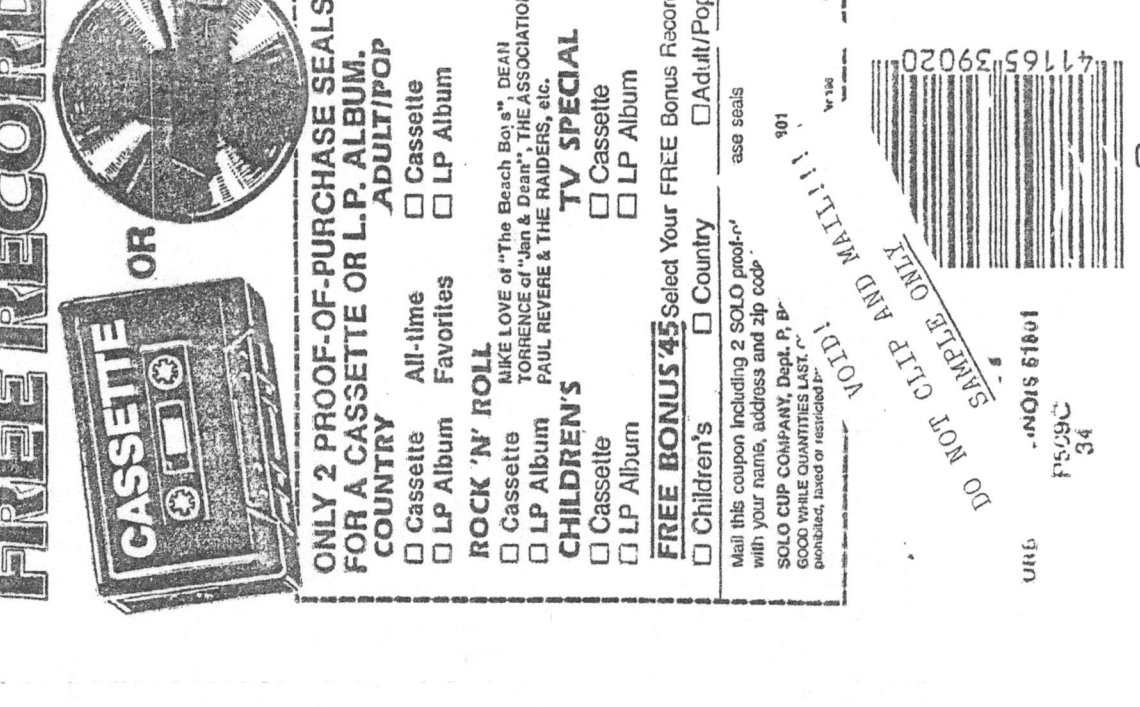

NEWSMAKERS

Move over, Clara Peller. Make room for Ethel Sway, 76, the newly crowned "Little Old Lady From Pasadena." To celebrate the 20th anniversary of their surf-sound hit, Jan & Dean are making a video version of the song, starring Sway in the title role. "You always think that all the good things happen to someone else," says the soon-to-be terror of Colorado Boulevard, who won her ticket to stardom by beating out 100 other aspirants with what judges called her "zaniness, energy, wisdom and zest for life." Those qualities will come in handy. "She'll be doing some drag-racing, some singing, and I guess she'll have to learn to break-dance," says Dean Torrence, adding that the Beach Boys—who have helped keep the song popular by playing it in their concerts—will also appear in the video, due for release in July.

'Little Old Lady' with Jan & Dean

Automobile Accident Almost "Killed" Career

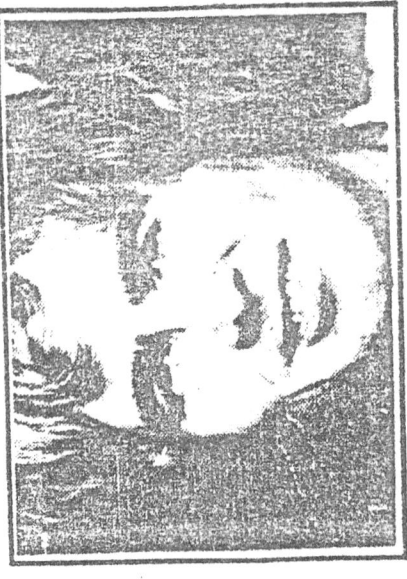

The recent high-rating TV movie on the life of Jan Berry about his near-fatal automobile accident some years back has prompted a Las Vegas show at the Marina Hotel entitled, "The Music of Jan & Dean." The road to success this second time around for the Marina showroom star has taken a few unexpected twists. He says, "After lying in a hospital bed not knowing if I was going to pull through, this engagement has even more impact on me than it would have had 20 years ago. It's a great feeling being here. It's a real thrill."

During an era where, "surf's up" could be heard enchoing all along Southern California's beaches, the original duo of Jan & Dean brought the carefree, sun-worshipping sound labeled, "Surf Rock" into the homes of millions. "Jenny Lee", Barry's first song, composed when he was only 17 years old, was the group's first number one million seller. It was an indication of what was to come. It was just a beginning for the string of top hits to follow, among them, "Dead Man's Curve," "Drag City," "Honolulu Lulu," "What's Your Name?", and "Surf City."

Ironically, the locale for Jan & Dean's 1964 hit recording, "Dead Man's Curve" in Los Angeles, was the place that nearly wrote Jan's epitaph when he was involved in that disasterous car accident.

After four years of intense therapy, Berry's strong will to perform, brought him once again to the forefront and to his Las Vegas debut.

So many who have lost hope and feel they can no longer work or make something of themselves because of a handicap, can learn from Berry's show of will and determination. The strength, compassion, and love that Jan has demonstrated to others has made it possible for them to cope more easily with what they have.

Berry explains, "I don't think I have ever tackled anything so hard like going through that therapy. So often it was hard and I didn't know if I would make it or not. There were days that I just wanted to give up. I don't really know what stopped me — it was just something — some little voice inside that kept saying,

'you've got to go on' and I kept thinking, I've got

to perform again. It was hard, but all the pain was worth it. I've made it to Las Vegas!"

May 15 thru 21, 1983

Surfin' Snow Country?
Jan & Dean in the Perspective of Switzerland

By Dan Bossard

How does a country full of snow and mountains treat a surf duo from sunny California? It's hard to get Jan & Dean stuff. Nearly the only way to hear Jan & Dean's music is buying records from dealers in foreign countries (mainly in England and the States). The usual record shops in Switzerland mostly have got no Jan & Dean records and you're a lucky person if you find one. The only ones I've seen were "20 Rock 'n' Roll Hits" (Rock 10) "Deadman's Curve" (Liberty 10011), a reissue of the Dore album (Dore 101) and "Folk 'n' Roll" (liberty 7431), but the last one was in an import shop.

What about Swiss releases? I know only of one Swiss compilation album including a few Jan & Dean (or should I say: Dean & Papa Doo Run Run) songs. It's a double album released through K-tel records and it's called "Beach Party," but that's back in 1978. Since then, no more Swiss records have ever featured any Jan & Dean songs.

Another way to hear Jan & Dean music is on the radio, but only in very few (and I have to emphasize: very few) shows.

We have a one-hour show called "oldies," which is every three weeks on the program and consists "only" of rock 'n' roll music from the '50s. But, since a few years, there's an annual special with surf music! In 1980, it was "Surf Oldies" (no more details available). In 1981, the show was called "Hot Rod Oldies" and featured 24 songs including "Drag City" by Jan & Dean, "I Gotta Drive" by the matadors, "hot rod USA" by the catalinas (incl. Hal Blaine and Leon Russell) and "Gas Money" by the Rip Chords.

In 1982, there were even two shows. The first one was again called "Surf Oldies" and included "Ride The Wild Surf", the only Jan & Dean or related song in this show.

The second one was "Summer Sounds Oldies," which I had the pleasure to put together the music for. The Jan & Dean songs were "Gonna Hustle You" ("Filet of Soul" version) and "Deadman's Curve" from the "Studio Out-Takes" bootleg. Other interesting songs were "Summer Means Fun" by the Legendary Masked Surfers, "Three Window Coupe" by the Rip Chords and the California Suns' "masked grandma", which is a lovely continue of "The Little Old Laky From Pasadena" and it goes something like this: "There's a little old lady, just a little bit meaner, than the little old lady from Pasadena..."

The DJ of all the "oldies" shows is a nice guy named Francois Murner. He has an unusual way of presentation, at least in Switzerland, because he is influenced by English and American DJs, so he sounds very refreshing in the otherwise so dull Swiss radio program. (Imagine: we have only one permitted broadcasting station in Switzerland and its program is... ooh, let's talk about more pleasant things!)

The reaction on the two surf shows this year was very big and very positive, and there is a certain interest in this kind of music, but it's difficult to imagine "Surf City" in " Snow Country"!

Another reason why surf music isn't as popular in Switzerland as it should be is that, there never was a surf music concert in our country. I think, if Jan & Dean ever should give a concert here, many people would like to go to their performance.

And that's the way we see the Jan & Dean thing here in Switzerland.

FOR MORE FROM DANNY, WRITE FOR SURFIN' AGAIN, D. BOSSARD, GOTTHELFWEG 9, 5036 OBERERTFELDEN, SWITZERLAND]

Goldmine
You Must Have Been A Beautiful

Reflecting a bit for the moment, we'd like to thank all of our favorite artists for the magic of cherished memories and the timeless gift of music. Now, with thoughts of holiday pleasures, *Goldmine* is proud to present not one but 10! New Year's Babies to welcome the upcoming year in style. It's *Goldmine's* "You Must Have Been A Beautiful Baby" contest, designed to bring you cheer! So, read on for details and resolve to mail your answers early. Goodbye Father Time! The New Year looks ten times better already!!

It's easy to enter. Just match the "Big Artist" with his or her "little baby" counterpart. Please submit your answers in the format below.

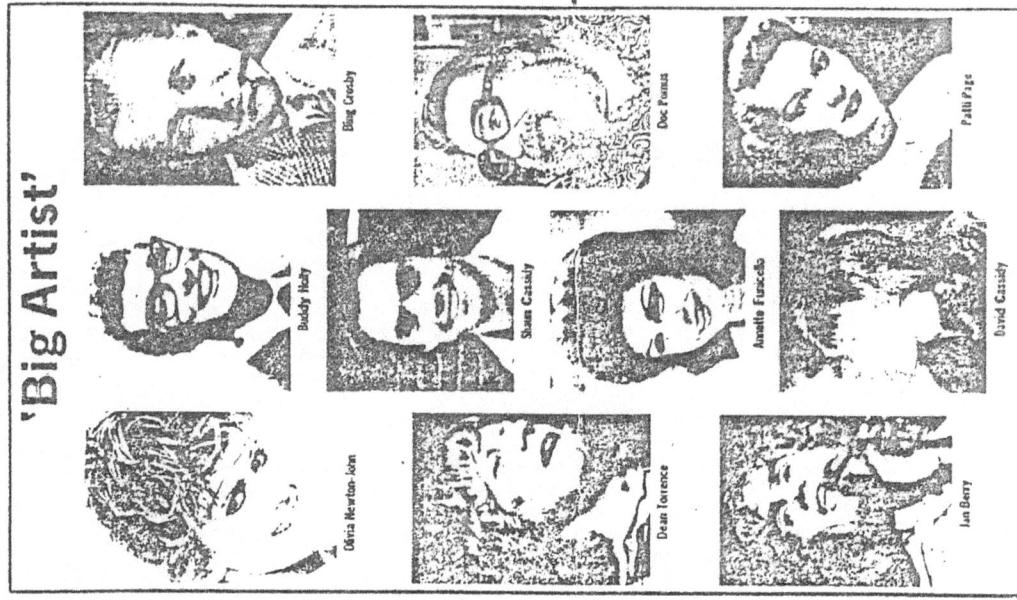

'Big Artist'

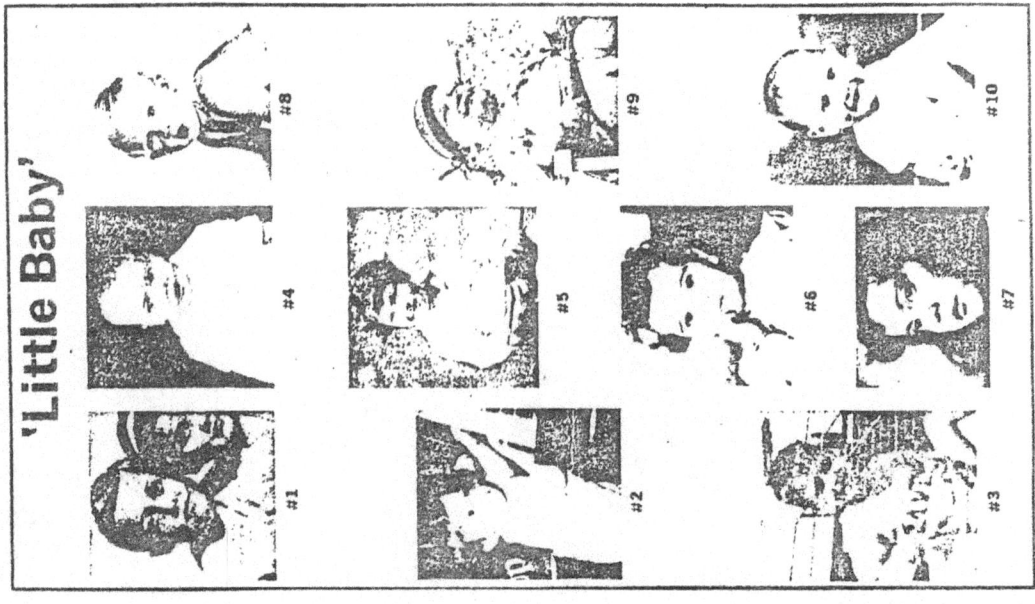

'Little Baby'